Paul B. Du Chaillu

Adventures in the Great Forest of Equatorial Africa

And the Country of the Dwarfs

Paul B. Du Chaillu

Adventures in the Great Forest of Equatorial Africa
And the Country of the Dwarfs

ISBN/EAN: 9783743385306

Manufactured in Europe, USA, Canada, Australia, Japa

Cover: Foto ©Andreas Hilbeck / pixelio.de

Manufactured and distributed by brebook publishing software (www.brebook.com)

Paul B. Du Chaillu

Adventures in the Great Forest of Equatorial Africa

ADVENTURES
IN
THE GREAT FOREST
OF
EQUATORIAL AFRI
AND THE
COUNTRY OF THE DWARFS

By PAUL DU CHAILLU
AUTHOR OF "THE LAND OF THE MIDNIGHT SUN," ETC.

WITH MAP AND ILLUSTRATIONS

ABRIDGED AND POPULAR EDITION

NEW YORK
HARPER & BROTHERS, FRANKLIN SQUARE
1890

By PAUL DU CHAILLU.

Adventures in the Great Forest of Equatorial Africa, and the Country of the Dwarfs. Abridged and Popular Edition. With Map and Illustrations. Post 8vo, Cloth, $1 75.

The Land of the Midnight Sun. Summer and Winter Journeys through Sweden, Norway, Lapland, and Northern Finland. With Map and 235 Illustrations. In Two Volumes. 8vo, Cloth, $7 50.

A Journey to Ashango-Land, and Further Penetration into Equatorial Africa. Illustrated. 8vo, Cloth, $5 00.

Stories of the Gorilla Country.—Wild Life Under the Equator.—Lost in the Jungle.—My Apingi Kingdom; with Life in the Great Sahara, and Sketches of the Chase of the Ostrich, Hyena, &c.—**The Country of the Dwarfs.** Five Volumes. Illustrated. 12mo, Cloth, $1 50 each.

Published by HARPER & BROTHERS, New York.

☞ *Any of the above works sent by mail, postage prepaid, to any part of the United States, Canada, or Mexico, on receipt of the price.*

Copyright, 1871, by HARPER & BROTHERS.

Copyright, 1890, by HARPER & BROTHERS.

All rights reserved.

Stereotyped by William Clowes & Sons, London.

PREFACE.

THE heroic exploits of Stanley and his followers have aroused a fresh interest in African exploration, and my former works on Equatorial Africa being now out of print, I have been encouraged by my publisher to condense into one popular volume, and to re-issue, the narrative of my journeys.

I may claim to be the first white man who penetrated into that vast and unbroken forest which, as I have elsewhere written, extends north and south of the equator, varying in breadth from two to three degrees on each side of it. Now and then, prairies looking like islands, resembling so many gems, are found in the midst of this dark sea of everlasting foliage.

In this great woody wilderness man is scattered and divided into numerous tribes. The forest, thinly inhabited by man, is still more scantily inhabited by those species of animals found in great number in almost every other part of Africa. There are neither rhinoceroses, zebras, giraffes, nor ostriches, and few of the many species of the antelope group, including elands and gazelles, are to be seen. Hence large carnivorous animals are scarce; the lion is quite absent, leopards and two or three species of hyenas and jackals only being found. There were no beasts of burden—neither horse, camel, donkey, nor cattle. The only true domesticated animals were goats, sheep, and fowls: I found the goats increasing in number as I advanced into the interior, and the fowls decreasing.

On the other hand, this region is peopled by a large number of venomous serpents, by several formidable kinds of ants, and by many strange varieties of apes, headed by the King of the African forest, the Gorilla.

In this strange and weird country I travelled alone, making friends with the various tribes, studying their language, and always being passed on from one to another with friendly commendation. I took no tent with me, but trusted entirely, when I was not residing in any village, to such temporary shelters, roofed with leaves, as the natives are accustomed to make for themselves.

No roads traverse this dense jungle; the villages and settlements of the different tribes, which are often separated by wide and desolate tracts of uninhabited country, are connected by narrow and tortuous paths, which form the only channels of communication. From these branch off occasional hunting tracks, which, after a score of miles, frequently lose themselves, or come to an abrupt termination; and woe betide the man who, without guide or knowledge of the paths, should lose himself in this inextricable labyrinth.

Before leaving New York for London to attend to the publication of "Explorations in Equatorial Africa," my much-esteemed friend and publisher, Mr. Fletcher Harper, said to me: "Paul Du Chaillu, your book is soon to be published in England. As you see, your name is on the title-page. I want now to give you some advice: Stick to it — stick to it." Astonished, I asked what he meant. He answered, with a smile, "Stick to it." Being then young and unsophisticated, I could hardly realize what he meant.

The bitter controversy which arose in England on the publication of my first book explains it. That bitterness has passed away, and has been almost forgotten—at any rate by myself—except in so far as it is associated with the names of those dear friends who there stood by me through it all—chief among them Sir Richard Owen, Sir Roderic Murchison, H. W. Bates, my venerable publisher, John Murray, and many others. The best of my specimens of gorillas are now in the Natural History Section of the British Museum; some are to be found in the United States; while my other collections are distributed among various museums, chiefly in America.

A few travellers, and Mr. Stanley at their head, have touched the outskirts of the country I traversed, and have confirmed by independent testimony my narrative, more especially on such points as the existence of tribes of cannibals and dwarfs—which I was the first to discover—the density and vast extent of the central forest of Africa, and the existence of a huge range of mountains to the eastward; but no white man, so far as I am aware, has been able to penetrate to the haunts of the gorilla and bring home specimens killed by himself since my time.

I ought to mention, in conclusion, that in order to avoid repetition and retracing my steps more than is necessary, I have so grouped my several journeys as to deal with each district separately; but to make this arrangement more clear, I now give a chronological table of my journeys according to years and months.

First Expedition.

1855. *October*, left New York.
" *December*, reached Africa.
1856. *January to March*, at Gaboon.
" *April*, started for Cape Lopez.
" *July* 27, started for Corisco to visit the Fans.
" *October*, returned to Corisco Bay, ascended the Moondah, and crossed to Gaboon country.
1857. *February* 5, started from the Gaboon for Commi country to explore the Ogobai.
1858. *February* 26, set out for Goumbi. Explored the Rembo and Ovenga country.
" *August* 13, returned to Biagano.
" *October* 10, started from Biagano for the Ashira and Apingi countries.
1859. Returned from Apingi country to Biagano.
" *June*, embarked for America.

Second Expedition.

1863-4. Explore again the Commi country.
1864. *October*, leave Goumbi for the Ashira country and Olenda's village.
1865. *March*, start for the Otando country and Mayolo's village.
" *May*, from Mayolo's village to the lands of the Aponos, Ishogos, Ashangos, etc., and the country of the dwarfs.
" *July*, fight with the natives, and retreat to the sea-shore.
" *September*, sail for England.

CONTENTS.

CHAPTER I.

The Gaboon—The Mpongwe tribe—The Mpongwe one of the great families of the negro race—Decrease of the Mpongwe and other tribes—Their villages and houses—Appearance of the Mpongwe—Their dress—Their cunning as traders .. .. 1—6

CHAPTER II.

Old King Glass—His death—Secret burial—Mourning customs—The election of a new king—Treatment before being made a king—Food—Plantation .. .. 6—10

CHAPTER III.

Corisco Island—The Mbengo tribe—Death of Tonda—Sorrowful scene—Departure for the Muni river—Mbango—Adventure at sea—Capture of a debtor—Lost in the Muni mangrove swamps—Arrival at Dayoko's—Reception .. .. 10—17

CHAPTER IV.

A king in Africa—Jealousy of the natives in regard to trade—Dayoko wants to keep me—Appearance of Mbousha—Death of a wizard—Departure for the interior—Ascent of the Muni—A Shekiani village—The Ntambounay and Noonday rivers—Mbene village—A new plantation—Reception by King Mbene—Offer of a wife .. 17—28

CHAPTER V.

Return of Dayoko's men—All alone—I am Mbene's white man—Different tribes—An ideal country for an African—Mbondemo houses—Polygamy—Its political aspect—Causes of quarrels and wars—Departure for the cannibal country—Among the hills—A strike for higher pay in the dense forest—Huts for travellers—A beautiful torrent—High mountains—A big snake—Snakes as food—Discovery of gorilla tracks—Fright of the women—Unsuccessful gorilla hunt—Return to the camp—Superstitions about gorilla—Starvation—Coming to a village .. .. 29—45

CHAPTER VI.

Hunger—Meeting with cannibals—They think I am a spirit—Great crowds of cannibals—Appearance of the Fans—Fan dress—Gorilla hunting—Fierce attack of a gorilla—His horrid appearance—Death of a gorilla—The Bakalai—Wailing of the Bakalai—Love of the people for tobacco .. .. 46—57

CHAPTER VII.

Departure for a Fan village—Cannibal practices of the Fans—Fierce appearance of the king—Head-dress of the Fans—A queen of the Fans—A Fan village—Signs of cannibalism everywhere—Refusal of cooked food—Ndiayai and his warriors—Weapons of the Fans—Drum, musical instruments .. .. 58—70

CHAPTER VIII.

Elephant hunting with the cannibals—The king hunts with me—Appearance of the forest—Man killed by an elephant—Ceremonies round a dead elephant—Habits of the elephant—Fan marriage ceremony—Eating those who die a natural death—Bravery of the Fans—Cannibalistic custom—Blacksmith—Pottery—Among the cannibal Oshebas—Bunbakai, king of the Oshebas—Dare not go further inland—Idol worship among the cannibals .. .. .. 70—87

CHAPTER IX.

Back to the coast—King Mbene gets a cannibal wife—The Fans regret my departure—Good-bye to the Fans and their mountains—The rains—Leopards—Mbicho villages—The Noya River—Wanga—King Alapay—Hunting with nets—Ferocious ants—The great forest—Over a mangrove swamp—A big snake .. .. 87—99

CHAPTER X.

Journey to Cape Lopez—Princess Akerni—A plantation—Prairie land—Caught in a storm—Mpongwe canoe-builders—Large size of canoes—Ogoul i-Limbai—Ogoula a great elephant hunter—Getting into canoes—Our predicament—The negroes great swimmers 100—107

CHAPTER XI.

Sangatanga—The royal residence—The Oroungou people—Visit to King Bango—The Mafouga—The king's crown—A ball given in my honour—Songs—Rum in plenty—Five reputed idols .. 108—115

CHAPTER XII.

Journey inland from Sangatanga—Preparations for hunting—The king gives me three great hunters—Beautiful appearance of the country—Buffaloes and elephants—Cool nights—Hippopotami—An approaching caravan—Mistrust—The village of Ngola—King Njambai—Shinshooko's house—Torturing a woman—Rescue—Appearance of the Shekianis—Their methods of warfare—My guns and watches are objects of wonder—Customs of the Shekianis—Our camp—Shooting two leopards—Superstitions in regard to leopard's tail and liver—Aboko kills an elephant—Buffaloes—Return to Sangatanga—The Oroungou burial-ground .. .. 115—134

CHAPTER XIII.

The Camma country—The coast line—Surf—The schooner *Caroline*—Crew—A tornado—Trouble at the mouth of the Fernand Vaz river—King Sangala and Ranpano—Sangala sends a hostage—Great palaver—Intense excitement—Discretion the better part of valour—Building my settlement—I have to be severe.. .. .. .. 135—144

CHAPTER XIV.

The Commi people—King Olenga-Yombi—I am obliged to attend a ball—Native love of rum—Fetich-houses—Mbuirri and Abambou—Ovengua—Ifouta tossed by a buffalo—A live young gorilla—How he was captured—His appearance—I call him "Joe"—He is untameable—His escape and recapture—Death of Joe—Shipping a young gorilla for London—Surprising gorillas in a plantain plantation—How gorillas walk—Another young live gorilla—How he was captured—The mother brought in not dead—Gorillas are often gregarious—Shooting hippopotami at night on shore—Habits of the hippopotamus—Combat between two hippopotami .. .. 144—166

CHAPTER XV.

Ascent of the Ogobai—The Anengue lake—King Damagondai—Damagondai lecturing his wives—King Shimbouvenegani—Shelters of the nshiego-mbouvé—Killing a nshiego-mbouvé; its appearance—Hunting the crocodile—Damagondai's idol—Troubles during the descent down the river .. .. 167—183

CHAPTER XVI.

The dry season—Migration of birds—Serpents—The ceremony of bola ivoga—Theory of the Commi about disease—Death of Ishungui—A greater doctor—Exorcising a sorcerer—Fear of witchcraft by the people—Capture of a young gorilla—Death of its mother—Death of the young gorilla—I am poisoned—Punishment and release of the poisoner.. .. .. 183—195

CHAPTER XVII.

King Quengueza sends his son to me as a hostage—Invitation to come to his country—Assembling the Biagano people—I leave my property in their hands—Rinkimongami appointed the keeper of my goods—Good-bye to Ranpano—Departure for Goumbi—Ascent of the Rembo—A man in ntchogo—Reception by Quengueza—Goumbi—Superstitions of King Quengueza—Ceremony for driving away the aniemba—The alumbi house—Hunting—Killing a gorilla—Ordeal—Capture of a young gorilla—Superstitions about gorillas—Bakalai villages—King Obindji—Trial by hot iron .. .. 195—218

CHAPTER XVIII.

I discover a new ape—The kooloo-kumba—Gouamba, or craving for meat—Troublesome flies—Malaouen—Numerous traces of gorilla—Killing a large male gorilla—Start for the ebony country—The ebony tree—Severe attack of fever—Take 150 grains of quinine in three days—Kindness of women during my illness—Death of a young wizard—Killing a nshiego-mbouvé—Capture of a young nshiego-mbouvé—His face is white—His mother is black—The young nshiego-mbouvé becomes tame—He turns darker as he grows older—Privileges of women—The idol said to have walked and talked .. 219—240

CHAPTER XIX.

Njambai—Worship of Njambai by women only—I get a peep inside the house of Njambai—Great wrath of the women—I am in a perilous position—Mbango and Quengueza take my part—Paying a fine—Gorilla hunting—Man killed by a gorilla—His gun bent—Gambo—The ibolai and igoogouai flies—The iboco and nchouna flies—Great number of parrots—The cloway wasp—Superstition in regard to different animals as food .. .. 240—252

CHAPTER XX.

Ants—The bashikouay ant—Its ferocity—Great moving armies of bashikouays—How they spread—Their mode of attack—They travel night and day—Every animal and insect flies before them—The white ants—Their buildings—Their habits—How they repair their houses—Their appearance—The ipi, or scaly ant-eater .. 253—262

CHAPTER XXI.

Subdivision of tribes—Tribes divided into clans—Chieftainship—The elders—Two kinds of slaves—Polygamy—Religious notions of the negroes—Idols—Fetiches and charms—Rabolo's fetich—The curse of witchcraft—The doctor—Power of the doctor .. .. 263—271

CHAPTER XXII.

The gorilla—Habitation of the gorilla—Habits of the gorilla—His food—Shyness of the female gorilla—Fierceness of the male—His enormous strength—Height of the gorilla—His appearance—Hands and feet of the gorilla—Hanno and Pliny on the gorilla—The chimpanzee—Difference between the chimpanzee and the gorilla—Habits of young chimpanzee—The nshiego-mbouvé, or bald-headed chimpanzee—The nkengo-nshiego—The kooloo-kamba 271–290

CHAPTER XXIII.

The Bakalai people—Tribes widely intermixed—Roving tendency of the Bakalai—Instability of their villages—Their quarrelsome habits—Their war customs—Marriage customs—Negroes' knowledge of human nature—Musical instruments 290–297

CHAPTER XXIV.

Another journey for the interior—Meeting of the people of Biagano—Good-bye to Biagano—Arrival at Goumbi—Death of Mpomo—Witchcraft ceremony—Drinking of the mboundou—Execution for witchcraft—Ilogo, a spirit living in the moon—Invocation of Ilogo—A species of manatee 298–308

CHAPTER XXV.

Arrival at Mpopo—Death of Querlaouen—Obindji enjoins Okendjo to take care of me—A cheery evening—Our entry into Ashira-land—Arrival at Akoonga—King Olenda sends men to fetch me—Extraordinary appearance of King Olenda—He receives me with great honour—The Ashira plain—Numerous villages—Appearance of the Ashira people—Dress—Mode of dressing the hair—Women's toilette—Pernicious effect of smoking wild hemp—Story of a leopard attacking a gorilla—Shelter of the nshiego-mbouvé—Starvation—Scramble for my cut hair 308–330

CHAPTER XXVI.

Preparations to go to the Apingi country—The Ovigui river—A dangerous bridge—The primeval forest—Beautiful brooks and rills—Travellers' shelters—Leopard attacking a buffalo—Remandji, king of the Apingi—A big river—Crossing the Rembo Apingi—Offer of a negro for supper—Stories about a cloven-footed race—I am made king—Am invested with the kendo—The kendo, the emblem of royalty—Tattooing—Supposed to be married to an Apingi woman—Industrious habits of the Apingi—Ownership in trees—Their knowledge of weaving—Powerful fetich to kill leopard 330–348

CHAPTER XXVII.

The ceremony of bongo—Ascending the Rembo Apingi—Apingi canoes—Apingi villages and houses—Great reputation of the Apingi fetiches—Quaint customs in regard to getting a wife—Spiders—Upsetting of a canoe—Apingi woman in the water—Customs regarding the dead—The Samba Nagoshi Falls—Grand and beautiful sight—Legend regarding the falls—The Rembo Okonda and the Rembo Ngouyai—Different tribes—Eastward from the Apingi country—No more shoes—Bleeding feet—Starvation—Farewell to the Apingi country 348–364

CHAPTER XXVIII.

A long absence—Wrecked in the breakers—Once again with my faithful Commi—Sangala, Makombé, Binkimongani dead—Ranpano and his superstitions—I receive fresh supplies—Departure for the interior—Arrival at Goumbi—Quengueza invokes the spirits of his ancestors—Departure from Obindji—Advice of Quengueza to my men—Once more in Ashira-land—A whole group of gorillas—Quarrels between my men and the Ashira—The small-pox—A terrible plague—Departure of Quengueza—Fearful effects of the plague—Death of King Olenda—A valley of the dead 364–380

CHAPTER XXIX.

Departure from the Ashira country—Crossing the Ovigui again—A village of slaves and their plantations—I am plundered—Illness of Macondai—He is left behind—A beautiful forest tract—Robbed again by my porters—The Koola nut—Hunger—The Mpegui nut .. 380–387

CHAPTER XXX.

Arrival in the Otando prairie—Máyolo—Present of food—Máyolo makes a speech—Illness of Máyolo—Arrival of Macondai—Surgical practice of the Otandos—A female doctor—The legend of Akenda Mbani—Protecting the village against witchcraft—My speech to Máyolo—Speech of Igala—Máyolo gets tipsy—Monkeys as food—I send men to Apono-land—Their reception—The people wonder at my powerful magnet—The Otando people—Native dogs 388–401

CHAPTER XXXI.

Start for Apono-land—An Apono village—Fright of the people—King Nchiengain—The village of Mouendi—The story of the sun and of the moon—Nchiengain and Máyolo drunk with palm wine—Their enthusiasm for going inland—The Aponos a merry people—They love to get tipsy—Leaving Nchiengain's village—Cross a large river—Ishogo and Apono villages—The village of Dilolo—A war cloud—A great meeting—The Apono village of Mokaba—Appearance and dress of the Aponos—The Aponos a warlike people—Iron workers—Their weapons—Aponos accompany me to the Ishogo country—Nchiengain returns to his country—Arrival among the Ishogos—The villages of Igoumbié and Yengué 401–409

CHAPTER XXXII.

The Apono country—The village of Mokaba—Large quantity of palm-trees—Palm wine a favourite drink—Many men with scars—The Ocuya performance—The Apono people—Fashion—Weapons of the Aponos—From Mokaba to Igoumbié—A large village—Singing at night 410–420

CHAPTER XXXIII.

From Igoumbié to Yengué—Discovery of a deserted village of the dwarfs—Curious houses of the dwarfs—Yengué—The king makes his appearance—Popularity of my red woollen caps—Presented with goats and fowls—Superstitions in regard to twins—The village of Mokenga—I am said to have moved a huge granite block—A village fetich-tree—Leopards—King Quembila—Panic among the Ishogos—Dismiss my Apono porters and guides—The Ishogo tribes—Appearance of the people—Women's head-dress—Wealth of an Ishogo man—The Ishogos are celebrated weavers 420–434

CHAPTER XXXIV.

I leave Mokenga—Engage Ishogo porters—The home of rain—The story of the rainy and dry seasons—Strike among the Ishogos for more pay—Drastic measures threatened—Among Ashango villages—Our entrance into Niembouai—Why chiefs do not show themselves at first—The Njavi, Abombo, and Ashangui tribes—Hear of a large river—A village idol—The mbuti men, or doctors 434–441

CHAPTER XXXV.

The dwarfs, or Obongos—Villages of dwarfs—Another deserted village of dwarfs—A new village—We approach with great caution—Flight of the dwarfs—Meeting some dwarfs—Their shyness—Leaving the dwarf village in despair—Return to their village—The people had fled—Cunning of the dwarfs—Laughable scene when measuring some of them—Appearance of the dwarfs—Modes of burial of the dwarfs—The dwarfs great trappers and hunters of game—Mode of life of the dwarfs—They are scattered all over the equatorial forests towards the east 441–449

CHAPTER XXXVI.

Departure from Niembouai—Onwards towards the
Appearance of the country—The village of
Numerous beehives—Ashangos—The Apono
the same—Appearance of the Ashangos—At
ants—Leave Niembouai Olomba—The villag
of a bride—Presentation of Ntchingo, or red p
paths to the Njavi country ..   ..   ..

CHAPTER XXXVII.

Arrival at Mouaou Kombo—True Ashango clans—
parture of the Niembouai and Mobana people—
—A palaver—Peace made—Return to the villa;
to the Njavi tribe—A terrible accident—A ma
Great panic among the natives—War drums b

CHAPTER XXXVIII.

A momentous pause—The head wife of a friendly
shout of war—The order of retreat—A deadly
Igala and I are wounded—My men narro\
desperate stand—Long rifle firing—Tumultuo
of my Commi men—Throwing away our heavy
—The enemy is cowed—Troubles threatene
Advice to my men in case I am killed or d
Olomba at night—Travelling through the fore
at a plantation—Friendly welcome—Stories
war-dish prepared between the people of Moba
—I am supposed to change my shape duri
Igoumbié—Farewell to the Ishogos—On our
shore—Meeting with Quengueza ..   ..

LIST OF ILLUSTRATIONS

	PAGE
Frontispiece.	
Map ..	*To face page* 1
Mpongwe Woman—Mode of Dressing the Hair	2
Mbondemo Man and Woman, showing manner of carrying Children and Burdens	36
Fan Warrior	47
Fan Woman and Child	49
Fan Shield and Spears	51
My First Gorilla	55
Ndiayai, King of the Fans	61
Fan Bowman	63
Poisoned Arrows, in a Skin Bag	64
Fan Knife and Axes	65
Grand Reception by the Cannibals	66
Fan Warriors	68
Fan Drum and Handja	69
The Handja	70
Elephant Battle among the Fans	72
Fan Blacksmiths	80
Fan Pottery	82
Fan Pipes	82
Fan Spoon	87
Crossing a Mangrove-Swamp	98
Horn and Bell of Iron	99
Shekiani Spoons	120
Wambee: the Shekiani Banjo	122
Encampment for the Night	124
Ncheri—a diminutive Gazelle	127
Commi Man and Woman	145
Native tossed by White Bull	150
Young Gorilla	151
River Navigation in Equatorial Africa	170
Nshiego-mbouvé (young)	175
Crocodile-hunting on Lake Anengue	178
Idol, Goddess of the Slaves	181
Ouganga exorcising a Sorcerer	188
Prisoner in Ntchogo	197
Reception at Goumbi	199
Kendo	215
Obindji in his Easy-chair	217
The Kooloo-kamba	221
Death of the Gorilla	225
Hunter killed by a Gorilla	243
The Bongo Antelope	251

LIST OF ILLUSTRATIONS.

	PAGE
The Bashikouay Ant, magnified to twice its natural size	253
Nests of Mushroom Ants and Tree Ants	256
Nests of Forest Ants	258
Ipi, or scaly Ant-eater	261
Whip, or the African Peace-maker	265
Gorilla's head	276
Gorilla, male	277
Gorilla, female	277
Gorilla, female	278
Gorilla, male	278
Gorilla, young	280
Gorilla, red rump	280
Gorilla, shedding teeth	280
Chimpanzees	282
Nshiego-mbouvé and young	283
Nshiego-mbouvés	285
Head of Kooloo-kamba	286
Kooloo-kambas	287
Ear of Kooloo-kamba	287
Skeleton of Man	288
Skeleton of Gorilla	289
Group of Bakalai	294
Ibeka: Musical Instrument of the Bakalai	297
Harp of Bakalai	297
Decapitation Scene at Goumbi	304
A Roll of Ashira Tobacco	316
Ashira Thread and Needle	317
Ashira Iron Weapons	318
Ashira Belles	319
Liamba Leaf, or Wild Hemp	322
Cynogale Velox	325
Nshiego-mbouvé in his Shelter	327
Ogana: an Ashira Housekeeper	329
Rude Bridge over the Ovigui	333
The Leopard and his Prey	336
Apingi Man and Woman with Ndengui or Green Cloth	342
An Apingi Village	350
The Kendo Squirrel	354
Wicker-work Rattle to drive the Devil out	361
Apingi tools	363
Opaitai, or Porter's Basket	368
Gorillas surprised in the Forest	373
Mokaba. An Apono Village	411
Ishogo Houses of Igoumbié, with Ornamented Doors	418
Ishogo Fashions.—Oblique Chignon	428
Ishogo Fashions.—Horizontal Chignon	429
Ishogo Fashions.—Vertical Chignon	430
Ishogo Fashions.—Male head-dress	431
Ishogo Loom and Shuttle	433
Approach to the Camp of the Obongo Dwarf	443
An African Group	451
Retreat from Ashango-Land	466

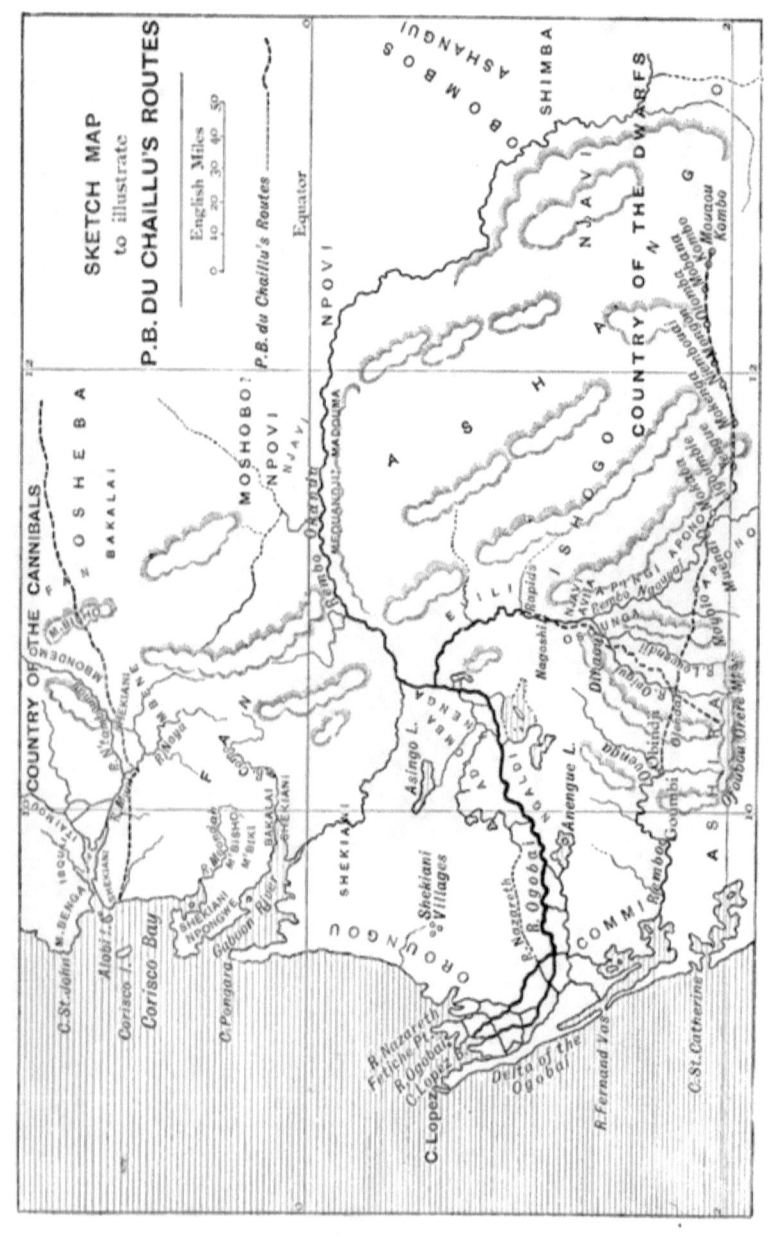

EXPLORATIONS AND ADVENTURES
IN
EQUATORIAL AFRICA.

CHAPTER I.

The Gaboon—The Mpongwe tribe—The Mpongwe one of the great families of the negro race—Decrease of the Mpongwe and other tribes—Their villages and houses—Appearance of the Mpongwe—Their dress—Their cunning as traders.

As a lad I left America for the Western Coast of Africa in the month of October, 1855. My purpose was to spend some years in the exploration of a region of territory lying between lat. 2° north and 2° south on the West Coast.

The coast-line of this region is dotted here and there with negro villages. The power and knowledge of the white man extend but a very few miles from the coast; and the interior was still a *terra incognita*. Of the natural history—which was the subject that interested me most—sufficient was known to assure me that here was a field worthy of every effort of an explorer and naturalist.

As I intended to remain a little time on the Gaboon to acclimatize myself more perfectly, I took up my residence among my friends of many years, the American missionaries, whose station is at Baraka, eight miles from the mouth of the river. Here I found a welcome and a hospitable home.

The Mpongwe, the Coast natives—once numerous, were, like so many of the African tribes, from various reasons entirely disappearing.

The fact of this mysterious and, to some extent, unaccountable extermination of certain tribes, who die out, leaving no mark behind them, is patent to every observer.

The Mpongwe are a branch of one of the great families of the negro race, which has moved gradually from the head-waters of the Nazareth down towards the sea-shore, extending its limits meantime to the north and south, until now they are found from the Gaboon River on the north to Cape St. Catherine on the south. A portion have taken possession of the sea-shore, and others are located inland. They have probably taken the place of other tribes who have disappeared in

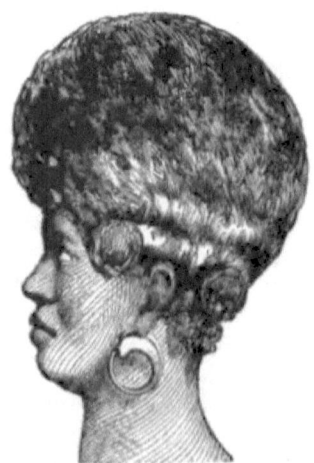

MPONGWE WOMAN—MODE OF DRESSING THE HAIR.

the strange way in which even the Mpongwe are now gradually lessening; the Ndina tribe is nearly gone, only three persons remaining of what was once a numerous people.

All the divisions of the Mpongwe speak the same language, with a difference of only a few words; though other tribes, sandwiched between, speak an entirely different tongue. I know only that there are eight different tribes now settled along the coast south of the Gaboon and in the interior, who speak the same language and have evidently a common origin.

The Mpongwe live in villages, which are generally located

with particular regard to the trading facilities afforded by the position, for these negroes are inveterate traders—in fact, the most intelligent and acute merchants on the coast. Their villages, though not extensive, have generally but one main street, on both sides of which the houses are built. Sometimes there are a few short cross-streets. In a considerable village, the main street is often 20 yards wide and 200 yards long. The houses, of course, vary in size according to the wealth of the owner. They are built of a kind of bamboo, which is obtained from a species of palm very plentiful hereabouts, and whose leaves also furnish them mats for the roofs. Indeed, this palm is one of the most generally useful products of the country to the negroes.

The houses are always of a quadrangular form, and from 20 to 100 feet in length or breadth. The principal room is in the centre. The floor is of clay, which is pounded hard, and by long use becomes a hard and clean flooring. Both houses and street are neatly kept.

The walls are built up by first driving stakes into the ground, and to these stakes the split bamboos are neatly tied. One set is tied outside and another inside, and the crevices which are left between are made close with the leaves of the palm-tree. Thus the walls are smooth and glossy, and perfectly clean.

The Mpongwe are the best-looking people I have seen, looking very much like the Mandigoes; of ordinary size and with pleasant negro features, but handsomer than the Congo tribes. The men wear a shirt, generally of English, French, or American calico, over which is wrapped a square cloth, which falls to the ankles. To this is added a *straw* hat for the head. Only the king is allowed to wear the high *silk* hat. The wealthier men and chiefs are fond of dress, and delight to show themselves in a bright military costume, sword and all.

The principal, and, in most cases, only garment of the women is a square cloth, which is wrapped about the body, and covers them from above the hips to just below the knees. On their bare legs and arms they delight to wear great numbers of brass rings, often bearing from twenty-five to thirty pounds of brass on each ankle in this way. This ridiculous vanity greatly obstructs their locomotion, and makes their walk a clumsy waddle.

The most characteristic trait of all the negro tribes I have seen is their great eagerness and love for trade.

Let me here give the reader an idea of African commerce. The rivers, which are the highways of the country, are, of course, the avenues by which every species of export and import must be conveyed from and to the interior tribes. Now, the river-banks are possessed by different tribes. Thus, while the Mpongwe hold the mouth and some miles above, they are succeeded by the Shekiani, and these again by other tribes, to the number of almost a dozen, before the mountains of the interior are reached. Each of these tribes assumes to itself the privilege of acting as go-between or middle-man to those next to it, and charges a heavy percentage for this office; and no infraction of this rule is permitted under penalty of war. Thus a tusk of ivory or a piece of ebony may belong originally to a negro in the far interior, and if he wants to barter it for "white man's trade," he dares not take it to a market himself. If he should be rash enough to attempt such a piece of enterprise his goods would be confiscated, and he, if caught, fined by those whose monopoly he sought to break down, or most likely sold into slavery.

He is obliged by the laws of trade to intrust it to some fellow in the next tribe nearer to the coast. He, in turn, disposes of it to the next chief or friend; and so ivory, or ebony, etc., etc., passes through probably a dozen hands ere it reaches the factory of the trader on the coast.

But this is only half the evil. Although the producer sold his ivory, and though it was re-sold a dozen times, all this trade was only a *commission* business with no advances. In fact, the first holder has *trusted* each successive dispenser with his property without any equivalent or "collateral" security. Now, when the last black fellow disposes of this piece of ebony or ivory to the white merchant or captain, he retains, in the first place, a very liberal percentage of the returns for his valuable services, and turns the remainder over to his next neighbour above. *He*, in turn, takes out a commission for *his* trouble and passes on what is left; and so, finally, a very small remainder—too often nothing at all—is handed over to the poor fellow who has inaugurated the speculation or sent the tusk.

The consequence is that the interior tribes—who own the most productive country—have little or no incentive to trade.

The trade in slaves is carried on in exactly the same way, except that sometimes an infraction of trade-laws, or some disturbance on account of witchcraft, causes a war between two tribes.

I have heard the negroes called stupid, but my experience shows them to be anything but that. They are very shrewd traders indeed; and no captain or merchant who is a new hand on the coast will escape being victimized by their cunning in driving a bargain.

Say that to-day the good ship *Jenny* has arrived in the river. Immediately every black fellow is full of trade. The ship is boarded by a crowd of fellows, each jabbering away, apparently at random, but all telling the same story.

Never was there such a dearth of ivory, or whatever the captain may want!

Never were the interior tribes so obstinate in demanding a high price!

Never was the whole coast so bare!

Never were difficulties so great!

There have been fights, captain!

And fever, captain!

And floods, captain!

And no trade at all, captain!

Not a tusk of ivory!

Now, while they are pretending that nothing is to be bought, that there is no ivory on the coast, all this time the cunning fellows have their hands full, and are eager to sell. They know the captain is in a hurry. The coast is sickly. The weather is hot. He fears his crew may fall sick or die, and he be left with a broken voyage. Every day is therefore precious to him; but to the black fellows all days are alike.

Even then, however, there are tedious hours of chaffering.

A negro has perhaps only one tusk to sell, and he is willing —as he must live on this sale for a long period of idleness— to give much time to its proper disposal. He makes up his mind beforehand how much more he will ask than he will eventually take. He brings his tusk alongside; spends the afternoon in bargaining, and probably takes it back ashore at dusk, to try again the next day; till at last, when he sees he cannot possibly get more, he strikes the bargain. I have known several days to be spent in the selling of a single tusk or a single cask of palm-oil.

Of course, the captain protests that he is not in a hurry— that he can wait—that they shan't tire *him* out. But the negroes know better; they know the fatal advantage their climate gives them.

When it is supposed that a captain or trader will return to the coast no more after his present voyage, then he is properly victimized, as then the native has no fear of future vengeance before him; and I have known many individuals who by the system of "trust" were all but ruined—getting scarce any return at all.

CHAPTER II.

Old King Glass—His death—Secret burial—Mourning customs—The election of a new king—Treatment before being made a king—Food— Plantation.

WHILE I was in the Gaboon old King Glass died. He had long been ailing, but stuck to life with a determined tenacity. He was a disagreeable old heathen, but in his last days became very devout—after his fashion. His idol was always freshly painted and brightly decorated; his fetich was the best-cared-for fetich in Africa; and every few days some great doctor was brought down from the interior, and paid a large fee for advising the old king. He was afraid of witchcraft— thought everybody wanted to put him out of the way by bewitching him; and in this country your doctor does not try to cure your sickness; his business is to keep off the witches.

The tribe had grown tired of their king. They thought, indeed, that he was himself a most potent and evil-disposed wizard, and though the matter was not openly talked about, there were few natives who would pass his house after night, and none who would be tempted inside by any slighter provocation than an irresistible jug of rum. Indeed, if he had not belonged to one of the most noble families of the Mpongwe tribe, I think he would perhaps have been killed, so rife was suspicion against him.

When he became ill at last everybody seemed very sorry; but several of my friends told me in confidence that the whole town hoped he would die; and die he did. I was awakened one morning early by the mournful cries and wails with which the African oftener assumes a sham sorrow than eases a real grief. All the town seemed lost in tears. It is a most singular thing to see the faculty the women of Africa have for pumping up tears on the slightest occasion, or on no occasion at all. There needs no grief or pain to draw the water. I have seen them shed tears copiously, and laughing all the while.

The mourning and wailing lasted six days. On the second the old king was secretly buried. The Mpongwe kings are always buried by a few of the most trustworthy men of the tribe in a spot which they only know of, and which is for ever hidden from all others. This custom arises from a vain belief of the Mpongwe that, as they are the most able and intelligent people of Africa, the other tribes would like much to get the head of one of their kings, with the brains of which to make a powerful fetich. Such an advantage they are not willing to give to their neighbours. Now, as it is customary to hang a flag or a piece of cloth where a Mpongwe is buried, these old men hung also a large piece of bright cloth over a spot where the king was *not* laid. Where he *was* put I cannot tell, because the secret was not told even to me.

During the days of mourning the old men of the village busied themselves in choosing a new king. This also is a secret operation. The choice is made in private, and communicated to the populace only on the seventh day, when the new king is to be crowned. But the king is kept ignorant of his good fortune to the last.

It happened that *Njogoni*, a good friend of my own, was elected. The choice fell on him, in part because he came of a good family, but chiefly because he was a favourite of the people and could get the most votes. I do not know that Njogoni had the slightest suspicion of his elevation. At any rate, if he had, he shammed ignorance very well. As he was walking on the shore, on the morning of the seventh day, he was suddenly set upon by the entire populace, who proceeded to a ceremony which is preliminary to the crowning, and which must deter any but the most ambitious men from aspiring to the crown. They surrounded him in a dense crowd, and then began to heap upon him every manner of abuse that the worst of mobs could imagine. Some spat in his face; some beat him with their fists; some kicked him; others threw disgusting objects at him; while those unlucky ones who stood on the outside, and could reach the poor fellow only with their voices, assiduously cursed him, his father, his mother, his sisters and brothers, and all his ancestors, to the remotest generation. A stranger would not have given a cent for the life of him who was presently to be crowned.

Amid all the noise and struggle, I caught the words which explained all this to me; for every few minutes some fellow, administering an especially severe blow or kick, would shout out, "You are not our king yet; for a little while we will do what we please with you. By-and-by we shall have to do your will."

Njogoni bore himself like a man and a prospective king. He kept his temper, and took all the abuse with a smiling face. When it had lasted about half-an-hour they took him to the house of the old king. Here he was seated, and became again for a little while the victim of his people's curses.

Then all became silent; and the elders of the people rose and said, solemnly (the people repeating after them), "Now we choose you for our king; we engage to listen to you and to obey you."

A silence followed, and presently the silk hat, which is the emblem of Mpongwe royalty, was brought in and placed on Njogoni's head. He was then dressed in a red gown, and received the greatest marks of respect from all who had just now abused him.

Now followed a six days' festival, during which the poor king, who had taken with the office also the name of his predecessor, was obliged to receive his subjects in his own house, and was not allowed to stir out; six days of indescribable gorging of food and bad rum—of beastly drunkenness and uproarious festivity. Numbers of strangers came in from surrounding villages to pay their respects; and all brought more rum, more palm-wine, and more food. Everything that tended toward festivity was given away, and all who came were welcome.

Old King Glass, for whom for six days no end of tears had been shed, was now forgotten; and *new* King Glass, poor fellow, was sick with exhaustion, for day and night he had to be ready to receive and be civil to all who came.

Finally, all the rum was drunk up, the allotted days were expired, and quiet once more began to reign. Now, for the first time, his new majesty was permitted to walk out and view his domains.

The vegetable food of the Mpongwe, and with little variation of most of the other tribes of this region near the sea-shore, consists of Indian corn, the plantain, yams, sweet potatoes, cassava (manioc), pumpkins, and pea-nuts. The last produce enormously, and considerable oil could be made from them if any one would give attention to their cultivation for this purpose. The forests abound in wild fruits and nuts, some of which are eaten; for instance, the pine-apple grows wild in all parts of this region.

Their plantations are never near their villages, and often many miles away. The consequence is, that during the dry season the Mpongwe villages are mostly deserted, all hands, men, women, and slaves, being busily engaged on their farms in preparing the soil for the crop which must be put down by the beginning of the rainy season. This is a busy time, as generally new clearings have to be made, for which the men cut down the trees and burn them, when the women come in and put in the crop. They use no ploughs or hoes, but only a little tool like a gardener's dibble, with which they turn up a piece of sod, put in a seed, cover it over, and pass on to the next. But rude as their agricultural knowledge is, they sometimes raise good crops.

The Mpongwe eat the meat of almost every animal found in the forest and river—deer, antelopes, wild boar. Civilization has taught them not to eat animals of other orders like the other natives, such as chimpanzee, crocodile, monkeys, rats, and so forth; such food is eaten by their slaves.

CHAPTER III.

Corisco island—The Mbengo tribe—Death of Tonda—Sorrowful scene—Departure for the Muni river—Mbango—Adventure at sea—Capture of a debtor—Lost in the Muni mangrove swamps—Arrival at Dayoko's—Reception.

It was my intention to proceed first on an exploration of the River Muni, and for this purpose I sailed from Gaboon for Corisco Island, where I was to get canoes and men to help me at least a part of the way up river.

The island is not more than twelve miles in circumference, with a population of about 1000 souls. The people are quiet, peaceable, and hospitable to strangers. They belong to the Mbenga tribe, the most enterprising traders and the most daring boatmen.

This tribe inhabits not only Corisco, but also the land about the neighbouring Capes Steiras and St. John. Their language differs somewhat from the Bakalai, but has, like that, no letter R, while the Mpongwe and its dialects abound in the use of this letter.

A few days before I left the island, *Tonda*, a Mbenga fellow, died, and at his funeral I was witness to a singular ceremony, akin to the "waking" of the body.

The mother of poor Tonda, who heard that I wished to see

NATIVE MOURNING.

him once more, led me to the house where the body was laid. The narrow space of the room was crowded; about two hundred women were sitting and standing around, singing mourning songs to doleful and monotonous airs. They were so huddled together that for a while I could not distinguish the place of the corpse. At last some moved aside, and behold! the body of my friend.

It was seated in a chair.

It was dressed in a black tail-coat and a pair of pantaloons.

It had several strings of beads about the neck.

Altogether, it was a ghastly sight, though the pallid face of death cannot be seen in the negro.

As I stood looking, filled with solemn thoughts, in spite of, or rather because of, perhaps, the somewhat ludicrous contrasts about me, the mother of Tonda approached.

She threw herself at the feet of her dead son, and begged him to speak to her once more.

And then, when the poor corpse did not answer, she uttered a shriek, so long, so piercing, such a wail of love and grief, that the tears came into my eyes. Poor African mother! she was literally as one sorrowing without hope; for these poor people count on nothing beyond the present life. For them there is no hope beyond the grave. "All is done," they say, with an inexpressible sadness of conviction that sometimes gave me a heartache. Truly, it is worth while to bear words of comfort and promise to such as these.

As I left the hut the wailing recommenced. It would be kept up by the women, who are the official mourners on these occasions, till the corpse was buried. Then the family and friends would lay aside their ornaments for many months, would refrain from dancing and all manner of merry-making, till at last all is forgotten again.

I made preparations for a long journey, in which I intended to explore the Muni to its head-waters; to cross, if possible, the Sierra del Crystal mountain, and see what kind of country and what manner of people were to be found there.

My voyage was to be made alone, so far as white companions were concerned. Mbango, a chief or head-man among the Corisco people, was engaged to accompany me, to introduce me to a friend of his, an influential king on the Muni.

We set out in Mbango's canoe on the 27th of July. The canoe was hewn out of a single tree. My crew consisted of twelve black fellows, besides Mbango, all armed with guns. I foresaw that, from the dread all the coast natives have of the cannibal tribes said to be living in the interior, I should have difficulty in carrying all my baggage. I therefore determined not to encumber myself with supplies of provisions or anything else that could be spared. My outfit consisted only of the following articles:—A chest containing 100 fathoms of prints, 19 pounds of white beads, a quantity of small looking-glasses, fire-steels and flints, a quantity of leaf tobacco. In addition to which came my greatest dependence, viz., 80 pounds of shot and bullets, 25 pounds of powder, and my guns.

The day on which we sailed was beautiful. There was a fine breeze, and we passed in rapid succession the islets which dot the Bay of Corisco, Leval, Banian, and Big and Little Alobi. I was in high spirits at the auspicious commencement of my trip, when one of those peculiar detentions occurred which arise out of the ill-regulated trade system of Africa, and which would be laughable were they not vexatious.

Mbango was a great trading man. Therefore Mbango had debts owing him. Now Mbango's debtors, like most debtors on the African coast, were not fond of paying, and I found that Mbango made a practice of lying in wait for them, seizing them, and robbing them of what they happened to have with them, as a kind of new way to pay old debts.

Accordingly, as we were sailing along, my steersman kept an unusually sharp look-out ahead. His care was presently rewarded. We saw a large boat sailing along down toward us carelessly, as though they had no enemies to dread. No sooner, however, were the boatmen near enough to recognize us than, with a little shout of surprise, they put about and sailed and paddled off in the utmost haste.

But Mbango also gave a little shout. He recognized in the same moment in the other boat a veteran poor debtor of his. Turning our boat after the other, he urged his men to paddle, and meantime shouted to the others to stop.

But the more he called "Stop!" the harder they paddled off.

Now our side became excited. Mbango called that he would fire upon them.

This only frightened them more.

Our men seized their guns, and (slyly shaking the powder out of the touch-holes, I must say to their credit) pointed directly at the flying boat.

Now the women even seized paddles and plied them vigorously.

Then our side fired a few random shots over the heads of the flying debtors. Still they paddled on.

By this time, however, it became apparent that our boat was the fastest. Presently, indeed, we overtook the other.

I had been sitting quietly watching the fun; but now, as we hauled alongside the enemy's boat, and I saw a good deal of fierce blood up on both sides, I began to remonstrate. I did not wish to see blood spilt, nor did I care to be upset in the scuffle; but my voice was drowned in the uproar. A desperate hand-to-hand fight began at once as we ranged alongside. How we escaped upsetting I do not yet understand. I was wet through; the canoe took in water—when suddenly the other canoe again gave us the slip.

Now the chase began again. Again we shouted, and the other side paddled as for dear life; but it was of no avail. Presently we again hauled alongside, and this time we made fast. Then came another fight, in the midst of which the boatmen, seeing they were about to be overpowered, suddenly leaped into the water and swam off. Mbango caught two of them, and took, besides, a woman prisoner; then coolly turned on his course again, saying to me with a smile that he had done a very good day's work. He explained that these people had long owed him a quantity of bar-wood, for which he had paid in advance, and, now that he had some of the party prisoners, they would soon settle up.

About a mile from the mouth of the Muni are Big and

Little Alobi, two small islets. The first has a few native villages, ruled by King Mpapay, who this day presented me with a chicken and a bunch of plantains, on which I made my dinner. In return I gave his negro majesty some heads of tobacco.

Here we remained over night, I sleeping ashore, while Mbango's favourite slave man kept watch over the boat.

The following morning several Muni River men came down to see me, having heard that I was about to go up the river; and in the afternoon we sailed with a favourable tide for the village of Mbango's friend, Dayoko. We had a fair wind, and the boat fellows availed themselves of it to lie about and do nothing, which they know how to do perfectly. These canoes do not sail *on* the wind at all; but *before* it, with their sails of country matting, they make very good headway.

Yesterday I measured our canoe—thirty-five feet long, three feet wide, and about three-and-a-half feet deep; made, as before said, out of one immense tree. The Muni, the river which I was now to ascend, empties its waters into the Bay of Corisco, in lat. 1° 2′ N., and long. 9° 33′. It is formed by the confluence of three other streams, the Ntongo, a stream of forty miles length, whose course is S.W. by W.; the Ntambounay, which runs an easterly course for thirty miles, and then turns to the south-west for forty miles more, when it disappears in the mountains; and the Noya, which runs from its rise sixty miles to the north-east, and then west for twenty miles more. The Ntambounay and the Noya both have their sources in the Sierra del Crystal. Their banks are sparsely populated by various tribes, speaking different dialects. The Muni is, like most of the rivers of the coast, bounded by mangrove swamps; but near the mouth, where we sailed to-day, the highlands were visible in the background, and made up a picturesque scene. The point forming one side of the bank at the mouth is high land, and on it several Shekiani villages are located, which look very pretty from the river.

As we ascended the river the banks became more swampy; and, at the distance of seventeen miles from the mouth, we came to a beautiful little island, formed by the junction of the Ntongo with the Muni.

Some miles above the mouth of the Ntongo, the Ndina empties its sluggish waters into the *Muni*. The Ndina is but a swampy creek, overrun with mangrove jungles, back of which are to be found some villages, to which the well-guided traveller is led by native paths which no one but an experienced woodman would perceive. It was the Ndina which we were now to ascend. As the tide was against us, and was stronger than the wind, we put down our sail, which had carried us along thus far, and the crew took to their paddles.

When we had pulled about twelve miles up the creek, through a continuous mangrove swamp, in which the sluggish current of the river often lost itself, I saw that my men began to look uneasy. Presently it leaked out that they had lost their reckoning. They had thought ere now to have arrived at Dayoko's village—our destination—and began to be discouraged.

So here was a pleasant prospect of passing the night in the swamp, where we were like to be eaten up by mosquitoes, whose buzz was already noisy, and whose sharp bills began to make themselves felt thus early in the afternoon.

In the midst of our perplexity a Mbenga boat came down the stream, and, on inquiry, its crew told us that Dayoko's village was yet a considerable way off. They gave us, however, the right direction—an important matter, as in the approaching gloom we were like to glide out of the main channel into some of the numerous side "reaches," or bayous, which lead in from the main stream. Thus encouraged, the men again took to their paddles, and, to show their joy, began to sing.

Presently we came to a very small collection of huts; and here I asked a fellow standing on the bank to guide us up to Dayoko's. He was ready to do so, but seeing probably that I was anxious to get ahead, thought to make a good bargain with me. He wanted two fathoms of cloth, two heads of tobacco, and two pipes. This was unreasonable, and I at once refused to have anything to do with him.

Nothing gives these people so poor an opinion of a white man as the discovery that they can victimize him in a bargain; and accordingly I was always careful to let no one get the better of me even in trifles. Fortunately the moon presently rose, and we were enabled to thread our way up the crooked creek, and found by-and-by the mouth of a smaller creek, at whose head Dayoko lives.

When we arrived the tide was out, and I had, in consequence, to wade through the stinking mud-bank which lay before, and, to some extent, defended the village. Such mud-banks, which at low tide are dry, emit a most offensive smell, and doubtless cause much sickness.

The noise of our approach awakened the whole village, and the men came down towards us, with their old trade muskets loaded, and ready for a fight should it prove, as oftens happens, a midnight raid of the enemy. These people have the luck of Ishmael; every man's hand seems against them, and their hand is against every man. They are constantly quarrelling, and scarce ever sleep without fear of a hostile incursion. The treacherous enemy comes down upon a sleeping village, and shoots the unsuspecting inhabitants through the chinks in their bamboo houses, then escapes under cover of the darkness. This is the style of warfare all over this part of Africa.

They were greatly rejoiced when they found us to be their friends the Mbenga. Visions of "trade" began to loom before them; they opened their arms, set up a shout of gladness, and immediately conducted us in state through the village to the house generally set apart in every considerable negro town for strangers.

Here a great fire was kindled, and presently Dayoko himself came in, his eyes not half opened, for he had but just waked up, and pretty soon the house was filled and surrounded by most of the men and women of the village.

Then began the "salutation"—a tedious formality among the African tribes. All the chief men of Dayoko, together with himself and his wives, sat round the fire, and, when all was hushed, *Mbango*, our head-man, began his oration. In this it is required that every most minute adventure and incident of the voyage up river shall be alluded to, and thus a catalogue made of everything that has happened. The speaker delivers himself in short sentences. All sit round silent and open-mouthed, and at intervals the chief men give little grunts of approbation. At last all was told, and, to my great satisfaction, *Mbango* sat down.

Immediately all ceremony was dropped; every man carried off his friend to have a talk about trade, night seeming no objection, and the women began to prepare some food, of which I stood in much need. I sat down before an immense basket of boiled plantains and a few boiled fish, and made a very hearty meal. This ended, I was shewn to my place in the house assigned me for sleeping, when I was glad enough to wrap myself in my mosquito-netting and sleep till daybreak.

CHAPTER IV.

A king in Africa—Jealousy of the natives in regard to trade—Dayoko wants to keep me—Appearance of Mbousha—Death of a wizard—Departure for the interior—Ascent of the Muni—A Shekiani village—The Ntambounay and Noonday rivers—Mbene village—A new plantation—Reception by King Mbene—Offer of a wife.

My first business on the following day was to talk to Dayoko about my expedition into the interior; to ask his permission to go, and obtain from him an escort.

A stranger going into an African village and seeing the chief or king living in a manner as simple and as needy as any of his subjects, would little expect that such a king possesses great authority in his own tribe, and wields great influence among his neighbours. Dayoko, for instance, was chiefly remarkable as the oldest living man in the village. He was a trader like the rest, a beggar like the rest, and was very glad to accept from me a propitiatory offering of an old dress-coat which, having done duty for a whole winter in New York, had been put away, with other cast-off garments, for this very purpose.

But Dayoko is the oldest and most influential chief among the Mbousha tribe. His age gives him great authority among his own people, and a judicious culture of the marriage relation has given the shrewd old fox no end of fathers-in-law in every tribe within a hundred miles. Now, to have a father-in-law in Africa means to have a friend in need, a man to whom you can confidently send a bit of ivory or bar-wood to sell, and whom you call on in an emergency where he can help you. In fact, the more wives a man has the more power he gains in this way, and women are chiefly valuable because by their means amicable and commercial relations are cultivated and subsist between the tribes. Dayoko was already an old man. He had begun to marry when quite young, had married, right and left, all about him ever since, and was now related to one or two great men in every tribe which he could by any means reach. Thus he promised to prove a most useful ally to me.

Though Dayoko's palace was no bigger than the hut of any of his well-to-do subjects, I found, as was to be expected, that he had more wives and more slaves than the others. And I found, too, that his voice in the councils was of great weight, and that, in certain cases, he possessed a veto power which rendered him supreme.

My first aim was to convince everybody that I did not want to *trade*.

Having established this point, I called Dayoko into my house and gave him the present with which a negotiation is generally opened. I gave him the coat before mentioned, about twenty yards of cotton cloth, some powder, some looking-glasses for his wives, and some gun-flints.

His majesty accepted graciously all my offering.

Then I spoke of going into the Fan or cannibal country.

Dayoko thought my project impossible.

I would die on the way, and he should have my death on his soul—a consideration which seemed to affect him greatly.

I should be murdered by the cannibals and eaten.

There was war on the river, and the tribes would not let me pass.

And so on

Seeing that I exhibited no signs of repentance, the old sinner turned on a new tack. *His* country was full of beasts and birds. Why not hunt here? and he would give me as many men as I wanted.

Finally, I told him, with a great show of firmness, that go I would, if not with his people, then with some one else.

Hereupon he relented, fearing probably that I would leave him, and that thus he should not make so much out of me as he calculated.

It is as well to add that I did not let any of his fellows peep into my chest. They are all greedy, and think that every white man is by nature a Crœsus, and owner of untold wealth in cloth, looking-glasses, gun-flints, powder, and tobacco.

It was at last determined that I should go under Dayoko's protection. So on the third day after my arrival I sent my Mbenga men back, and was now left alone among my new friends. I am to wait for a party going to Mbene's people, who lived farther up river, and in whose charge Dayoko proposes to put me. If they do not come, I shall get an escort of his Mbousha men.

Meantime, numbers of the neighbouring tribes come daily to see me. Most of these have never seen a white man before, and are filled with astonishment at my long hair, at my white skin—it is really tanned a very dark brown by this time—and at the clothes I wear. They stand about me in such crowds that often I am half-suffocated with the stench which their uncleanly bodies give out.

While waiting, I amused myself with hunting.

I have still to wait for the people Dayoko promises. This will make some detention, as they are here on agricultural intents, and the men are out all day cutting trees, and the women clearing the ground; everything is busy bustle. This is the dry season, and now all planting must be done, for in a few weeks the rains come on, and then it is too late.

The dry season is delightful in Africa. It is the season of flowers, of birds—who flit through bushes at all hours, and charm one with their meteor-like flight—of everything pleasant.

These Mbousha look very much like the Shekiani people. They have the usual negro features, and are of medium height. They are less warlike than the Shekianis, but quite as superstitious and cruel, as I had occasion to know. I heard one day, by accident, that a man had been apprehended on a charge of causing the death of one of the chief men of the village. I went to Dayoko, and asked about it. He said yes, the man was to be killed; that he was a notorious wizard, and had done much harm.

So I begged to see this terrible being.

I was taken to a rough hut, within which sat an old, old man, with wool white as snow, wrinkled face, bowed form, and shrunken limbs. His hands were tied behind him, and his feet were placed in a rude kind of stocks. This was the great wizard. Several lazy negroes stood guard over him, and from time to time insulted him with opprobrious epithets and blows, to which the poor old wretch submitted in silence. He was evidently in his dotage.

I asked him if he had no friends, no relations, no son, or daughter, or wife to take care of him. He said sadly, "No one."

Now, here was the secret of this prosecution. They were tired of taking care of the helpless old man, who had lived too long, and a charge of witchcraft by the greegree man was a convenient pretext for putting him out of the way. I saw at once that it would be vain to try to save him.

I went, however, to Dayoko, and argued the case with him. I tried to explain the absurdity of charging a harmless old man with supernatural powers; told him that God did not permit witches to exist; and finally made an offer to buy the old wretch, offering to give some pounds of tobacco, one or two coats, and some looking-glasses for him—goods which would have bought me an able-bodied slave.

Dayoko replied that for his part he would be glad to save him, but that the people must decide; that they were much excited against him; but that he would, to please me, try to save his life.

During the night following I heard singing all over the town all night, and a great uproar. Evidently they were preparing themselves for the murder. Even these savages cannot kill in cold blood, but work themselves into a frenzy of excitement first, and then rush off to do the bloody deed.

Early in the morning the people gathered together, with the fetich-man in their midst. His blood-shot eyes glared in savage excitement as he went around from man to man getting the votes to decide whether the old man should die.

In his hands he held a bundle of herbs, with which he sprinkled three times those to whom he spoke. Meantime a man was stationed on the top of a high tree, whence he shouted from time to time, in a loud voice, "*Jocoo! Jocoo!*" at the same time shaking the tree strongly.

"*Jocoo*" is *devil* among the Mbousha, and the business of this man was to keep away the evil spirit, and to give notice to the fetich-man of his approach.

At last the sad vote was taken. It was declared that the old man was a most malignant wizard; that he had already killed a number of people; that he was minded to kill many more, and that he must die. No one would tell me how he was to be killed, and they proposed to defer the execution till my departure, which I was, to tell the truth, rather glad of. The whole scene had considerably agitated me, and I was willing to be spared the end. Tired and sick at heart, I lay down on my bed about noon to rest and compose my spirits a little. After a while I saw a man pass my window, almost like a flash, and after him a horde of silent but infuriated men. They ran toward the river.

Then, in a little while, I heard a couple of sharp, piercing cries, as of a man in great agony, and then all was still as death.

I got up, guessing the rascals had killed the poor old man, and turning my steps toward the river, was met by the crowd returning, every man armed with axe, knife, cutlass, or spear, and these weapons, and their own hands and arms and bodies, all sprinkled with the blood of their victim. In their frenzy they had tied the poor wizard to a log near the river-bank, and then deliberately hacked him into many pieces. They finished by splitting open his skull and scattering the brains in the water. Then they returned, and, to see their behaviour, it would have seemed as though the country had just been delivered from a great curse.

These Africans suppose that no cruelty is too great to practise upon a wizard; and this kind of legalised murder, though it temporarily excites their passions, does not seem to afflict them with any remorseful feelings at all.

The following day we were to start for the interior. Dayoko gave me two of his sons to be of my party—a piece of real good luck for me. Also, he sent messages to all the neighbouring tribes to command good treatment for me.

The men asked to be paid before we started—a dangerous practice, as they are likely to run away. But as they were Dayoko's men, and he had treated me well, I thought best to agree. They are real extortioners. I had to pay for canoes, for mat sails, for paddles, for every least thing necessary for the outfit; and every fathom of cloth or string of beads that could be got from me on any pretext I was relieved of. Then, to make them happier, I went to their wives, who had all been very kind to me, and gave each some tobacco to solace her in her husband's absence.

At last, and just before we were to start, when all was ready and the men were gathered, I had again to assure Dayoko that I did not at all intend to trade, but only to hunt for the gorilla, and visit the mountains and their inhabitants.

So at last we were off. My party consisted of two sons of Dayoko, myself, and several men to carry my chests and guns. Mbene, the Mbondemo chief, for whose place we are bound, is to take me into the heart of the Sierra del Crystal, and then "perhaps we shall cross over beyond."

We started in canoes, and paddled up a creek which led into the Muni. The course of the stream was dotted and interrupted by many small islands, the shores of which were bordered with graceful palms. Evidently we had got out of the dull and dreary region of mangrove swamps.

Towards night we reached a Shekiani village, where we had to stop all night. It was a most uncomfortable night. I never saw natives so excited as were these savages at the appearance of my chests. Their cupidity was excited by what they thought must be fabulous riches in my possession, and I was told at once by a head-man that I could not pass to the interior without paying to this Shekiani town a tribute of six shirts, 100 fathoms of cloth, three great-coats, and a great quantity of looking-glasses, files, and beads, etc.

As the excitement seemed to grow the longer I stayed, I ordered my men to lie in my hut, thinking that the fear of killing members of a friendly tribe might deter them from firing in upon me during the night. I lay quietly down, with my double-barrelled gun by my side, ready for instant action, fully resolved to sell my life at as dear a rate as possible. Meantime, Dayoko's sons went out to palaver with the chief.

I did not sleep a wink all night. All night the crowd surrounded my house, talking, shouting, singing, and in the greatest excitement. At last, about four o'clock, things became a little quieter, and towards daylight those who were not asleep were still.

As early as I could go out I called on the king, and told him that my chests contained only powder, shot, and other heavy things necessary for my journey; and also I gave his majesty a few fathoms of cloth, and distributed a few leaves of tobacco among his big men; at which all were much satisfied. They asked for rum, but that I never give to these natives, and so refused of course. Finally we left them, many of the people following us along the river, and wishing us good luck and speedy return.

We left our large canoe at the Shekiani village, and passed up the Ntambounay into the Noonday River, making in this day, Tuesday, August 19th, a toilsome journey of twenty-nine miles, twelve of which were on the Noonday.

The landscape continued beautiful on the Ntambounay. The palms lining the river-banks, and the numerous small islands which stud its smooth and glass-like bosom, the occasional gazelles which started away from the water-side as our canoe swept into sight, the shrill cries of various monkeys gazing at us in astonishment and terror, the clear sky and the magnificent solitude of these forests which surrounded us, and through the trees of which we saw only at considerable intervals the smoke curling up which announced a village hid in the wilderness: all this was a constant delight to every sense.

As we were sailing lazily along, I espied two eagles sitting on some high trees about eighty yards off. Willing to give my fellows a taste of my quality, I called their attention to the birds, and then brought both down with my double-barrel. They could hardly believe their eyes for surprise, such shooting being almost miraculous to them. When they had got a little over their astonishment, I heard them say, "Ah! if he had fought those Shekiani fellows last night, how many he *would* have killed!"

In the far distance the ranges of the Sierra del Crystal could be seen, the second and higher range rising above the first. The river we were ascending seemed to abound in fish, which jumped frequently out of the water in pursuit of their insect prey; and the bright-blue kingfishers shot across the water hither and thither, breaking the quiet with their shrill screams.

As we got higher up the Noonday the stream became narrow, and finally almost dwindled away. Part of its course lay through a tangled thicket or jungle of aloe-trees, whose sharp thorns tore our clothes, and wounded me so that I was covered with blood. We had here a fair sample of African "river" travel. The aloe-jungle grew, in many places, right into the narrow stream, and so filled it up that, had I not seen it, I should never have believed that a canoe could pass through. In several places we had to get out and carry the canoe over fallen trees which entirely barred our progress, and all through it was a battle with the jungle, and a passage through a swamp rather than fair navigation. Yet this is the only highway of this country, by which the natives bring all their ivory, ebony, and india-rubber, etc., to the coast; for even this is better than travelling *through* the almost impenetrable jungle on foot, in which case their poor women have to bear the heavy loads on their shoulders.

Dark came on before we had reached Mbene's town, which was the nearest settlement, and I had the ugly prospect before me of passing the night in this deadly swamp. Fortunately I had fallen in, at the Shekiani town, with a son of King Mbene; and this good fellow, now, seeing my men wearied out and unable to go farther, volunteered to hurry on to his father's town and bring assistance. How far it was we knew not; but he went off.

We waited an hour, but no help arrived. Then I sent out two of my men to meet the party and hurry them on. Two hours more passed, and I had begun to despair of help, when loud shouts ringing through the woods gave us notice of the approach of our friends; and presently rushed in among us King Mbene himself, his face radiant with smiles, and shouting a welcome to me. He was followed by a large party of men and women, who took up my boxes and other things. Mbene took one of my guns, and, thus relieved, we hurried on to the town or encampment of my royal friend, which proved to be about six miles off.

The people had been here such a little while that they had not had time to cut a road to the river, so that the few miles we traversed from the river-side were of the roughest. Happily, elephants are plentiful hereabouts, and when we could we walked in their huge tracks—the rushing of a herd effecting quite a clearing in the woods, though everything grows up again with marvellous rapidity.

I expected to come to a town. My astonishment was great when I found, instead of the usual plantations of plantain-trees which surround the collection of huts which make up an African village, an immense mass of timber thrown down helter-skelter, as though a hurricane had passed through this part of the forest. It appeared that Mbene's people had their village at some distance off, but came here to make new plantations, and this was their way of making a clearing. It is the usual way among these tribes. The men go into the forest and choose a site for the plantation; then cut down the trees in any way, just as luck or fancy may direct; let everything lie till the dry season has sufficiently seasoned the great trees, when they set fire to the whole mass, burn it up, and on its site the women then plant their manioc, maize, and plantains.

It was only with the greatest difficulty, and with many tears from thorns and trips from interposing boughs, that I got through this barrier, than which they could not have made a better wall of defence for their village. For, once get an enemy entangled in such a piece of ground, and they could pepper him at their convenience, without fear of retaliation.

At last, when my patience was entirely gone, and my few clothes were literally hanging in ribbons about me, we arrived at the camp. Here we were received in grand African style. Guns were fired, the people shouted and danced, everybody was as jolly as though everybody's brother had just come back rich, and I was immediately installed under a shed, whither the king graciously followed me with a present—very welcome indeed—of a goat and some bunches of plantains.

The plantain is the bread of all these tribes. Lucky would they be if they always had such bread to eat; but their thriftless habits leave them without even the easily-cultivated plantain, and force them to eke out a wretched subsistence from the wild roots, nuts, and berries which are found in the forests.

Mbene's village or encampment is situated at the foot of the first granite-range of the Sierra del Crystal. The forest-clad hill-sides were visible in the distance, and were to me a delightful spectacle. The people had not as yet built themselves houses, but were living in camp, under rude sheds composed of leaves spread thickly over four-forked sticks planted in the ground. Here each head of a family gathered his wives, children, and slaves about him, and rested in safety and peace. One of the best constructed of these sheds—one whose stick stood upright, and whose leafy roof was water-tight—was given me, and here I presently fell soundly asleep, after first placing my two chests near my head.

On rising the next morning, I found that we were really not more than ten or fifteen miles from the hills. Yesterday evening we could see two ranges; the lower 500 or 600 feet high, and the farther and higher from 2000 to 3000 feet high.

It is beyond these hills that the Fans—the cannibal tribe—live, and the gorilla also has here his home.

Mbene excused himself for what he thought a shabby reception of me. He said that his people had but just come here; that the men had been busy all the dry season cutting down trees and clearing the woods. He said that they had had very little to eat; had been obliged to beg food of the neighbouring tribes, and half the time had nothing to eat but the nut of a sort of palm, of the sap of which they make a kind of intoxicating drink. This nut is very bitter. It is shaped like an egg, with rounded ends. To prepare it, it is divested of its husk and soaked in water for twenty-four hours, when it loses in part its exceedingly bitter taste, and becomes tolerably palatable to a hungry man. Sometimes hunger presses them to eat the nut without soaking it—I have been compelled to do so—and it is then excessively disagreeable.

I saw at once that it would not do for me to stay long with Mbene, for I could not live as these people do; and my own stores, though I had a few crackers and sea-biscuits left, would not last long, and ought to be kept for possible sickness.

The negro tribes of this region are half the time in a state of starvation by their utter improvidence. They seem unable to cope with want, even with so fertile a country as theirs to help them. Such encampments as this of Mbene's are common among all the tribes. Their agricultural operations are of the rudest kind, and, from the necessity of seeking out the most fertile soil, as well as from general habit, they prefer to go a distance from their villages to clear and plant the ground. They never plant two successive years in the same place, and have, therefore, much labour in clearing the ground every time. And, after all, it is not uncommon for a village to lose all the fruits of its labours by the incursions of a herd of elephants, who trample down what they do not eat up. This happens especially to plantain plantations.

The encampment is called an *olako*. An *olako* is a romantic scene to look at, particularly in the night, when every family has its fire, near which its beds are made under the *shades* before described. But hunger spoils the prettiest romance; and I would have given up the camp willingly for a good roast fowl or a sufficient supply of bread.

I told Mbene that as his place had no food to offer I must go farther; explained to him my objects; and finally it was agreed that his brother Ncomo should accompany me with a party as far as the *Fan* tribe. So much was settled without difficulty; but still several weeks passed ere my company was ready to start. The king's wives supplied me with mats for my bed, and under these I put dry leaves enough to make a soft couch. On each side of the bed I built a fire to keep off the mosquitoes, which were very troublesome, and thus I tried to sleep at night. My days were spent in hunting.

I ought to add that, with usual African hospitality, my kingly friend offered me a wife on my arrival at his place. This is the common custom when the negroes wish to pay respect to their guests, and they cannot understand why white men should decline what they consider a mere matter of course.

The mosquitoes penetrated through the smoke of my fires, and bit me so that I could scarce sleep on the first night after my arrival, and, to make matters yet more unpleasant, the rain poured on me through a leaky place in my leafy shelter.

I went to make arrangements with Ncomo for an early start, and found that his women had gone out to beg food for their trip. Mbene gave me a chicken for my dinner—an unusual luxury. But I had to shoot my fowl before eating it. The natives build no perches for their poultry, and the consequence is that the chickens fly to roost in the topmost branches of the trees, where they are safe from predatory attacks of all kinds, either by their owners or by wild beasts.

When I declined Mbene's offer of a "wife," he said, "Oh well, she can at any rate wait on you and cook for you;" and so I am lucky enough to have a good cook. The negroes use a good deal of pepper in their cooking, which I think healthy for this climate.

CHAPTER V.

Return of Dayoko's men—All alone—I am Mbene's White Man—Different tribes—An ideal country for an African—Mbondemo houses—Polygamy—Its political aspect—Causes of quarrels and wars—Departure for the cannibal country—Among the hills—A strike for higher pay in the dense forest—Huts for travellers—A beautiful torrent—High mountains — A big snake—Snakes as food — Discovery of gorilla tracks—Fright of the women—Unsuccessful gorilla hunt—Return to the camp—Superstitions about gorilla—Starvation—Coming to a village.

TO-DAY (August 20th, 1856), I sent back Dayoko's men, and am now in Mbene's power and at his mercy. He is a very good fellow, and I feel myself quite safe among his rough but kindly people. I have found it the best way to *trust* the people I travel among. They seem to take it as a compliment, and they are proud to have a white man among them. Even if a chief were inclined to murder, it would not be profitable in such a case, for the exhibition of his white visitor among the neighbouring tribes does more to give him respect and prestige than his murder would.

They speak of me now as "Mbene's white man." Before, I was "Dayoko's white man." The title has comfort and safety in it, for it would be a great insult to Mbene for any stranger to molest *his* white man, and it is to his own honour to feed him as well as he can.

Of course, one must have tact enough to satisfy the chief with occasional little presents, given him generally in private, so that his people may not beg from him, and given, also, not as though you wished to conciliate—for it will not do to show any symptoms of fear, however much cause there may be—but apparently as friendly gifts.

This is the only safe way to get ahead in this country, and I never found a chief whose "white man" I was for the time but would help and further my plans and journeys.

Dayoko's men are to return to Mbene's camp in three months to look for me, and I have to be back, if possible, by that time.

The women have brought in a supply of the bitter palm

seeds and of other fruits, mostly more palatable than that bitter abomination, but unfortunately not so plentiful. Among these is a round nut the size of a large walnut, containing three or four oily kernels, each of the size of a peanut; when these were roasted they were not disagreeable. And there was a remarkable magnificent fruit which I never saw before, resembling in general shape a bunch of grapes, each grape olive-shaped, and the whole of a bright scarlet colour. It was really a splendid sight to see these glowing bunches hanging from the trunks of the trees which bear them. The seed is larger than that of the olive; the skin not so thick as that; and the pulp is quite juicy and of a pleasant flavour.

The *Mbondemo* tribe is allied to the *Mbisho*, *Mbiki*, *Mbousha*, *Ibouay*, *Acoa*, and *Shekiani* tribes. The speech of all these tribes is nearly alike. They can all understand each other. Also, they have the same general customs and superstitions, and the same nomadic habits. The *Mbondemo* live or have their towns in the mountains of the interior east of Cape Lopez, and in that tract of country which extends from north of the Muni to the Moondah River.

Mbene had moved his village twice, his present removal making the third. I asked what reasons moved him to these changes. The first time, he said, a man had died there, and the place was "not good" after that. The second time he was forced to move because they had cut down all the palm-trees, and could get no more *mimbo* (palm-wine), a beverage of which they are excessively fond, though they take no pains to preserve the trees out of the soft tops of which it is made. But these are very plentiful all over the country; and it seems easier for them to move than to take care of the trees surrounding their settlements, useful as they are to them; for they furnish not only the wine they love, but the very bitter nut I mentioned before, which often keeps them from starvation. A country which has plenty of palm-trees, plenty of game, a good river, and plenty of fish, is the ideal region of a Mbondemo settler or squatter.

The Mbondemo houses are mostly of uniform size, generally from twelve to fifteen feet long, and eight or ten feet wide.

They are built on both sides of a long and tolerably wide street, and invariably join each other. The chief's house and the palaver-house are larger than the others. The ends of the street are barricaded with stout sticks or palisades, and at night the *doors* or gates of the village are firmly closed, and persons approaching, if they cannot explain their intentions, are remorselessly shot down or speared. The houses have no windows, and doors only on the side towards the street; and when the door of the street is locked, the village is, in fact, a fortress. As an additional protection, however, they often cut down thorny brushwood and block up the surrounding approaches; and, also, they always locate the village on the top of the highest hill they can find in the region where, for the time being, they squat. All this shows—what is the truth—that they are a quarrelsome, though not a brave race. They are continually in hot water with their neighbours, and never know when they are to be attacked.

Within, the Mbondemo house is divided by a bark partition into two rooms; one the kitchen, where also everybody sits or lies down on the ground about the fire; the other the sleeping apartment. This last is perfectly dark; and here are stowed their provisions and all their riches. To ascertain how large a family any Mbondemo householder has, you have only to count the little doors which open into the various sleeping apartments: "So many doors, so many wives," it was explained to me. The houses are made of bark and a kind of jointless bamboo, which is got from the trunk of a particular palm. The strips are tied to posts set firmly into the ground, with rope made from the vines of the forest. The roofing is made of matting. The houses are neither so large, so substantially built, nor so good-looking as those of the Mpongwe.

To-day (21st) my men have been getting ready their guns for enemies or game. The tribes of Africa have so many petty causes of quarrel that they are always in danger of a fight. They are so bound together by ridiculous superstitions of witchcraft, and by the entangling alliances of polygamy, and greatly also by their want of good faith in trade, that no man can say where or why an enemy is waiting for his life.

I have already spoken of the system of intermarriages by which a chief gains in power and friends. But there are other means of securing allies. For instance, two tribes are anxious for a fight, but one needs more force. This weakling sends one of its men secretly to kill a man or woman of some village, living near but having no share in the quarrel. The consequence is, *not*, as would seem most reasonable, that this last village takes its revenge on the murderer, but, strangely enough, that the murderer's people give them to understand that this is done because *another* tribe has insulted them, whereupon, according to African custom, the two villages join, and together march upon the enemy. In effect, to gain a village to a certain side in a quarrel, that side murders one of its men or women, with a purpose of retaliation on somebody else.

A man pays goods or slaves for his wife, and regards her therefore as a piece of merchandise. Young girls—even children in arms—are married to old men for political effect. The idea of love, as we understand it, seems unknown to these people. The inhabitant of the sea-coast has no hesitation in bartering the virtue of his nearest female relatives, nor are the women averse from the traffic, if only they be well paid.

Adultery with a black man is punishable by fine among all the tribes, and this law, which is strictly executed, is the cause of a most singular state of things. Husband and wife combine to rob some fellow with whom the woman pretends to carry on an intrigue, making sure of being discovered by the husband, who thereupon obtains a recompense sufficient to heal his wounded honour, and upon which he and his wife and accomplice are able to live for some time.

Unlawful intercourse with the women of a neighbouring tribe or village is the cause of nearly all the "palavers," and wars, and fights in Africa. If a tribe wants to fight, they *make* this the cause by getting one of their women to intrigue with a man of the other tribe or village; and even if they do not want to fight, they are often forced into it.

Then the system of intermarrying involves half-a-dozen tribes in the quarrel of two. Each chief calls on his fathers-in-law to assist, and thus the country is thrown into uproar; property is unsafe, and becomes almost valueless to them; agricultural operations are impeded, and whole villages gradually disappear from the scene of contention, either by migrating, starving out, or being killed out.

The women not only provide all the food, they are also the beasts of burden in this part of Africa. My party from Mbene's town consisted of Mbene's two sons, *Miengai* and *Maginda*, a young man named *Pouliandai*, and half-a-dozen stout women to bear my heavy chests and other luggage, and food for the journey.

We started at length on the morning of August 24th. The natives had done what they could to gather food beforehand for the trip, but the result was poor enough. My own supplies were by this time completely exhausted. The half-dozen biscuits I had in reserve were for sickness or a great emergency. Besides this, they had succeeded in getting several large bunches of plantains and a good many of the bitter palm-nuts, and that was all the commissariat.

I took with me 70 pounds of shot, 19 pounds of powder, and 10 pounds of arsenic for killing and preserving my specimens; also my chests, containing cloth, tobacco, beads, &c., to buy food and give presents to the natives we should meet. I made *Miengai* carry the shot, as the women had already enough. But my men were all loaded with goods on their own account, consisting of brass kettles, iron pots, jugs, &c., and about 100 pounds of salt, put up in little packages of three or four pounds.

The packing of the women is a subject of great importance. They carry their loads in heavy, rude baskets, suspended down the back; and it is necessary that these should be carefully arranged, with three or four inches of soft tree-fibre next to the back to prevent chafing.

When all was arranged—when everybody had taken leave of all his friends, and come back half-a-dozen times to take leave over again, or say something before forgotten— when all the shouting and ordering, and quarrelling were done, and I had completely lost patience, we at last got away.

In about five miles' travel we came to the banks of the Noonday River, which is here a narrow, but clear and beautiful stream, so clear that I was tempted to shoot a fish of curious shape I saw swimming along as we stood on the bank.

I fired a charge of small shot into him; but no sooner had I pulled the trigger than I heard a tremendous crash on the opposite bank, above six or seven yards across, saw some small trees torn violently down, and then came the shrill trumpetings of a party of frightened elephants. They had been standing in dead silence on the opposite bank in the jungle, whether watching us or not we could not tell. I was sorry I fired, for we crossed the stream close by, and might have killed one but for the fright they got, which sent them out of our reach.

After crossing the Noonday, and travelling ten miles in a north-east direction, we reached a range of granite hills, which are a part of the Sierra del Crystal mountains. The hills were very steep. I ate a few boiled plantains, then we ascended the crooked and poorly-marked path up-hill, which wound its devious course about immense boulders of granite and quartz, which, scattered along the declivity, gave the country a very strange look.

This range was about 600 feet high, and the summit formed a table-land three miles long, which also was strewed with the immense quartz and granite boulders.

Passing this table-land, we came to another tier of hills, steeper and higher than the first, which also had to be surmounted. In this kind of travelling I find that the natives had a great advantage over me. They use their bare feet almost as monkeys do theirs. Long practice enables them to catch hold of objects with their toes, and they could jump from rock to rock without fear of falling, while I, with thick shoes on, was continually slipping.

We were yet on the first plateau when *Miengai* suddenly made me a sign to keep very still. He and I were in advance. I thought he had discovered a herd of elephants, or perhaps a leopard. He cocked his gun, and I mine, and there we stood for five minutes in perfect silence. Suddenly Miengai sent a "hurrah" rolling through the forest, which was immediately answered by shouts from many voices at no great distance, but whose owners were hid from us by the rocks and trees. Miengai replied with the fierce shout of the Mbondemo warriors, and was again answered. Going a little farther on, we came in sight of the encampment of a large party, who proved to be some of Mbene's people just returning from a trading expedition to the interior.

It was a curious picture. They lay encamped about their fires to the number of about a hundred—young and old, men and women; some gray and wrinkled, and others babes in arms. They had evidently travelled far, and were tired out. They had collected india-rubber, and had in charge some ivory, and were now about to take these goods to Mbene or some other river chief, to be sent down from hand to hand to the "white-man market."

Here even I noticed the cruel way in which the women are obliged to work. The Mbondemo men lay about the fires, handling their spears and guns, and talking or sleeping, while the women were doing the cooking and making the camp comfortable, and such of the children as could walk were driven out to collect firewood for the night.

Being tired ourselves, we built our camp-fires near the party, and I had the opportunity next day to see them get under way. The men carried only their arms, and most of them were armed to the teeth. The women and larger children carried, in the usual baskets, suspended along the back, the food—of which they seemed to have a good supply—the ivory and india-rubber, and besides—still in the basket—such of the babies as could by no means get along alone. The old people were not exempt from light burdens, though they had to totter along with the help of long sticks.

The whole party were very thinly clothed, even for Africa. They had with them an old chief, to whom they seemed to pay much reverence, and *he* was constantly waited upon by his wives, of whom he seemed to have several with him. I gave them a little salt, for which they seemed very grateful

Next morning we broke up before daylight, after eating a very scanty breakfast of a few cooked plantains. It rained all day, and consequently we tramped all day in the mud, wet through, and chilly. About noon we met another large party of travelling Mbondemo returning from the interior.

MBONDEMO MAN AND WOMAN, SHOWING MANNER OF CARRYING CHILDREN AND BURDENS.

They had never seen a white man before, and stared at me with all the eyes they had. I fear my appearance gave them but a poor idea of white people. I was clothed in only a blue drill shirt and trowsers, both wet, and the latter muddy. They begged for some tobacco "to warm them selves," and a few leaves which I gave them made them perfectly happy.

Among this party were two fellows, named Ngolai and Yeava, who were from Mbene's village, and well known to Mbene's sons. These offered to go with us if we would give them food, as theirs was nearly gone, and Miengai and Maginda promising this much, they at once joined our party.

After a walk of about eighteen miles in the rain, through thick woods, and over a rough hilly country (and in a general direction of E.S.E.), we came to our camp, and to my delight found very large and commodious huts ready for us. This is a highway, it seems, of this country, though no signs of a road are visible, and different parties of traders had built and kept up these very neat and comfortable sheds.

We built great fires and made ourselves comfortable. I had three fires lit about my bed of brush, hung up my wet clothes to dry, and, after comforting myself with a little brandy, went to sleep in much more than usual snugness, not knowing the "palaver" which was in store for me on the morrow.

When we got up, much refreshed, my men came and said they were tired, and would not go a step farther if I did not pay them more cloth.

They seemed in earnest, and I was, as may be imagined, in considerable trouble of mind. To return now, when I had proceeded so far, was not to be thought of. To be left alone would have been almost certain death, and to give what they demanded was to set a bad precedent to my guides. Finally, I determined to put on a bold front. I went into the crowd, told them—pistols in hand—that I should not give them any more cloth; that neither could I permit them to leave me, because their father, Mbene, had given them to me to accompany me to the *Fan* tribe. So far, I told them, they must go with me, or else—here I motioned with my pistols—there would be war between us. But, I added, if they were faithful, I would give each something additional when the trip was done.

After a consultation among themselves, they finally said that they were pleased with what I said, and were my friends.

Hereupon, with great lightness of heart at my escape from an ugly dilemma, I shook hands with them, and we set out on the journey.

It was ten o'clock before we made a start on this day. We were now approaching the second mountain-range of the Sierra del Crystal, and passing through a wild country, densely wooded, rough, and strewn along the higher ground with immense boulders, which gave an additional wildness to the scene. Up, and up, and up we struggled, through a forest more silent than I recollect to have noticed in Africa before. Not even the scream of a bird or the shrill cry of a monkey to break the dark solitude—and either would have been welcome.

Nothing was heard but the panting breathings of our party, who were becoming exhausted by the ascent, till, at last, I thought I heard a subdued roar as of a fall of water. It grew plainer as we toiled on, and finally filled the whole air with its grand rush; soon turning a sharp corner of a declivity and marching on a little way, the torrent literally burst upon our sight. It was an immense mountain-torrent dashing down-hill at an angle of twenty-five or thirty degrees, for not less than a mile right before us, like a vast, seething, billowy sea. The river-course was full of the huge granite boulders which lie about here as though the Titans had been playing at skittles in this country; and against these the angry waters dashed as though they would carry all before them, and, breaking, threw the milky spray up to the very tops of the trees which grew along the edge.

Where we stood at the foot of the rapids the stream took a winding turn down the mountain; but we had the whole mile of foaming rapid before us, seemingly pouring its mass of waters down upon our heads.

These were the head-waters of the Ntambounay.

Drinking a few handfuls of its pure, clear, cool water, we travelled onward, still up-hill and partly along the edge of the rapids. In another hour we reached a clear space where a Mbondemo village had once stood; this was the summit.

From this elevation—about 5000 feet above the ocean level—I enjoyed an unobstructed view as far as the eye could reach. The hills we had surmounted the day before lay quietly at our feet, seeming mere mole-hills. On all sides stretched the immense virgin forests. And far away in the east loomed the blue tops of the farthest range of the Sierra del Crystal, and, as I strained my eyes toward those distant mountains which I hoped to reach, I began to think how this wilderness would look if only the light of civilization could once be fairly introduced among the black children of Africa. I dreamed of forests giving way to plantations of coffee, cotton, and spices; of peaceful negroes going to their contented daily tasks; of farming and manufactures; of churches and schools; and, luckily raising my eyes heavenward at this stage of my thoughts, saw pendent from the branch of a tree beneath which I was sitting an immense serpent, evidently preparing to gobble up this dreaming intruder on his domains.

My dreams of future civilization vanished in a moment. Fortunately my gun lay at hand. I rushed out so as to "stand from under," and, taking good aim, shot my black friend through the head. He let go his hold, and, after dancing about a little on the ground, lay dead before me. He measured a little over thirteen feet in length, and his fangs proved that he was venomous.

And now that civilization of which I had mused so pleasantly a few minutes before received another shock. My men cut off the head of the snake, and, dividing the body into proper pieces, roasted it and ate it on the spot; and I— poor, starved, but *civilized* mortal!—stood by, longing for a meal, but after a while I had to learn also how to eat snake or starve.

When the snake was eaten, and I, the only empty-stomached individual of the company, had sufficiently reflected on the disadvantages of being bred in a civilized country, we began to look about the ruins of the village near which we sat. A degenerate kind of sugar-cane was growing on the very spot where the houses had formerly stood, and I made haste to pluck some of this and chew it for the little sweetness it had. But, as we were plucking, my men perceived what instantly threw us all into the greatest excitement. Here and there the cane was beaten down, torn up by the roots, and lying about in fragments which had evidently been chewed.

I knew that these were fresh tracks of the gorilla, and joy filled my heart. My men looked at each other in silence, and muttered *Nguyla*, which is as much as to say in Mpongwe *Ngina*, or, as we say, gorilla.

We followed these traces, and presently came to the footprints of the so-long-desired animal. It was the first time I had ever seen these footprints, and my sensations were indescribable. Here was I now, it seemed, on the point of meeting face to face that monster of whose ferocity, strength and cunning the natives had told me so much; an animal scarce known to the civilized world, and which no white man before had hunted. My heart beat till I feared its loud pulsations, and my feelings were really excited to a painful degree.

By the tracks it was easy to know that there must have been several gorillas in company. We prepared at once to follow them.

The women were terrified, and we left them a good escort of two or three men to take care of them and reassure them. Then the rest of us looked once more carefully at our guns—for the gorilla gives you no time to re-load, and woe to him whom he attacks! We were armed to the teeth. My men were remarkably silent, as they were going on an expedition of more than usual risk; for the male gorilla is literally the king of the African forest.

As we departed from the camp, the men and women left behind crowded together, with fear written on their face. Miengai, Makinda, and Ngolai set out in one party, and myself and Yeava formed another, for the hunt. We determined to keep near each other, that in emergency we might be at hand to help each other. And for the rest, silence, coolness, and a sure aim were the only cautions to be given.

As we followed the tracks we could easily see that there were four or five of them; though none appeared very large. We saw where they had run along on all fours, the usual mode of progression of these animals; and where, from time to time, they had seated themselves to chew the canes they had borne off. The chase began to be very exciting.

We had agreed to return to the women and their guards, and consult upon final operations when we should have discovered their probable cause; and this was now done. To make sure of not alarming our prey, we moved the whole party forward a little way to where some leafy huts, built by passing traders, served for shelter and concealment. And having here stowed the women—who have a lively fear of the terrible gorilla, in consequence of various stories current among the tribes of women having been carried off into the woods by the fierce animal—we prepared once more to set out in chase, this time hopeful to get a shot.

Looking once more to our guns, we started off. I confess that I had never been more excited in my life. I had heard of the terrible roar of the gorilla, of its vast strength, its fierce courage, if, unhappily, only wounded by a shot. I knew that we were about to pit ourselves against an animal which even the leopard of these mountains fears.

We descended a hill, crossed a stream on a fallen log, and presently approached some huge boulders of granite. Alongside of this granite block lay an immense dead tree, and about this we saw many evidences of the very recent presence of the gorillas.

Our approach was very cautious. We were again divided into two parties. Makinda led one and I the other. We were to surround the granite block behind which Makinda expected the gorillas to be found. Guns cocked and in hand, we advanced through the dense wood, which cast a gloom even in mid-day over the whole scene. I looked at my men, and saw plainly that they were in even greater excitement than myself.

Slowly we pressed on through the dense brush, fearing almost to breathe lest we should alarm the beasts. Makinda was to go to the right of the rock, while I took the left. Unfortunately, he circled it at too great a distance. The watchful animals saw him. Suddenly I was startled by a strange, discordant, half-human, devilish cry, and beheld four young gorillas running towards the deep forests. We fired, but hit nothing. Then we rushed on in pursuit; but they knew the woods better than we. Once I caught a glimpse of one of the animals again, but an intervening tree spoiled my aim, and I did not fire. We ran till we were exhausted, but in vain. The alert beasts made good their escape. When we could pursue no more we returned slowly to our camp, where the women were anxiously expecting us.

As I saw the gorillas running—on their hind legs—they looked fearfully like hairy men; their heads down, their bodies inclined forward, their whole appearance was like men running for their lives. Take with this their awful cry, which, fierce and animal as it is, has yet something human in its discordance, and you will cease to wonder that the natives have the wildest superstitions about these "wild men of the woods."

In our absence the women had built large fires and prepared the camp, which was not so comfortable as last night's, but yet protected us from rain. I changed my clothes, which had become wet through by the frequent torrents and puddles we ran through in our eager pursuit, and then we sat down to our supper, which had been cooked meantime.

As we lay about the fire in the evening before going to sleep the adventure of the day was talked over, and of course there followed some curious stories of the gorillas. I listened in silence to the conversation, which was not addressed to me, and was rewarded by hearing the stories as they are believed, and not as a stranger would be apt to draw them out by questions.

One of the men told a story of two Mbondemo women who were walking together through the woods, when suddenly an immense gorilla stepped into the path, and, clutching one of the women, bore her off in spite of the screams and struggles of both. The other woman returned to the village, sadly frightened, and related the story. Of course, her companion was given up for lost. Great was the surprise, therefore, when, a few days afterward, she returned to her home. She related that the gorilla had misused her, but that she had eventually escaped from him. This and many similar stories I subsequently found to be devoid of all credit.

"Yes," said one of the men, "that was a gorilla inhabited by a spirit." Which explanation was received with a general grunt of approval.

They believe, in all this country, that there is a kind of gorilla—known to the initiated by certain mysterious signs, but chiefly by being of extraordinary size—which is the residence of certain spirits of departed negroes. Such gorillas, the natives believe, can never be caught or killed; and, also, they have much more shrewdness and sense than the common animal. In fact, in these "possessed" beasts, it would seem that the intelligence of man is united with the strength and ferocity of the beast. No wonder the poor African dreads so terrible a being as his imagination thus conjures up.

One of the men told how, some years ago, a party of gorillas were found in a cane-field tying up the sugar-cane in regular bundles, preparatory to carrying it away. The natives attacked them, but were routed, and several killed, while others were carried off prisoners by the gorillas; but in a few days they returned home uninjured, with this horrid exception: the nails of their fingers and toes had been torn off by their captors.

Some years ago a man suddenly disappeared from his village. It is probable that he was carried off by a tiger; but as no news came of him, the native superstition invented a cause for his absence. It was related and believed that, as he walked through the wood one day, he was suddenly changed into a hideous large gorilla, which was often pursued afterwards, but never killed, though it continually haunted the neighbourhood of the village.

Here several spoke up and mentioned names of men now dead whose spirits were known to be dwelling in gorillas.

Finally, the story which is current among all the tribes who at all know the gorilla was rehearsed, viz.: that this animal lies in wait in the lower branches of trees, watching for people who go to and fro; and, when one passes sufficiently near, grasps the luckless fellow with his powerful feet, and draws him up into the tree, where he quietly chokes him.

Many of the natives agree, I say, in ascribing to the animal this trait of lying in wait for his enemies and drawing them up to him by his "lower hands," as they may properly be called. But I have little doubt that this story is incorrect. Of course, the secluded habits of this animal, which lives only in the darkest forests, and carefully shuns all approach to man, help to fill the natives with curious superstitions regarding it.

This day we travelled fifteen miles, ten of which were easterly, and five to the south-east.

The next day we went out on another gorilla-hunt, but found no traces at all.

We rose early next morning, and trudged off breakfastless. There was not a particle of food among us. We crossed several streams, and travelled all day through a forest of an almost chilling gloom and solitude, ascending, in the midst, the steepest and highest hill we have so far met with. I suppose it to be part of the third range of the Sierra.

I felt vexed at the thoughtlessness of my men, who ought to have provided food enough to last us. But I ought to praise the poor fellows, for, though long hungry themselves, they gave me the greater part of the few nuts they found.

This is one of the hardest days' travel I had accomplished. We made twenty miles in a general direction of east, though some deductions must be made for deviations from a straight line.

The forest seemed deserted. Not a bird even to kill. We heard the chatter of a few monkeys, but sought in vain to get near them for a shot.

The next morning I woke up feeble, but found that the fellows had killed a monkey, which, roughly roasted on the coals, tasted delicious. To add to our satisfaction, Makinda presently discovered a bee-hive in the hollow of a tree. We smoked the bees out and divided the honey, which was full of worms, but was nevertheless all eaten up. We were so nearly famished that we could scarce wait for the hive to be emptied. No sooner was the honey spread out on leaves and laid on the grass, than everyone of the men was ready to clutch the biggest piece he could lay his hand on and eat away. There might have been a fight, to prevent which I interposed, and divided the whole sweet booty into equal shares, reserving for myself only a share with the rest. This done, everyone—myself included—at once sat down and devoured honey, wax, dead bees, worms, dirt, and all, and our only sorrow was that we had not more.

We had a hard time getting through old elephant tracks, which were a better road then the path through the jungle. Saw no animals, but met with several gorilla-tracks.

Towards two o'clock the men began to be very jolly, which I took to be a sign of our approach to a village. Presently they shouted, and, looking up towards the face of a hill before us, I saw the broad leaves of the plantain, the forerunner of an African town. Since we left Mbene's town these were the first human habitations we had met with, and I was not a little refreshed by the sight.

But alas! as we approached we found no one coming out to meet us, as is the hospitable way in Africa, and when we got to the place we found it entirely deserted. It was an old town of Mbene's people. Presently, however, some *Mbicho* people living near, relatives of Mbene's, came to see us, and gave us some plantains. But I could not get what I needed most—a fowl.

The *Mbichos* were in great amazement. None had ever seen a white man before. They thought me very singular.

We spent the evening in our houses drying and warming ourselves. It was much better than the forest, even though it was only a deserted town.

I judged myself here about 150 miles from the coast. With the exception of a Mbicho town near by, we were now surrounded on three sides by *Fan* villages, and shall make the acquaintance of these cannibals in a very short time.

CHAPTER VI.

Hunger—Meeting with cannibals—They think I am a spirit—Great crowds of cannibals—Appearance of the Fans—Fan dress—Gorilla hunting—Fierce attack of a gorilla—His horrid appearance—Death of a gorilla—The Bakalai—Wailing of the Bakalai—Love of the people for tobacco.

NEXT day Mbene came, which gave me great relief, for he is a steadier and more influential man than his sons. He was exhausted from his travels, and when I told him we needed food, he immediately set off to a Fan village a few miles off for a supply. Unable to wait for his return, I started off with my men to meet him, hoping perhaps to shoot something by the way. My hunger accelerated my movements, and pretty soon I found myself half a mile ahead of my companions and in sight of a chattering monkey, who dodged me whenever I took aim at him, and whom I vainly tried to get down off his perch on the high tree where he lived.

After watching this animal for some time, I happened to look down before me, and beheld a sight which drove the monkey out of my mind in an instant. Judge of my astonishment when before me I saw a *Fan* warrior, with his two wives behind him. I was at first alarmed, but immediately saw that all three were quaking with deadly terror. The man's shield shook and rattled, to such a degree was he frightened; his mouth stood open—the lips were fairly white; one of his three spears had fallen to the ground, and the other two he held in a manner betokening great fear.

The women had been carrying baskets on their heads, but these had been thrown to the ground, and they stood in perfect silence and terror looking at me.

They all thought, it appeared afterwards, that I was a spirit who had just come down out of the sky. As for me, my first thought, when I took in the situation, was—Suppose these people grow desperate with fear, then I may have a poisoned arrow launched at me. And if they got over their terror ere my companions arrived, then I was likely to have a spear sent through me, unless I were quicker than my antagonist and shot him, which I by no means desired to do; for, aside from the hatred of unnecessary bloodshed, I should by such a course have endangered my life among his countrymen.

I smiled and tried to look pleasant, in order to reassure

FAN WARRIOR.

them a little; but this only made matters worse. They looked as though upon the point of sinking to the ground.

Then I heard the voices of my men behind coming up, and presently I was safe, and the Fan people were relieved of their terror. Miengai smiled to see it, and told the man he need not regard me as a spirit, for I was his father's white man, come from the sea-shore on purpose to visit the Fan. Then I gave the women some strings of white beads, which did more than anything else to ease their fears.

On our return we found that Makinda had brought some plantains, but no fowl. I had now been a week without tasting flesh, except only the monkey we shot on the way, and felt very much in need of something better.

For the rest of the day we held levée in my house. Great crowds of *Fan* from the neighbouring villages came to see me. The men did not appear very much frightened, but the women and children were excessively so. But all kept at a very respectable distance. One glance from me toward a woman or child sufficed to make these run off.

If I was not frightened, I was at least as much surprised by all I saw as the Fan could be. These fellows, who now for the first time saw a white man, were to me an equal surprise, for they are real, unmistakeable cannibals. And they were, by long odds, the most remarkable people I had thus far seen in Africa. They were much lighter in shade than any of the coast tribes, strong, tall, well-made, and evidently active; and they seemed to me to have a more intelligent look than is usual to the African unacquainted with white men.

The men were almost naked. They had no cloth about the middle, but used instead the soft inside bark of a tree, over which in front was suspended the skin of some wild-cat or other animal. They had their teeth filed, which gives the face a ghastly and ferocious look, and some had the teeth blackened besides. Their hair or "wool" was drawn out into long thin plaits; on the end of each stiff plait were strung some white beads, or copper or iron rings. Some wore feather caps, but others wore long queues made of their own wool and a kind of tow, dyed black and mixed with it, and giving the wearer a most grotesque appearance.

Over their shoulders was suspended the huge country knife, and in their hands were spears and the great shield of elephant-hide, and about the necks and bodies of all was hung a variety of fetiches and greegrees, which rattled as they walked.

FAN WOMAN AND CHILD.

The Fan shield is made of the hide of an *old* elephant, and only of that part which lies across the back. This, when dried and smoked, is hard and impenetrable as iron. The shield is about three feet long by two-and-a-half wide.

Their fetiches consisted of fingers and tails of monkeys; of human hair, skin, teeth, bones; of clay, old nails, copper chains, shells; feathers, claws, and skulls of birds; pieces of iron, copper, or wood; seeds of plants; ashes of various substances; and I cannot tell what more. From the great variety and plenty of these objects on their persons, I suppose these *Fan* to be a very superstitious people.

The women, who were even less dressed than the men, were much smaller than they. These, too, had their teeth filed, and most had their bodies painted red, by means of a dye obtained from the bar-wood. They carried their babies on their backs in a sling or rest made of some kind of tree-bark and fastened to the neck of the mother.

Such were the strange people who now crowded about me, examining every part of my person and dress that I would allow to be touched, but especially wondering at my hair and my feet. The former they could not sufficiently admire. On my feet I had boots; and as my trousers lay over these, they thought, naturally enough, that these boots were my veritable feet, and wondered greatly that my face should be of one colour and the feet of another. I showed myself to as good advantage as I could, and surprised them very much— as I wished to do—by shooting a couple of swallows on the wing in their presence. This was thought a wonderful feat. They all went off at four o'clock, promising to return to-morrow and bring me some fowls.

These *Fan* belong, I should think, to a different family of the negro race from the coast natives, or indeed any tribes I have seen before. Their foreheads do not seem so compressed; but it is curious that in many the head runs up into a kind of peak or sugar-loaf. This indicates a low scale of intelligence; but it must be said, to these people's credit, that they are in some things much more ingenious than their neighbours. They extract iron from the ore, and show great ingenuity, with such poor implements as they have, in making their weapons, as the illustrations I give of those in my collection will show.

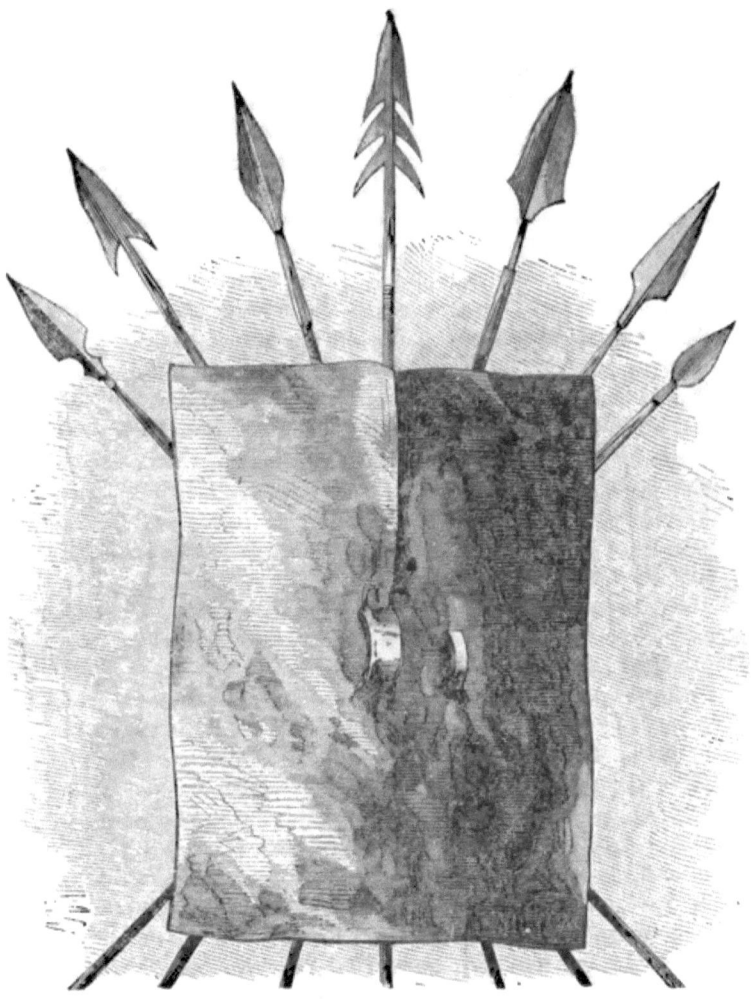

FAN SHIELD AND SPEARS.

I spent the day chiefly in looking about the town and neighbourhood—really doing nothing. As I walked along, a Fan woman gravely asked me why I did not take off my clothes? She felt sure they must be a great hindrance to me, and if I would leave off these things I should be able to walk more easily.

The next day we went out all together for a gorilla-hunt. The country hereabout is very rough, hilly, and densely crowded; consequently, hunting is scarcely to be counted sport. But a couple of days of rest had refreshed me, and I was anxious to be in at the death of a gorilla.

We saw several gorilla-tracks, and about noon divided our party, in the hope of surrounding the resting-place of one whose tracks were very plain. I had scarce got away from my party three hundred yards when I heard the report of a gun, then of three more, going off one after the other. Of course I ran back as fast as I could, and hoped to see a dead animal before me, but was once more disappointed. My Mbondemo fellows had fired at a female, had wounded her, as I saw by the clots of blood which marked her track, but she had made good her escape. We set out at once in pursuit; but these woods are so thick, so almost impenetrable, that pursuit of a wounded animal is not often successful. A man can only creep where the beast would run.

Night came upon us while we were still beating the bush, and it was determined to camp out and try our luck again on the morrow.

We started early, and pushed for the most dense and impenetrable part of the forest, in hopes to find the very home of the beast I so much wished to shoot. Hour after hour we travelled, and yet no sign of gorilla. Only the everlasting little chattering monkeys—and not many of these—and occasionally birds. In fact, the forests of this part of Africa —as the reader has seen by this time—are not so full of life as in some other parts to the south.

Suddenly Miengai uttered a little *cluck* with his tongue, which is the native's way of showing that something is stirring, and that a sharp look-out is necessary. And presently I noticed, ahead of us seemingly, a noise as of some one breaking down branches or twigs of trees.

This was the gorilla, I knew at once, by the eager and

satisfied looks of the men. They looked once more carefully at their guns, to see if by any chance the powder had fallen out of the pans; I also examined mine, to make sure that all was right; and then we marched on cautiously.

The singular noise of the breaking of tree-branches continued. We walked with the greatest care, making no noise at all. The countenances of the men showed that they thought themselves engaged in a very serious undertaking; but we pushed on, until finally we thought we saw through the thick woods the moving of the branches and small trees which the great beast was tearing down, probably to get from them the berries and fruits he lives on.

Suddenly, as we were creeping along, in a silence which made a heavy breath seem loud and distinct, the woods were filled with the tremendous barking roar of the gorilla.

Then the underbrush swayed rapidly just ahead, and presently before us stood an immense male gorilla. He had gone through the jungle on all-fours; but when he saw our party, he raised himself erect and looked us boldly in the face. He stood about a dozen yards from us, and was a sight I think I shall never forget. Nearly six feet high (he proved four inches shorter), with immense body, huge chest, and great muscular arms, with fiercely-glaring large deep gray eyes, and a hellish expression of face, which seemed to me like some nightmare vision; thus stood before us this king of the African forest.

He was not afraid of us. He stood there, and beat his breast with his huge fists till it resounded like an immense bass-drum, which is their mode of offering defiance; meantime giving vent to roar after roar.

The roar of the gorilla is the most singular and awful noise heard in these African woods. It begins with a sharp *bark*, like an angry dog, then glides into a deep bass *roll* which literally and closely resembles the roll of distant thunder along the sky, for which I have sometimes been tempted to take it where I did not see the animal. So deep is it that it seems to proceed less from the mouth and throat than from the deep chest and vast paunch.

His eyes began to flash fiercer fire as we stood motionless on the defensive, and the **crest of short** hair which stands on his forehead began **to twitch rapidly up** and down, while his powerful fangs were shewn as he again sent forth a thunderous roar. And now truly he reminded me of nothing but some hellish **dream-creature—a being** of that hideous order, half-man, half-beast, **which we find pictured by** old artists in some representations of the infernal regions. He advanced **a few steps**—then stopped to utter that hideous roar again—advanced again, and finally stopped when **at a** distance of about six yards from us. And here, just as he began **another** of his roars, beating his breast in **rage, we fired and killed** him.

With a groan which **had** something terribly human in it, and yet was full of brutishness, he **fell** forward on his face. The body shook **convulsively** for **a few minutes,** the limbs moved **about in a struggling way, and** then all was quiet—death had **done its work, and I had** leisure to examine the huge body. It proved to be five feet eight inches high, and **the muscular development** of the arms and breast showed **what immense strength** it had possessed.

My men, though rejoicing at our luck, immediately began to quarrel about the apportionment of the meat—for they really eat this creature. I saw that they would come to blows presently if I did not interfere, and therefore said I would myself give each man his **share, which** satisfied all. As we were too tired **to return to our** camp of last night, we determined to **camp here on the** spot, and accordingly soon had some shelters erected and dinner going **on.** Luckily one **of the** fellows shot a deer just **as** we began to camp, and on its meat **I feasted** while my **men ate** gorilla.

I noticed that they very carefully saved the brain, and was **told that charms were** made of this—charms of two kinds. Prepared **in one way,** the charm gave the wearer a strong hand for the hunt, and in another it gave him success with women. This evening we had gorilla stories again—but all to the same point already mentioned, that there are gorillas inhabited by human spirits.

We returned **to our** deserted village **next** day, and found a **division of travelling** Bakalai **in possession.** These people,

with whom fortunately I could speak, had lived on the Noya, some distance from here. They were now moving to be near some of their tribe. I asked why they left their former village, and learned that one morning one of their men, while out bathing in the river, had been shot. Hereupon they were seized with a panic, believed the town attacked by witches, and at once resolved to abandon it and settle elsewhere. They had all their household goods with him—chests, cloth, brass kettles, wash-basins, pans, &c., as well as a great quantity of yams, plantains, and fowls.

They were glad to get some tobacco from me, and I was glad to barter a little away for provisions.

At sunset every one of them retired within doors. The children ceased to play, and all became quiet in the camp where just before had been so much life and bustle. Then suddenly arose on the air one of those mournful, heart-piercing chants which you hear among all the tribes in this land—a wail whose burden seems to be, "There is no hope." It was a chant for their departed friends; and as they sang, tears rolled down the cheeks of the women, fright marked their faces and cowed their spirits—for they have a belief that at the sunset hour the evil spirits walk abroad among them.

I listened to try to gather the words of their chants; but there was a very monotonous repetition of one idea—that of sorrow at the departure of some one.

Thus they sang:

> "*We chi noli lubella pe na beshe.*
> Oh, you will never speak to us any more,
> We cannot see your face any more;
> You will never walk with us again,
> You will never settle our palavers for us."

And so on.

These poor people lead dreadful and dreary lives. Not only have they to fear their enemies among neighbouring tribes, as well as the various accidents to which a savage life is especially liable, such as starvation, the attacks of wild beasts, &c., but their whole lives are saddened and embittered by the fears of evil spirits, witchcraft, and other kindred superstitions under which they labour.

After they had chanted for half-an-hour, they came over to my house with various fowls and other food to buy "white man's tobacco" to cheer them on their journey. I was very glad to trade with them, and bought fowls, plantains, sugar-cane, and pine-apples. In Western Africa, men, women, and children all smoke. They never chew, unless they learn the practice of the whites; but smoking seems to be a very grateful occupation to them.

The next morning all was bustle in camp. The Bakalai were cooking a meal before setting out on their travels. It is astonishing to see the neatness with which these savages prepare their food. I watched some women engaged in boiling plantains, which form the bread of all this region. One built a bright fire between two stones. The others peeled the plantains, then carefully washed them—just as a clean white cook would—and, cutting them in several pieces, put them in the earthen pot; this was then half filled with water, covered over with leaves, over which were placed the banana peelings, and then the pot was placed on the stones to boil. Meat they had not, but roasted a few ground-nuts instead; but the boiled plantains they ate with great quantities of Cayenne pepper.

Next day we had promised to go among the *Fans* to live, so to-day we went hunting again. I had no padlock to my house, and was in a quandary how to leave what would certainly be stolen—all my provisions. Fortunately, I bethought me of some sealing-wax, and went to work to seal up my door with pieces of twine, to the great amusement of the rascally Miengai, who saw his game baulked, but could not help laughing. This evening, as I sat in my house, tired, I perceived a smell of burning meat. Stealing out, I found my fellows sitting about a fire and roasting an animal which I could not recognize. Their duty is to bring me all they kill, but they evidently did not. They seemed much ashamed, and I told them they need not come to me for more powder.

CHAPTER VII.

Departure for a Fan village—Cannibal practices of the Fans—Fierce appearance of the king—Head-dress of the Fans—A queen of the Fans—A Fan village—Signs of cannibalism everywhere—Refusal of cooked food—Ndiayai and his warriors—Weapons of the Fans—Drum, musical instruments.

THE next morning we moved off for the Fan village, and now I had the opportunity to satisfy myself as to the cannibal practices of these people. I was satisfied but too soon. As we entered the town I perceived some bloody remains which looked to me to be human; but I passed on, still incredulous. Presently we passed a woman who solved all doubt. She bore with her a piece of the thigh of a human body, just as we should go to market and carry thence a chop or steak.

The whole village was much excited, and the women and children greatly scared at my presence. All fled into the houses as we passed through what appeared the main street —a long lane—in which I saw here and there human bones lying about.

At last we arrived at the palaver-house. Here we were left alone for a while, though we heard great shoutings going on at a little distance. I was told by one of them afterwards that they had been busy dividing the body of a dead man, and that there was not enough for all. The *head*, I am told, is a *royalty*, being saved for the king.

Presently they flocked in, and before long we were presented to the king. This personage was a ferocious-looking fellow, whose body, naked with exception of the usual cloth about the middle, made of the bark of a tree, was painted red, and whose face, chest, stomach and back were tattooed in a rude but very effective manner. He was covered with charms, and was fully armed, as were all the Fans who now crowded the house to see me.

I do not know if the king had given himself a few extra horrid touches to impress me; but if so, he missed his mark, for I took care to retain a look of perfect impassiveness.

CHAP. VII.   A FAN KING AND QUEEN.   59

All the Fans present wore queues, but the queue of *Ndiayai*
the king was the biggest of all, and terminated in two tails,
in which were strung brass rings, while the top was ornamented with white beads. Brass anklets jingled as he
walked. The front of his middle-cloth was a fine piece of
tiger-skin. His beard was plaited in several plaits, which
also contained white beads, and stuck out stiffly from the face.
His teeth were filed sharp, and coloured black, so that the
mouth of this old cannibal, when he opened it, put me uncommonly in mind of a tomb.

The queen, who accompanied her lord, and who was
decidedly the ugliest woman I had ever seen, and very old,
was called Mashumba. She was nearly naked, her only
article of dress being a strip of the Fan cloth, dyed red, and
about four inches wide. Her entire body was tattooed in the
most fanciful manner; her skin, from long exposure, had
become rough and knotty. She wore two enormous iron
anklets—iron being a very precious metal with the Fan—
and had in her ears a pair of copper ear-rings two inches in
diameter, and very heavy. These had so weighed down the
lobes of her ears that I could have put my little finger easily
into the holes through which the rings were run.

I think the king was a little shaken at sight of me. He
had been originally much averse to the interview, from a
belief that he would die in three days after seeing me.
Finally Mbene reassured him.

Mbene was in his glory. He had charge of a white man,
among a people whom he himself feared, but who he saw
feared, in turn, *me*, whom he knew very well. He told the
Fan king that he had brought him a spirit, who had come
many thousands of miles across *the big water* to see the Fan.

The king replied that this was well, and sent off his queen
—the ugly one—to prepare me a house. And after a few
more civilities, but very little formality of any kind, his
majesty withdrew.

Presently I was conducted to my house. The village was
a new one, and consisted mostly of a single street about 800
yards long, on which were built the houses. The latter were
small, being only eight or ten feet long, five or six wide, and

four or five in height, with slanting roofs. They were made of bark, and the roofs were of a kind of matting made of the leaves of a palm-tree. The doors run up to the eaves, about four feet high, and there were no windows. In these houses they cook, eat, sleep, and keep their store of provisions, the chief of which is the smoked game and smoked human flesh, hung up to the rafters.

All the Fan villages are strongly fenced or palisadoed, and by night they keep a careful watch. They have also a little native dog, whose sharp bark is the signal of some one approaching from without. In the villages they are neat and clean, the street being swept, and all garbage—except, indeed, the well-picked bones of their human subjects—is thrown out.

After visiting the house assigned me, I was taken through the town, where I saw more dreadful signs of cannibalism in piles of human bones, mixed up with other offal, thrown at the sides of several houses. I find that the men, though viewing me with great curiosity, are not any longer afraid of me, and even the women stand while I approach them. They are a more manly and courageous race than the tribes towards the coast.

Then we returned to the king, where we were presented to his four wives, who showed uncommon dislike to my presence. Mbene is in great glee, as wherever he goes he is surrounded with Fan fellows, who praise him for being the friend of the spirit. Indeed, he has always been proud of this, and tells now, with no little pleasure, to the astonished Fans, that two before me have visited him, which is a fact.

Towards evening we retired to our houses. I called the king into mine, and gave him a large bunch of white beads, a looking-glass, a file, fire-steel, and some gun-flints. His face was fairly illuminated with joy, and he took his leave, highly pleased. Presently afterwards one of the queens brought me a basket full of bananas. Some of these were already cooked, and these I at once refused, having a horrid loathing of the flesh-pots of these people. I stated at once my fixed purpose to have all cooking done for me in my own

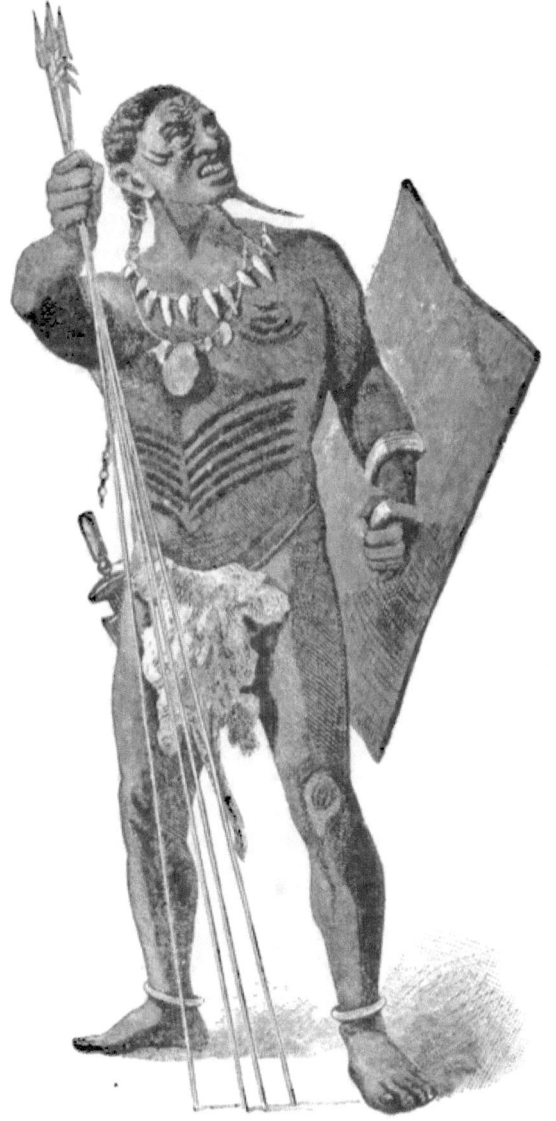

NDIAYAI, KING OF THE FANS.

kettles, and mean to be involved in no man-eating—even at second-hand.

Shortly after sunset all became silent in the village, and everybody seemed inclined to go to sleep. I barred my door as well as I could with my chest, and lying down on the dreadful bed which was provided for me, placed my gun by my side ready for use. For though they be ever so friendly, I cannot get it out of my head that these people not only kill people, but eat them, and that some gastronomic caprice might tempt them to have me for a dinner while I am among them.

I said dreadful bed. It was a frame of bamboos, each about an inch in diameter. Of course it was rough; and I found my bones aching so in the morning, that I might as well have slept on a nail-heap or on a pile of cannon-balls. But I slept, and was not interrupted, though, on going out next morning, I saw a pile of ribs, leg and arm bones, and skulls (human) piled up at the back of my house, which looked horrid enough to me. In fact, symptoms of cannibalism stare me in the face wherever I go, and I can no longer doubt.

I had told the king that I should like to see him dressed in war array, so this morning (September 1st) he called upon me with his queen and a cortège of his chiefs. The body was again painted red; he wore a shield of elephant's hide, and was armed for the offensive with three spears and a little bag of poisoned arrows. His head was splendidly decorated with the red feathers of a *touracaw* (corythaix); his teeth were painted very black; and his whole body was covered with greegrees and fetiches, to protect him from death by spears, guns, and witches.

Everybody admired the head-dress of Mashumba, the queen. It was a cap of white beads. These beads form the most desired ornaments of the blacks, and, with tobacco and powder, are the best trade a traveller can take into the interior.

Ndiayai remarked that, while surrounded by his warriors, he feared nothing, and spoke of the bravery of his people; and I am ready to believe them an unusually warlike tribe.

CHAP. VII.   NATIVE WEAPONS.   63

They pointed out one man to me who bore the name of "*Leopard*," because of his bravery. He had killed many of their enemies, and also many elephants.

They have a great diversity of arms. Among the crowd to-day I saw men armed with cross-bows, from which are shot either iron-headed arrows, or the little, insignificant-looking, but really most deadly, poison-tipped arrows. These are only slender, harmless reeds, a foot long, whose sharpened ends are dipped into a deadly vegetable poison which these people know how to make. The arrows are so light that that they would blow away if simply laid in the groove of

FAN BOWMAN.

the bow. To prevent this, they use a kind of sticky gum, a lump of which is kept on the under side of the bow, and with which a small spot in the groove is lightly rubbed. The handle of the bow is ingeniously split, and by a little peg, which acts as a trigger, the bow-string is disengaged, and, as the spring is very strong, sends the arrow to a great distance, and, light as it is, with great force. They are good marksmen with their bows, which require great strength to bend. They have to sit on their haunches, and apply both feet to the middle of the bow, while they pull with all their strength on the string to bend it back.

The larger arrows have an iron head, something like the

sharp barbs of a harpoon. These are used for hunting wild beasts, and are about two feet long. But the more deadly weapon is the little insignificant stick of bamboo, not more than twelve inches long, and simply sharpened at one end. This is the famed poison-arrow—a missile which bears death wherever it touches, if only it pricks a pin's-point of blood. The poison is made of the juices of a plant which was not shown me. They dip the sharp ends of the arrows several times in this sap, and let it get thoroughly dried into the wood. It gives the point a red colour. The arrows are very carefully kept in a little bag, made neatly of the skin of some wild animal. They are much dreaded among the tribes about here, as they can be thrown or projected with such power as to take effect at a distance of fifteen yards, and with such velocity that you cannot see them at all till they are spent. This I have often proved myself. There is no cure for a wound from one of these harmless-looking little sticks—death follows in a very short time.

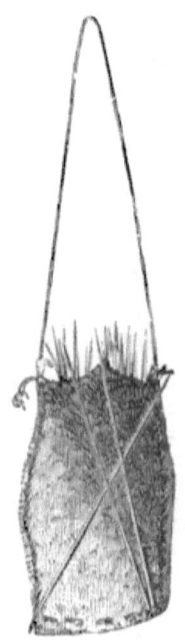

POISONED ARROWS, IN A SKIN BAG.

Some of the Fans bore on their shoulders the terrible war-axe figured on the following page, one blow of which quite suffices to split a human skull. Some of these axes, as well as their spears and other iron-work, were beautifully ornamented with scroll-work, and wrought in graceful lines and curves which spoke well for their artisans.

The war-knife, which hangs by the side, is a terrible weapon for a hand-to-hand conflict, and, as they explained to me, is designed to thrust through the enemy's body; they are about three feet long. There is another huge knife also worn by some of the men now in the crowd before me. This is over a foot long, by about eight inches wide, and is used to cut down through the shoulders of an adversary. It must do tremendous execution.

CHAP. VII.   FAN WEAPONS.   65

Then there is a very singular pointed axe, which is thrown from a distance. The figure (1) will give the reader an idea of the curious shape of this weapon. When thrown it strikes with the *point* down, and inflicts a terrible wound. They use it with great dexterity. The object aimed at with this axe is the head. The point penetrates to the brain, and kills the victim immediately; and then the round edge of the axe is

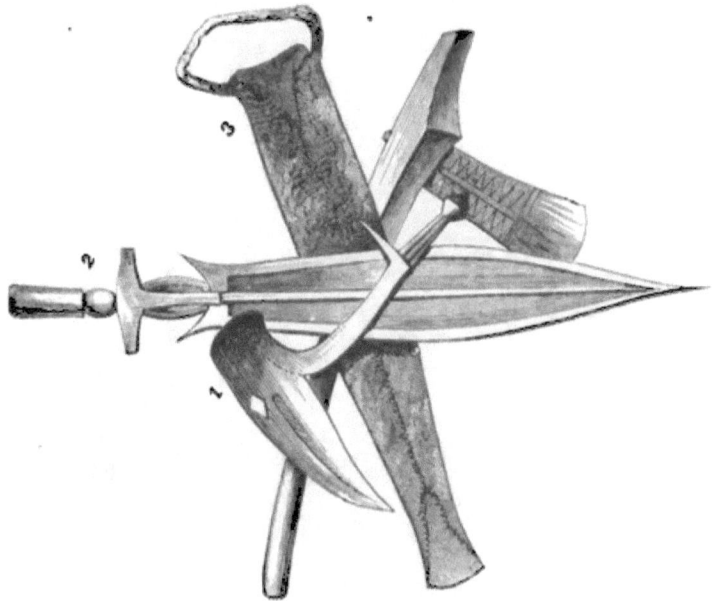

FAN KNIFE AND AXES.
1. Tomahawk.   2. Knife.   3. Sheath.   4. War-axe.

used to cut the head off, which is borne away by the victor as a trophy.

The spears, which are six to seven feet in length, are thrown by the natives with great force, and with an accuracy of aim which never ceased to surprise me. They make the long slender rod fairly whistle through the air. Most of them can throw a spear effectively to the distance of from twenty to thirty yards.

GRAND RECEPTION BY THE CANNIBALS.

Most of the knives and axes were ingeniously sheathed in covers made of snake-skins, or human skin taken from some victim in battle. Many of these sheaths are ingeniously made, and are slung round the neck by cords, which permit the weapon to hang at the side out of the wearer's way.

The only weapon of defence is the huge shield of elephant's hide; but this is even bullet-proof; and as it is very large —three-and-a-half feet long by two-and-a-half broad—it suffices to cover the whole body.

Besides their weapons, many of the men wore a smaller knife—but also rather unwieldy—which served the various offices of a jack-knife, a hatchet, and a table-knife. But, though rude in shape, they used it with great dexterity.

It was a grand sight to see so many stalwart, martial, fierce-looking fellows, fully armed and ready for any desperate foray, gathered in one assemblage. Finer-looking men I never saw; and I could well believe them brave, did not the completeness of their armoury prove that war is a favourite pastime with them. In fact, they are dreaded by all their neighbours, and, if they were only animated by the spirit of conquest, would soon make short work of the tribes between them and the coast.

To-day several hundred Fans from the surrounding villages came in to see me. Okolo, a great king among them, gave me his knife, saying it had already killed a man. To-night there is a great dance in honour of the arrival of a spirit (myself) among them. This dance was the wildest scene I ever saw. Everybody was there; and I, in whose honour the affair was, had to assist by my presence. The only music was that of a rude drum—an instrument made of a certain kind of wood, and of deer or goat skins. The cylinder was about four feet long, and ten inches in diameter at one end, but only seven at the other. The wood was hollowed out quite thin, and the skin stretched over tightly. To beat it the drummer held it slantingly between his legs, and with two sticks beat furiously upon the upper, which was the larger, end of the cylinder.

This music was accompanied with singing, which was less

FAN WARRIORS.

CHAP. VII. *MUSICAL INSTRUMENTS.* 69

melodious even than the drumming. As for the dancing, it was an indescribable mixture of wildness and indecency.

They had an instrument of another kind, and of so ingenious a construction that it is not altogether unworthy of more civilized people. This, which they call the handja, consists of a light reed frame, 3 feet long by 1½ broad, into

FAN DRUM AND HANDJA.

which are set and securely fastened a set of hollow gourds, covered by strips of a hard red wood found in the forests. Each of these cylinders is of a different size, and all are so graduated that the set forms a regular series of notes. A handja generally contains seven. The performer sits down, lays the frame across his knees, and strikes the strips lightly with a stick. There are two sticks, one hard, the other soft, and the principle is the same on which music has been produced in France from a series of glasses. The tone is very clear and good; and though their tunes are very rude, they can play them with considerable skill. Each gourd has a little hole on the side, covered with the skin of a spider.

One of the consequences of the dance is that we are to

THE HANDJA.

have a great elephant-hunt, and women are busied in cooking food and men in preparing arms for this great game. The few guns owned by the Fans have been carefully furbished up, and I have prepared my two for action, expecting great things from such desperate hunters as these.

CHAPTER VIII.

Elephant hunting with the cannibals—The king hunts with me—Appearance of the forest—Man killed by an elephant—Ceremonies round a dead elephant—Habits of the elephant—Fan marriage ceremony—Eating those who die a natural death—Bravery of the Fans—Cannibalistic custom—Blacksmith—Pottery—Among the cannibal Oshebas—Bunbakai, king of the Oshebas—Dare not go further inland—Idol worship among the cannibals.

About five hundred men assembled for the hunt on the morning of September 4th. They were divided into different parties, each of which set out for the part of the forest assigned it. Meantime *Ndiayai* and I went together to the general rendezvous, a walk of about six hours through the woody and mountainous country which I have already described. The march was conducted in perfect silence, and every care was taken not to alarm any game which might be near our track. Arrived at our halting-place, we immediately began to build our camp, and had hardly got our shelters constructed when it began to rain.

The next morning we set out for the hunting-ground. And here a most remarkable sight presented itself. The elephant, like most other great beasts, has no regular walk or path, but strays somewhat at random through the woods in search of food; but it is his habit, when pleased with a neighbourhood, to remain there for a considerable time, and not to let any small matter drive him away. Now, of this the Fan take advantage. The forests here are full of rough, strong, climbing-plants, running up to the top of the tallest trees. These creepers they tear down, and with them ingeniously, but with much labour, construct a kind of huge fence or obstruction, not sufficient to hold the elephant, but quite strong enough to check him in his flight and entangle him in the meshes till the hunters can have time to kill him. Once caught, they quietly surround the huge beast, and put an end to his struggles by incessant discharges of their spears or guns.

Presently a kind of hunting-horn was sounded, and the chase began. Parties were stationed at different points of the *barrier* or "tangle," as we will call it, which had an astonishing extent, and must have cost much toil to make. Others stole through the woods in silence and looked for their prey.

When they find an elephant they approach very carefully. The object is to scare him and make him run toward some part of the barrier—generally not far off. To accomplish this, they often crawl at their full length along the ground, just like snakes, and with astonishing swiftness.

The first idea of the animal is flight. He rushes ahead almost blindly, but is brought up by the barrier of vines. Enraged, and still more terrified, he tears everything with

his trunk and feet. But in vain; the tough vines, nowhere fastened, give to every blow, and the more he labours, the more fatally he is held.

Meantime, at the first rush of the elephant the natives crowd round; and while he is struggling in their toils they are plying him with spears, often from trees, till the poor wounded beast looks like a huge porcupine. This spearing does not cease till they have killed their prey.

To-day we killed four elephants in this way. It was quite an exciting time to the natives, though I confess of less interest to me after I had seen the first killed. It seemed monotonous and somewhat unfair; nevertheless, there is sufficient danger about it. The elephants about here have the reputation of holding man in slight fear, and the approach and attack are work for the greatest courage and presence of mind. Even then fatal accidents occur. To-day a man was killed. I was not present at the accident, but he seems to have lost his presence of mind, and when the elephant charged with great fury at a crowd of assailants, he was caught, and instantly trampled under foot.

When his companions saw that he was dead, they in turn grew furious, and actually pursued the elephant, which was making its escape, charged upon it, and so beset it with spears, that in a few minutes it was dead. I never saw men so excited with rage. They began even to cut the dead animal to pieces for revenge.

They have certain precautionary rules for these hunts, which shew that they understand the animal. For instance, they say you must never approach an elephant but from behind, as he cannot turn very fast, and you have time to make your escape after firing. Great care is necessary that the vines which are so fatal to the elephant do not also catch his pursuers. I was told that it was not unfrequent for a man to be thus hopelessly entangled, and then deliberately killed by the elephant. Often it becomes necessary for the hunters to retreat, and, as they can scarce outrun the great heavy animal, at such times all hands take refuge in trees, which they climb with astonishing swiftness—almost like monkeys. Even then, however, a man must select a stout tree; and *Ndiayai* told me of a case where a small sapling was pulled down by an enraged beast, and the occupant had a narrow escape for his life.

Now followed the rites with which they offer thanks for a good day's hunt to the idol who, in their belief, guides their fortunes. Without these preliminary rites, no meat is touched.

First comes the whole party and dances around the elephant, while the medicine or greegree men cut off a portion —invariably from one of the hind legs—of each elephant. This was the meat intended for an offering to the idol. This meat was put into baskets, afterward to be cooked under the direct superintendence of the greegree man and the men who killed the particular animal. Finally, the whole party danced about the baskets and sang songs to their idol, begging for another such good hunt as this one.

The king was of opinion that if this ceremony were neglected they would get nothing next time; but thought their songs and dances would please the idol, who would give them even more elephants in future.

The sacrificial meats are taken into the woods, where it is probable they regale some panther—if the shrewd medicine-man does not himself come and eat them. And the body of the poor fellow who was killed to-day is, I am told, to be sent to another Fan village, *to be sold and eaten*. This seems the proper and usual end of the Fans. They will not eat their own people.

The elephants were cut up the next day, and the meat was all hung up to be *smoked*, which these natives understand how to do.

The persistence with which the elephant in this part of the country sticks to a spot which affords him such leaves as he best likes, is very remarkable. It is in part, probably, from a scarcity of his favourite trees. I have seen them remain for days in the immediate vicinity of such a set of fences as I have described, where the natives, of course, each day killed some. Sometimes, too, they will almost enter the towns, pulling down the small trees, and breaking branches off the larger, to get the food which best suits their taste. Often, however, they leave a neighbourhood at the first attack, when the natives follow and make new fences.

They have another way of killing elephants, which I saw used in the woods this day, and have often seen since. They discover a walk or path through which it is likely that a herd or single animal will soon pass. Then they take a piece of very heavy wood, which the *Bakalai* call *hanou*, and trice it up into a high tree, where it hangs, with a sharp point, armed with iron, pointing downward. It is suspended by a rope, which is so arranged that the instant the elephant touches it—which he cannot help doing if he passes under the *hanou*—it is loosed, and falls with tremendous force on to his back, the iron point wounding him, and the heavy weight generally breaking his spine.

It is generally supposed that the elephant is found only in the plains; but, from various observations in this region, I conclude that the animal also frequents the mountains and rough high country. Their tracks are frequently met with among the mountains, and several times I have scarcely been able to believe my eyes when I saw plainly the foot-prints of the huge animal in spots which it could only have attained by the ascent of almost precipitous hill-sides—ascents which we found it difficult to make ourselves.

The elephant-meat, of which the Fan seem to be very fond, and which they have been cooking and smoking for three days, is the toughest meat I had tasted, and when it has been boiled for two days, twelve hours each day, it is still tough. I cannot explain its taste, because we have no flesh which tastes like it; but the flavour is not unpleasant.

As we were returning, I learned from the king a very curious particular of the Fan customs, of which I did not suspect any of these West African tribes. It appears that they never marry their girls before they have arrived at the age of puberty, and that they have a care for the chastity of their young women. I had already remarked, what I suppose is the natural result of the Fan custom, that these people have more children by far than either the Shekiani, Bakalai,

Mbicho, Mbondemo, Mbousha, or any of the interior tribes I have seen north of the equator. Those tribes are gradually but surely disappearing, but the Fans seem likely to survive.

The Fan marriage ceremonies are very rude, but are an occasion of great jollity. Of course, the husband has to buy his wife, and the shrewd father makes a bargain with him as well as he can, putting on a great price if the man's love is very ardent; so that I was told it sometimes took years before a man could buy and marry his wife. If trade with the sea-shore were better it would not be so hard; but as "trade" is the most precious thing, "trade goods" are always expected as payment for a wife. Hence their bravery as hunters; for ivory is one of the chief articles they send down to the coast; and though, after a hunt like that before related, the meat is shared, the ivory belongs to those who killed the animal, who have, however, to divide the proceeds with their immediate relatives. Copper and brass rings, white beads, and the copper pans called neptunes on the coast, are the chief articles of trade which are a legal tender for a wife among the Fans.

When a wedding is in prospect the friends of the happy couple spend many days in obtaining and laying in great stores of provisions—chiefly smoked elephant-meat and palm-wine. They engage hunters to keep up the supply, and accumulate enough to feed the great numbers who are expected to come. When all is ready, the whole town assembles, and, without any ceremony, but merely as a public sale, as it were, the father hands his daughter to her husband, who has generally already paid her price.

The "happy pair" are, of course, dressed finely for the occasion. The bridegroom is attired in a feather head-dress of glowing colours; his body is oiled; his teeth are black and polished as ebony; his huge knife hangs at his side; and if he can kill a leopard or panther, or other rare animal, its skin is wrapped about his middle in a graceful way. The bride is very simply dressed, or rather she is (like all the Fan women) not dressed at all. But for this occasion she is *ornamented* with as many bracelets as she can get, of brass or copper, and wears her woolly locks full of white beads.

When all are assembled, and the bride is handed over to her lord, a general jollification ensues, which lasts sometimes for many days. They eat elephant-meat, get tipsy on palm-wine, dance, sing, and seem to enjoy themselves very much, until at last wine grows scarce, and the crowd returns to an involuntary sobriety.

While I was talking to the king some Fans brought in a dead body which they had bought in a neighbouring town, and which was now to be divided. I could see that the man had died of some disease. I confess I could not bear to stay for the cutting up of the body, but retreated when all was ready. It made me feel sick. I remained till the infernal scene was about to begin, and then retreated. Afterwards I could hear them from my house growing noisy over the division.

Eating the bodies of persons who have died of sickness is a form of cannibalism of which I had never heard among any people, so that I determined to inquire if it were indeed a general custom among the Fans, or merely an exceptional freak. They spoke without embarrassment about the whole matter, and I was informed that they constantly buy the dead of the Osheba tribe, who, in return, buy theirs. They also buy the dead of other families in their own tribes, and, besides this, get the bodies of a great many slaves from the Mbichos and Mbondemos, for which they readily give ivory, at the rate of a small tusk for a body.

Until to-day I never could believe two stories—both well authenticated, but seeming quite impossible to anyone unacquainted with this people—which are told of them on the Gaboon. A party of Fans who came down to the sea-shore once actually stole a freshly-buried body from the cemetery, and cooked it and ate it among them; and at another time a party conveyed a body into the woods, cut it up, and smoked the flesh, which they carried away with them. The circumstances caused a great fuss among the Mpongwe, and even the missionaries heard of it, for it happened at a village not far from the missionary grounds, but I never credited the stories till now, though the facts were well authenticated by witnesses.* In fact, the Fan seem regular ghouls, only they practise their horrid custom unblushingly and in open day, and have no shame about it. I have seen here knives covered with human skin, which their owners valued very highly.

To-day the queen brought me some boiled plantain, which looked very nice; but the fear lest she should have cooked it in some pot where a man had been cooked before—which was most likely the case—made me unable to eat it. On these journeys I have fortunately taken with me sufficient pots to do my own cooking.

They are the finest, bravest-looking set of negroes I have seen in the interior, and eating human flesh seems to agree with them, though I afterwards saw other Fan tribes whose members had not the fine air of these mountaineers. As everywhere else, locality seems to have much to do with it. These were living among the mountains, and had all the appearance of hardy mountaineers.

The strangest thing about the Fans (next to their hideous cannibalism) is their constant encroachments upon the land westward. Year by year tribes of Fan are found nearer the sea-shore; town after town is being settled by them on the banks of the Gaboon; and in the country between the Gaboon and the Moondah they have come down to within a few miles of Point Obendo. In fact, they seem a stirring race, and more enterprising than the Bakalai, Mbondemo, Mbicho, and even the Mpongwe; and I think will leave these gradually behind and take possession themselves of the whole line of sea-shore.

It has been supposed that these Fans are, in fact, the *Giaghi* or *Jaga*, who formerly invaded the kingdom of Congo,

---

* These stories seem so incredible, and even the fact that these people actually buy and eat the corpses of their neighbours—resting as it does upon my statement alone—has excited so much evident disbelief among friends in this country to whom I have mentioned this custom, that I am very glad to be able to avail myself of the concurrent testimony of a friend, the Rev. Mr. Walker, of the Gaboon mission, who authorises me to say that he vouches for the entire truth of the two stories above related.

and who seem to have been a similar people. The fact is, however, that in my later journeys to the head-waters of the Nazareth, and into the interior, south of the present location of the Fans, I could find no tribes who knew anything of such a people. Now, the migration of the Fans is so slow a process that, whichever way they move, it is impossible they should not be remembered by the tribes among whose villages they have scattered their own; and were they indeed the Jaga of the south, I must have come on their traces somewhere. Moreover, all the Fans, when asked whence they came, point to the north-east, or east-north-east. No matter how many different men or villages you put this question to, the answer is always the same.

The Fans tattoo themselves more than any of the other tribes I have met north of the equator, but not so much as some to the south. The men are less disfigured in this way than the women, who take great pride in having their breasts and abdomen entirely covered with the blue lines and curves. Their cheeks also are fully marked in various figures, and this, with the immense copper and iron rings which weigh down the lobes of their ears, gives them a hideous appearance.

They have considerable ingenuity in manufacturing iron. The articles of trade which they wish for most seem to be white beads—used for ornaments everywhere in this part of Africa—and vessels of copper and brass. The "neptune"— a plate of yellow copper, which has long been one of the standard articles of trade imported hither by the merchants, and which is found very far in the interior—the Fans cut up, and it seems to pass as a kind of medium of exchange.

Iron ore is found in considerable quantities through the Fan country cropping out at the surface. They do not dig into the ground for it, but gather what lies about. To get the iron they build a huge pile of wood, heap on this a considerable quantity of the ore broken up, then comes more wood, and then fire is applied to the whole. As it burns away, wood is thrown on continually, till at last they perceive, by certain signs, that they have made the iron fluid. All is then permitted to cool, and they have now *cast* iron.

To make this malleable and give it temper, they put it through a most tedious series of heatings and hammerings, till at last they turn out a very superior article of iron and steel, much better than that which is brought to them from Europe. It is a fact that, to make their best knives and arrow-heads, they will not use the European or American iron, but prefer their own. And many of their knives and

FAN BLACKSMITHS.

swords are really very finely made, and, for a rude race, beautifully ornamented with scroll-work on the blades.

As blacksmiths, they very far surpass all the tribes of this region who have not come in contact with the whites. Their warlike habits have made iron a most necessary article to them; and though their tools are very simple, their patience is great, and, as the reader will perceive from the pictures of their arms, they produce some very neat workmanship.

The forge is set up anywhere where a fire can be built. They have invented a singular bellows, composed of two short, hollowed cylinders of wood, surmounted by skins accurately fitted on, and having an appropriate valve and a wooden handle. The bellows-man sits down, and moves these coverings up and down with great rapidity, and the air is led through small wooden pipes into an iron joint which emerges in the fire.

The anvil is a solid piece of iron of the shape seen in the illustration. The sharp end is stuck into the ground, and the blacksmith sits alongside of his anvil and beats the iron with a singular hammer, which is simply a piece of iron weighing from three to six pounds, and in shape a truncated cone. It has no handle, but is held by the smaller end, and, of course, the blows require much more strength. It is a little curious that, with all their ingenuity, they should not have discovered so simple a thing as a handle for a hammer.

Time is of no value to a Fan, and the careful blacksmith spends often many days and even weeks over the manufacture of a small knife, while weeks and months are used to turn out a finished war-knife, spear, or brain-hatchet. The small, graceful, and often intricate lines with which the surfaces of all their best weapons are very beautifully ornamented are all made by the hand and a chisel-like instrument, struck with the hammer. They evince a correct eye, and a good deal of artistic taste.

They have also some skill in forming pottery, though the only objects of clay they use are the cooking-pot and the pipe. The former is in shape much like our common iron cooking-pot. It is remarkable chiefly for the very regular shape they give it merely by hand, for of the lathe they are, of course, ignorant. When the clay is moulded it is set in the sun to dry, and afterwards thoroughly baked in the fire. Pipes are made in the same way, but the stems are always of wood. Many of the Fan had *iron* pipes, which they seemed to prefer to those of clay.

Water is carried or kept in gourds, and in jugs made of a kind of reed tightly woven and afterward coated with a kind of gum. This gum is first softened in the fire, and then thickly laid over the outside of the vessel. When completed,

FAN POTTERY.
1. Cooking-pot.   2. Water-jar.   3. Palm-wine Bottle

it forms a durable, water-tight vessel; but it is necessary, before using it, to keep it standing in water for a fortnight, to take away the disagreeable taste of the gum.

FAN PIPES.

They smoke leaves which looked to me like a kind of wild tobacco, and which seem to grow plentifully here.

The meat of the elephant is their chief subsistence, while the ivory is their only export article, and, therefore, very important to them, as thereby they get their brass, copper, kettles, looking-glasses, flints, fire-steels, and beads, which have become almost necessities to them. Of all these, however, they set the greatest value on copper and brass.

Their agricultural operations are very rude, and differ but little from those of the surrounding tribes. Like them, they cut down the trees and brush to make a clearing, burn everything that is cut down, and then plant their crop in the cleared space. The only agricultural instrument they have is a kind of heavy knife or cutlass, which serves in place of an axe to cut down trees, and for many other purposes, such as digging the holes in which they plant their manioc or plantains.

Their staple food is the manioc, a very useful plant, because it yields a large return, and is more substantial food than the plantain. It is cultivated by cuttings; and one little stem, stuck carelessly into the ground in their manner, produces in a season two or three large roots the size of a yam. They also boil the leaves and eat them, and they make excellent "greens."

Besides manioc they have plantains, two or three kinds of yams, splendid sugar-cane, and squashes, all of which they cultivate with considerable success; but the manioc is the favourite. Enormous quantities of squashes are raised, chiefly for the seeds, which, when pounded and prepared as they know how to do, are much prized by them, and by me too. At a certain season, when the squash is ripe, their villages seem covered with the seeds, which everybody spreads out to dry. When dried, they are packed in leaves and placed over the fireplaces in the smoke, to keep off an insect which also likes them. The process of preparation is very tedious. A portion of seeds is boiled, and each seed is divested of its skin. Then the mass of pulp is put into a rude wooden mortar and pounded, a vegetable oil being mixed with it. When all is well mixed, a portion is finally cooked over a charcoal fire, either in an earthen pot or in a plantain leaf. It is then very sweet, and I think nourishing, and certainly quite pleasant.

Of the mortars above mentioned every Fan family possesses at least one. They are of wood, and are in fact troughs, being two feet long by two or three inches deep and eight wide. Besides these, every village owns and uses in common two or three immense mortars (also of wood), which are needed to pulverize the manioc-root. When it is reduced to flour it is made into little cakes, which may be kept for several days. They are also very fond of red pepper, which plant is found in abundance near all the villages.

While on the subject of food, I ought to say that they do not sell the bodies of their chiefs, kings, or great men. These receive burial; and consequently they do not eat *every* body that dies. It may be that when people die of some peculiar disease they are not eaten.

Slavery does not seem very prominent among them, though a great many of the Fans themselves are yearly sold for slaves to the coast traders on account of witchcraft accusations, debts, adultery, &c.

So vague and unsatisfactory were the rumours I heard of country and people in the farther interior that I shall not make any guess at the condition of that vast region. Only I think it quite likely that, as the Fan and Osheba tribes point eastward as the place of their origin, their manners and customs, with such knowledge as they have of iron and of poison, and such changes in life as the different circumstances of the country may necessitate, may be characteristic of the tribes beyond.

On September 10th, Ndiayai, the king, took me over to an Osheba town some miles away, whose king was his friend. The town, the people, the arrangements, everything looked just as in the Fan town. I should not have known they were of a different tribe had not Ndiayai assured me it was so. I imagine they are not very far apart, however. Like the Fans, the Osheba look warlike, and are tall; their women are smaller, and hideously ugly, and tattooed all over their bodies. A large part of their intercourse with the Fan village consists in the interchange of dead bodies, and I saw as many human bones lying about the Osheba village as among the Fans.

King Bunbakai, the Osheba chief, seeing that his friend

Ndiayai did not die after having seen me, decided to come out and have a look at me himself. He was a sociable old fellow, dressed in the Fan style, and every way acting as a Fan king might. We stayed with him several days, as I had come in great part to see what lay farther east toward the interior, and how I should get farther. But I was now come to my *ultima thule*. After every inquiry, made with the help of my Mbondemo followers, I could get only this information:—that beyond the Osheba village, two or three days' journey off, there lived other tribes, also cannibals, whose names my informants did not know. It was said, however, that they were warlike, and used poisoned arrows. When I desired to advance in that direction the people seemed unwilling, even afraid, to accompany me; assuring me that on account of the wars at present in existence between tribes there, any party attempting to visit either side would run the risk of being waylaid with poisoned arrows by the other.

I had a great desire to go on, but confess that these stories and some other considerations cooled my ardour. I was completely at the mercy of the Fans, and should be still more so if I advanced, for Mbene's men would not go farther. And I could not forget that the Fans, though apparently well disposed toward me, had a great penchant for human flesh, and might—by one of those curious freaks which our tastes play us—be seized by a passionate desire to taste me. To fall sick among them would be to tempt them severely and unjustifiably. Then I had not goods enough to carry me among a strange people and also bring me back; and I feared that, left in poverty, I should fail to receive among them the respect and obedience which the beads, tobacco, and powder, copper and brass rings of a white man always obtain for him. Moreover, the Fan language is such a collection of *throat* sounds that I not only could not get to understand it, but could not for some time distinguish any words. The Osheba is yet worse; and harsher, ruder, or more guttural sounds I never heard made. Now, as Mbene's men would not go with me, nor even stay long here, I was like to be left without an interpreter; and to go among any new tribes beyond the mountains entirely unable to hold communication with them would have been labour almost altogether in vain. I therefore determined to make some longer stay with King Ndiayai, and then return by a new route to the seashore.

The Fans are a very superstitious people. *Witchcraft* seems to be a very common thing to be accused of among them, and the death-penalty is sternly executed. They set little value on life; and as the dead body has its commercial value, this consideration too, probably, has its weight in passing sentence of death.

Polygamy is a fertile source of quarrels and bloodshed among them.

They have a great reverence for charms and fetiches, and even the little children are covered with these talismans, duly consecrated by the doctor or greegree man of the tribe. They place especial value on charms which are supposed to have the power to protect their owner in battle. Chief among these is an iron chain, of which the links are an inch and a half long by an inch wide. This is worn over the left shoulder, and hanging down the right side. Besides this, and next to it in value, is a small bag, which is suspended round the neck or to the side of the warrior. This bag is made of the skin of some rare animal, and contains various fragments of others, such as dried monkeys' tails, the bowels and claws of other beasts, shells, feathers of birds, and ashes of various beasts. All these are of the rarer animals, in order that there may not be too many charms of one kind, which would diminish their value and power.

The chief village of each clan of the Fans has a huge idol, to whose temple all that family gather at certain periods to worship. This worship consists of rude dances and singing. The idol-houses are mostly surrounded by a number of skulls of wild animals, prominent among which I recognized the skull of the gorilla. To take away or disturb these skulls would be counted sacrilege, and worthy of death. I do not think they offer human sacrifices.

The non-cannibal tribes do not intermarry with their cannibal neighbours, as their peculiar practices are held in too great abhorrence. Trade is, however, likely to break down this barrier. Within two or three years the ivory of the Fans has so far excited the cupidity of their neighbours that two or three chiefs, among whom Mbene was one, have been glad to take Fan girls to wife, in order thus to get the influence of a Fan father-in-law. The poor Fans, who are farthest of all from the coveted white trade, are but too glad to get a son-in-law nearer the seashore; and I have little doubt but in a few years they will even succeed in intermarrying with other tribes to a considerable extent.

The Fan have left the impression upon me of being the most promising people in all Western Africa. They treated me with unvarying hospitality and kindness; and they seem to have more of that kind of stamina which enables a rude people to receive a strange civilization than any other tribe I know of in Africa. Energetic, fierce, warlike, decidedly possessing both courage and ingenuity, they are disagreeable enemies; and I think it most probable that the great family or nation of which they are but a small offshoot, and who should inhabit the mountainous range which subsequent explorations convince me extends nearly if not quite across the continent—that these mountaineers have stayed in its course the great sweep of Mohammedan conquest in this part of Africa.

FAN SPOON.

CHAPTER IX.

Back to the coast—King Mbene gets a cannibal wife—The Fans regret my departure—Good-bye to the Fans and their mountains—The rains—Leopards—Mbicho villages—The Noya River—Wanga—King Alapay—Hunting with nets—Ferocious ants—The great forest—Over a mangrove swamp—A big snake.

WE now began to make ready for our return to the sea. I was to go as far as his village with Mbene, and thence take my new route. Mbene had since our arrival obtained a daughter of King Ndiayai for his wife; a point of great exultation to this politic old negro, who rejoiced that so rare an honour should fall to him, and hoped to receive large consignments of ivory from his father-in-law's people, on which he would pocket a profitable percentage.

The Fans seemed very sorry that I was about to leave them, and all expressed a wish for my return. Ndiayai gave me a native knife as a token of remembrance, which was as much as receiving a be-diamonded snuff-box from another sovereign—for knives are precious in Africa. I offered a large price to another man for a superb knife he had, but could not get it. His father had given it to him, he said, and he could not part with it.

So at last we were fully ready, and left the Fans and their mountains. These mountains have a climate which is by no means African in the popular conception. Since we have been here we have had rain during every night; and it has been so much clouded that I do not think the sun has shone clearly for three consecutive hours on any day in as many weeks. The country seems well watered, and the soil is exceedingly fertile. The climate is, of course, much healthier than it is on the rivers near the coast, and the people in consequence are more robust and energetic.

The warriors of this part of Africa—with the exception of the Fans and Osheba—are not overstocked with courage. They applaud tricks that are inhumanly cruel and cowardly, and seem to be quite incapable of open hand-to-hand fight. To surprise man, woman, or child in sleep, and kill them then; to lie in ambush in the woods for a solitary man, and kill him by a single spear-thrust before he can defend himself; to waylay a woman going to the spring for water, and kill her; or to attack on the river a canoe much smaller and weaker than the attackers: these are the warlike feats I have heard most praised and seen oftenest done in this part of Africa.

The rainy season had by this time (September) fairly set in in these mountains, and the thunder, lightning, and heavy showers are common both day and night. We find great comfort in **using the** shelters erected and conscientiously **kept** in repair by **the caravans or** trading-parties of **negroes who** pass over this track. **They** give at least some shelter from the everlasting rains. **We** have found them kept in **good** repair wherever we have been. It is customary for every party **to** do what repairs are necessary.

On our way back we saw many elephant-tracks, but no **animals.**

At night the cries **of** leopards often awoke me; but they were not very near us, our fires probably keeping them off. I **had** four distinct **fires** about my **shed,** and these I now carefully poked up **and** fed, **that no hungry leopard** might be tempted to rush across the lines; and **then returned** to sleep.

One day we saw a strange water-snake, whose body **was** black, with rings of bright yellow along the whole length. **My men** were much alarmed when they saw it, for they said **its bite was mortal; they tried** to kill it with their spears, **but it managed to escape them.** They told me that besides being poisonous it **was very** good to eat, and gave as a caution that the head must **be cut off** immediately it is killed, in order, I suppose, to prevent **its fangs from fastening on** any part of the body.

At last, after some hard travelling, **the** forest being very dense, and often swampy, while numerous streams, bridgeless, of course, had to be crossed on crazy logs, **we came to a** small creek leading into the Noya, which was only **two or** three hundred yards distant. We seized on **two canoes we** found empty, and **as** these would not hold all our party, **I put in** all my goods and as many men as I could make room **for,** and made the others promise to wait till we sent a canoe **for** them, which was likely to be soon. Sure enough, scarce **had we emerged into** the Noya (a noble stream, refreshing to **look upon after** the wretched creeks which had been crossed **for two days at very** frequent **intervals), than we met a** couple **of women fishing in** two **canoes. I promised them some** leaves of tobacco if they would **go and bring along the men, and** they were only too glad **to do so.**

Thus we descended the Noya. The banks here are clothed

with trees of a pleasant shape and a dark evergreen verdure, which made a favourable contrast to the immense gloomy mangrove-swamps which line all these rivers near the seashore. Here and there we saw little native villages peeping through the woods, looking so quiet and pleasant that for the moment I could forget the horrors of witchcraft and other cruelties which rule even in these peaceful groves.

Towards afternoon we came to the village of a chief named Wanga, Mbene's friend, who had sent a message to me to stop at his place on my way down. We were received with acclamation; all the people turned out to see me, and there was the usual singing, dancing, and cutting capers. The chief took me immediately to his own house, the best in the town; but I was not destined to remain quiet, for presently the house and all the neighbourhood began to fill up with people eager to take a look at me. I was this time doubly a hero; for they had heard of my trip to the Fan country, and had prophesied that I should be killed and eaten by those terrible people, of whom all these tribes seem to stand in great awe. Now that I was come back in safety, they openly proclaimed that I must be the lucky owner of a fetich of very remarkable powers. The king complimented me on my safe return, and asked why I cared to see the cannibals and go to their country.

When I answered that I went there to shoot birds and animals strange to me, there went up a general shout of astonishment, and I fear I lost some of the confidence and admiration of the hearers, for they could scarce give credence to what appeared so foolish. Nevertheless, Wanga invited me to stay as long as I pleased with him.

Next morning I noticed the beautiful situation of Wanga's village, which I had been too weary to appreciate the night before. It lay on the edge of a steep bank overhanging the Noya. Immediately behind the town was a heavy forest of grand old trees, many of vast size, both for height and thickness. The undergrowth was tolerably dense, and huge vines stretched from tree to tree, like gigantic snakes.

I spent several days in the villages near here, and was

everywhere received with kindness and also with curiosity. The natives had never seen a white man before, and, of course were full of surprise, and alarm too, for a time. Others, who were more experienced, asked curious questions about the manners and customs of the white people. When I told them that a man was put into prison for having two wives, both men and women set up a shout of wonder, but seemed to think that, though the white man's country must be a great country, the white men were themselves more lucky than wise.

Wanga had promised me a new set of guides if I would stay some days with him; accordingly, I sent Mbene's men back, with proper acknowledgments, and prepared for a start with my new guides.

We were to go down the Noya for a few miles and then take the land, leaving our canoes to return.

I wanted very much to go off privately, but that would not do. The king and the whole village, male and female, about two hundred people, came down to bid me good-bye, and I had to shake hands all round, which took more time than I cared to spare for the purpose. But it was the last pleasure I was ever likely to do to a people who had received me with very great kindness. One feels a strange softness about the heart on leaving one of these simple African villages, where, a stranger in a strange land, he has yet been treated kindly, and all his wants supplied. The people seem really sorry to see you go; and as you leave, thinking that in all human probability you will never meet these kind people again, you feel sorrier than you expected.

We descended the Noya for a few miles, hailed at every turn by the inhabitants of villages who wished us to stop; and then abandoned our canoes and took to the land. For some miles it was very swampy, and the loads of my men made travelling difficult and tedious. I had now with me the entire results of this expedition, and this formed no light burden, even for the stout, finely-made negro fellows I had. The people along the Noya are a fine-looking race, not above, but up to, the "middle height," with rather intelligent features, and not very black. They seem to live very happily in their villages, though, of course, all the vices and superstitions of Africa infect them, and often make brutes of them.

Presently we came to high land, and then the landscape regained somewhat of the beauty it had about Wanga's village, while we were able to push ahead faster over the solid ground. Towards sunset we reached a place called Ezongo, where the inhabitants, seeing our heavy loads, and supposing that I brought them vast and unheard-of amounts of trade, turned out with the greatest amount of enthusiasm to welcome me.

Their ardour cooled somewhat when they learned the contents of my packages, and I found in the course of the evening that the rascally chief or king of Ezongo, thinking I must place a great value on things I had gone so far to get, had determined to hold me till I paid a heavy price to get away.

I was very angry at this outrage; and for a while things looked as though I should have trouble. I determined not to submit to an imposition which would leave me empty-handed and defenceless, even if it would have answered to let any one of these fellows impose on me under any circumstances. There seemed likely to be a palaver. I determined to fight for my rights, but was, of course, anxious to get all settled peaceably. The king, urged on by his people, who seemed a greedy set of rascals, insisted on his price. At last, my Mbicho guides from the Noya tried to settle the matter. They were wise enough to get the king to come to me with them alone. I gave the rascal a coat and an old shirt, and told him what was literally true—that I was very poor, and could not pay what his people wanted, and that he must be on my side. He went out at once and harangued the turbulent extortioners. I watched the result with considerable anxiety; but at last, seeing that he would succeed, paid my Wanga-town guides, and prepared to set out for Yoongoolapay, a village whose chief I had seen on the coast some time before, when he made me promise to pay him a visit on my return from the interior.

I was now commercially so reduced that I had only a few

white beads left to pay to my guides, and was glad enough to be getting down towards the territory of a man who knew me, and would probably trust me.

We arrived at our destination late in the afternoon, and were received with great demonstrations of joy. My old friend, King Alapay, was very glad to see me, and asked me to stay some days, which, being very much worn out with constant exposure and anxieties, I determined to do. His village is situated upon a high hill overlooking the surrounding country, and a beautiful stream skirts the foot of the hill.

A considerable number of independent Mbicho villages lie here within a circuit of a few miles, and live in great harmony with each other, all having prudently intermarried to such a degree that they are really one large family. I was made welcome among them all, and spent some very pleasant days in hunting, and particularly in that kind of sport called here ashiga-hunting, or net-hunting—a practice very common among the Bakalai tribes.

This singular sport is very much practised in this part of Africa, and, as it is generally successful, is a local amusement, and brings out the best traits of the natives. I was always very fond of it.

The nets are made of the fibre of the pine-apple plant, and also with the fibres of a kind of tree, which are twisted into stout threads. They are from sixty to eighty feet long and four to five feet high, and every village owns several. But as few villages have sufficient to make a great spread, generally several unite in one grand hunt and divide the proceeds: the game caught in any net being the share of its owners.

The first day we went out, half-a-dozen villages met together at an appointed place, the men of each bringing their nets. Then we set off for a spot about ten miles off, where they had a clearing in the dense woods which had been used before. We moved along in silence, so as not to alarm the animals who might be near our ground. The dogs —for dogs are used for this hunt—were kept still and close together.

Finally we arrived on the ground, and the work of

spreading the toils began. Each party stretched a single net, tying it up by vines to the lower branches of trees; but as all worked in one direction, and each took care to join his and his neighbour's net together, we in a very short time had a line of netting running in a wide half-circle, and at least half-a-mile long.

This done, a party went out on each side to guard the sides and prevent escape, and the rest of us were then ready to beat the bush. We started at about a mile from the nets, and, standing about fifty yards from each other, advanced gradually, shouting and making what noise we could, at the same time keeping our guns in readiness to bring down anything which should come in our way. The sport would have been less exhausting had not the jungle been so dense. Though this very spot was frequently used for net-hunting, and therefore more cleared than the neighbouring wilder wood, yet we were obliged to proceed almost step by step, and every native was armed, besides his gun, with a kind of heavy cutlass or *machete*, with which it was necessary literally to hew out a way, the vines making a net-work which only the beasts of the forests could glide through without trouble.

As we advanced, so did the men who guarded the flanks, and thus our party gradually closed on the prey, and presently we began to hear shots. I heard the shots, but could see nothing, and had only to hold my own gun in readiness, and pray that my neighbour might not shoot me by mistake; for they are fearfully reckless when on a chase.

At last we came in sight of the nets. We had caught a gazelle of a very minute size—a pretty little animal—which does not grow to be larger than a pointer. It is very graceful, and ought to make a pretty pet, though I have never seen one tamed. There were several other little quadrupeds, and a large antelope was held and shot before I came up; and another antelope, being shot at and missed, rushed forward and got entangled in the net.

Having drawn this cover, we gathered up the nets and the dogs—who enjoyed the sport vastly—and walked off to try another place.

I do not wonder at all at the bad shots the natives make.

Wherever I have been among them my shots have excited astonishment; and this not so much because my guns are better, as because I have good powder, and they do not know how to load a gun. The negro idea is to put in as much powder as he dares, and on top of this as much old iron as he can afford to throw away in one shot. If the powder was of only average strength they would blow themselves to pieces, but the traders on the coast make it very mild by adulterations; and I have actually seen bits of iron of various shapes rammed into a gun till it was loaded to within a few inches of the muzzle. Consequently, the recoil is heavy; they dare not hold the guns to their shoulders, and blaze away very much at a venture.

Walking over to another part of the forest, about three-quarters of an hour distant, we again spread our nets. Here we had better luck, catching a number of antelopes, deer, and some smaller animals. This seemed enough for one day, of which I was very glad, for I was tired out.

Before breaking up, all the game caught was laid together, that all might see it. And now I had opportunity to notice the curious little dogs, about a foot high, and sharp-eared, who had been of such material assistance driving the animals into our toils. They were standing looking at their prizes with eager and hungry eyes. They do not look very intelligent, but are of the greatest use in this sport, because when they bark the game is never far off, and thus they warn the hunters. Often they go out on hunts for themselves; and it is no unusual thing for half-a-dozen dogs to drive an antelope to the neighbourhood of their village, where they give tongue, and the hunters come out and kill their quarry.

I was glad to go to sleep early, but was scarce soundly asleep when I was turned out of the house by a furious attack of the *bashikouay* ants. They were already all over me when I jumped up, and I was bitten terribly. I ran out into the street and called for help. The natives came out, and lights were struck, and presently I was relieved. But now we found that the whole village was attacked. The great army was pouring in on us, doubtless excited by the smell of meat in the houses; and my unfortunate antelope had probably brought them to my door. All hands had to turn out for defence. We built little cordons of fire, which kept them away from places they had not yet entered, and thus protected our persons from their attacks; and towards morning, having eaten everything they could get at, they left us in peace. As was to be expected, I found my antelope destroyed—literally eaten up.

The vast number, the sudden appearance, the ferocity and voracity of these frightful insects never cease to astonish me. Last night they poured in literally by millions and billions, and only when many fires were lighted were they forced from that direct and victorious course which they generally hold. Then, however, they retreated in parties, and with the greatest regularity, vast numbers remaining to complete the work of destruction.

The negroes of the villages differ but little from those on the coast, except that they are *dirtier*. The women seem to lay on the oil and red earth thicker than their husbands; seem to wear dirtier cloths about their middles, and are actually less endurable when gathered in a crowd about a fire, as is their wont, than the men.

I noticed a custom or superstition which is common to all the tribes I have visited, and the reason or supposed reason for which I have never been able to persuade any one to tell me. On the first night when the new moon is visible all is kept silent in the village; nobody speaks but in an undertone; and in the course of the evening King Alapay came out of his house and danced along the street, his face and body painted in black, red, and white, and spotted all over with spots the size of a peach. In the dim moonlight he had a frightful appearance, which made me shudder at first. I asked him why he painted thus, but he only answered by pointing to the moon, without speaking a word.

There are other and varying ceremonies in different tribes to welcome the new moon; but in all the men mark their bodies with charmed chalk or ochre; and no one has ever been prevailed on to tell me the meaning of the rites or the particulars of the belief. I suppose the common men do not know it themselves.

Our path lay through an immense forest—a grand solitude, gloomy and, even at midday, unpenetrated by the sun. Here the silence was only made more striking by the occasional shrill scream of a parrot or the chatter of a monkey. We saw no other animals, though elephant-tracks abounded.

The biggest ivory of the coast comes from this belt under the equator. I have seen a tusk whose weight was 110 pounds, but this was an extraordinary instance; the most weigh from twenty to fifty pounds.

Alapay's head-wife, at his village, made me a quantity of igouma, or cassava-bread, the day before we started, so that with a little fish and some plantains I was not likely to starve, even if we did not enter any villages on the way. The igouma is made by pounding and making a paste of the cassava. This paste when boiled becomes very thick and firm, and it is then shaped into loaves a foot long and four or five inches in circumference, and permitted to dry, when it becomes hard and tough, and may be kept several weeks, though it becomes sour and unfit for a civilized stomach generally after two or three days. But it will not do to be squeamish in Africa, which, with all its tropical richness of vegetation, is as good a place to starve in as any man could desire.

As we neared a stream, we came to a mangrove-swamp. It was high tide, and there was not a canoe to be had. To sleep on this side among the mangroves, and be eaten up by mosquitoes, was not a pleasant prospect, and to me there seemed no other. But my men were not troubled at all. We were to cross over, quite easily too, on the roots which projected over the water's edge, and which lay from two to three feet apart at irregular distances. It seemed a desperate venture; but they set out, jumping like monkeys from place to place, and I followed, expecting every moment to fall in between and stick in the mud, perhaps to be attacked by some noxious reptile whose rest my fall would disturb. I had to take off my shoes, whose thick soles made me more likely to slip. I gave all my baggage and guns and pistols to the men, and then commenced a journey whose like I hope never to take again. We were an hour in getting across—

an hour of continual jumps and hops. In the midst of it all a man behind me flopped into the mud, calling out "Omemba!" in a frightened voice.

Now, "omemba" means *snake*. The poor fellow had put his hand on an enormous black snake, and, feeling its cold, slimy scales, let go his hold and fell through. All hands immediately began to run faster than before, and to shout and make all kinds of noises to frighten the serpent. But the poor animal also took fright, and began to crawl away among the branches as fast as he could. Unfortunately, his fright led him directly towards some of us; a general panic now ensued, everybody running as fast as he could to get out of the way of danger. Another man fell into the mud below, and added his cries to the general noise. I came very near getting a mud-bath myself, but luckily I escaped. But my feet were badly cut up.

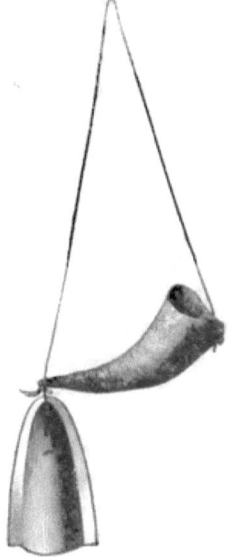

HORN AND BELL OF IRON,
TO KEEP THE DEVIL OUT. THE BELL IS SOUNDED TO DRIVE OUT THE EVIL SPIRITS, WHILE THE GOOD ONES COME INTO THE HORN.

CHAPTER X.

Journey to Cape Lopez—Princess Akerai—A plantation—Prairie land—Caught in a storm—Mpongwe canoe-builders—Large size of canoes—Ogoula-Limbai—Ogoula a great elephant hunter—Getting into canoes—Our predicament—The negroes great swimmers.

FROM the Gaboon I prepared myself for a trip to Cape Lopez, south of the Equator.

When all was ready, I placed all my goods, and guns, and ammunition in one of the immense canoes which the Mpongwe make, and we started for Mbata Creek, on which lay the plantation of King Rompochombo.

We entered the Mbata Creek at 4 P.M., and paddled up and up, the stream growing narrower all the time, and more overhung with trees, till about midnight the men had to pull the canoe through the brushwood, which made more swamp than creek. This brought us soon to the end of the creek, and then we found ourselves on the royal plantation.

The king was at his town on the coast, but had given orders to have me forwarded on to Cape Lopez, Sangatanga, the chief town of the cape, being about sixty miles from Mbata.

My baggage was immediately taken to the king's first wife's house. Though so late, or rather now getting *early*, the people were not asleep. It is a singular habit the Africans have—they do not sleep at night, but lie about their fires, and smoke and tell stories, dozing off all day afterwards. I was not surprised, therefore, to find the Princess Akerai lying, with three or four other women near a huge fire (the thermometer was at 85°), smoking her pipe, and saying she was glad to see me.

However, all was busy in an instant. The princess hurried off to cook me some plantains and fish which her slaves were preparing, and which I greatly enjoyed, for our day's journey had made me hungry. A fire was built in the centre of the floor of the house which I was to occupy, and around this several of the king's wives assembled, while the queen busied herself in preparing a corner for my sleeping accommodation.

For bed I had a mat—simple enough, but not so hard for the bones as the bamboo couch I had enjoyed at Mbene's or in the cannibal country; and there was added to my mat, in this case, the unusual luxury of a mosquito netting, by help of which I was able to enjoy a good sleep.

The village, which lies at the head of the Mbata Creek, is surrounded by a fertile prairie, which was now in full cultivation. The people have a great many slaves, and the women seem really to have a taste or liking for agricultural operations. Here I saw on every hand, and for several miles in all directions, fields of ground-nuts, plantains, corn, sugar-cane, ginger, yams, manioc, squash (a great favourite with all the negroes); while near their little huts were growing the paw-tree, the lime, the wild orange, together with abundance of plantains and pine-apples. They seemed even to care for animals, for everywhere I saw goats and the diminutive African chickens.

The queen rules supreme, managing everything, and ordering the labour of the slaves and the succession of the agricultural operations. Occasionally, she sets her own hand to the planting, which is the labour of the women, the men cutting down and burning the bushes, which spring up with such rapidity wherever the African soil is left for a season untouched.

As I intended to spend some months in the Cape Lopez country, I had brought a very inconvenient quantity of luggage, which was to be transported overland to Sangatanga from here, Mbata being the head of navigation in this direction—to carry all this required some thirty men. These I asked the queen for next morning, saying that I would give each man five fathoms of cotton cloth, some beads, and tobacco. She made no difficulty, but, of course, several days were required to get everything ready for a start.

Finally, all was prepared, and we started. Our way led us for ten or twelve miles through a fine prairie, interspersed with occasional hills, and making altogether a beautiful country for agriculture. South of the Gaboon the country changes very much, and is generally less rough and better adapted to the growing of yams and other farm-products than any I had seen before. Here, as we travelled along, we came occasionally upon the huts of slaves who lived here, far away from their Mpongwe masters on the coast, and tilled the soil on their own account, sending a tribute of its products down to the seaside whenever canoes came up the Mbata for it. They seemed quite happy, as they were certainly independent, for slaves. The old men and women lay lazily in front of their little huts, smoking; and on every hand were smiling fields of plantains, manioc, pea-nuts, and yams.

Towards twelve o'clock we approached the sea, and could hear the distant boom of the surf. Presently the sky, before clear, became overcast, and before long we were in the midst of a wild storm—almost a tornado. It thundered and lightened violently, and rained as it rains only in Africa. We rushed for a little hut we saw before us, and were kindly received by an old negro and his wife, who lived there. In about an hour the storm was over, and the sky was again clear. These storms are frequent here in the season, and sometimes do much damage, tearing down trees, and overwhelming the plantations in ruin.

Half-an-hour's walk brought us to the beach, along which we now had to walk. The soft sand made our journey exhausting; I was forced to take off my shoes, as I sank down above my ankles at every step. This lasted the whole day, and I was glad when night came and we stopped. On one side was the rolling sea, and on the other the dark green forests, coming down in seemingly impenetrable masses nearly to the shore. Every mile or so a creek cut its way through this mass of green, and wound its devious course into the interior, having a curious appearance—canal-like—from the way in which the vegetation began on the very banks, in the same solid masses which presented their fronts seaward. It was a real solitude, the roar of the sea breaking the grim silence of the forest only to make that more impressive. From time to time we recognized the lonesome cry of the chimpanzee, which is the chief inhabitant of these wilds.

Just at sunset we came upon a beautiful little prairie or

natural clearing, situated quite in the middle of the woods, and received an unexpected welcome from the owner of some huts we saw in front of us. He proved to be a Mpongwe, named Mbouma, whom I had known at the Gaboon. He had come hither to spend the dry season in making canoes, the trees surrounding his little clearing being of unusual size. He had chosen for the scene of his labours one of the prettiest spots I have seen. The little prairie was a mile long, by perhaps one-third of a mile wide, perfectly clear, and covered with a luxuriant growth of grass, which, when the sun lay on it next morning, shone with a golden glory. The very beasts of the forest seemed to rejoice in its brightness; monkeys leaped nimbly along the trees on its skirts, and the song of the birds in the morning gave a charm to the whole scene which few of the African wilds can boast.

Mbouma had moved hither temporarily, but with his whole family—wives, children, and slaves. They had built shelters, rude but sufficient leaf-roofed huts.

He showed me some immense trees he had cut down, and which were intended for canoes. Several of these vessels were already completed and ready to launch. A Mpongwe canoe is sometimes of very considerable size. Mbouma had one finished, which was 60 feet long, 3½ feet wide, and 3 feet deep. The process of canoe-building is very simple. The tree is felled, cut to the requisite length, divested of limbs, if any are in the way, and then fire is applied to burn out the inside. This fire is carefully watched and guided till all the inside is eaten away. Then the *mpano*, the native adze, is used to trim all off neatly, and to give shape to the outside. They know very well how to do this; and their larger canoes are very stout and reliable craft, in which considerable coasting voyages are sometimes made. Unfortunately the making of the canoe is mostly the least part of the work. The canoe-tree (for only one kind of tree is used for this purpose) grows almost invariably some miles away from the water, and the unlucky boat-builder's greatest undertaking is the launch. Often they have to transport a sixty-foot canoe eight or ten miles overland to the nearest creek or river. In this case they cut a path through the woods, and on this lay rollers two feet apart, on which, with much trouble, the little vessel is pushed along.

Mbouma was very fortunate in his choice of locality. His farthest canoe was but two miles from the seashore, and he thought his labour easy enough. But he was forced to send all his canoes by sea to the Gaboon.

Little prairies like this of Mbouma's occurred constantly between this and Sangatanga, the head town of the Oroungous. They were great reliefs to the dreary journey.

We continued to skirt the seashore, our aim being to gain a Shekiani village, where we purposed to stop the night.

We reached a village where the chief, Ogoula-Limbai by name, turned out to meet us at the head of his whole village, which consisted of thirty men, sixty or seventy women, and a prodigious number of children. I was welcomed and conducted to a house—a real house—the most convenient and substantial I had met with among the wild negroes. It was high, had a plank floor, and was really wonderful for a savage chief's abode. It had several rooms partitioned off with planks; and when I had rested and talked awhile I was asked into another room, where a new surprise awaited me. The walls of this room were covered with wall-paper, and all around were hung little pictures of saints. A table was covered with a real cotton cloth, on which was my dinner, which I was now asked to eat. The *pièce de résistance* was a splendid roast of boar-meat, juicy and fragrant. The wild boar is very plentiful hereabouts, and makes a very fine roast. The animal is black.

Ogoula has the reputation of being the greatest hunter of elephants in all the country about here. As he could speak Mpongwe, he told me some of his adventures, which proved that he was indeed a daring and expert fellow. Going out to the hunt one day, he met two elephants. Being alone he had but one gun, and would have retreated and watched for a safer chance; but the great beasts saw him and did not give him any opportunity of escape. He was obliged to make a stand; and taking good aim he killed one elephant. Unfortunately it was the female, and the male, seeing its partner fall, immediately rushed at him. He turned to retreat, and caught his foot in a trailing creeper. The more he struggled the more he became entangled, and meantime his pursuer was tearing down everything in its way, and was almost on top of him when he got his foot loose, and swung himself into a young sapling which stood at hand. Scarce had he done this, when the elephant trumpeting with rage, was beneath him. It seized the sapling with its trunk and swayed it violently back and forth, determined to pull it down. But as it swung on one side, Ogoula, nimble through desperation, was able to catch at another which stood near, and when the elephant seized this, he gave himself a great swing and caught the outstretched branch of a huge full-grown tree, from which he clambered to a safe height where he could afford to laugh at the vain rage of his enemy.

The negroes are not generally good marksmen, but they have great nimbleness and considerable presence of mind, and often escape in situations where a white man would most likely be killed.

As my men were very much exhausted with the weight of my baggage, I asked Ogoula to let me have a canoe, which he did. The road to Sangatanga by sea was a little further, but a good deal easier than along the yielding sand of the seashore; so the luggage was to be put in the canoe, and I and part of the people to go with it.

I slept on a sofa-bed—another relic of the Portuguese—with a negro boy to fan me, and a torch by whose smoke it was hoped the musquitoes would be driven off. As the natives here, including Ogoula himself, are great thieves, my things were placed in a room near mine, where my men slept.

About one o'clock I woke up, roused up the men, and proceeded to the seashore. Here we found ourselves in a position so common, and so characteristic of the negroes' dealings, that I will describe it. I had bargained for a canoe and paid for it, expecting, of course, to have it in such a condition that we could use it.

Now we could find no paddles. I went to Ogoula, who said they must have been stolen, but offered a new set for two fathoms of cloth and two bottles of rum.

I refused, point-blank, to be cheated.

Ogoula frowned—looked blacker than usual, in fact, and declined to help us.

There was much "palaver," and finally one of my men gave his own cloth and got the paddles. I was very angry, but could do nothing; and happily Ogoula was just in the same state. He thought himself ill-used that I had given him no rum (which I never carried for the natives), but could do nothing—but cheat. Had I not been escorted by Rompochombo's men, no doubt I should have had trouble—probably been robbed.

We now put our things aboard, got in, and put off. The surf was high, the boat deep-laden, and, unluckily, we got caught in a mountain of a breaker, which turned us over in an instant but a few yards from the shore, and sent us all into the water, which, fortunately for me, was not deep.

Here was another mess. We got ashore again, kindled an immense fire, and then my men, who were, as all the coast negroes are, good divers, set out, and in an amazingly short time fished up everything we had lost but one or two small packages. I was very glad to find my guns again, for without them I should have been in a bad plight. The powder, fortunately, had been so carefully packed that it was not injured; and, as for the rest, I came off very well.

Last of all, the paddles were hunted up. They had been washed ashore a long distance off. Then we lay down by the fire till dawn and dried ourselves, and, when day broke, I had all the things again put into the boat, and sent the men off to make their way round, determining myself to walk overland.

While we lay about the fire, I kept a good look-out for my friend Ogoula, and was rewarded by seeing his rascally face peering at us through the darkness. He came down when he saw himself discovered, and expressed himself very sorry; but I felt certain that if we had been in confusion I should have been plundered. These negroes seem to be unable to keep their hands off property that has been cast ashore by the sea, no matter how slight the accident.

I set out with a man to carry my gun and show me the way. Towards noon we came to a village, where, fortunately, we got something to eat, for I was very hungry. In the afternoon we came to the Shark River; rightly named, for its mouth was actually alive with huge sharks, which swam about our frail canoe as we crossed in such an outrageously familiar manner that I was rather glad to get safely across.

The negroes boast that they can swim the river without danger if only they have nothing red about them; and, in fact, all my men swam across without accident, first carefully concealing those parts of their scanty dress which might have the obnoxious colour. They also offered to take me over on their backs; but this I refused, from a fear that the sharks might make an exception in my case to their general rule. These fish are here held sacred—which may have something to do with their harmlessness. The natives believe that if they were to kill one there would be no safety from their attacks thereafter. It is certainly very singular that they should not attack men in the water, for on any other of the numerous points on the coast where they abound a man would be instantly killed did he venture among them.

The prairies grow larger and more important as the traveller approaches Sangatanga, and in the interior they form a still larger portion of the country. The change is very curious and very decided, as north of the Gaboon such a thing as a clear patch is almost unknown; all being vast, dense, hardly penetrable forest. All the interior, from Gaboon to Sangatanga and Nazareth River, is hilly, rolling land, and contains large prairie tracts, where the buffalo has his home and pasture. Each clearing is lined with dense, evergreen forests, where the buffalo spends his days, grazing only by night; and these forests shelter the elephant, leopard, and all the varied fauna of these woods, which abound much more in game than the country north of the Gaboon.

I did not reach Sangatanga till a little before dark, having travelled sixteen hours, counting an hour's rest on the way.

CHAPTER XI.

Sangatanga—The royal residence—The Oroungou people—Visit to King Bango—The Mafouga—The king's crown—A ball given in my honour —Songs—Rum in plenty—Five reputed idols.

THE hills above Sangatanga assume very fantastic shapes, and are many of them quite steep. Along their sides, where they are bare, they are covered with thousands of the curious hills of the white ants which abound hereabouts.

Sangatanga is set upon a tolerably high hill fronting the sea-shore, between which and the town, a distance of about two miles, stretches a lovely prairie, about which are scattered numerous little villages. The view is charming, for, turning the eye upwards from the landscape which lies at one's feet, the beholder sees before him the boundless stretch of the ocean, whose billows seem pouring in to overwhelm the shore. I never tired of this fine landscape, which was doubly refreshing after my long and tedious journeys in the unpicturesque regions north of the Gaboon, where the coast-line almost everywhere is a deadly swamp, and the interior an interminable forest.

At the top of the hill was the royal residence, where dwelt the king of the Oroungou tribe. He is a powerful chief, and his tribe—over whom he rules almost as a despot by his personal influence—are a thriving and influential people.

Cape Lopez proper is in lat. 0° 36′ 10″ S., and long. 8° 40′ E. from Greenwich. It takes its name from the Portuguese, who formerly called it Cape Lopez Gonsalvez. It is chiefly a long sandy point projecting into the sea, on which it gains somewhat every year. This point protects the bay, which is quite large and full of shallows and banks, so that vessels are obliged to anchor far from the shore. The cape looks from the sea something like overflowed land. The point is so low that the bushes and trees growing on it seem from a distance seaward to be set in the water.

The indent of the bay is about fourteen miles, and several small rivers empty their waters into it near its base. The Nazareth, a more considerable stream, also has its mouths here, as well as the Fetich River, one of its branches. The bay has frequent banks and shallows, but the water is very deep near the cape itself, and vessels of large size may sail in, almost or quite touching the land without danger.

The inner shores of the bay are swampy and overgrown with mangroves, which come quite down to the water's edge, in their usual gloomy and impenetrable masses. The water here is brackish, from the large quantity of fresh water brought down by the Nazareth and other streams. This part of the coast has a gloomy, dirty, sickly appearance—the black waters rushing into the sea, the long mangrove-flats sending up noisome exhalations, and filling the air with a pungent and disagreeable odour of decaying vegetation. The bay abounds with all sorts of delicious fish, and the cape itself is a famous place for turtle.

King Bango, if he were not a drunken vagabond, might be a prosperous king. Back from the seashore the land becomes higher and hilly, the mangroves give place to forests of palm and more useful woods, and fine prairies dot the country quite thickly. The whole of this district was then given to the slave-trade.

In the morning after my arrival the king sent his mafouga (his intendant, major-domo, herald, and secretary of state) to the village where I had stopped, to ascertain who was the white man who had come, and what was his business.

The Oroungo language being almost identical with the Mpongwe, I was able to converse with the mafouga, and informed him that I was too tired to speak to or see anyone, but that next day I would see the king.

At eight o'clock the following morning I accordingly prepared for my visit to King Bango, or Pass-all—the last being the name given him by the traders. The royal palace is surrounded by a little village of huts, in which reside the royal wives, of whom there are really a vast number (over 300), as the king takes pride in keeping up the largest harem to be found on this part of the coast.

As I entered the village the mafouga met me, with the king's cane borne aloft, and inquired, in an official voice, my business, and if I desired to see the king.

I answered, Yes—somewhat disgusted at so much ceremony, though the crowd of loyal subjects who had followed me up were hugely pleased.

I was asked to wait awhile, and presently (the royal wives having put the finishing touches to their toilets, perhaps) I was admitted to the palace.

It was an ugly hole of a house, set on pillars, and of two stories. The lower story consisted of a dark hall, flanked on each side by rows of small dark rooms, looking uncommonly like cells. At the end of the hall was a staircase, steep and dirty, up which the mafouga piloted me. When I had ascended, I found myself in a large room, at one end of which was seated King Bango, surrounded by about a hundred of his wives, and with his interpreter and some of his principal men standing near him.

The king—a middle-sized, not over-clean, dissipated-looking negro, dressed very lightly in a shirt and a dilapidated pair of pantaloons—wore on his head a crown which had been presented to him by some of his friends the Portuguese slavers, and over his shoulders a flaming yellow coat with gilt embroidery all over it—apparently the cast-off coat of some rich man's lackey in Portugal or Brazil. The crown was shaped like those commonly worn by actors on the stage, and was probably worth when new about two pounds. But his majesty had put around it a new band or circlet of pure gold, which must have been worth at least forty pounds. He was very proud of this crown. He sat on a sofa, and held in his hand a cane, which officiated as sceptre.

Most of his wives present wore silks. I was presented to the queen or head wife, an old woman, and by no means pretty.

The king remarked that the slave-trade no longer prospered. He complained of the English, who were the cause of this stagnation, and feared much that in a few years more he would be left without customers.

He next addressed me in French, and told me he had been to Brazil and also to Portugal, having lived two years in Lisbon, and knew how to read Portuguese—a bit of knowledge which must have been handy in his business affairs.

It was easy to see that his foreign travel had done him little good.

He told me that the entire village on the hill was occupied by his family and slaves, and that about two hundred of his men were now in the country on his plantation. To my question of how many children he had, he replied that he did not know the exact number, but at least six hundred, which, from after observation, I consider a fair estimate.

The next morning that absurd personage, the mafouga, who was evidently the result of his royal master's visit to Lisbon, came down to my house to announce that the king would return my visit in the afternoon. Accordingly, at two o'clock I arranged my little hut, and presently a great beating of drums announced that King Bango was under way. Soon a great procession of people appeared, at the head of whom the king was borne in a hammock. I went out to meet him, and found, to my surprise, that he could not move. I thought, at first, that he was dead-drunk, but was presently informed that his left arm and leg were paralyzed. His people lifted him out of his hammock and seated him on a seat which I had prepared, and here six of his wives surrounded him with fans. The rest of his family who were present also crowded around, and I soon perceived that all the women were drunk. His majesty had called at one of the slave-factories on his way to my house, and there rum had been served out to the whole cortège. Evidently the royal ladies had managed to get more than their share.

Bango was dressed as yesterday, except that he had on a new crown, which I asked to see. He took it off. I found that it was also a tawdry concern, but enriched with gold to the value of at least a thousand dollars. It contained some poor imitations of precious stones, and was evidently thought an object of great value and beauty by its possessor. After praising its beauty, I returned it; whereupon his majesty tried to pick a quarrel, saying that neither Portuguese, English, French, Spaniards, or Americans had ever before asked him to take off his crown, and that he thought I intended to insult him. Of course I said I had a great desire to behold, near to, such a beautiful object, which seemed to pacify him. He informed me that this crown had been given him by a celebrated slave-trader on the coast, well known under the name of Don Jose, and that it was sent as a special gift from one of the richest firms of Rio Janeiro, who had dealt largely with him.

While we were talking, one of the women was slyly kicking me on the shins and winking at me, which I sincerely hoped the king, her husband, would not see, as I had no desire to arouse his jealousy. When we ceased, all the women began to ask for rum, which I refused, but gave them instead several heads of tobacco, and then formally presented the king with two large pieces of cloth. This put him in good humour, and, after some refreshments, he set out for home.

The next night a ball was given by the king in my honour. The room where I had been first received was the ball-room. When I arrived, shortly after dark, I found about one hundred and fifty of the king's wives assembled, many of whom were accounted the best dancers in the country. Shortly afterwards singing began, and then a barrel of rum was rolled in and tapped. A good glassful was given to each of the women, and then the singing recommenced. In this the women only took part, and the airs were doleful and discordant. The words I could not always catch; but here is a specimen:—

> "When we are alive and well,
> Let us be merry, sing, dance, and laugh;
> For after life comes death;
> Then the body rots, the worms eat it,
> And all is done for ever."

When everybody was greatly excited with these songs, the king, who sat in a corner on a sofa with some of his favourite wives next him, gave the signal for the dance to begin. Immediately all rose up and beat a kind of tune or refrain to accompany the noise of the tam-tams or drums. Then six women stepped out and began to dance in the middle of the floor. The dance is not to be described. Any one who has seen a Spanish fandango, and can imagine its lascivious movements tenfold exaggerated, will have some faint conception of the postures of these black women. To attain the greatest possible indecency of attitude seemed to be the ambition of all six. These were relieved by another set of six in course of time, and so the ball went on for about two hours, when, what with occasional potations of rum and the excitement of the dance and noise, the whole assemblage got so uproarious that I had thoughts of retreating; but the king would not suffer it. He and all the people seemed to enjoy it all exceedingly.

Next women came out, one at a time, and danced their best (or worst) before a closely-critical audience, who, watching every motion with jealous eyes, were sure to applaud by audible murmurs of pleasure at every more than usually lewd *pas*. At last this ceased, and two really pretty young girls came out hand in hand and danced before me. I was told that they were daughters of the king, and he desired that I should take them for my wives.

Finally the room began to smell too high for me, and, as the revelries were getting madder all the time, I slipped out and betook myself to my hut to sleep.

Near the king's house I passed three little houses, in which I was then told were deposited five idols, which, I knew, were considered the most powerful on all the coast from Banoko to Mayombai. They are thought to be the great protectors of all the Oroungou tribes, and are themselves placed near the king's house, who delights to do them honour, and whom they protect from all evil.

The five idols are deposited in three houses. Pangeo, a male idol, is married to Aleka, and the two stand together in one house. Pangeo is the special protector of the king and his people, and watches over them by night, keeping off every evil.

Makambi, a second male idol, is married to Abiala, and they have a second house to themselves. Poor Makambi is a powerless god, his wife having usurped the power. She holds a pistol in her hand, with which it is supposed she can kill any one she pleases: for which reason the natives fear her greatly. She protects them from various evils: and when they are sick they implore her to make them well, and bring her presents of food to propitiate her.

Last comes a bachelor-god, Numba, who is the Oroungou Neptune and Mercury in one, keeping off the evils which are likely to come from beyond sea and ruling the waves. He has the third house all to himself.

These idols are all large, and very rudely carved and ornamented. The people seem to place great value upon them. I offered 20 dollars for one, but was told I could not buy it for 100 slaves even, which is as much as to say that it was not to be bought.

The next day I wandered about the town watching the lazy negroes, and did not return to my house till after dark. I struck a match and set fire to a torch to go to bed by; and casting my eyes about to see if anything had been disturbed, noticed something glittering and shining under my *akoko* or low bamboo bedstead. I did not pay much attention to the object, which did not seem important by the dim light of the torch, till, just as I approached the bed to arrange it, I saw that the glitter was produced by the shining scales of an enormous serpent which lay quietly coiled up there within two feet of me. My first motion was to retreat behind the door; then I bethought me how to kill it. But unfortunately my two guns were set against the wall behind the bed, and the snake was between me and them. As I stood watching and thinking what to do, keeping the doorway fairly in my rear for a speedy retreat, I noticed that my visitor did not move, and finally I mustered up courage to creep along the floor to the bedside and quickly grasp one gun. Happily it was loaded very heavily with large shot. I placed the muzzle fairly against one of the coils of the serpent, and fired, and then ran out.

At the report there was an instant rush of negroes from all sides, eager to know what was the matter. They thought some one had shot a man, and then run into my house for concealment. Of course they all rushed in after, helter-skelter; and as quickly rushed out again, on finding a great snake writhing about the floor. Then I went in cautiously to reconnoitre; happily my torch had kept alight, and I saw the snake on the floor. My shot had been so closely fired that it had cut the body fairly in two, and both ends were now flopping about the floor. I gave the head some blows with a heavy stick, and thus killed the animal; and then, to my surprise, it disgorged a duck, which it had probably swallowed that afternoon, and then sought shelter in my hut to digest it quietly. This pretty sleeping companion measured eighteen feet in length.

CHAPTER XII.

Journey inland from Sangatanga—Preparations for hunting—The king gives me three great hunters—Beautiful appearance of the country—Buffaloes and elephants—Cool nights—Hippopotami—An approaching caravan—Mistrust—The village of Ngola—King Njambai—Shinshooko's house—Torturing a woman—Rescue—Appearance of the Shekianis—Their methods of warfare—My guns and watches are objects of wonder—Customs of the Shekianis—Our camp—Shooting two leopards—Superstitions in regard to leopard's tail and liver—Aboko kills an elephant—Buffaloes—Return to Sangatanga—The Oroungou burial-ground.

I ASKED the king for permission to go into the interior on a hunting expedition; he immediately gave me twenty-five men to carry my luggage and help me in my undertaking. Of these, three were his majesty's own slaves, and reputed the greatest hunters in the country. They were the providers of the royal table, and passed their lives in the hunt and in the bush. They killed elephants on his account, bringing him home the ivory.

I desired to penetrate into the hitherto unexplored interior of this latitude till we should meet the Nazareth River, which I was told we should do at the distance of about one hundred miles to the east. For their services I agreed to give the men twenty fathoms of cotton cloth each, if they behaved themselves faithfully towards me.

As we were to meet elephants, leopards, buffaloes, and the gorilla, I provided myself with a good supply of bullets. I was told that game was very plentiful in all the region I was now to visit, people being scarce, and the country more favourable than in those regions north of the Gaboon.

At half-past five we were already on the march, myself

ahead, with Aboko, my head-man, and Niamkala, the next best, at my side, and four other hunters, and twenty-three young men, as bearers and assistants, following us.

The way led through some beautiful prairies, each surrounded by dark forests, and seeming like natural gardens planted in the wilderness. It does not need much time to get into the "backwoods" here. By three o'clock Aboko announced to me that we were now where any moment we might come upon elephant or buffalo; and in a short time, sure enough, we saw a bull standing deer-like upon the edge of the wood, watching us. He stood for some minutes, safe out of range, and then turned into the wood, evidently not liking our appearance. We ran round to intercept his tract, and I waited at one pass in the wood for Aboko and two others to get clear round and drive the bull towards me. Suddenly I saw something approaching me out of the deep gloom of the forest, but, not looking closely, took it to be one of my men. It came towards me, and I walked unsuspiciously forward to a clear space. Here the thing caught sight of me, and, with a shrill scream, ran back into the woods. Then first I knew that in the dark (for in these forests daylight is almost shut out) I had mistaken a chimpanzee for a man. I was vexed; for the beast was but about thirty yards off when it ran, and I could have shot it easily. Presently my men returned, and had a hearty laugh at me for my mistake.

At six we camped in the midst of a prairie, my men collecting from the nearest forest an immense quantity of firewood, and building fires which must have been visible at a great distance. Our supper was of roast venison and plantains —good enough for such hungry fellows as we; and shortly after seven, we stretched ourselves with our feet to the fires, and wrapped up, I in my blankets, and the men in whatever they could get together of leaves and grass. No wonder the poor fellows love a fire. They are very lightly dressed, and the winds here, near the equator as it is, in the dry season are very cold when the sun is not up to warm them. I could not rest well for cold, though I had a thick blanket about me.

The night was clear and very chilly for Africa, and I could not sleep, though I had placed my boxes to windward for shelter. So about two o'clock I roused everybody up to move on, thinking it easier to keep warm in motion than while lying still. The men were very glad. Poor fellows! they had suffered more than I. Fortunately it was bright moonlight, and we could see our way clearly across the prairie. A couple of hours' sharp walking brought us to a thick wood so situated as to shelter us from the wind. Here we quickly built a tremendous fire, and again stretched out for a short nap, which lasted till six, or sunrise, when the cry of the gray partridge (*Francolinus squamatus*) aroused us.

Sunrise found us under way again; and before us a fine stretch of prairie, on whose farther borders were quietly grazing several herds of buffaloes, which quickly ran into the woods. While they remained they gave the wild country a singularly civilized appearance. It looked like a great grazing farm in June, with cattle, and hay almost ready for harvest; a fine, quiet, old-country picture here in the wilds of Africa.

Towards nine o'clock we came to a large pool or lakelet, and here I saw for the first time a hippopotamus. A dozen of these vast unwieldy creatures were sporting and snorting in the water, now popping their huge unshapely heads out, and then diving to the bottom. Aboko persuaded me not to kill any of them, as he justly remarked we could not have got them out of the water; and the proper way is to take them when they come on shore at night to feed.

Shortly after we came to an open space, and saw in the distance what I took at first to be a herd of buffalo, but which proved to be a caravan approaching us. When they saw us they prepared for trouble—for here there is no law, and every man's hand is against his brother. The greater number hid in the grass; and, after some reconnoitring, four fellows, well armed, came towards us to ask if it was peace or war. When they saw me, they were at once filled with surprise, and, losing their fears in their amazement at seeing a white man in the interior, began to shout out to their company to come and see the *Otangani*.

They were bound south and west with tobacco, salt, and goods, and intended to bring back slaves and ivory. They were Shekianis, who are the prevailing people in the interior hereabouts. We reached about the middle of the afternoon the village of Ngola, the residence of a Shekiani chief named Njambai, a vassal of King Bango, who had sent word by Aboko that I was to be entertained as long as I liked to stay and hunt. It contained about fifty neat houses, running in a double row along a long street, in the African fashion. But the whole place had a pleasing look of neatness which was not peculiarly African. It lies sixty miles due east from Sangatanga.

As we approached, the women caught sight of me and ran screaming into the houses. It is curious that nothing excites so much terror in an interior African village as the appearance of a white man. The women and children run for their lives, and seem to be afraid that the mere sight of a white will kill them. Here, however, the men did not seem to be afraid, as my cannibal friends were; and, though Njambai had never before seen a white man, he received me very courteously. Aboko delivered King Bango's message, to which Njambai replied to me that he owned all the country hereabouts, and I should have as many men to help me hunt it as I wished. All which being satisfactorily arranged, I was escorted to the house of the king's brother, which, being the most commodious in the town, was set apart for my use.

I did not go out the next day, and counted myself lucky that I did not, for I was able to save the life of a poor woman who was being killed with the most horrible tortures. After dinner, as I was reading, I heard a woman crying out as if in great pain. On my asking what was the matter, a man told me the king was punishing one of his wives; and some others hinted that I had better go and try to save her life. I hurried over to the king's house, and there, in front of the veranda, a spectacle met my eyes which froze my blood with horror. A woman, naked, was tied by the middle to a stout stake driven into the ground. Her legs were stretched out and fastened to other smaller stakes, and stout cords were bound round her neck, waist, ankles, and wrists. These cords were being twisted with sticks, and when I arrived the skin was already bursting from the terrible compression. A great crowd of spectators was standing around, not much excited. I suppose they were used to such scenes.

I walked up, and, taking the king by the arm, asked him to release the poor wretch for my sake, and not to kill her. When I spoke, the twisting ceased. The executioners seemed willing enough to suspend operations. The king hesitated, and was not willing to be balked of his revenge. He walked into his house. I followed him, and threatened to leave his town immediately if he did not release her. Finally he gave in, and said, "Let her loose yourself. I give her to you."

I rushed immediately, and, being unable to untie the savage cords, cut them with my knife. The poor creature was covered with blood. Some of the ropes had penetrated so deeply that the flesh had burst open, and she bled freely. But she was not seriously hurt. I went immediately in to the king and made him promise me that he would not punish her again. Then I asked what she had done to deserve such punishment. He said she had stolen the bead belt which he usually wore around his waist and given it to her lover— a heinous offence truly.

Then, to change the current of his ebony majesty's thoughts, I pointed out to him a small bird sitting upon the top of a high tree near his house, and said I could kill that bird. He said it was impossible, as I knew he would. I sent for my gun, took aim, and brought down the bird, amid the loud shouts of his majesty and the populace. They examined my gun, which had a *cap*-lock, and was a great wonder to them, as, of course, they use only flint-locks. Then they said I had a greegree or fetich to help me shoot. No one who had not a powerful charm could do such things, they thought.

Then, to clinch their good-humour, I brought out my match-box and struck a light. This has never failed to get me a great reputation among the interior negroes. It is a trick which seems to them the most marvellous of all, and these Shekianis were never tired of seeing me "make fire."

The Shekiani tribe, and those people who are closely allied

to them and speak various dialects of their language, occupy a portion of the sea-shore and interior as far as 80 miles from the sea—from the banks of the Muni and Moondah down as far south as the banks of the Ogobay. Through this great extent of country they are scattered in villages, having nowhere any central point of union. Still they manage to keep up their nationality. In some parts they are most numerous near the coast; in others they range as the second, third, and even fourth tribe inland. Thus they are settled near the mouth of the Muni and Moondah, and inhabit the sea-shore between the latter river and the Gaboon; while south of the Gaboon they have given way to the Mpongwe, and have their villages in the interior.

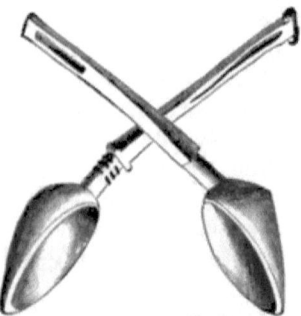

SHEKIANI SPOONS.

In person they are of ordinary size, generally light-coloured for negroes. They are warlike, treacherous, much given to trading, and are real cheats. They are ardent hunters, and have sufficient courage and great skill in woodcraft, being very lithe and active, light of foot, and cunning in their manœuvres to approach their prey. They are quarrelsome, and have constant "palavers," either with their own villages or those of other tribes. They have but little clan feeling, and the intercourse between neighbouring villages of Shekiani is not always friendly, and scarcely ever intimate. The men, in common with all other African men I have met, have little or no taste for agriculture; they leave the culture of the ground to their women and slaves.

In their warfare cunning plays a most important part.

They laugh at the courage of the white man who faces his enemy, and delight most in ambushes and sudden surprises. If one man has a quarrel with another, he lies in wait for him, shoots him as he is passing by the way, and immediately retreats. Then, of course, the dead man's friends take up his quarrel; then ensue other ambushes and murders; frequently a dozen villages are involved in the palaver, and the killing and robbing goes on for months and even years, each party acting as occasion offers. This breeds a feeling of insecurity which is destructive to all settled habits. Often, to escape assassination, a whole village moves away and builds anew at some distance; and perhaps then the enemy reaches them, or new complications arise, giving cause for new murders.

Withal, they are not bloodthirsty, but simply careless of human life, passionate, and revengeful.

Polygamy, of course, prevails among them, and takes rank as a political institution.

Though chastity is not valued for itself, adultery is a serious offence among townsmen. It is punished by fines, graduated according to the means of the offender; and many men are sold annually into slavery where the fine cannot be levied in any other way. Sometimes the guilty man compromises by working for a certain time for the injured husband, and sometimes blood alone heals the difficulty.

Each man has generally a head or chief wife—mostly the woman he married first; and for anyone to have criminal intercourse with this woman ranks as a most heinous crime, for which the offender is at least sold into slavery. When the husband forms new marriage connexions, and, as often happens, his new bride is but a child, she is then put under the care and guardianship of the head wife, who brings her up to the proper age. They marry also with their slave-women; but the children of these women, though free, have less influence and position among the people than the children of free women. Frequently the women desert their husbands for abuse or other causes, and run off to other villages; and, as it is a point of honour to return no fugitives of this kind, here is another fertile source of palaver and war.

The women are treated very harshly. The men take care to put all the hardest work on their wives, who raise the crops, gather firewood, bear all kinds of burdens; and, where the bar-wood trade is carried on, as it is now by many Shekiani villages, the men only cut down the trees and split them into billets, which the women are then forced to bear on their backs through the forests and jungle down to the river-banks, as they have but rude paths, and beasts of burden are unknown in all this part of Africa. This is the most severe toil imaginable, as the loads have to be carried often six or seven miles or more.

The Shekiani tribe, like all other African tribes, is divided into clans, and, though these clans grow very large sometimes, marriage between members of the same clan is prohibited. Children add much to a man's consequence, especially boys; and a fruitful woman enjoys, for this reason, great favour. In cases where, as frequently happens, the head of the

WAMBEE: THE SHEKIANI BANJO.

family is old and decrepit, the mother of many children has no questions asked her. They know nothing scarcely of the care of children, and lose a great proportion through mistaken treatment in infancy.

Though they have villages, they may almost be called a nomadic people. They are continually moving about the country, shifting their quarters for such causes as a palaver with a neighbouring town, the death of the chief, or a belief that their village is bewitched. Then they gather up all their household goods, and, collecting what provisions they can, move off in a body, sometimes many weary miles away.

Their superstitions, similar to many of other tribes, are of the most degrading and barbarous character. I shall mention here only that the belief in witchcraft is general, and causes much misery; while of idols, evil and good spirits, greegrees, fetiches and charms, there seems no end.

In different localities the Shekianis are known by sub-names, and the chief of these are the Mbondemo or Ndemo, the Mbicho, the Ntaimou, and the Acoa—the last inhabiting the interior between the Gaboon and Cape Lopez—the Mbiki, the Mbousha, and the Ibouay. All these speak dialects of the Shekiani, but hold themselves to be separate tribes.

We were now about fifteen miles from Njambai's village; I concluded to make my permanent camp in a pretty prairie, where we were near water, and had a wide stretch of forest on one side of us for our hunts. The men thought it a good place, one likely to afford us good sport, especially as the lake was likely to draw beasts to its banks to drink. Accordingly, we spent a whole day in arranging our encampment in such a way as to make everything comfortable and secure. Fortunately it is now the dry season, and we have no rain, but only the cold night-winds to fear. With branches of trees we built ourselves shelters which should protect us from the wind. I had my boxes piled in a solid mass to windward of my own bed; and, having locked everything up, threatened to shoot the first man who stole anything from me. Then we built light roofs of leafy branches over our sleeping-places, arranged the fires, and behold! a village. In the midst of our work came ten slaves of Njambai laden with plantains, which the good fellow had sent after me—a most welcome supply.

When all was done, and we were ready for supper, I again warned my men to be honest and keep their fingers at home. They are good fellows; but I have found that, while all savages steal, in this part of the country—where the slave-trade prevails, and where the negroes have come in contact with the lowest class of whites—they are much greater thieves than is even usual with them. So I threatened to kill the first man I caught troubling my property—to shoot without mercy; "and then," said I, with great sternness, "when I have blown your brains out, I will settle the matter with your king."

To which Aboko coolly replied that this arrangement was

not likely to do them any particular good—another little specimen of African humour.

Of course, they all protested loudly that they were honest; but I knew their temptations, poor fellows! and had more confidence in their faith that I would certainly kill the thief than in their good resolutions.

When this little matter was settled, we drew around the fire. The sun was just setting. In a huge kettle suspended over the fire was boiling a quantity of the juicy buffalo-meat; before us was a great pile of roasted plantains; and so, seating ourselves about the immense fire, for the evening was growing chilly, we took a hearty supper together.

After dinner they drank a jug of palm-wine, which had been brought from Ngola; and then, to crown their feast with the greatest delight of all, I went to my box, and lifting the lid, while the shining black faces peered at me with saucer-eyes of expectation, took out a huge head of Kentucky tobacco. This "brought down the house," so to speak; there was a wild hurrah of joy as I distributed a good portion to each, and in a few minutes all were lying about the fire smoking, with that peculiar air of utter content into which the African falls so readily at the slightest opportunity of fire and tobacco-smoke. Then ensued wild stories of hunting-adventures, of witchcraft, and evil spirits, well fitting the rude picturesque surroundings; and they lay there talking and talking till at last I was obliged to remind them that it was late, and time to feel sleepy.

The next morning (June 1st) Aboko and I went out in search of elephants, while Niamkala went with some other men to hunt for wild boar, and, if he could find them, gorilla and chimpanzee. I had poor luck, killing only a few small monkeys and birds, of no value; but as we were returning to the camp I had quite unexpectedly, as such good luck generally comes, the great shot of the day. As Aboko and I were walking carelessly along, I heard the cry of a gray partridge near by, and turned back to get a shot if possible, as they are fine eating. As I pushed into the grass—we were just on the edge of the forest—I saw suddenly several buffalo, one of which I made sure of, as he stood a little in advance of the rest, and the grass was high enough for a stealthy approach. Aboko and I advanced slowly towards the unconscious bull, who stood a fair mark; and I was about to raise my gun when Aboko made a quick sign to hold still and listen. As we stood perfectly motionless I heard, at apparently a little distance before us, a low purring sound, which might have been taken by a careless ear for the sound of the wind passing through the grass. But to Aboko's quick ear it betokened something else. His face grew very earnest, and he whispered to me "Njego," which is Shekiani for leopard.

The noise continued, and we moved slowly and very cautiously a few steps ahead to get a position where we could see over the grass. The position was not a pleasant one. The leopard comes out generally by night only, and nothing but extreme hunger will bring him out of his lair in open day. Now, when he is hungry, he is also unusually savage and quick in his motions. We knew the animal was near, but could not by any means get a sight of him. As the wind blew from it towards us, I perceived plainly a strong and peculiar odour which this animal gives out, and this proved more decidedly that it could not be far off. The thought passed through my mind—was *it* watching us? Did its eyes penetrate the grass which we could not see through? If so, was it perhaps getting ready to spring?

Meanwhile our buffalo-bull stood stupidly before his herd not twenty yards from us, utterly innocent of the presence of so many of his formidable enemies, and little suspecting the curious circumstances to which he was about to owe his life.

Just then we moved a little to one side, and, peering through an opening in the grass, I beheld an immense leopard, a female, with a tiny little leopardling near her side. The beast saw us at the same moment, turning her head quickly at some slight noise we made. She had been watching the buffalo so intently as not to notice our approach. As I watched her, it seemed to me as though a curious look of indecision passed over her face. She, too, had more game than she had looked for, and was puzzled which to attack first. Her long tail waved from side to side, and her eyes glared as she sought for a moment for a decision. But I saved her the trouble; for in less time than it takes to write it down I had put a ball into her head, which, luckily for us, relieved her of further care for prey. At the same time Aboko fired into the little leopard and killed it.

I thought the men would have lost their senses for joy when we called them to get our prizes. The leopard is one of the most feared animals of these forests. The gorilla is said to kill the leopard, but is not so dangerous to man as this great cat. Thus it is considered a great feat to kill one of these animals, and the whole camp was alive with excitement. Guns were fired, and everybody shouted aloud

NCHERI—A DIMINUTIVE GAZELLE.

In the midst of this noise Niamkala came into camp with some wild boars and a ncheri—a curious little beast—which were a welcome addition to our bill of fare.

Then, after supper, the men painted themselves and sang songs over the leopards till I made them go to sleep, which was not till towards morning. They danced, they sang songs of victory, they abused and exulted over the deceased leopard. They addressed comical compliments to its beauty—and it is really a most beautiful animal. They shouted, "Now you will kill no more people! Now you will eat no more hunters! Now you cannot leap on your prey!" And so on, till the mummery grew past laughing at.

The next morning, however, I first learned the full extent of their rejoicing, and the great importance attached to the killing of this feared beast. I was drawn to where we had suspended the body to keep the ants from it by a noise of angry quarrelling, and found Niamkala asserting his determination to have the end of the leopard's tail, while the rest of the hunters were all asserting equal rights to it, and the non-combatants, the bearers of our luggage, looked on in envious silence, evidently wishing they could also put in claims. On inquiry, I found that the lucky possessor of the end of a leopard's tail was sure to be fortunate among the women, and could, in virtue of this powerful charm, win as many hearts as he might desire.

Laughing at them, I reserved the desired tail for him among them who should behave best, and thought I had settled the quarrel. But now came a fresh division. Aboko, Niamkala, and Fasiko each wanted the whole brain of the animal. For a few minutes a fight seemed imminent on this head, which seemed even more strenuously disputed than the other. I discovered that the brain, if properly dried and mixed with some other charm called *monda*, and the nature of which I could not understand, gave its possessor dauntless courage and great fortune on the hunt. And I was so happy as to persuade my three hunters—who really needed no such amulet to patch up their courage—that a part was in this case as good as the whole.

This settled, I found that the liver was laid before me. As this had no value or interest for me, I was going to kick it aside and walk off, but was stopped and entreated to take off the gall, and myself destroy it. This was to be done to save the whole party from future trouble. It appears that the negroes believe the gall of the leopard to be deadly poison, and my men feared to be suspected of having concealed some of this poison by their friends or enemies at Sangatanga. To settle which beforehand I was now to destroy it, and afterwards to bear witness for them, if by chance they were accused of poisoning. Of course I did so, though convinced that this is a mere superstitious belief.

A strange and horrid form of monomania is sometimes displayed by these primitive negroes. An instance was related to me so circumstantially by Akondogo, chief of one of the Commi villages, and so well confirmed by others, that I cannot help fully believing in all the principal facts of the case.

Poor Akondogo said that he had had plenty of trouble in his day; that a leopard had killed two of his men, and that he had a great many palavers to settle on account of these deaths.

Not knowing exactly what he meant, I said to him, "Why did you not make a trap to catch the leopard?" To my astonishment, he replied, "The leopard was not of the kind you mean. It was a man who had changed himself into a leopard, and then became a man again." I said, "Akondogo, I will never believe your story. How can a man be turned into a leopard?" He again asserted that it was true, and gave me the following history:—

Whilst he was in the woods with his people, gathering india-rubber, one of his men disappeared, and, notwithstanding all their endeavours, nothing could be found of him but a quantity of blood. The next day another man disappeared, and in searching for him more blood was found. All the people got alarmed, and Akondogo sent for a great Doctor to drink the mboundou, and solve the mystery of these two deaths. To the horror and astonishment of the old chief, the doctor declared it was Akondogo's own child (his nephew and heir), Akosho, who had killed the two men. Akosho was sent for, and, when asked by the chief, answered that it was truly he who had committed the murders; that he could not help it, for he had turned into a leopard, and his heart longed for blood; and that after each deed he had turned into a man again. Akondogo loved his boy so much that he would not believe his own confession, until the boy took him to a place in the forest where lay the two bodies, one with the head cut off, and the other with the belly torn open. Upon this, Akondogo gave orders to seize the lad. He was bound with ropes, taken to the village, and there tied in a horizontal position to a post, and burnt slowly to death, all the people standing by until he expired.

But on careful inquiry, I found it was a case of monomania in the boy Akosho, and that he really was the murderer of the two men. It is probable that the superstitious belief of these morbidly imaginative Africans in the transformation of men into leopards, being early instilled into the minds of their children, is the direct cause of murders being committed under the influence of it. The boy himself, as well as Akondogo and all the people, believed he had really turned into a leopard, and the cruel punishment was partly in vengeance for witchcraft, and partly to prevent the committal of more crimes by the boy in a similar way, for, said they, the man has a spirit of witchcraft.

Elephants are not very plentiful in this region, at least at this season, and seem to travel a good deal, not finding their feed in such abundance as to induce them to stay long in one place. We had travelled nearly the whole of the 7th, when at last, late in the afternoon, we came across our quarry. Emerging from a thick part of the forest into the plain which bordered it, we saw to our left, just upon the edge of the wood, a solitary bull-elephant. The huge animal stood quietly by a tree, unconscious of our presence. I was struck with the vast bulk of this giant of the forests. The eye and mind had leisure to dwell upon his size, and the place was well adapted to comparisons. Trees seemed but small saplings to me when I measured them with the immense beast which was standing placidly near them.

But there was not much time for this feeling. What we had to do was to kill him, though I felt a sense of pity at destroying so great a life. I was very anxious to get the first shot myself, but, after taking in all the chances of approach, was compelled to admit that I could not manage it with any certainty. The grass was burned in every direction to leeward of him, and, we dared not risk approaching him from the windward for fear he should smell us.

I was therefore reluctantly compelled, as a sensible hunter, to resign in favour of Aboko, whose eyes glistened with pleasure, at the opportunity of showing his skill.

Cocking his musket, he dropped down into the short grass, and began to creep up to the elephant, slowly, and on his belly. It was a splendid piece of woodcraft. We stood behind some trees, whither we had all retired to consult, and watched Aboko as he glided through the grass, for all the world like a huge boa-constrictor; for the slight glimpses we caught of his back, as he moved farther and farther away from us, resembled nothing so much as the folds of a great serpent winding his way on.

Finally we could no longer distinguish any motion. Then all was silence and impatient waiting, suddenly broken by the sharp report of a gun ringing through the wood and over the plain, and eliciting screams of surprise from sundry scared monkeys and birds who had perhaps watched the secret approach with us, though from a better point of view. As the smoke cleared away I saw the huge beast helplessly tottering, till it finally threw up its trunk and fell in a dead mass at the foot of a tree. The men began to shout with excitement at such a good shot, and we all hurried up to the shapeless black mass, whose flesh was yet quivering with the death-agony. Aboko's bullet had entered its head below the ear, and, striking the brain, was at once fatal.

Aboko began to make fetich-marks on the ground around the body, and, this done, we took an axe which we had carried along and broke the skull, in order to get out the two tusks. These belonged to Aboko of right, but, as he was King Bango's slave, he was bound to give one to that sable tyrant. The proceeds of the other would be divided among the party, Aboko retaining, of course, the most considerable share. The tusks weighed but 30 pounds each.

We slept that night near our prize, about which the natives built a ring of fire to keep off intruders. The next morning, when news came into camp of our luck, all the fellows hurried out to bring in the meat, which was immediately smoked, and was to be carried into Sangatanga to be sold and given away.

I never saw men happier than these poor fellows. They ate nothing but meat, but ate such quantities that several of them have got sick, and I have been obliged to give them laudanum in brandy to cure their diarrhœa. The camp is full of meat. I had to have a separate shanty built on one side and to leeward of the camp, where all the meat is now smoked and kept, as I could not stand the smell.

The 16th and 17th were passed in shooting birds about the camp, some of which I have stuffed, but no new species. The men had meantime been hunting and exploring in various directions; and as they reported that great herds of buffalo (*Bos brachicheros*) frequented every night a prairie situated about ten miles from our camp, I determined to have a set-to.

We set out towards sunset of the 17th, and by 8 o'clock reached the forest which bounded the prairie in which we hoped to find our game. Securing for ourselves safe hiding-places in the woods on the edge of the plain, we lay down and waited.

Now, waiting is tedious; but waiting in a cold night from 8 to 2 o'clock, every moment expecting what does not come, is apt to try the patience. Mine was entirely gone, and I wished myself comfortably under my blanket in camp, when suddenly the buffaloes came. Aboko heard them coming, and presently a herd of about twenty-five stately animals emerged from the woods and scattered quietly about the grassy plain. The moon was going down, and we could see from our hiding-place the long shadows of the buffaloes silently gliding one way and another, but never near enough to us for a shot. Soon they felt quite at ease and began feeding, ever and anon gambolling sportively with each other. Seeing them engaged, we crawled upon them with great care, and at a snail's speed. We had almost got within safe range when a sudden change of wind discovered us to them. They snuffed up the air suspiciously, and instantly gathering together disappeared in the woods.

We reached King Bango's residence on the afternoon of the 23rd. The men who were his slaves immediately surrendered to him a great part of what they had brought in, whether meat or ivory; and then, protesting that this was all, were let go about their business, and to tell their adventures to their excited townsmen, amid whose enthusiastic acclamations we had entered the town.

My men came on the 27th to be paid. We parted with great good-feeling. If I ever want them they will be glad to come with me; and I should be glad to have them, for they were a very good set of fellows.

To the reader there may seem little real difference in condition between slave and freeman in Africa, but in reality the difference is quite as great here as it is in other and more civilized slave-holding nations. Even in this rude Cape Lopez country to be born of a slave mother is a disgrace, and debars the unfortunate from much of the respect and authority which his daily companions enjoy, and this though the child so born is in reality free, as it follows the condition of the father. The slave, in Africa, does not speak for himself. If he is in trouble, if there is an "adultery palaver," a "stealing palaver," or "trading palaver," his master must speak for him, and clear him if possible.

Near Fetich Point is the Oroungou burying-ground, which I went to visit. It was distant about half a day's pull in a canoe. It is a grove of noble trees, many of them of magnificent size and shape. The natives hold this place in great reverence, and refused at first to go with me on my contemplated visit, even desiring that I should not go. I explained to them that I did not go to laugh at their dead, but rather to pay them honour. But it was only by the promise of a large reward that I at last persuaded Niamkala, who was of our party, to accompany me. The negroes visit the place only on funeral errands, and hold it in the greatest awe, conceiving that here the spirits of their ancestors wander about, and that these are not lightly to be disturbed. I am quite sure that treasure to any amount might be left here exposed in perfect safety.

The grove stands by the sea-shore. It is entirely cleared of underbrush, and, as the wind sighs through the dense foliage of the trees and whispers in the darkened, somewhat gloomy grove, it is an awful place, even to an unimpressible white man. Niamkala stood in silence by the strand, while I entered the domains of the Oroungou dead.

They are not put below the surface. They lie about beneath the trees in huge wooden coffins, some of which, by their new look, betokened recent arrivals; but by far the greater number were crumbling away. Here was a coffin falling to pieces, and disclosing a grinning skeleton within. On the other side were skeletons, already without covers, which lay in dust beside them. Everywhere were bleached bones and mouldering remains. It was curious to see the brass anklets and bracelets in which some Oroungou maiden had been buried still surrounding her whitened bones, and to note the remains of goods which had been laid in the same coffin with some wealthy fellow, now mouldering to dust at his side. In some places there remained only little heaps of shapeless dust, from which some copper, or iron, or ivory ornament gleamed out to prove that here, too, once lay a corpse.

Passing on to a yet more sombre gloom, I came at last to the grave of old King Pass-all, the brother of his present majesty. The coffin lay on the ground, and was surrounded on every side with great chests which contained the property of his deceased majesty. Among these chests and on the top of them were piled huge earthenware jugs, glasses, mugs, plates, iron pots and bars, brass and copper rings, and other precious things which this old Pass-all had determined to carry at last to the grave with him. And, also, there lay around numerous skeletons of the poor slaves who were, to the number of one hundred, killed when the king died, that his ebony kingship might not pass into the other world without due attendance.

One day I saw a negro carpenter fellow go into his private fetich-house, and was lucky enough to be able to watch his motions without being discovered. He first built a little fire in the middle of the hut, then stripped and marked his body with white chalk, making very peculiar and careful stripes on one of his arms and in the centre of his breast. While doing this, which took some time, he kept up a constant mumbling of words which I could not understand, but which were doubtless prayers addressed to his fetich. Then the fire was extinguished and the hut was shut. When he came out I laughed at him; but he took the whole matter very seriously, of course, and told me that the spirit *Numba*, which has its dwelling in the ocean, had gone into his chest, and would kill him if he had not exorcised it by the ceremony I saw. This spirit, Numba, has also something to do with the moon, but what I could not discover.

CHAPTER XIII.

The Camma country—The coast line—Surf—The schooner *Caroline*—Crew—A tornado—Trouble at the mouth of the Fernand Vaz river—King Sangala and Ranpano—Sangala sends a hostage—Great palaver—Intense excitement—Discretion the better part of valour—Building my settlement—I have to be severe.

The "Camma country" begins to the south of Cape Lopez in lat. 0° 40′ S., and extends to the southward as far as the River Camma, in lat. 1° 50′ S., and to the east for about fifty miles from the coast. It is a well-watered region; the Mexias, and some minor branches of the great Ogobay River, running into the sea in its northern bounds, while the Fernand Vaz, the Camma, and the Setti have their mouths farther down, at various points of the Camma coast.

The coast-line is generally low and swampy; a heavy surf makes landing difficult, except at a few points protected by the shape of the land; and the shore, viewed from the sea, has so monotonous an aspect that seamen find it difficult to recognize their whereabouts, even after considerable experience of the coast. The mouths of the rivers, however, are readily recognized by the great streams of fresh water which they send with considerable force into the sea, discolouring it for some distance from shore, as also by the breakers on the bars which line their mouths.

The surf on the coast is much the worst during the dry season, or from June to September. During the rains landing is much easier; but even then one needs skilful natives and the best canoes.

I knew by experience that I should meet with more than usual difficulties in my attempts to penetrate into the interior. The natives here had never heard of me; they had had so little intercourse with whites that they were even more jealous than those to the north; and I expected nothing less than to have, in the first place, to win their confidence and respect by living among them near the coast for a considerable time. For this reason I made preparations for an absence of from fourteen to twenty months, during which I expected to be entirely alone.

When all was ready I went on board the *Caroline*—and should have been glad to have come immediately ashore again. My captain was a Portuguese negro, Cornillo by name. The crew, who numbered no less than seven, were Mpongwe, Mbenga, and Croomen, no more than two of whom could understand each other, and not a soul could understand the captain. To add a little more to this confusion of tongues, I brought on board two Mpongwe men and their wives, who were to serve me as headmen, interpreters, and for other purposes in the new locality where I intended to make my home.

We got on board at daylight, and by dint of steady shouting and a great deal of loafing about, with a little work now and then, we got the anchor up just at dusk. The captain did not much like that we should leave port on Friday, but I told him I would take the responsibility. No sooner had we got out into the swell than every man (and woman) on board, except the captain, got sea-sick. The cook was unable to make breakfast next morning, the men were lying about looking like dying fish, and in the canoe which we had on deck, Oyaya, one of my Mpongwe men, sea-sick himself, was vainly striving to comfort his newly-married wife, who was more sea-sick than he.

We hoped to get down to the Camma region in five days. But on the 5th, our sailing-day, and for three successive days thereafter, we had light head winds and a head current, and on February 10th we were caught in such a storm as I hope never to be in at sea again.

The steering had gone on so badly when the captain was below that I was forced to stand watch. I was sleeping soundly, having steered for four hours, and had been perhaps an hour in my berth, when I was awakened by the captain's voice giving orders to take down the mainsail. I jumped on deck immediately, knowing there must be at least a heavy squall coming. But no sooner did I cast my eye to leeward than I saw how imminent the danger was. This coast is troubled by frequent squalls of wind, lasting, in general, but a short time, but of terrible violence, and followed by torrents of rain. Such a squall was now coming up. The black clouds which had gathered about the horizon were becoming lurid white with startling quickness. It seemed almost as though they were lit up by lightning. This was the wind, which would now in a moment be upon us. As yet, all was still.

I turned to see if the mainsail was down, but found nothing done to meet the squall. The captain was shouting from the wheel, the men were running about, half-scared to death, also shouting, and in the pitchy darkness (for I could not actually see my hands when held close before my eyes) no one could find the halliards. In the midst of our trouble the wind came roaring down. I seized a knife determined to cut everything away; but just then somebody let go the halliards, and, in the nick of time the mainsail came halfway down. Just then the squall broke upon us with the roar and force of a tornado. The jibs flew away in rags in a moment. The vessel sank over on her beam-ends. The water rushed on to her decks, and the men sung out that we were drowning, as, in fact, we should have been in a very few minutes. Happily the wind shifted a little, and by the light of some vivid lightning we seized on the mainsail and pulled it down, holding it so that the wind should not catch it again.

So she righted, and in about twenty minutes the squall died off, and was succeeded by a driving rain, pouring down in such torrents, that we could get no protection from it even below.

The next morning we had no jibs, and our other sails were severely damaged. This did not help us along very fast. It was not till the 13th that we made the land; but now no one on board knew where we were, not even our captain, who brings up every day an old quadrant, about the use of which he knows as much as a cow does about a musket. At last a canoe came off to ask me to land to start a factory, as they had plenty of ivory and palm-oil and other trade. If I had gone ashore I should probably have found not a gallon of oil, not the smallest tusk of ivory. The great anxiety of every one of these negroes is for a factory, just as a western townbuilder's chief desire is for a railroad. They lie, and beg, and almost force a white man ashore, thinking themselves safe if they can induce him to set up a little factory and trust them with some goods; for they do not, as a general thing, intend to pay him.

However, a speculative friend in the canoe informed us we were off Cape St. Catherine, and therefore a good many miles south of the mouth of the Fernand Vaz; so we turned about to retrace our steps. Sailing close in shore, at every village we passed we were hailed by canoes full of negroes begging us to start a factory in their place. In some villages we could even see the large house, looking very fine from the sea, but doubtless poor enough seen close to, which was intended for the great factory which should make everybody rich. This house was generally surrounded by huts, in which lived the natives waiting for their commercial millennium, which, alas! never comes. I paid no attention to their entreaties, and was even firm enough, to the surprise of everybody, to decline a magnificent offer of two slaves made by the natives of Aniambia, or Big Camma, who came off with a message from their king.

At last we came to the mouth of the Fernand Vaz, and our fame and the disappointment of the natives had gone before us. It had been determined in the Gaboon that I should set up my establishment in the town of King Ranpano. As the *Caroline* passed Ranpano's sea-village, of course a canoe came off to beg me to land. But they evidently had little hope; and their surprise was extravagant when I assented, and told them I had come on purpose to set up a factory with them.

I never saw men so anxious for trade as these wild Africans are. They remind me of what is said of Western land speculators, and really they have quite as much enterprise and quite as sanguine a temperament as those worthies.

Ranpano's men, in whose town it had been determined I should set up my establishment, wanted much to hug me, and were so extravagant in their joy that I had to order them to keep their hands off. I sent one of my men in their boat to bear a message to the king, and took one of theirs for a pilot, being now anxious to get across the intricate bar and fairly into the river before dark. As we sailed along into the river, boats shot out to meet us belonging to different villages, and presently I had a crowd alongside anxious to board us and sufficient almost to sink us. They took me for a slaver at first, and immediately called out their names in Portuguese. One was Don Miguel, another Don Pedro, another Don Francisco. They began to jabber away in Portuguese, which I do not understand, so I set my captain at them, who had some difficulty in pursuading them that I came on no such errand. They belonged to Elindé, a town just at the mouth of the Fernand Vaz, whose king is named Sangala. They praised the greatness and power of Sangala, and decried poor Ranpano, until I had to order all hands ashore for the night, being anxious to get a good quiet sleep to prepare for to-morrow.

During the night a fellow named Nchouga came off to see me. He was brother to the king of Cape Lopez. The king, falling sick, accused this Nchouga of bewitching him; whereupon the latter, to save his life, fled the country and came down to get protection from Sangala, his father-in-law. This is one of the uses of fathers-in-law.

Nchouga now came off to tell me that Sangala was master of all the river, and that he would not let me go up to Ranpano's, who was only a vassal of the great Sangala. Therefore he advised me as a friend to go ashore at Elindé. Fortunately, I knew Mr. Nchouga.

Next morning (14th) Sangala sent off a boat for me. I took two interpreters, and, on my arrival in Elindé, which is about two miles from the river's mouth, was conducted to the best house. Hither came Sangala presently, drunk, and attended by a great crowd of eager subjects. He grew very angry when I stated my intention of passing up the river and going into the interior; declared I should not; he was the big king, and I must settle in his town.

We had some sharp words, and I explained to his majesty that I saw through all his lies. Then he said he would not make any *palaver* if I would have a factory in his town too.

I refused, but offered to *dash* him—give him some presents.

He refused this offer. And now, Ranpano having come,

and assuring me that I should be backed up, I told Sangala I should force my way up.

All this time rain was pouring down. When the talk ended Ranpano took me in his canoe to his river-village, a town which the people had but just started, their real town being on the sea. Thither (to the sea-town) we went next day. I found it a very substantial place for an African town, having some good houses, and looking much like a Mpongwe village. But I saw that my goods could not be brought hither without great trouble, nor my specimens of natural history shipped through the surf without great danger, and so told Ranpano I must live on the river; whereupon he gave me at once as much land as I wanted, and I am to have houses built for myself.

Meantime the excitement had spread over the country, and all Ranpano's friends gathered to help fight Sangala. It was really a droll but exciting scene to see canoe after canoe come in, loaded with armed men, drums beating, and all hands shouting and waving swords, guns, and spears. All were prepared to assist Ranpano's white man, and all were anxious to burn and plunder Elindé. King Ritimbo, who has a factory in his own town, kept by a Mpongwe fellow, and belonging to a New York house, had two canoes and fifty men. King Mombo, from Sanguibuiri, had also two canoes; in short, we had in all no less than twenty big canoes, and could muster, on the morning of the 17th, about three hundred men, most of whom were drunk on palm-wine, and as noisy and as ready for fight as drunkenness will make an African.

Drums were beaten, and songs sung, and guns fired, as we paddled down the river; all hands had their faces painted white, which is a sign of war, and were covered with fetiches, greegrees, and other amulets. One who did not know the genuine and never-failing cowardice of the Africans, would have supposed these terrible fellows bent upon the most bloody of raids. I was not disappointed when, sighting Sangala's town, they pushed over to the other shore out of the way, and took care to keep the *Caroline* between the enemy and themselves.

We found that Sangala had also gathered his friends, and had about one hundred and fifty men ready for fight. These fellows were painted more outrageously than my side, having red as well as white applied in broad stripes. They looked like so many devils, shouting and firing off guns—each side knowing the common lack of courage, and thinking it prudent to scare the other in advance.

There was a grand palaver, in the midst of which I sent word to Sangala that if he stopped me I would blow his canoes out of the water with grape-shot, and then go and bring a man-of-war to finish him up. (This threat of a man-of-war always strikes terror into their guilty consciences.) I loaded my guns and pistols, and made my men put good charges into their pieces, and awaited the event.

Presently a boat came to ask me ashore, Sangala sending his chief wife to be hostage for my safety. I determined to go ashore, and, to show these negroes that I had no fear of them, took the woman along with me, to her great joy. Ranpano and his brother kings protested against my rashness, as they thought it. All this had its effect upon them, and Ranpano was evidently impressed, as also was old Sangala.

We met on neutral ground outside his town. His army was drawn up in battle array, and made a fine savage display, many of the men, in addition to their paints, wearing beautiful leopard-skins about their waists. They came up to us at a full trot when we were seated, and made as though they would spear us all; but it was only a kind of military salute. After this, Sangala said he would let me pass up for a barrel of rum. I refused to give rum, but was obliged to give him 16 dollars, also a number of pieces of cloth and other things, and then the great quarrel was settled.

Ranpano was delighted. He said he would no more be king, but install me in his place, and made the greatest promises of good treatment. We loaded seventeen canoes from the *Caroline*, and pulled up to the village where I was to make my home and headquarters for some time; and, to my great astonishment, though we did not reach the town till after dark, not a thing was stolen. The next day the schooner was emptied; and, I am glad to say, they stole not a single article from me. While I was thinking over a plan for my house, on the evening of my arrival, in came Ranpano with his head wife to get his present. He came slily, that his people might not see him; and I made him happy with ten pieces of cloth, a gun, a neptune,* a kettle, and some beads and other trifles.

The next day everybody was set to work. I chose the site for the house, a beautiful little spot in the high prairie about one hundred and fifty yards distant from the huts of the village. It faced the river which I was to explore, and where a school of hippopotami were playing about every day on a shoal; had a grove at its back, and a rivulet of clear spring-water rippling along one side.

Hither every day the men brought me the long straight branches of a kind of palm growing by the river-side, which are used for the sides of a native house. Some gathered the leaves of the same tree, from which mats for roofing are made, and others went through the woods collecting wild vines, with which to tie the poles or bamboos together, and long slender poles to set up at the corners to tie the bamboo sides up to. The women cleaned the ground, and every evening huge piles of building-material were laid at my feet, of which I accepted what was good, and sent away the rest.

Everything went on very pleasantly until the 10th of April, when pay-day came for my men. I had settled with some, when a fellow for whose labour I had promised him twenty-four dollars in goods, had the impudence to ask forty for his party. I refused, whereupon one of the workmen threatened me with his knife. Here was a very bad case indeed, and one of which I felt that I must make an example. I ran for my gun, and threatened to shoot the fellow, who was put out of my way by his friends. Then I called for the king, and demanded that the rascal should be sent to my house in chains.

He said "Yes," but evidently did not want to find him; and I, who felt that I must make an example of the man if I looked for peace and respect in the future, only insisted the more that they should catch him.

* A flat copper dish to boil salt water in order to procure the salt.

At last, seeing that they only pretended, I sent for my Croomen and began to pack up my goods, saying I would go back to the Gaboon, and would not stay among such men.

The king came to me, and upon his knees begged me not to go; and finally, seeing I was determined, set off with some men for the plantation where they had stowed the offender. He was one of the oldest and most influential people of the town, and they were very loth to give him up.

On the next day (the 12th) the man, whose name was Ovenga, was brought in. The excitement was intense. The people were gathered in a crowd, and talked over the matter; the king looked almost pale with anxiety, and Ovenga himself shook like a leaf. I demanded that he should be tied, brought to my house, and severely flogged. They begged that his cloth might not be taken off, as it would be a disgrace to expose an old man. To this I consented; but sat, with a hard, stern face, waiting for the poor criminal. When at last he stood bound before me, I scolded him well for his attempt to cheat, and made much of the enormity of his threat. Then I said I could pay only what I had promised; that it was a great outrage to threaten with a knife; that his own people acknowledged my justice in flogging him, but that, as they did not know "white man's fashions" in such matters, I had determined to forgive him, and not flog him at all; with which I set him free.

Instantly thunders of applause rang through the village, guns were fired, singing and dancing began all over, and never was such a set of jolly fellows. It was the only way to treat them. If I had passed Ovenga's threat by, I should probably have been murdered at some future time.

On the 13th of April I took possession of my new place, which, being quite a village, I have called Washington.

At the back of my house is a wide extent of prairie. In front is the river Npoulounai winding along; and I can see miles on the way which I shall soon explore. Its banks are lined with mangroves; and, looking up stream almost any time, I can see schools of hippopotami tossing and tumbling on the flats.

As I am entirely at the mercy of the negroes now, I am

very strict, but entirely just, in my dealings; making myself obeyed, and that without loss of time.

CHAPTER XIV.

The Commi people—King Olenga-Yombi—I am obliged to attend a ball—Native love of rum—Fetich-houses—Mbuirri and Abambou—Ovengua—Ifouta tossed by a buffalo—A live young gorilla—How he was captured—His appearance—I call him "Joe"—He is untameable—His escape and recapture—Death of Joe—Shipping a young gorilla for London—Surprising gorillas in a plantain plantation—How gorillas walk—Another young live gorilla—How he was captured—The mother brought in not dead—Gorilla are often gregarious—Shooting hippopotami at night on shore—Habits of the hippopotamus—Combat between two hippopotami.

AND now, having finished my village, I will say a word about the people. They are very much like the Mpongwe, and have the same language, with a few local variations. The women here, also, wear on their legs a large number of brass rings.

They call themselves *Commi*. They possess the sea-shore from south of Cape Lopez to Cape St. Catherine, having also one or two villages on the Mexias. Their chief town is Aniambia, once a large and flourishing place.

Every enterprising Commi fellow builds a few huts for a village in what he thinks an advantageous situation; then builds a big house for the factory which is to come; and then does nothing for the remainder of his life but wait for this blissful coming. It does not occur to him to collect ivory, or oil, or india-rubber. He prefers rather to lie in wait for passing vessels, and try with his most honeyed words to persuade some luckless captain ashore.

I bought a splendid canoe, which I hoped would be serviceable to me in my up-river explorations. I was now anxious to be off, and determined to make a short trip to the sea-shore by way of Aniambia. This would carry me first about thirty-five miles up the Fernand Vaz, and then across the land.

CHAP. XIV.   THE FERNAND VAZ.   145

The mouth of the Fernand Vaz is obstructed by bars, on which the sea breaks with considerable violence; but the channel has generally three, and in the rainy season four, fathoms of water. The banks at the mouth are low; and it

COMMI MAN AND WOMAN.

is not only a difficult land-fall to make from sea, but a very dreary piece of land when made.

On the morning of the 14th we set out. I had satisfied myself that Ranpano was anxious to have me remain in his town, as were also his people: and I had little fear of injury to my things in my absence so long as this good opinion of me was kept up. I therefore called the people together before my departure, and said that I had perfect confidence in them; that I was *their* white man, and had come to them through much difficulty and danger (*cheers*); that Sangala people wanted me, but I was determined to live with the honest folks of Biagano (*great cheering*); that I was going away for a few days, and hoped to find my goods all safe when I came back.

At this there were great shoutings of "You can go!" "Do not fear!" "We love you!" "You are our white man!" "We will take care!" and so on; amid which my sixteen men seized their paddles and we set off for Aniambia, which lies on the sea-shore, near a point north of Cape St. Catherine, and sufficiently sheltered to make a safe landing-place.

The king, Olenga-Yombi, came in from his plantation when he heard the joyful news that a white man had arrived, and I made him a formal visit. He was a drunken old fellow, surrounded by a crowd of the chief men of the town. His majesty had on a thick overcoat, but no trousers; and, early as it was, had already taken a goodly quantity of rum or palm-wine. I was invited to sit at his right hand. I told him I had come to purchase a little ivory and to hunt, having heard that there was game in his country. After presenting him with a few strips of cloth, some pipes, and several heads of tobacco, which put him in a good temper, he declared I was a good white man, and should go wherever I chose.

On the next evening (17th), the king held a grand dance in my honour. This is an honour I abominate, but one which cannot be declined, because the natives enjoy it too much themselves. All the king's wives, to the number of forty, and all the women of the town and neighbourhood were present. Fortunately the dance was held out in the street, and not in a room. The women were ranged on one side, the men opposite. At the end of the line sat the drummers beating their huge tam-tams, which make an infernal and deafening din, enough to distract a man of weak nerves. And, as though for this occasion the tam-tams were not entirely adequate, there was singing, and shouting, and a series of brass kettles, which also were furiously beaten; while, as a last and most ingenious addition, a number of boys sat near the drummers beating on hollow pieces of wood. It is curious what a stirring effect the sound of the tam-tam has on the Africans; they lose all control over themselves at its sound, and the louder and more energetically the horrid drum is beaten, the wilder are the jumps of the male African, and the more disgustingly indecent the contortions of the women.

As may be imagined, to beat the tam-tam is not a labour of love. The stoutest negro is worn out in an hour at furthest, and for such a night's entertainment as this a series of drummers is required.

The people enjoyed it vastly, their only regret being that they had not a barrel of rum to drink in the pauses of the dance. But they managed to get just as drunk on palm-wine, of which a great quantity was served out. The excitement became greatest when the king danced. His majesty was pretty drunk, and his jumps were very highly applauded. His wives bowed down to his feet while he capered about, and showed him the deepest marks of veneration, while the drums and kettles were belaboured more furiously than ever.

The next day I visited the two fetich-houses. Aniambia enjoys the protection of two spirits of very great power, named Abambou and Mbuirri. The former is an evil spirit, the latter is beneficent. They are both worshipped; and their accommodations, so far as I was permitted to see, were exactly alike.

They were housed in little huts, each about six feet square and six feet high. The fetich-man, who is also doctor and town-oracle, led me to where they stood together at the end of the village, and respectfully opened the doors for me to look into his holy places.

In the house of Abambou I saw a fire, which I was told is not permitted to go out. I saw no idol, but only a large chest, on the top of which lay some white and red chalk and some red parrot-feathers. The chalk is used to mark the bodies of the devout on certain occasions when vows are made. The feathers were probably part of the trappings of the spirit.

Abambou, the devil of the Commi, is a wicked and mischievous spirit, who lives near graves and in burial-grounds, and is most comfortably lodged among the skeletons of the dead. He takes occasional walks through the country; and, if he is angry at anyone, has the power to cause sickness and death. The Commi cook food for him, which is deposited in lonely places in the woods; and then they address him in a flattering manner, and ask him to be good to them, and, in consideration of their gifts, to leave them alone. I was present once at a meeting where Abambou was being addressed in public. They cried continually, "Now we are well! Now we are satisfied! Now be our friend, and do not hurt us!"

The offerings of plantain, sugar-cane, and ground-nuts are wrapped in leaves by the free men, but the slaves lay them on the bare ground. Sometimes Abambou is entreated to kill the enemies of him who is making the sacrifice. A bed is made in Abambou's house, and here he sometimes comes to rest himself when he is tired of going up and down the coast. At the new moon great quiet reigns in the Commi villages, and then the people pray to their spirits, of whom each family or subdivision of the tribe owns two, kept in a small hut in the village of the oldest chief of that family.

Mbuirri, whose house I next visited, is lodged and kept much as his rival. He is a good spirit, but has powers much the same as Abambou, so far as I could see. Being less wicked, he is not so zealously worshipped.

There is a third and much dreaded spirit, called Ovengua. This is the terrible catcher and eater of men. He is not worshipped, and has no power over diseases. But he wanders unceasingly through the forests, and catches and destroys luckless travellers who cross his path. By day he lives in dark caverns, but at night he roams freely; and even sometimes gets into the body of a man, and beats and kills all who come out in the dark. Sometimes, they relate, such a spirit is met and resisted by a body of men, who wound him with spears, and even kill him. In this case his body must be burned, and not even the smallest bone left, lest a new Ovengua should arise from it. There are many spots where no object in the world would induce a Commi negro to go by night, for fear of this dreadful monster. It is really a frightful superstition to an ignorant and credulous people, and I do not wonder at their fear.

They have a singular belief that when a person dies who has been bewitched, the bones of his body leave the grave one by one, and form in a single line, which line of bones gradually become an Ovengua.

I set out early on the 19th to try and get a shot at some buffalo, which were said to be in the prairie at the back of the town. Ifouta, a hunter, accompanied me, and met with an accident through losing his presence of mind. We had been out about an hour, when we came upon a bull feeding in the midst of a little prairie surrounded by a wood which made our approach easy. Ifouta walked around opposite to where I lay in wait, in order that, if the animal took alarm at him, it might run towards me; and then began to crawl, in the hunter fashion, through the grass towards his prey. All went well till he came near enough for a shot. Just then, unluckily, the bull saw him. Ifouta immediately fired. The gun hung fire, and he only wounded the beast, which, quite infuriated, as it often is at the attack of hunters, immediately rushed upon him.

It was now that poor Ifouta lost his presence of mind. In such cases, which are continually happening to those who hunt the *Bos brachicheros*, the cue of the hunter is to remain perfectly quiet till the beast is within a jump of him, then to step nimbly to one side, and let it rush past. But Ifouta got up and ran.

Of course, in a moment the bull had him on his horns. It tossed him high into the air once, twice, thrice, ere I could run up, and by my shouts, draw its fury to myself. Then it came rushing at me. But my guns do not hang fire, and, as I had a fair shot, I killed it without trouble.

NATIVE TOSSED BY WHITE BULL.

CHAP. XIV. A LIVE YOUNG GORILLA. 151

Ifouta proved to be considerably bruised, but, on the whole, more scared than hurt; and when I had washed him in a creek close by, he was able to walk home.

I found, on my return, that all the Biagano people had moved from the sea-shore and built themselves huts near my house. I had reason to fear for my fowls and goats; but, on remonstrating, was assured by all hands that they would not steal from me, and that they did not want to live away from their white man. Tobacco was what brought them to me. They thought they would get none unless they were near me.

On the 4th of May, some hunters who had been out on my account brought in a young gorilla *alive!*

YOUNG GORILLA.

It was a little fellow of between two and three years old, two feet six inches in length, and as fierce and stubborn as a grown animal could have been.

My hunters, whom I could have hugged to my heart, took him in the country between the Rembo and Cape St. Catherine. By their account, they were going, five in number, to a village near the coast, and walking very silently through the forest, when they heard what they immediately recognized as the cry of a young gorilla for its mother. The forest was silent. It was about noon; and they immediately determined to follow the cry. Presently they heard it again. Guns in hand, the brave fellows crept noiselessly towards a clump of wood, where the baby gorilla evidently was. They knew the mother would be near; and there was a likelihood that the male, the most dreaded of all, might be there too. But they determined to risk all, and, if at all possible, to take the young one alive, knowing what a joy it would be for me.

Presently they perceived the bush moving; and crawling a little further on in dead silence, scarce breathing with excitement, they beheld, what has seldom been seen even by the negroes, a young gorilla, seated on the ground, eating some berries which grew close to the earth. A few feet further on sat the mother, also eating of the same fruit.

Instantly they made ready to fire; and none too soon, for the old female saw them as they raised their guns, and they had to pull triggers without delay. Happily, they wounded her mortally.

She fell. The young one, hearing the noise of the guns, ran to his mother and clung to her, hiding his face, and embracing her body. The hunters immediately rushed toward the two, hallooing with joy as they ran on. But this roused the little one, who instantly let go his mother and ran to a small tree, which he climbed with great agility, and there he sat and roared at them savagely.

They were now perplexed how to get at him. No one cared to run the chance of being bitten by this savage little beast, and shoot it they would not. At last they cut down the tree, and, as it fell, dexterously threw a cloth over the head of the young monster, and thus gained time to secure it while it was blinded. With all these precautions, one of the men received a severe bite on the hand, and another had a piece taken out of his leg.

As the little brute, though so diminutive, and the merest baby for age, was astonishingly strong and by no means good-tempered, they could not lead him. He constantly rushed at them. So they were obliged to get a forked stick in which his neck was inserted in such a way that he could not escape, and yet could be kept at a safe distance. In this uncomfortable way he was brought into the village.

There the excitement was intense. As the animal was lifted out of the canoe in which he had come a little way down the river, he roared and bellowed, and looked around wildly with his wicked little eyes, giving fair warning that if he could only get at some of us he would take his revenge.

I saw that the stick hurt his neck, and immediately set about to have a cage made for him. In two hours we had built a strong bamboo house, with the slats securely tied at such distances apart that we could see the gorilla and it could see out. Here the captive was immediately deposited; and now, for the first time, I had a fair chance to look at my prize.

It was a young male gorilla, evidently not yet three years old, fully able to walk alone, and possessed, for its age, of most extraordinary strength and muscular development. Its greatest length proved to be, afterwards, two feet six inches. Its face and hands were very black, eyes not so much sunken as in the adult. The hair began just at the eyebrows and rose to the crown, where it was of a reddish-brown. It came down the sides of the face in lines to the lower jaw much as our beards grow. The upper lip was covered with short coarse hair; the lower lip had longer hair. The eyelids very slight and thin. Eyebrows straight, and three-quarters of an inch long.

The whole back was covered with hair of an iron-gray, becoming dark nearer the arms, and quite white about the *anus*. Chest and abdomen covered with hair, which was somewhat thin and short on the breast. On the arms the hair was longer than anywhere on the body, and of a grayish-black colour, caused by the roots of the hair being dark and the ends whitish. On the hands and wrists the hair was black, and came down to the second joints of the fingers, though one could see in the short down the beginning of the long black hair which lines the upper parts of the fingers in the adult. The hair of the legs was grayish-black, becoming blacker as it reached the ankles, the feet being covered with black hair.

When I had the little fellow safely locked in his cage, I

ventured to approach to say a few encouraging words to him. He stood in the furthest corner, but, as I approached, bellowed and made a precipitate rush at me; and though I retreated as quickly as I could, succeeded in catching my trouser-legs, which he grasped with one of his feet and tore, retreating immediately to the corner furthest away. This taught me caution for the present, though I had a hope still to be able to tame him.

He sat in his corner looking wickedly out of his gray eyes, and I never saw a more morose or more ill-tempered face than had this little beast.

The first thing was, of course, to attend to the wants of my captive. I sent for some of the forest-berries which these animals are known to prefer, and placed these and a cup of water within his reach. He was exceedingly shy, and would neither eat nor drink till I had removed to a considerable distance.

The second day found Joe, as I had named him, fiercer than the first. He rushed savagely at anyone who stood even for a moment near his cage, and seemed ready to tear us all to pieces. I threw him to-day some pine-apple leaves, of which I noticed he ate only the white parts. There seemed no difficulty about his food, though he refused now, and continued during his short life to refuse, all food except such wild leaves and fruits as were gathered from his native woods for him.

The third day he was still morose and savage, bellowing when any person approached, and either retiring to a distant corner or rushing to attack. On the fourth day, while no one was near, the little rascal succeeded in forcing apart two of the bamboo rails which composed his cage, and made his escape. I came up just as his flight was discovered, and immediately got all the negroes together for pursuit, determining to surround the wood and recapture my captive. Running into the house to get one of my guns, I was startled by an angry growl issuing from under my low bedstead. It was Master Joe, who lay there hidden, but anxiously watching my movements. I instantly shut the windows, and called to my people to guard the door. When Joe saw the crowd of black faces he became furious, and, with his eyes glaring, and every sign of rage in his little face and body, got out from beneath the bed. We shut the door at the same time and left him master of the premises, preferring to devise some plan for his easy capture rather than to expose ourselves to his terrible teeth.

How to take him was now a puzzling question. He had shown such strength and such rage already, that not even I cared to run the chance of being badly bitten in a hand-to-hand struggle. Meantime, Joe stood in the middle of the room looking about for his enemies, and examining, with some surprise, the furniture. I watched with fear lest the ticking of my clock should strike his ear, and perhaps lead him to an assault upon that precious article. Indeed, I should have left Joe in possession, but for a fear that he would destroy the many articles of value or curiosity I had hung about the walls.

Finally, seeing him quite quiet, I despatched some fellows for a net, and opening the door quickly, threw this over his head. Fortunately we succeeded at the first throw in fatally entangling the young monster, who roared frightfully, and struck and kicked in every direction under the net. I took hold of the back of his neck, two men seized his arms and another his legs, and thus held by four men this extraordinary little creature still proved most troublesome. We carried him as quickly as we could to the cage, which had been repaired, and there once more locked him in.

I never saw so furious a beast in my life as he was. He darted at everyone who came near, bit the bamboos of the house, glared at us with vicious and sullen eyes, and in every motion showed a temper thoroughly wicked and malicious.

As there was no change in this for two days thereafter, but continual moroseness, I tried what starvation would do towards breaking his spirit; also, it began to be troublesome to procure his food from the woods, and I wanted him to become accustomed to the civilized food which was placed before him. But he would touch nothing of the kind; and as for temper, after starving him twenty-four hours, all I gained was that he came slowly up and took some berries from the forest out of my hand, immediately retreating to his corner to eat them.

Daily attentions from me for a fortnight more did not bring me any further confidence from him than this. He always snarled at me, and only when *very* hungry would he take even his choicest food from my hands. At the end of this fortnight I came one day to feed him, and found that he had gnawed a bamboo to pieces slily and again made his escape. Luckily, he had but just gone; for, as I looked around, I caught sight of Master Joe making off on all fours, and with great speed, across the little prairie for a clump of trees.

I called the men up, and we gave chase. He saw us, and before we could head him off made for another clump. This we surrounded. He did not ascend a tree, but stood defiantly at the border of the wood. About one hundred and fifty of us surrounded him. As we moved up he began to yell, and made a sudden dash upon a poor fellow who was in advance, who ran, tumbled down in affright, and, by his fall, escaped, but also detained Joe sufficiently long for the nets to be brought to bear upon him.

Four of us again bore him struggling into the village. This time I would not trust him to the cage, but had a little light chain fastened around his neck. This operation he resisted with all his might, and it took us quite an hour to chain securely the little fellow, whose strength was something marvellous.

Ten days after he was thus chained, he died suddenly. He was in good health, and ate plentifully of his natural food, which was brought every day for him; he did not seem to sicken until two days before his death, and died in some pain. To the last he continued utterly untameable; and, after his chains were on, added treachery to his other vices. He would come sometimes quite readily to eat out of my hand, but while I stood by him would suddenly—looking me all the time in the face to keep my attention—put out his foot and grasp at my leg. Several times he tore my pantaloons in this manner, quick retreat on my part saving my person; till at last I was obliged to be very careful in my approaches. The negroes could not come near him at all without setting him in a rage. He knew me very well, and trusted me, but evidently always cherished a feeling of revenge even towards me.

After he was chained, I filled a half-barrel with hay and set it near him for his bed. He recognized its use at once, and it was pretty to see him shake up the hay and creep into this nest when he was tired. At night he always again shook it up, and then took some hay in his hands, with which he would cover himself when he was snug in his barrel.

I subsequently embarked another live gorilla for Europe, and hoped that he would arrive safely and gratify the world of London with a sight of this rare and wonderful ape in the living state; unfortunately, he died on the passage. He did very well for a few weeks, I am told, as long as the supply of bananas lasted which I placed on board for his sustenance. The repugnance of the gorilla to cooked food, or any sort of food except the fruits and juicy plants he obtains in his own wilds, will always be a difficulty in the way of bringing him to Europe alive. I had sent him consigned to Messrs. Baring, who, I am sure, never had any such consignment before. I promised the captain that he should receive one hundred pounds if he succeeded in taking the animal alive to London.

During the few days he was in my possession he remained, like all the others of his species that I had seen, utterly untractable. The food that was offered to him he would come and snatch from the hand, and then bolt with it to the length of his tether. If I looked at him he would make a feint of darting at me, and in giving him water I had to push the bowl towards him with a stick, for fear of his biting me. When he was angry I saw him often beat the ground and his legs with his fists, thus showing a similar habit to that of the adult gorillas which I described as beating their breasts with their fists when confronting an enemy. Before lying down to rest, he used to pack his straw very carefully as a bed to lie on. He used to wake me in the night by screaming suddenly, and in the morning I more than once detected him in the attempt to strangle himself with his chain, no doubt through rage at being kept prisoner. He used to twist the chain round and round the post to which it was attached until it became quite short, and then pressed with his feet the lower part of the post until he had nearly done the business.

One lovely morning, when going quietly along the borders of a large plantation, I heard, in the grove of plantain-trees towards which I was walking, a great crashing noise, like the breaking of trees. I immediately hid myself behind a bush, and was soon gratified with the sight of a female gorilla; but before I had time to notice its movements, a second and a third emerged from the masses of colossal foliage; at length no less than four came into view.

They were all busily engaged in tearing down the larger trees. One of the females had a young one following her. I had an excellent opportunity of watching the movements of the impish-looking band. The shaggy hides, the protuberant abdomens, the hideous features of these strange creatures, whose forms so nearly resemble man, made up a picture like a vision in some morbid dream. In destroying a tree, they first grasped the base of the stem with one of their feet and then with their powerful arms pulled it down, a matter of not much difficulty with so loosely-formed a stem as that of the plantain. They then set upon the juicy heart of the tree at the bases of the leaves, and devoured it with great voracity. While eating they made a kind of clucking noise, expressive of contentment. Many trees they destroyed. Now and then they stood still and looked around. Once or twice they seemed on the point of starting off in alarm, but recovered themselves and continued their work. Gradually they got nearer to the edge of the dark forest, and finally disappeared. I was so intent on watching them, that I let go the last chance of shooting one almost before I became aware of it.

The next day I had no expectation of seeing gorillas in the same plantation, and was carrying a light shot gun, having given my heavy double-barrelled rifle to the boy to carry. The plantation extended over two hills, with a deep hollow between, planted with sugar-cane. Before I had crossed the hollow I saw on the opposite slope a monstrous gorilla, standing erect and looking directly towards me. Without turning my face I beckoned to the boy to bring me my rifle, but no rifle came—the little coward had bolted, and I lost my chance. The huge beast stared at me for about two minutes, and then, without uttering any cry, moved off to the shade of the forest, running nimbly on his hands and feet.

I had excellent opportunity of observing, during these two days, the manner in which the gorillas walked when in open ground. They move along with great rapidity and on all fours, that is, with the knuckles of their hands touching the ground. When the gorillas that I watched left the plantain-trees, they moved off at a great pace over the ground, with their arms extended straight forwards towards the ground, and moving rapidly. I may mention also that having now opened the stomachs of several freshly-killed gorillas I have never found anything but vegetable matter in them.

My old friend Akondogo brought me a young living gorilla, the largest I had ever seen captured alive. Like Joe, this one showed the most violent and ungovernable disposition. He tried to bite every one who came near him, and was obliged to be secured by a forked stick closely applied to the back of his neck. This mode of imprisoning these animals is a very improper one if the object be to keep them alive and to tame them, but, unfortunately, in this barbarous country, we had not the materials requisite to build a strong cage. The injury done to this one by the forked stick eventually caused his death.

One day one of my men came in with the startling news that three live gorillas had been brought, one of them full grown. I had not long to wait; in they came. First, a very large adult female, bound hand and foot; then her female child, screaming terribly; and lastly a vigorous young male, also tightly bound. The female had been ingeniously secured by the negroes to a strong stick, the wrists bound to the upper part and the ankles to the lower, so that she could not reach to tear the cords with her teeth. It was dark, and the scene was one so wild and strange that I shall never forget it. The fiendish countenances of the Calibanish trio, one of them distorted by pain, for the mother gorilla was severely wounded, were lit up by the ruddy glare of native torches.

The young male I secured by a chain which I had in readiness, and gave him henceforth the name of Tom. We untied his hands and feet; to show his gratitude for this act of kindness he immediately made a rush at me, screaming with all his might; happily the chain was made fast, and I took care afterwards to keep out of his way. The old mother gorilla was in an unfortunate plight. She had an arm broken and a wound in the chest, besides being dreadfully beaten on the head. She groaned and roared many times during the night, probably from pain.

I noticed next day, and on many occasions, that the vigorous young male, whenever he made a rush at any one and missed his aim, immediately ran back. This corresponds with what is known of the habits of the large males in their native woods; when attacked they make a furious rush at their enemy, break an arm or tear his bowels open, and then beat a retreat, leaving their victim to shift for himself.

The wounded female died in the course of the next day; her moanings were more frequent in the morning, and they gradually became weaker as her life ebbed out. Her death was like that of a human being, and afflicted me more than I could have thought possible. Her child clung to her to the last, and tried to obtain milk from her breast after she was dead. I photographed them both when the young one was resting in its dead mother's lap. I kept the young one alive for three days after its mother's death. It moaned at night most piteously. I fed it on goat's milk, for it was too young to eat berries. It died the fourth day, having taken an unconquerable dislike to the milk. It had, I think, begun to know me a little. As to the male, I made at least a dozen attempts to photograph the irascible little demon, but all in vain. The pointing of the camera towards him threw him into a perfect rage, and I was almost provoked to give him a sound thrashing. The day after, however, I succeeded with him, taking two views, not very perfect, but sufficient for my object.

The capture of the female was the first instance that had come to my knowledge of an adult gorilla being taken alive. The place where they were found was on the left bank of the Fernand Vaz, about thirty miles above my village. At this part a narrow promontory projects into the river. A woman, belonging to a neighbouring village, had told her people that she had seen two squads of female gorillas, some of them accompanied by their young ones, in her plantain field. The men resolved to go in chase of them, so they armed themselves with guns, axes, and spears, and sallied forth. The situation was very favourable for the hunters; they formed a line across the narrow strip of land and pressed forward, driving the animals to the edge of the water. When they came in sight of them, they made all the noise in their power, and thus bewildered the gorillas, who were shot or beaten down in their endeavours to escape. There were eight adult females altogether, but not a single male. The negroes thought the males were in concealment in the adjoining woods, having probably been frightened away by the noise.

It is clear that, at certain times of the year, the gorillas go in bands more numerous than those I saw in my former journey. I have myself seen two of these bands of gorillas, numbering eight or ten, and have had authentic accounts from the natives of other similar bands. It is true that, when gorillas become aged, they seem to be more solitary, and to live in pairs, or, as in the case of old males, quite alone. I have been assured by the negroes that solitary and aged gorillas are sometimes seen almost white; the hair becomes grizzled with age, and I have no doubt that the statement of their becoming occasionally white with extreme old age is quite correct.

Gorillas are attracted to this district by the quantity of a little yellow berry, called *mbimo*, growing there on a tree resembling the African teak, and by the abundance of two other kinds of fruits, of which they are very fond, and which grow on the sandy soil of this part of the coast-land; one of these fruits is called *nionien*, about the size of a nectarine, and of the colour of the peach, but not having the rich bloom of this fruit; it is produced by a shrub that creeps over the sandy soil; the other resembles in size and colour the wild plum, and is a fruit of which I am myself very fond.

The gorilla is of migratory habits at some seasons of the year. He is then not found in the districts usually resorted to by him when the berries, fruits, and nuts are in season.

On the 20th of May I went up the river about five miles to shoot hippopotami. There was here a place in the river shallow enough for them to stand in and play around; and here they remained all day, playing in the deep water, or diving, but for the most part standing on the shallows, with only their ugly noses pointed out of the water, and looking, for all the world, exactly like so many old weather-beaten logs stranded on a sand-bar. We approached slowly and with caution, to within thirty yards of the herd, without seeming to attract the slightest attention from the sluggish animals. Stopping there, I fired five shots, and, so far as I could see, killed three hippopotami. The ear is one of the most vulnerable spots, and this was my mark every time. The first shot was received with but little attention; but the struggles of the dying animal, which turned over several times, and finally sank to the bottom, seemed to rouse the herd, who began to plunge about and dive down into the deep water. The blood of my victims discoloured the water all around, and we could not see whether those which escaped were not swimming for us.

Presently the boat received a violent jar, and, looking overboard, we perceived that we were in the midst of the herd. They did not, however, attack us, but were rather, I imagine, anxious to get away. We, too, pulled out of the way as fast as we could, as I was not anxious to be capsized. Of the dead animals we recovered but one, which was found two days after on a little island near the river's mouth.

I now determined to go on a night hunt after hippopotami. These animals come ashore by night to feed. As I have said before, the Fernand Vaz runs for many miles parallel with the sea-shore, separated from the sea by a strip of sandy prairie. On this prairie the river-horses feed, and the "walk" of a herd is easily discernible at a great distance, looking very much like a regular beaten road, only their immense tracks showing who are its makers. In the path no grass grows; but the ground is hard, and solidly beaten down by their constant passage to and fro. It is curious that they will not even leave such a walk if they have been attacked there, but come back without fail. This gives the hunter a great advantage.

We chose a moonlight night, and paddled up to the vicinity of one of these "walks," where Igala, my hunter, and I set out by ourselves. I had painted my face with a mixture of oil and soot, which is a prudent measure in a white hunter in Africa, where the beasts seem to have a singularly quick eye for anything white. We chose the leeward side of the track, for the hippopotamus has a fine sense of smell, and is easily alarmed at night, feeling, probably, that on land his sluggish movements and huge bulk have their disadvantages. We lay down under shelter of a bush and watched. As yet none of the animals had come out of the water. We could hear them snorting and splashing in the distance, their subdued snort-like roars breaking in upon the still night in a very odd way. The moon was nearly down, and the watch was getting tedious, when I was startled by a sudden groan, and, peering into the half-light, saw dimly a huge animal, looking doubly monstrous in .the uncertain light. It was quietly eating grass, which it seemed to nibble off quite close.

There was another bush between us and our prey, and we crawled up to this in dead silence. Arrived there we were but about eight yards from the great beast. The negroes who hunt the hippopotamus are sometimes killed. The animal, if only wounded, turns most savagely upon its assailant; and experience has taught the negro hunters that the only safe way to approach it is from behind. It cannot turn quickly, and thus the hunter has a chance to make good his escape. This time we could not get into a very favourable position, but I determined to have my shot nevertheless, eight yards being safe killing distance, even with so poor a light as we had by this time.

Igala and I both took aim. He fired; and, without waiting to see the result, ran away as swiftly as a good pair of legs could carry him. I was not quite ready, but fired the moment after him; and, before I could get ready to run—in which I had not Igala's practice—I saw there was no need to do so. The beast tottered for a moment, and then fell over dead.

This closed our night's sport, as none of the herd would come this way while their companion lay there. So we returned home, poor Igala remonstrating with me for not running as he did, this being, as it appeared, considered one of the chief accomplishments of the hippopotamus-hunter. Our good luck created great joy in the village, where meat was scarce.

The feet of the hippopotamus are curiously constructed, to facilitate their walking among the reeds and mud of the river-bottoms, and swimming with ease. The hoof is divided into four short, apparently clumsy, and unconnected toes; and they are able, by this spread of foot, to walk rapidly even through mud. I have seen them make quick progress, when alarmed, in water so deep that their backs were just on the river-level.

After watching for a great many times the movements of the hippopotamus, I became assured that the huge crooked tusks, which give its mouth so savage an appearance, are designed chiefly to hook up the long river-grasses on which the animals feed in great part. Often I have seen one descend to the bottom, remain a few minutes, and re-appear with its tusks strung with grass, which was then leisurely chewed up. They make the whitest of all ivory, and in the Camma country the beasts are much hunted for the sake of the tusks, as the dentists of Europe make a demand for this white ivory.

The animals consort together here in flocks of from three to thirty. They choose shallows in the rivers, where the depth of the water allows them to keep their footing, and yet have their whole bodies submerged. Here they remain all day, swimming off into the deeps and diving for their grassy food, gambolling in the waves, and from time to time throwing up a stream of water two or three feet high. This is done with a noise like "blowing," and is doubtless an effort for breath. It is pleasant to watch a flock peacefully enjoying themselves, particularly when they have two or three young among them. The little fellows, who are comically awkward, play about their dams, and I have often seen them seated on the back of the mother, and chasing each other about the shoals.

They prefer parts of the rivers where the current is not very swift, and are therefore to be found in all the lakes in the interior. Also, they like to be near their grass-fields. They are very fond of a particular coarse grass which grows on these prairies, and will travel considerable distances to hunt this up, always returning, however, before daylight. Their path overland is very direct. Neither rocks, nor swamps, nor bushes can prove formidable obstacles to a water-beast of such bulk; and one of their peculiarities is that they will always return to the water by the same road they came. Some of their favourite grass was growing on a little plain at the back of my house, and several times I found hippopotamus-tracks not more than fifty yards from the house. They had not feared to come as near as this; though, probably, if the wind had been from me to them, they would have avoided the place.

They always choose a convenient landing-place, one where the bank has a long and easy incline, and this they use till they have eaten up all the provender which lies in that vicinity. Before going ashore they watch for an hour, and sometimes for two hours, near the landing, remaining quiet themselves and listening for danger. The slightest token of the hunter's presence on such occasions sends them away for that night. If no danger appears, they begin to wander ashore in twos and threes. I never saw more than three of a herd grazing together; and during their stay ashore they place more dependence on their ears than on their eyes. I have watched closely in many hunts, and am convinced that the beast walks along with his eyes nearly shut. This makes the approach easier, though their hearing is very quick; and it is common to get within three or four yards before firing. I generally tried to get at least as near as four yards, and found my most successful aim to be at a spot near the shoulder, and one just behind the ear.

When playing in the water this animal makes a noise very

much resembling the grunt of a pig. This grunt it also utters when alarmed at the near approach of man. The stuffed skin loses its original colour, so that our stuffed specimens do not give a true idea of the clay-colour of the live beast. Its excrement is like the horse's, but smaller and dryer.

When enraged, or suddenly disturbed, it utters a kind of groan, a hoarse sound, which can be heard at a considerable distance. They are very combative among themselves, and I often saw marks on their bodies of desperate conflicts. One, a male, which I killed, had its thick hide lacerated in a frightful manner in numerous stripes, from a fight. The young males suffer particularly in these encounters, as they are much imposed upon by the grown males, who are jealous of them. Their principal weapons of offence are their huge tusks, with which they strike most savage blows.

I once witnessed a combat between two hippopotami. It occurred in broad daylight. I was concealed on the bank of the stream, and had been for some time watching the sports of a herd, when suddenly two huge beasts rose to the surface of the water and rushed together. Their vast and hideous mouths were opened to their widest possible extent; their eyes were flaming with rage, and every power was put forth by each to annihilate the other. They seized each other with their jaws; they stabbed and punched with their strong tusks; they advanced and retreated; were now at the top of the water, and again sank down to the bottom. Their blood discoloured the river, and their groans of rage were hideous to listen to. They showed little powers of strategy, but rather a piggish obstinacy in maintaining their ground, and a frightful savageness of demeanour. The combat lasted an hour. It was evident that their tusks could not give very dangerous wounds to such thickly-protected bodies as theirs. At last one turned about and made off, leaving the other victorious and master of the field.

CHAPTER XV.

Ascent of the Ogobai—The Anengue lake—King Damagondai—Damagondai lecturing his wives—King Shimbouvenegani—Shelters of the Nshiego Mbouvé—Killing a Nshiego Mbouvé; its appearance—Hunting the crocodile—Damagondai's idol—Troubles during the descent down the river.

AFTER poor Joe Gorilla died I prepared to set out upon my explorations up river.

We were to make a start on the evening of May 27th, and on that morning I called king and people together, and gave them charge of my property.

I next counted my ten goats in their presence, and told them I wanted no leopard-stories told me when I came back —at which they shouted and laughed, and declared neither they nor the leopard should touch them.

I had twelve stout paddlers in my canoe.

We found the Npoulounay for the first eight miles to run through the mangrove-swamps, which render navigation so disagreeable. Above that the banks became higher and clearer.

About sixty miles from Biagano we came to a fork in the river. We took the right branch. A few miles further up there was another tributary, which we entered, as this led to the lake. The stream was here about two hundred yards wide, but with very low, marshy banks, and no wood. Immense fields of reeds and other water-weeds covered the marshy soil as far as we could see from our little canoe, and gave the landscape an aspect of utter desolation. The stream had scarce any current, the water was turbid, and the smell of decaying vegetation exceedingly unpleasant. In the far distance beyond the plains we could see the outlines of hills and higher plains. Where these join the marsh, crocodiles are found in great plenty, as I was told now by the natives, and found for myself afterwards.

While I was wondering at the change in this sluggish river from the rapid-flowing Ogobai, we came suddenly to what seemed the end of navigation in this direction. The river was here as wide as at the mouth, but closed suddenly. Paddling round the shore, to try for some possible outlet, for it would be too bad to have taken so much trouble to get into this nasty cul-de-sac, we found at length a stream, not more than six yards wide, which poured with a tolerably rapid current into what seemed to me now only a lagoon. Up this narrow avenue we pushed, much doubting where it would lead us, for none of my men had been here before, and I was going by guess-work.

As we ascended the narrow, deep little stream, it branched off in several places, and became gradually narrower, till at last we were pushing our canoe laboriously along through a deep, crooked ditch, not more than two yards wide, and overhung with tall reeds, on which great numbers of birds were balancing themselves, as though enjoying our dilemma.

For two hours we pushed along in this way, and I was upon the point of giving up and returning, when we suddenly emerged into the long-looked-for lake of Anengue. A body of water, at least ten miles wide, and dotted with various beautiful wooded isles, was spread suddenly before our gladdened eyes. On one side the lake is bounded by hills which come close down to the shore. On the other the hills recede, and between them and the water lies a dreary extent of low marsh. Several villages were in sight, all located at the summit of hills, and towards one of these we pushed with what speed we could, for all hands were tired and hungry.

There are very few villages between Biagano and the Anengue—we counted but seven; and yet the country seems habitable enough. I was struck with the immense height of some of the palm-trees which lined the banks. They were really giants even in these primitive woods.

From the 1st to the 10th of June I spent in exploring the lake and its islands. I find everywhere deep water enough for steamers of moderate draught to have free play. The whole country around is literally filled with the india-rubber vine.

Game is not very abundant in this part of the country, and the animal most hunted is the porcupine. They hunt with dogs, which track the truculent little beast to its lair or burrow, whence it is dug out by the men. The dogs hunted by scent, and never barked at a deserted hole.

Here it burrows among the huge boulders which cover the ground. I noticed that the dogs were very careful not to touch the animal till they were sure it was dead, having probably had sad experience of its sharp spines.

It is as well to add here that, though most of the West African villages have crowds of dogs, I could never learn of a case of hydrophobia, nor did the natives even know of such a disease as madness in dogs.

Later in the season, when I came again, the appearance of the lake had changed. Now the surface of the Anengue was dotted with numberless black mud-banks, on which swarmed incredible numbers of crocodiles. We actually saw many hundreds of these disgusting monsters sunning themselves on the black mud and slipping off into the water to feed. I never saw so horrible a sight. Many were at least twenty feet long; and, when they opened their frightful mouths, looked capable of swallowing our little canoes without trouble.

I determined to have a shot at these beasts, who seemed noways frightened at our approach. Making my men paddle pretty well in, I singled out the biggest of a herd, and lodged a ball in his body by way of the joints of his forelegs, where the thick armour is defective. He tumbled over, and, after struggling in the water for a moment, sank into the mud. His companions turned their hideous snaky eyes down at him in momentary surprise, but did not know what to make of it, and dropped back to their sluggish comfort. I shot another, but he sank also; and as my men did not like to venture in the black mud after them, we got neither.

Paddling carefully past great numbers of crocodiles, into whose ready jaws I was by no means anxious to fall, and past several native villages, we at last reached the town of my old friend Damagondai, who stood upon the shore ready to receive me. He was dressed in the usual middle-cloth of the natives, and a tarnished scarlet soldier-coat, but was innocent of trousers. But his welcome was none the less hearty, though the unmentionables were lacking.

A great crowd was assembled, visitors not being frequent here; and when the presence of a wonderful white man became known, the anxiety of the people to see me knew no bounds. Quarters were provided for me by the king, who was rejoiced to see me, and sent me a goat; which, in this part of the country, where they have no tame cattle, is as much as half-a-dozen bullocks would be in South Africa.

His village, which contains about fifty huts, lies on some high ground at a little distance from the water; and the people came to meet us on the shady walk which connects them with the lake. Everybody seemed glad to see us. I distributed presents of tobacco, gave the king some cloth, and put him in a good humour, though he could scarce forgive me for not bringing him rum also. I noticed in the middle of the village a strongly-built goat-house, which is a sign that leopards sometimes come this way.

Damagondai put all his village at my disposal, and suggested that I had better pick out two or three of the best-looking girls for wives for myself. He was somewhat amazed when I declined this pleasant offer, and insisted upon it that my bachelor life must be very lonely and disagreeable.

The king is a tall, rather slim negro, over six feet high, and well put together, as most of these men are. I suppose in war or in the chase he had the usual amount of courage, but at home he was exceedingly superstitious. As night came on he seemed to get a dread of death. He grew querulous; told the men to stop their noise; and at last began to groan out that some of the people wanted to bewitch him in order to get his property and his authority. Finally he got excited, and began to curse all witches and sorcerers; said no one should have his wives and slaves.

The old fellow began to lecture his wives, telling them to love him and to feed him well, for he had given a great deal of money and goods to their parents for them, and they were a constant expense and uneasiness to him; to all which the poor women listened with great respect; and no doubt made up their grateful hearts to give their lord and master a good breakfast next morning.

At last this dreariest of African nights got too slow for

the people, who suddenly struck up a dance and forgot all about witchcraft. And I, too, was tired, and went to my dreams.

The Anengue people, though they intermarry with their neighbours the Commi, are not permitted to come down to the sea-shore for trade. This would disturb the monopoly, and monopoly is the most sacred thing in West Africa. The consequence is that they have no energy or life among them.

On the 5th, the day after our arrival, Damagondai took me across the lake to the village of one Shimbouvenegani, a king with a big name and a small village, who lives fifteen miles off, at the eastern end of the lake.

We found the king with the long name not at his village, but at his *olako*, a place temporarily erected in the woods when the people of a village want to hunt, or fish, or pursue agriculture. They had chosen a charming spot in the woods just upon the shores of the lake, which here had high, abrupt banks, and looked more like a pleasant river than a lagoon. Their mosquito-nets were hung up under the trees, and every family had a fire built, and from the pots came the fragrant smell of plantains and fish cooking. We were seated at a rude table, and presently Shimbouvenegani came up, rejoiced to see me. The usual ceremony of introduction was gone through, Damagondai relating that he had brought his white man over here because game was plenty, and to do a favour to his friend the king.

The latter was a meagre negro of between sixty and seventy years old, dressed in a very dirty swallow-tailed coat, and in what had been—so I imagined—some thirty or forty years ago a silk or beaver hat.

The people gathered about to examine my hair—that constant marvel to the interior negroes; and presently some large pots of palm-wine were brought, whereupon all hands proceeded to celebrate my arrival among them. I added some tobacco, and then their happiness was complete.

Meantime Damagondai had presented me to his eldest son, Okabi, who lived in this village. It is curious that in this country the eldest son of a chief always lives abroad. Okabi hurried off to contrive a little shelter of tree-branches for my use, put up a table for me, and arranged his *akoko* or bed for my sleeping; then gave me in charge to his two wives, who were to take care of me.

The next morning Shimbouvenegani sent me some plantains and a quantity of sugar-cane by the hands of a young black woman, who also brought a message that she was to be my wife. I had to decline the matrimonial proposal, which seemed to grieve the black nymph, while her royal master was merely surprised, but evidently thought that it was right I should do as I pleased.

This day we went out on a hunt—one of those hunts which are marked with the brightest of red ink in my calendar. On this day I discovered a new and very curious ape.

As I was trudging along, rather tired of the sport, I happened to look up at a high tree which we were passing, and saw a most singular-looking shelter built in its branches. I asked Okabi whether the hunters here had this habit of sleeping in the woods, but was told, to my surprise, that this very ingenious nest was built by the *Nshiego Mbouvé*, an ape, as I found afterwards, which I put in the genus *Troglodytes*, and called *Troglodytes calvus*; an animal which had no hair on its head.

I saw at once that I was on the trail of an animal till now unknown to the civilized world. A naturalist will appreciate the joy which filled me at this good fortune. I no longer felt tired, but pushed on with renewed ardour and with increased caution, determined not to rest till I had killed this nest-building ape. One such discovery pays the weary naturalist-hunter for many months of toil and hardship. I felt already rewarded for all the inconveniences and expenses of my Commi trip.

I saw many of these nests after this, and may as well say here that they are generally built about fifteen or twenty feet from the ground, and invariably on a tree which stands a little apart from others, and which has no limbs below the one on which the nest is placed. I have seen them at the height of fifty feet, but very seldom. This choice is probably made that they may be safe at night from beasts, serpents, and falling limbs. They build only in the loneliest parts of the forest, and are very shy, and seldom seen even by the negroes.

Okabi, who was an old and intelligent hunter, was able to tell me that the male and female together gather the material for their nests. This material consists of leafy branches with which to make the roof, and vines to tie these branches to the tree. The tying is done so neatly, and the roof is so well constructed, that until I saw the nshiego actually occupying his habitation, I could scarce persuade myself that human hands had not built it. It throws off rain perfectly, being neatly rounded at the top for this purpose. The material being collected, the male goes up and builds the nest, while the female brings him the branches and vines. The male and female do not occupy the same tree, but have nests not far apart.

From all I have observed, I judge that the nshiego is not gregarious. The nests are never found in companies; and I have seen even quite solitary nests occupied by very old nshiegos-mbouvé, whose silvery hair and worn teeth attested their great age. These seemed hermits who had retired from the nshiego world.

They live on wild berries, and build their houses where they find these. When they have consumed all that a particular spot affords, they remove and build new houses, so that a nest is not inhabited for more than eight or ten days.

We travelled with great caution, not to alarm our prey, and had a hope that, singling out a shelter and waiting till dark, we should find it occupied. In this hope we were not disappointed. Lying quite still in our concealment (which tried my patience sorely), we at last, just at dusk, heard the loud peculiar "Hew! Hew! Hew!" which is the call of the male to his mate. We waited till it was quite dark, and then I saw what I had so longed all the weary afternoon to see. A nshiego was sitting in his nest. His feet rested on the lower branch; his head reached quite into the little dome of a roof, and his arm was clasped firmly about the tree-trunk. This is their way of sleeping.

After gazing till I was tired through the gloom at my poor sleeping victim, two of us fired, and the unfortunate beast fell at our feet without a struggle or even a groan.

We built a fire at once, and made our camp in this place, that when daylight came I might first of all examine and skin my prize. The poor ape was hung up, to be out of the way of the bashikouay and other insects, and I fell asleep on my bed of leaves and grass, as pleased a man as the world could well hold.*

NSHIEGO MBOUVÉ (YOUNG).

Next morning I had leisure to examine the nshiego. I was at once struck with the points of difference between it and the chimpanzee. It was somewhat smaller than the chimpanzee I had killed; but its great distinction was its bald head. This is its mark. This specimen was 3 feet 11 inches high or long. It was an adult. Its skin, where there is no hair, is black, in its natural state. The throat,

* For description of the animal, see 'Proceedings of the Boston Society of Natural History,' June, 1860.

breast, and abdomen are covered with short and rather thin blackish hair. On the lower part of the abdomen the hair is thinnest; but this is not perceived unless looked at carefully, as the skin is the colour of the hair. On the legs the hair is of a dirty gray mixed with black.

The shoulders and back have black hair between two and three inches long, mixed with a little gray. The arms, down to the wrist, have also long black hair, but shorter than in the gorilla. The hair is much thinner, in general, than on the gorilla, and the skin is not so tough. I noticed that the bare places, where the hair is worn off by contact with hard substances in sleeping, were different from the bare places which are so conspicuous on the chimpanzee.

There is a yet greater difference between this animal and the gorilla. It is not nearly so powerful as that monster. Its chest is of far less capacity; its muscular development is not on the same prodigious scale; its arm is a little longer; and the fingers of the gorilla are not only shorter, but also much more powerful than those of the nshiego mbouvé. There is also a similar difference in the fingers of the feet. The largest nshiego I shot measured a few inches over four feet in height, and its spread of arms was almost seven feet.

The hair of the nshiego is blacker, longer, and glossier than that of the gorilla. The latter has his head covered with hair, while the former is bald, both male and female. The nose of the nshiego is not so prominent as the gorilla's; the mouth is wider; the ears are much larger; the chin is rounder than that of the gorilla, and has some thin, short hairs on it. The posteriors of the nshiego are bare, and there the skin is white. The eyebrows of the nshiego are of thin black hair, but long. The side of the face is thinly covered with hair, commencing about the middle of the ear.

I sent my prize into the olako, and on our way back we had the good luck to kill another. This was a very old animal, with venerable aspect, silvery hair, and decayed teeth. It measured 4 feet 4 inches. Its weight was so considerable that, to carry it, we had to take out its intestines. I found in the stomach only some leaves. On my return to the olako I stuffed my two prizes, ready to send home.

On the 9th we had a great crocodile-hunt. The people were very glad, as they seem extravagantly fond of the meat. They kill more or less every day at this village, and so at the others; but the negroes are so lazy that they were glad to let me go and save them the trouble. The crocodile has not much meat on him, so that, though some were killed every day, the village was never sufficiently supplied.

We went in canoes. These canoes are of a very singular construction; quite flat-bottomed, very light draught, about fifty feet long, and not more than two broad. They are ticklish craft. The oarsmen stand up and use paddles seven feet long, with which they can propel one of these boats at a very good rate. The canoes are, of course, easily capsized—the gunwale being but a few inches above the water; but they do not often tip over. What surprised me most was the way the negro paddlers stood up at their work all day without tiring.

The negroes hunt the crocodile both with guns and a kind of harpoon. They have very poor guns, and powder is a scarce article with them; so the harpoon is most used. The vulnerable part of the animal is near the joints of his forelegs, and there they endeavour to wound it. Though so many are killed, they do not decrease in numbers, nor, strange enough, do they seem to grow more wary. As we started out we saw them swimming about in all directions, and lying on the mudbanks sunning themselves. They took no notice of our boat at all. As we were to shoot, we were obliged to look for our prizes on the shore, for, if killed in the water, they sink and are lost. Presently we saw an immense fellow extended on the bank among some reeds. We approached cautiously; I took good aim, and knocked him over. He struggled hard to get to the water, but he had been hit too surely. His strength gave out ere he could reach it, and with a few final kicks he was dead. We got one more, and then they brought another canoe, and capsizing it along the shore, rolled the dead monsters in and paddled off for the village. One measured eighteen and the other twenty feet in length. I never saw more savage-looking jaws. They

were armed with most formidable rows of teeth, and looked really as though a man would be a mere bite for them.

During the heat of the day these animals retire to the reeds, where they lie sheltered. In the morning and late afternoon they come forth to seek their prey. They swim with great silence, making scarce even a ripple on the water, and make pretty good progress. The motion of the paws in swimming is like that of a dog, over and over. They can stand quite still on top of the water, when they may be seen looking about them with their dull, wicked eyes. They sleep in the reeds, not for long in the same place. Their eggs they lay in the sand on the islands in the lake, covering them over with a layer of sand. The great abundance of fish in the lake makes them increase as fast as they do. The negroes seemed rather indifferent to their presence, and certainly did not view them with the loathing and horror they inspired in me.

On the 11th I went on a hunt. Coming home, I found near the water the hole or burrow of an *ogata*. This is a species of alligator which lives near pools, and makes a long hole in the ground with two entrances, in which it sleeps and watches for prey. The ogata is a night-roving animal, and solitary in its habits. It scrapes this hole with its paws with considerable labour. It lives near a pool, for the double reason, I imagine, that it may bathe, and because thither come bock, for which it lies in wait in its hole. The negroes tell me that the ogata rushes out with great speed upon any wandering animal, and drags it into the hole to eat it. When they discover one of these holes they come with their guns—which are generally loaded with iron spikes—and watch at one end, while a fire is built at the other entrance. When it becomes too hot, the ogata rushes out and is shot. I killed one, which proved to be seven feet long. It had great strength in its jaws, and very formidable teeth.

As we were paddling along, on our return to Damagondai's town, I perceived in the distance ahead a beautiful gazelle, looking meditatively into the waters of the lagoon, of which from time to time it took a drink. I stood up to get a shot, and we approached with the utmost silence. But just as I raised my gun to fire, a crocodile leaped out of the water, and, like a flash, dived back again with the struggling animal in its powerful jaws. So quickly did the beast take his prey that, though I fired at him, I was too late. I do not think my bullet hit him. I would not have believed that this huge and unwieldy animal could move with such velocity; but the natives told me that the deer often falls prey to the crocodile.

On the 14th I gave Shimbouvenegani two pieces of cotton cloth, some tobacco, and beads, and returned to Damagondai's town. Here I found a canoe from King Ranpano, who had sent to inform me that a vessel was on the coast by which I could send things to America if I wished. I determined to go down immediately and send some specimens off.

The people of the Ogobay and the Anengue are of the same tribe with the sea-shore Commi. They intermarry; their customs and superstitions are the same; their palavers are the same; and, though they are more peaceable, they have the will to be just as great rascals. The country behind the river-swamps is very rich in all manner of tropical products, and ebony is found in the hills; but to transport heavy substances twenty miles to the river or lake-shore, in a country where there are no roads, is too much trouble for these lazy fellows—for which reason very little is cut. The copal-tree is also found, as well as the india-rubber vine. They raise sugar-cane in great quantities, yams, ground-nuts, plantains, manioc, and sweet potatoes. The chief commercial produce of the country at present is ivory, of which a small quantity is brought down every year.

In Damagondai's town I was so fortunate as to become possessed of one of their idols or *mbuitis*. It is a mistake to suppose that these natives worship their greegrees and fetiches. Wherever I have been I have found the headman or chief of each family in possession of an idol, which was worshipped by that family. This whole matter is kept so secret that, unless the traveller pays particular attention, he may live in a village for weeks, and not know of this idol's existence.

Damagondai's idol was a female figure, with copper eyes and a tongue made of a sharp sword-shaped piece of iron. This

A FEMALE IDOL.

IDOL, GODDESS OF THE SLAVES.

explained her chief attributes; she cuts to pieces those with whom she is displeased. She was dressed in a Shekiani cloth, covering her from the neck down. She is said to speak, to walk, to foretell events, and to take vengeance on her enemies. Her house is the most prominent one in the whole village. She comes to the people by night, and tells them in their sleep what is going to happen. In this way, they asserted, my coming had been foretold. They worship her by dancing around her, and singing her praises and their requests. Sometimes a single man or woman comes to prefer a request; and once I saw the whole village engaged in this rite. They offer her sugar-cane and other food, which they believe she eats.

I tried to buy this goddess, but, ugly as she is, Damagondai said no money would purchase her. But he insinuated that for a proper price I could have the goddess of the slaves. These poor fellows were absent on the plantations, and after council with his chief men, the king determined to tell them that he had seen their mbuiti walk off into the woods. I packed her up and took her off with me, and now give her portrait.

In the afternoon news came that Oshoria, the king of a town situated at the junction of the Anengue and Ogobai rivers, intended to stop me on my way down and exact tribute for my passage. Poor King Damagondai was much troubled. He sent his brother down with a present of a plate, a mug, and a brass pan to propitiate him. I was very angry, and determined to put down Mr. Oshoria. We cleaned our guns, and I prepared my revolver; and next morning we set out without waiting for the king's brother's return, greatly to the dismay of these peaceable people.

When we came in sight of Guaibuiri, Oshoria's village, I saw that some of my fellows began to show the white feather. I therefore told them I would blow out the brains of the first man who failed to fight to the death, at the same time pointing to my revolver as the intended instrument of death. They have a great respect for this wonderful revolver; and immediately answered me, "We are men."

So we pulled up to the village. On the shore stood about one hundred and fifty fellows armed with spears and axes, led by ten men who had guns. I went immediately up to them, revolver in one hand and double-barrelled gun in the other. At this piece of bravado they became very civil, and instead of firing at my party received us peaceably.

Damagondai's brother hurried down to meet me, and announced that there was no palaver. I was then led to where the quarrelsome Oshoria stood, whom I reproached for his conduct, telling him that if anybody had been killed the palaver would have been on his head. He said he had been vexed that I did not stop to see him on my way up; and after making further excuses, added, "Aoué olomé;" which means, "Thou art a man;" an expression used in several ways, either to designate a smart man, or a rascal, or, in the best sense, a very brave man. I was content to accept it as an intended compliment.

I was presented with fruits and fowls, and we were presently the best of friends; and when I brought down a little bird which sat on a very high tree, they all declared I must have a very big shooting-fetich, and respected me accordingly; and to show them I was not afraid of them I spent the night at their village.

Leaving this place, we got back to Biagano without further trouble.

My coming back was fortunate, for in a few days after came a high and mighty visitor from far up the River Rembo. King Quengueza, of whom I had often heard from the Commi men, lives up the Rembo about ninety miles, and is king over a large tribe of people. He was a man whom I had not even hoped to see here, and whose influence and friendship I was very glad to have. He came down some months before in considerable state, in three canoes, with three of his favourite wives, and about one hundred and thirty men. When he saw me he was much astonished, and said he had heard of me for a great hunter, and had expected to see a tall and stout man, and not such a feeble body as mine. He was now convinced, he said, that I must have a brave heart, to hunt as I did.

Fortunately the king and I could talk together without an interpreter, so that I did not need any Commi to confound my words and misrepresent my wishes.

The king told me there were plenty of gorilla and nshiegos in his country, and that if I would come I should have liberty and protection to hunt and do what I pleased. I was ready to go immediately, but he said the fall of the rainy season would be the best time, and so I put my visit off.

I had sent the kind-hearted old fellow off well contented, with his canoes full of presents of iron bars, brass rods, &c. He promised me great sport, and an introduction to some tribes of whom even these Commi knew nothing, and who are, therefore, beyond even their *ultima Thule*. To do him greater honour, my people fired a salute as he started off, with which he was highly delighted—as an African is sure to be with any noise.

CHAPTER XVI.

The dry season—Migration of birds—Serpents—The ceremony of bola ivoga—Theory of the Commi about disease—Death of Ishungui—A great doctor—Exorcising a sorcerer—Fear of witchcraft by the people—Capture of a young gorilla—Death of its mother—Death of the young gorilla—I am poisoned—Punishment and release of the poisoner.

THE dry season was now setting in in earnest. It is curious that most of the birds which were so abundant during the rainy season had by this time taken their leave, and other birds, in immense numbers, flocked in to feed on the fish, which now leave the sea-shore and the bars of the river-mouth, and ascend the river to spawn.

The breakers on the shore were now frightful to see. The coast was rendered inaccessible by them even to the natives, and the surf increased to that degree at the mouth of the river even, that it was difficult to enter with a canoe. Strong breezes prevailed, and though the sky was constantly overcast, no drop of rain fell. The thermometer fell sometimes to 64° of Fahrenheit, and I suffered from cold, as did also the poor natives, who make no provision of thick clothing for such weather, though it is the same every year. The grass on the prairies was dried up to powder. The ponds are dried up; only the woods keep their resplendent green.

At this season the negroes leave their villages and work on their plantations. Biagano was almost deserted; all hands were on the plantations; the women harvesting the crop of ground-nuts, one of the staples of this country, and the men building canoes and idling around. Their plantations are necessarily at some distance off, as the sandy prairie is not fit to cultivate, being only, in fact, a deposit of the sea.

Fish, particularly mullet, were so abundant in the river that sometimes, when I took my evening constitutional in a canoe on the water, enough mullet leaped into the boat to furnish me a breakfast next day.

Birds flocked in immense numbers on the prairies, whither they came to hatch their young.

The ugly marabouts, from whose tails our ladies get the splendid feathers for their bonnets, were there in thousands. Pelicans waded on the river-banks all day in prodigious swarms, gulping down the luckless fish which came in their way. I loved to see them swimming about in grave silence, and every moment grabbing up a poor fish, which, if not hungry, they left in their huge bag, till sometimes three or four pounds of reserve food thus awaited the coming of their appetite.

I found great flocks of the *Ibis religiosa* (the sacred Ibis of the Egyptians), which had arrived over-night, whence I could not tell.

Ducks of various kinds built their nests in every creek and in every new islet that appeared with the receding waters. Cranes, too, and numerous other waterfowl flocked in, every day bringing new birds. All come, by some strange instinct, to feed upon the vast shoals of fish which literally filled the river.

On the sea-shore I sometimes caught a bird, the *Sula capensis*, which had been driven ashore by the treacherous waves to which it had trusted itself, and could not, for some mysterious reason, get away again.

And finally, every sand-bar is covered with gulls, whose shrill screams are heard from morning till night as they fly about greedily after their finny prey.

Land birds are equally plentiful; but I have time to enumerate only one curious species. This is the bee-eater, of which I discovered two new species. The common one is the *Meropicus bicolor*, with breast of a gorgeous roseate hue, and looks as he flies about like a lump of fire. The bee-eaters feed on bees and flies, and are remarkable for the nests they build. These are holes in the ground, always on the edge of some bank or acclivity, and in these they sleep at night.

Serpents are not so common as in the rainy season, but do not altogether abandon the country, as I had reason to discover one night. I had retired to rest, but was roused by a tremendous fluttering among my chickens. I rushed out immediately, expecting to catch a thief, but found nobody; and as the houses were not broken into, returned to my own room, thinking it was only a false alarm. But I was no sooner in than I rushed out again, for, in the dim light, I found myself upon the point of stepping upon a huge black snake. I had my gun in my hand, and lost no time in blowing his head to pieces with cold lead. He was ten feet long, and of a kind whose bite is said by the negroes to be fatal. The hideous beast was just swallowing one of my chickens when I killed it. It had been among the fowls, which accounted for the noise I heard. The negroes rushed in when they heard the report of my gun, and with great joy cut off the head of their enemy.

Now the river was covered with muddy islands, left dry and covered with reeds; among which sported the flamingo —a bird not seen here in the wet season. All these reedy islets were submerged when I passed up last May.

From August 18th to the 31st I was badly ill with dysentery and symptoms of malignant fever, contracted, probably, in the Anengue marshes. In three days I took one hundred and fifty grains of quinine, and thus happily succeeded in breaking the force of the fever, which was the more dangerous of the two diseases.

By September 9th I was pretty strong again, and the people came to ask me if I was willing for them to *bola ivoga*, that is, to make a terrible noise with their ceremonious breaking of the mourning-time. I gave my consent, and next day great numbers of canoes came down to help in this ceremony. When any one of importance dies, the tribe or town cease to wear their best clothes, and make it a point to go unusually dirty. This is to mourn. Mourning lasts from a year to two years. As for the breaking up of mourning, this shall now be described.

The man who had died left seven wives, several slaves, a house, a plantation, and other property. All this the elder brother inherits, and on him it devolves to give the grand feast. For this feast every canoe that came brought jars of *mimbo* or palm-wine. Sholomba and Jombuai, the heir, had been out for two weeks fishing, and now returned with several canoe-loads of dry fish. From their plantations quantities of palm-wine were brought in. Everyone in the village furbished up his best clothes and ornaments. Drums and kettles were collected; powder was brought out for the salutes; and at last all was ready for bola ivoga.

The wives of the deceased seemed quite jolly, for to-morrow they were to lay aside their widows' robes and to join in the jollification as brides. The heir could have married them all, but he had generously given up two to a younger brother and one to a cousin.

At seven o'clock in the morning three guns were fired off to announce that the widows had done eating a certain mess, mixed of various ingredients supposed to have magical virtues, and by which they are released from their widowhood. They now put on bracelets and anklets, and the finest calico they had. About nine all the guests sat down on mats spread about the house of deceased and along the main street. They were divided into little groups, and before each was set an immense jar of mimbo. All began to talk pleasantly, till suddenly the Biagano people fired off a volley of about one hundred guns. This was the signal for the drinking to begin. Men, women, and children set to; and from this time till next morning the orgies were continued without interruption. They drank, they sang, they fired guns, and loaded them so heavily as they got tipsy, that I wonder the old trade-guns did not burst; they drummed on everything that could possibly give out a noise; they shouted; and the women danced—such dances as are not seen elsewhere. They are indecent in their best moments. The reader may imagine what they were when every woman was furiously tipsy, and thought it a point of honour to be more indecent than her neighbour.

Next day, about sunrise, Jombuai came to ask me to assist at the concluding ceremony. His brother's house was to be torn down and burned. When I came they fired guns, and then, in a moment, hacked the old house to pieces with axes and cutlasses. When the ruins were burned, the feast was done. And this is to go out of mourning among the Commi.

Hardly were the rejoicings done, when Ishungui, the man who had faithfully taken care of my house in my absence, lay at death's door. He had gone out on Jombuai's fishing-excursion, caught cold, and had now a lung fever. I knew when I saw him that he must die, and tried to prepare his mind for the change. But his friends by no means gave him up. They sent for a distinguished fetich doctor, and under his auspices began the infernal din with which they seek to cure a sick man.

The Commi theory of disease is that Abambou (the devil) has got into the sick man. Now this devil is only to be driven out with noise, and accordingly they surround the sick man and beat drums and kettles close to his head; fire off guns close to his ears; sing, shout, and dance all they can. This lasts till the poor fellow either dies or is better—unless the operators become tired out first, for the Commi doctors either kill or cure.

Ishungui died. He left no property, and his brother buried

him without a coffin in a grave in the sand, so shallow that, when I chanced to come upon it some days after, I saw that the wild beasts had been there and eaten the corpse. The mourning lasted but six days; and as there were no wives or property, so there was no feast. The relatives of the deceased slept one night in his house, as a mark of respect; and then all that remained was to discover the person who had bewitched the dead man. For that a young man, generally healthy, should die so suddenly in course of nature was by no means to be believed.

A canoe had been despatched up the lake to bring down a great doctor. They brought one of Damagondai's sons, a great rascal, who had been foremost in selling me the idol, and who was an evident cheat. When all was ready for the trial, I went down to look at the doctor, who looked literally *like the devil.* I never saw a more ghastly object. He had on a high head-dress of black feathers. His eye-lids were painted red, and a red stripe, from the nose upward, divided his forehead into two parts. Another red stripe passed round his head. The face was painted white, and on each side of the mouth were two round red spots. About his neck hung a necklace of grass and also a cord, which held a box against his breast. This little box is sacred, and contains spirits. A number of strips of leopard and other skins crossed his breast, and were exposed about his person; and all these were charmed, and had charms attached to them. From each shoulder down to his hands was a white stripe, and one hand was painted quite white. To complete this horrible array, he wore a string of little bells around his body.

He sat on a box or stool, before which stood another box containing charms. On this stood a looking-glass, beside which lay a buffalo-horn containing some black powder, and said in addition to be the refuge of many spirits. He had a little basket of snake-bones, which he shook frequently during his incantations; as also several skins, to which little bells were attached. Near by stood a fellow beating a board with two sticks. All the people of the village gathered about this couple, who, after continuing their incantations for awhile,

14

at last came to the climax. Jombuai was told to call over the names of persons in the village, in order that the doctor might ascertain if any one of those named did the sorcery. As each name was called the old cheat looked in the glass to see the result.

During the whole operation I stood near him, which seemed to trouble him greatly. At last, after all the names were called, the doctor declared that he could not find any "witch-man," but that an evil spirit dwelt in the village, and many of the people would die if they continued there. I have a suspicion that this final judgment with which the incantations broke up was a piece of revenge upon me. I had no idea till next day how seriously the words of one of these (*ouganga*) doctors is taken.

The next morning all was excitement. The people were scared; they said their *mbuiri* was not willing to have them live longer there; that he would kill them, &c. Then began the removal of all kinds of property and the tearing down of houses; and by nightfall I was actually left alone in my house with my Mpongwe boy and my little Ogobai boy, Makondai, both of whom were anxious to be off.

Old Ranpano came to beg me not to be offended; that he dared not stay, but would build his house not too far away; that the mbuiri was now in town: he advised me as a friend to move also; but nobody wished me ill—only he must go, &c.

I did not like to abandon my houses, which had cost me money and trouble, and where I was more comfortably settled than I had ever before been in Africa. So I called a meeting of the people, and tried to induce some of them to come over and live with me. Now, though they loved tobacco, though they worshipped trade, though they had every possible inducement to come and live near me, "their white man," as they called me, it was only with the greatest difficulty I could get some men who had already worked for me to come over and stay in my place. These began immediately to build themselves houses, and by October 8th the little village was built, of which I was now, to my great surprise, offered the sovereignty. I remembered how the new king was made in the Gaboon; and though it seemed romantic to be the chief of a negro town in Africa, the thought of the contumely which precedes the assumption of royalty deterred me. Finally the men determined to have me as the chief next to Ranpano, and with this my ambition was satisfied.

On the 1st of November I went in a canoe, with guns and provisions, up to Irende, a town about forty miles up the Fernand Vaz. Hereabouts there was likelihood of some good hunts; so I had been told. In fact, we killed a number of wild red pigs, and some beautiful, but very shy, red gazelles. It is a curious circumstance—which I think I ascertained to be a fact—that on this part of the Fernand Vaz the gorilla lives only near the left bank, and the chimpanzee only near the right bank of the stream, until one reaches the Rembo River.

On the 9th I started for the town of my old friend Makaga, where I was heartily received. We went out on a gorilla-hunt on the 10th, but took too many men, and probably made too much noise; for we saw none, and returned next day with our trouble for our pains. On the 13th I went out with only one hunter, and he took me to a part of the country full of the wild pine-apple. The gorilla is very fond of the leaves of this plant, of which it eats the white stems. We saw great quantities thus eaten away, therefore we hoped to find here the beasts themselves.

About noon, Mbele, my hunter, was some distance ahead, when suddenly I heard his gun fired. I ran up and found he had shot at and killed a female gorilla about half-grown.

Coming back we heard the cry of the gorillas off at one side of our path. We approached, but were discerned, and came up only to see four young animals making off on their all-fours into the woods. I noticed that in their trot their hind legs seemed to play in between their arms; but they made very good speed.

Before we got to town again I shot a *mboyo*, a very shy animal, of the wolf kind, with long yellowish hair and straight ears. I have often watched these beasts surrounding and chasing small game for themselves. The drove runs very well together; and as their policy is to run round and round, they soon bewilder, tire out, and capture any animal of moderate endurance.

I found this a great gorilla country; the animals even approached the town early in the morning, and I found that I need not make long journeys in order to reach the hunting-ground. But they are very difficult of approach; the slightest noise alarms them and sends them off. It is only once in a way that you can surprise an old male, and then he will fight you.

On the 25th I got another young gorilla. This time I was accessory to its capture. We were walking along in silence, when I heard a cry, and presently saw before me a female gorilla, with a tiny baby gorilla hanging to her breast and sucking. The mother was stroking the little one, and looking fondly down at it; and the scene was so pretty and touching that I held my fire, and considered—like a soft-hearted fellow—whether I had not better leave them in peace. Before I could make up my mind, however, my hunter fired and killed the mother, who fell without a struggle.

The mother fell, but the baby clung to her, and, with pitiful cries, endeavoured to attract her attention. I came up, and when it saw me it hid its poor little head in its mother's breast. It could neither walk nor bite, so we could easily manage it; and I carried it, while the men bore the mother on a pole. When we got to the village another scene ensued. The men put the body down, and I set the little fellow near. As soon as he saw his mother he crawled to her and threw himself on her breast. He did not find his accustomed nourishment, and I saw that he perceived something was the matter with the old one. He crawled over the body, smelt at it, and gave utterance, from time to time, to a plaintive cry, "Hoo, hoo, hoo," which touched my heart.

I could get no milk for this poor little fellow, who could not eat, and consequently died on the third day after he was caught. He seemed more docile than the others I had, for he already recognised my voice, and would try to hurry towards me when he saw me. I put the little body in alcohol, and sent it to Doctor Wyman, of Boston, for dissection.

The mother we skinned; and, when I came to examine her, I found her a very singular specimen. Her head was much smaller than that of any other gorilla I ever saw, and the rump was of a reddish-brown colour. These are peculiarities which made this specimen different from all others I have seen. I called her, therefore, the gorilla with the red rump.

On the 29th and 30th of November I took my last hunts near Makaga's place. I found gorilla growing scarce. I had hunted them too perseveringly; so I determined to return to Biagano to make ready for my trip up the Rembo.

I found all safe, and at once prepared for my next trip. This, however, was put off by one of those accidents which happen in these barbaric countries once in a while. On the 5th of December I was poisoned by my cook. He was a Sangatanga fellow, who had been sent to me from the Gaboon because I could not stand the cooking of my Biagano friends. He had served in the Cape Lopez slave-factories, and had there learned treachery and thieving. For a time he behaved well; but by-and-by I began to miss things, and made sure, after watching the Commi fellows pretty closely, that the thief could be none other but my cook.

On this day I was preparing a tiger's skin which Igala, my hunter, had killed the night before, and had to send cook for something in my storehouse. He came back without the key, which he said was lost. I told him if he did not get it before night I would punish him.

I had Sholomba, a native prince, to dine with me, and we had fowls, chicken-soup, and a goat for dinner. It happened that Sholomba's family hold chickens in abhorrence as food, believing that one of their ancestors had been cured of a deadly disease by the blood of a fowl; therefore he ate of the goat. I took two plates of chicken-broth, and had scarce finished the last when I was seized with frightful pains and vomiting, and diarrhœa set in, and lasted all night. I never suffered such frightful torments.

When I was first taken sick I called Boulay, the cook, who

said he had put nothing in the soup; but when charged with poisoning, turned and fled into the woods. The next afternoon, when I was somewhat easier, my people brought the wretch in. He had fled down river, but had been caught. Ranpano and all were very angry, and demanded the life of him who had tried to kill *their* white man. It was proved that he had gone into my storehouse with the key he said was lost; and, after some prevarication, he admitted that he had taken two tablespoonfuls of the arsenic I always had at hand there, and put it in my soup. I owe my life to his *overdose*; consequently to a kind Providence.

Ranpano kept Boulay in chains till I was well enough to sit in judgment over him. Then it was determined that he should suffer death; but I interfered, and desired that he should be let off with one hundred and ten lashes with a whip of hippopotamus-hide. Eleven of the stoutest *freemen* of the town were chosen to administer the punishment, and when it was over Boulay was again put in chains.

Bad news travels even in this country, where there are neither mails nor post-roads. Boulay had brothers in Cape Lopez, who in some way heard of his rascality. They were troubled at this disgrace to their family, and appeared before me one day with four slaves in their train. They thanked me for not killing their brother, which, they said, I had a right to do. They said, "Boulay has conducted himself as a slave in trying to poison his master." Then they begged me to give him to them and to spare his life, and handed over to me the four slaves they had brought as an equivalent.

The brothers were old, venerable, and honest-looking men. They evidently grieved deeply for the crime of their kinsman. I told them that in my country we did not "make palaver for money;" that I might have killed their brother, according to their own laws. Then I called Boulay, and told him how meanly he had treated me; then, taking off his chains myself, I handed him over to his brothers, with the four slaves they had given me. They thanked me again and again. Ranpano forbade Boulay ever to return, and so they went back to Cape Lopez.

I found myself, after some weeks, not only entirely re-

covered from the effects of the arsenic, but also cured of a
fever which had long beset me. Where quinine has ceased
to affect the traveller in Africa, solutions of arsenic are
sometimes administered, and with good effect, in fever cases.

CHAPTER XVII.

King Quengueza sends his son to me as a hostage—Invitation to come to
his country—Assembling the Biagano people—I leave my property
in their hands—Rinkimongami appointed the keeper of my goods—
Good-bye to Ranpano—Departure for Goumbi—Ascent of Rembo—
A man in ntchogo—Reception by Quengueza—Goumbi—Superstitions
of King Quengueza—Ceremony for driving away the aniemba—The
alumbi house—Hunting—Killing a gorilla—Ordeal—Capture of a
young gorilla—Superstitions about gorillas—Bakalai villages—King
Obindji—Trial by hot iron.

TOWARDS the close of January, 1858, when I was thinking of
King Quengueza and of my approaching visit to him, the old
fellow sent down his eldest son to me with a lot of ebony,
and his youngest son, a boy of ten, who was to be left with
me. Quengueza sent word that I must come soon; that I
should have his escort to go to the far interior, and that he
was ready to cut ebony for me. Meantime, lest I should be
afraid to trust myself in his hands, he sent his young son,
who was to remain in Ranpano's hands as hostage for my
safety. "You see," he sent word, "I am not afraid of you.
You may trust me."

This message determined me to get ready at once for my
trip. I packed my goods and put my house in order, and at
last called together the people of Biagano for a serious talk.
I knew they were opposed to my taking trade-goods to the
interior, but I could not go without. I therefore told them
that I not only now was, but intended to remain, *their* white
man; that I took goods only to pay my way, and that my
explorations would help their trade, while I only wanted to
hunt. At the same time I told them, if they did not help
me with canoes I should leave them and never come back.

They were glad to let me go where I wished, and to help me as far as I needed help.

Next day I had a more formal ceremony still. In my houses remained about two thousand dollars' worth of ebony and goods, together with ivory, all my specimens not sent to America, and various other things of value. These were to remain, and I had to trust to the honour of a parcel of black fellows for their safety.

Accordingly I took Ranpano and some of his head-men all over the premises, showed them everything I had which was to remain; then said, "Give me a man to keep all safe, that I, who am your white man, may lose nothing."

They gave me at once old Rinkimongami, the king's brother, to whom I promised good pay if my things were kept safe.

Then I distributed tobacco to all the people; and next morning (February 26th) we set off for Goumbi, Quengueza's place.

I had to take my big boat, because no canoe would hold all the goods, powder and shot, guns and provisions I required. I had 26 guns, 150 pounds of lead, 200 pounds of coarse trade-powder, 30 pounds of fine powder for myself, about 10,000 yards of cotton cloth, 400 pounds of beads, and quantities of iron and brass pots, kettles, and pans; caps, coats, shirts, looking-glasses, fire-steels, flints, knives, plates, glasses, spoons, hats, &c., &c. This is an African explorer's outfit. For this I hoped to get not only friendly treatment, but ebony, ivory, and wax, and perhaps india-rubber.

We were fifteen in all in my boat. Another canoe, with other fifteen men, followed us. In my own boat, Jombuai, a fellow from my own town, and who had married some wives up the Rembo, was the head man; Quengueza's little boy was of our party, and also the brave little Makondai, whom I had at first determined to leave behind, as being too small to stand the fatigues of such a journey. The little fellow entreated so to be taken with us that I at last consented. He behaved like a trump, and I had no occasion to regret my confidence in him.

When we had got a few miles up river the slaves of Jom-

CHAP. XVII.   *ASCENT OF REMBO.*   197

Imai came down to bid him good-bye, and brought him a
large quantity of plantains—a welcome accession to our
provision-store. A few miles up and we were clear of the
mangroves, and the river began to widen, and its shores
became beautiful. Fine palms lined the banks, and seemed
even to guard them from the encroachments of the full river,
which ran along quite level with its banks.

We pulled nearly all night, and by noon of the next day

PRISONER IN NTCHOGO.

reached Monwé Island, thirty-five miles from the mouth of
the river, but only about ten miles from the sea. Here we
took a rest, the heat being excessive.

A little above Monwé the Fernand Vaz becomes much narrower. It then takes an easterly direction; and from this
point upward it is known to the natives as Rembo, which
means "The River." At Quayombi several small islands

divide the river temporarily into different channels, without, however, seriously obstructing the navigation.

The land which divides the river into three here we found to be mere mud-banks, half-overflowed and covered with reeds. When we got into the main stream I found it suddenly narrower, but a full rushing tide, two hundred yards wide, and from four to five fathoms in depth all along, with no shallows or other impediments to navigation.

On the 28th we passed numerous villages, my men shouting, singing, and firing guns, and the people gazing at us from shore in great wonder. In the afternoon I went ashore at the village of "Charley," a quarrelsome fellow, who had become known to white traders some years before by seizing and imprisoning a whole canoe-load of negroes who had been sent up on a trading expedition. He put them into a very uncomfortable kind of stocks called *ntchogo*, which consists of a heavy billet of wood in which the feet are stuck, and a lighter billet into which the hands are secured. Thus the man is helpless both against men and against mosquitoes and flies; and here the poor fellows were kept till the trader, who was waiting in a ship, sent up a ransom for them.

The two chiefs treated me very well, and said they felt friendly towards me, as indeed they showed by killing in my honour the fatted calf (it was a goat), and sending besides some chickens and plantains. They were much alarmed at the charmed pistol (one of Colt's revolvers), which I fired off to show them how many of them I could kill without stopping.

About one o'clock the next day (the 29th) we came to Goumbi, the residence of King Quengueza. Here we were received in a most triumphant manner. I could not make myself heard for shouts and the firing of guns. The whole population of Goumbi crowded down to the shore to see me; and I was led up in procession to an immense covered space, capable of holding at least a thousand people, and surrounded by seats. These were quickly filled up by the people, among whom I presently found there were strangers from various parts of the interior, drawn thither by the news that I was coming up to Goumbi, and now gazing at me, and

RECEPTION AT GOUMBI.

especially at my hair, with the greatest wonder in their countenances.

A large high seat was appointed for me, and another close to it was for Quengueza, who presently arrived, and, with a face beaming with joy, shook hands with me.

He is an old, white-woolled negro, very tall, spare, and of a severe countenance, betokening great energy and courage, which he has, and for which he is celebrated all over this country. He is a very remarkable man, considering his opportunities; and has more natural intelligence than any other negro I met in Africa. He made haste to explain to me that, as he was in mourning for his brother, who had died two years ago, he could not dress finely. He had on a finely-knit black cap, and a cloth of black also, both of Ashira make, and really beautiful; no shirt—which article is not allowed to mourners—and an American coat too small for him.

When he had done welcoming me, I called his little son, Akoonga, whom he had sent me as a hostage, and who had been brought up in my canoe. When he came forward, I said to the king, in a loud voice, that the people might hear, "You sent your son to me to keep, so that I might feel safe to come to you. I am not afraid. I like you, and can trust you. I believe you will treat me and my men rightly; and therefore I have brought your little son back to you. I do not want him for safety."

At this there was tremendous shouting, and all the people seemed overjoyed.

Then I reminded the king of his promise to let me go into the interior, and to help me. The king and the people shouted approval. Then I said I had come to benefit them. I had brought goods, and would buy their ebony and ivory, as much as they would get. At this announcement the shouts and rejoicings grew boundless and obstreperous. I had touched—as I expected—their most sensitive nerve.

The king then rose to reply. There was immediately a dead silence—for Quengueza is honoured by his people. He first gave me a large house, which he pointed out to me. It had a verandah with seats in front. Then he turned to the people, and said:—

"This is my *ntangani* (white man). He has come from a far country to see me. I went down to beg him to come up to me. Now he has come. Let no one do any harm to his people. For him I need not speak. Give food to his people. Treat them well. Do not steal anything. A big palaver would come on you."

Then he addressed himself to the Ashira and Bakalai, who were present, saying, "Beware! Do not steal my white man, for if you should make the attempt, I would sell you all."

This closed the ceremonies.

Goumbi is ninety-five miles from the mouth of the river. It is the last town of the Commi; and is important because it commands the whole of the upper river, so far as the natives are concerned, by a hereditary right. The Abouya clan, who reside in Goumbi, and of whom Quengueza is the chief, claim, and are allowed to have, the sole right of trading up river. Sometimes they allow a few down-river Commi who have wives in Goumbi to go up and cut ebony; but even this privilege is sparingly granted, and for all intents and purposes Quengueza has a monopoly of all the commerce with the rich country beyond, and really considers the people who live above him as his vassals.

It is very singular that among all these people descent and inheritance are taken from the mother. The son of a Commi man by a woman of another tribe or nation is not counted a Commi; and to narrow it down to families, to be a true Abouya (citizen of Goumbi), it is necessary to be born of an Abouya mother. If only the father were Abouya, the children would be considered half-breeds.

Up to Goumbi there is safe navigation for little steamers in almost every month of the year, and with light-draught steamers at any time. The river is deep and narrow, and the banks steep all the way up. About fifteen miles above Quayombi the current becomes stronger. Here the hills come down to the river, receding however above. The country seemed fertile and productive; and the number of villages we passed on our way argues well for its fertility.

On the 1st of March I received a visit from one Igoumba, a

chief of the Ashiras, an interior people. He had fled from his home because he had been accused of practising sorcery. Also several Bakalai chiefs came to see me, and asked me to visit their country.

Quengueza was all this time perfectly happy. He danced, and sang, and made jokes, and altogether was as jolly as though all his wishes and desires had been gratified at once. He gave me back his little boy, Akoonga, to stay with me; and, as Makondai is already my steward, the young prince has been appointed to wash my dishes. I gave Quengueza his present of fifty yards of cloth, a gun, a neptune, and some beads, &c. He was greatly pleased, and promised again that I should go into the interior as far as he had authority and influence.

Nevertheless he is curiously superstitious. For a year he had not passed down a street which leads most directly to the water, but had always gone a roundabout way. This was because when he came to the throne this street was pronounced to be bewitched by an enemy of his; and he was persuaded that if he passed by it he would surely die. Several times efforts had been made by distinguished doctors to drive away the witch which there lay in wait; but the king, though he believed in sorcery, had not much faith in the exorcisers or doctors.

A last attempt to drive off the *aniemba* or witch was made on the night of March 2nd–3rd. A famous doctor from the far-off Bakalai country had been brought down to perform this act. His name was Aquailai. The people gathered in great numbers under the immense *hangar* or covered space in which I had been received, and there lit fires, around which they sat. The space thus covered was one hundred and fifty feet long by forty wide, and roofed with bamboo and leaves. About ten o'clock, when it was pitch-dark, the doctor commenced operations by singing some boasting songs, recounting his power over witches. This was the signal for all the people to gather into their houses and about their fires under the *hangar*. So much haste did they make, that two women, failing to get home, and afraid to go farther through the streets, took refuge in my house.

Next all the fires were carefully extinguished, all the lights put out; and in about an hour more not a light of any kind was in the whole town except mine. I gave notice that white men were exempted from the rules made in such cases, and this was allowed. The most pitchy darkness and the most complete silence reigned everywhere. No voice could be heard even in a whisper, among the several thousand people gathered in the gloom.

At last the curious silence was broken by the doctor, who, standing in the centre of the town, began some loud babbling of which I could not make out the meaning. From time to time the people answered him in chorus. This went on for an hour, and was really one of the strangest scenes I ever took part in. I could see nothing but the faces of the two women in my house, who were badly frightened, poor things! as, in fact, all the people were. The hollow voice of the witch-doctor resounded curiously through the silence; and when the answer of many mingled voices came through the darkness, it really assumed the air of a serious, old-fashioned incantation scene.

At last, just at midnight, I heard the doctor approach. He had bells girded about him, which he jingled as he walked. He went separately to every family in the town, and asked if the witch which obstructed the king's highway belonged to them. Of course all answered, "No." Then he began to run up and down the bewitched street, calling out loudly for the witch to go off. Presently he came back and announced that he could no longer see the aniemba, and that doubtless she had gone, never to come back. At this all the people rushed out and shouted, "Go away! go away! and never come back to hurt our king!"

Then fires were lit, and we all sat down to eat. This done, all the fires were once more extinguished, and all the people sang wild songs until four o'clock. Then the fires were again lit.

At sunrise the whole population gathered to accompany their king down the dreaded street to the water.

Quengueza, I know, was brave as a hunter and as a warrior. He was also intelligent in many things where his people were very stupid. But the poor old king was now horribly afraid. He was assured that the witch was gone; but he evidently thought himself walking to almost certain death. He would have refused to go if it had been possible. He hesitated, but at last determined to face his fate, and walked manfully down to the river and back amid the plaudits of his loyal subjects.

I was at first puzzled to know the meaning of certain miniature huts which are seen standing behind or between the dwelling-houses, and which are held sacred. No one but the owner himself is allowed to enter these little huts; but Quengueza's great friendship for me overcame his African scruples in my case; and I was permitted, on my return from the interior, to examine his *alumbi*-house. These erections are spoken of by the natives as fetich-houses; and if, perchance, a stranger is allowed to peep into one, he sees a few boxes containing chalk or ochre, and upon a kind of little table a cake of the same, with which the owner rubs his body every time he goes on a fishing, hunting, or trading expedition. The chalk is considered sacred, and to be smeared with it serves as a protection from danger. If you are a great friend, the chalk of the alumbi will be marked upon you on your departure from the residence of your host. But the boxes generally contain also the skulls of the ancestors of the owner, at least those relatives who were alive during his own life-time; for, on the death of such a relative, his or her head is cut off and placed in a box full of white clay, looking like chalk, where it is left to rot and saturate the chalk; both skull and saturated chalk being then held sacred. The skulls of twin children are almost always used for the alumbi.

When a guest is entertained of whom presents are expected, the host, in a quiet way, goes from time to time into the fetich-house and scrapes a little bone-powder from a favourite skull, and puts it into the food which is being cooked as a present to the guest. The idea is that, by consuming the scrapings of the skull, the blood of their ancestors enters into your body, and thus, becoming of one blood, you are naturally led to love them, and grant them what they wish.

By the 6th, matters began to be put in train for some hunting-expeditions. Food was scarce in town on account of the great number of strangers present; but the king's thirty wives—he has only this moderate number—bring food for me and my men every day. Quengueza has given me **Etia**, his favourite hunter and slave, for a guide in the bush. This Etia is a fine-looking old man, a native of the far interior, whence the king bought him many years ago. He lives now on a little plantation outside of town, where he had a neat house and a nice old wife, who always treated me in a kind motherly way. Etia's business is to supply the royal larder with "bush-meat;" and he hunts almost every week for this purpose.

Also, Quengueza gave me Mombon, his overseer, chamberlain, steward, man of business, factotum; the man whose place it was to take care of the king's private affairs, set his slaves to work, oversee his plantations, and who had the care of the keys of the royal houses. Mombon was to see that I was made comfortable in town.

A man's wealth is reckoned here, first by the number of slaves he owns, next by the number of wives, and then by the number of chests. Chests are used to secure goods in. Therefore chests have come to be the synonym here for property of this kind, as banks indicate money with us. Now, chests, to be secure, must have locks, and therefore locks of American make are in great demand all over this country. Native locks are not very secure. But as locks secure chests, so keys are worn in great numbers as the outward symbol of ownership in locks and chests and property. And I found shams even in Goumbi, for several of my Commi friends had a great array of chests, most of which were empty; and indeed it is the mode to collect as many boxes as you can, no matter if you have nothing to put in them.

Some of their houses have locks also. But to have a lock you must have a door; and though this door is a very narrow, shabby affair, a whole great tree must be whittled down with their rude axes to make the board which shall answer for a door. Therefore doors are a luxury in Goumbi, as indeed also on the coast.

15

On the 8th we started for a two days' hunt. Etia and Gambo, the latter a son of Igoumba, an Ashira chief, and a noted hunter, and a few others, with myself, made up the party. We set out from Etia's house, where the old fellow had skulls of elephants, hippopotami, leopards, and gorillas ranged around as trophies of his prowess. Gambo was an ill-looking fellow, by reason of being much pitted with the small-pox; but he had fiery eyes, good courage, and a kind heart, as I discovered.

I was amused at a remark Quengueza made, as we started from the town together. "See," said he, to some people, "how hunters love each other! No matter if they come from different nations, and are different people. See how my white man loves these black hunters!"

We had been going through the woods about three hours, when at last we came upon fresh gorilla-tracks. Etia now set out by himself, while Gambo and I walked silently in another direction. The gorilla is so difficult of approach that we had literally to *creep* through the thick woods when in their vicinity. The dead silence and the tediousness of the approach, together with the fact that the hunter cannot expect to see his enemy till he is close upon him, while even then the gloom of the forest makes him but dimly visible—all this makes the hunt of this animal most trying to the nerves. For it is in the hunter's mind that if he misses—if his bullet does not speed to the most vital point—the wounded and infuriated animal will make short work of his opponent.

As we crept silently along, suddenly the woods resounded with the report of a gun. We sped at once towards the quarter whence the report came, and there found old Etia sitting complacently upon the dead body of the largest *female* gorilla I ever saw. He had hit her fatally with his first ball. The total height of the animal was 4 feet 7 inches; length of the hand, $7\frac{1}{2}$ inches; length of the foot from the hair comprising the heel, $8\frac{1}{2}$ inches; round of hand above the thumb, $9\frac{1}{4}$ inches; ditto under the thumb, 9 inches. *Length of the fingers (hands)*: thumbs, $1\frac{2}{5}$ inches; first finger, 4 inches; second, $4\frac{1}{4}$ inches; third, $3\frac{3}{4}$ inches; fourth, $3\frac{1}{2}$ inches. *Circumference of the fingers (hands)*; thumb, $2\frac{3}{4}$ inches; first finger, $3\frac{1}{2}$ inches; second,

4 inches; third, 3½ inches; fourth, 3 inches. *Circumference of the toes*: thumb, 3½ inches; first finger, 2¾ inches; second, 2¼ inches; third, 2½ inches; fourth, 1¾ inches. This was a huge animal for a female, for these are always much smaller than the males.

The next morning I heard a great commotion on the plantation, and learned that an old doctor, named Olanga-Condo, was to drink the *mboundou*. This is an intoxicating poison, which is believed by these people to confer on the drinker—if it do not kill him—the power of divination. It is much used in all this part of the country to try persons accused of witchcraft. A poor fellow is supposed to have bewitched his neighbour, or the king, and he is forced to drink mboundou to establish his innocence. If the man dies he is declared a witch. If he survives he is innocent. This ordeal is much dreaded by the negroes, who often run away from home and stay away all their lives rather than submit to it. The doctors have the reputation of being unharmed by the mboundou * and I am bound to admit that Olanga drank it without serious consequences. Nevertheless it is a deadly and speedy poison. I have seen it administered, and have seen the poor drinker fall down dead, with blood gushing from his mouth, eyes, and nose in five minutes after taking the dose. I was told by a native friend that sometimes, when the mboundou-drinker is really hated, the dose is strengthened secretly; and this was the case, I suppose, in those instances where I saw it prove

---

* I gave to Prof. John Torrey, of New York, some of the leaves and root of this remarkable plant for chemical analysis, and insert here the note in which he communicates his opinion as to its properties and chemical affinities.

"From the intensely poisonous quality of the root, and the symptoms which result from its administration, there can be little doubt that the active principle is a vegeto-alkali belonging to the *Strychnine* group. Under a powerful glass, I have not been able to detect any crystalline salt in the bark. The taste of the infusion is extremely bitter. The *ligneous* portion of the bark is much less active, is very hard, and, from the numerous annual rings, it must be of very slow growth.

"The mboundou pretty certainly belongs to a natural order that contains many venomous plants—viz., the LOGANIACEÆ; and, from the peculiar veining of the leaves, it is probably a species of *Strychnos* belonging to that section of the genus which includes *S. nux vomica*."

fatal. I have also been assured by negroes that sometimes the veins of the person who drinks it burst open.

This time I overlooked the whole operation. Several of the natives took the root and scraped it into a bowl. Into this a pint of water was poured. In about a minute fermentation took place: the ebullition looked very much like that of champagne when poured into a glass. The water then took the reddish colour of the cuticle of the mboundou root. When the fermentation subsided, Olanga was called by his friends. The drinker is not permitted to be present at the preparation of the mboundou, but he may send two friends to see that all is fair.

When Olanga came he emptied the bowl at a draught. In about five minutes the poison took effect. He began to stagger about. His eyes became bloodshot. His limbs twitched convulsively. His speech grew thick;* and other important symptoms showed themselves, which are considered as a sign that the poison will not be fatal. The man's whole behaviour was that of a drunken man. He began to babble wildly; and now it was supposed that the inspiration was upon him. Immediately they began to ask him whether any man was trying to bewitch Quengueza. This question was repeated several times. At last he said, "Yes, some one was trying to bewitch the king." Then came the query, "Who?" But by this time the poor fellow was fortunately hopelessly tipsy, and incapable of reasonable speech. He babbled some unintelligible jargon, and presently the palaver was declared over.

While he was being questioned, about one hundred people sat around with sticks in their hands. These they beat regularly upon the ground, and sung in a monotone—

"If he is a witch, let the mboundou kill him.
If he is not, let the mboundou go out."

The whole ceremony lasted about half an hour; and when

* A frequent and involuntary discharge of the urine is the surest indication that the mboundou will have no fatal effect, as it proved with Olanga, otherwise it is generally followed by death. The very words employed by the men when any one drinks the poison seem to imply what are its usual consequences.

it was over the people dispersed, and Olanga, who had by that time partially recovered, lay down to sleep. I was told that this old Olanga could drink the poison in very considerable quantities and at frequent intervals, with no other ill effect than this intoxication. This gave him, of course, a great name among these superstitious people.

Accusations of sorcery are really the cause of very many troubles and miseries among these people. On the 11th Obindji's younger brother was brought up on a charge of having bewitched to death his elder brother, Obindji's predecessor. This man had been dead a year, and his poor brother had already drunk mboundou three times to establish his innocence. Still the charge was pushed. He gave away some slaves for peace' sake. But now his brother-in-law demanded another trial. I interfered and procured his release, at least while I am here.

Next day (the 10th) we were to go to a considerable distance, to a spot where Etia gave me hopes we should catch a young gorilla alive, perhaps. This I was most anxious of all to do. I would have gone through any hardships and peril to get one large enough to be kept alive.

This time we had a large party: Etia, Gambo, myself, and ten men, each armed and laden with provisions for a couple of days. The men were covered with fetiches and charms. They had painted their faces red, and had cut their hands—this bleeding of the hands being done for luck. The fellows were very nearly naked—but this is their usual habit.

As for me, I had also made extra preparations. I had blackened my face and hands with powdered charcoal and oil, and my blue drill-shirt and trousers and black shoes made me as dark as any of them. My revolver hung at my side, with ammunition-bag and brandy-flask. My rifle lay upon my shoulder. All this excited the admiration of the crowd who assembled to see us set out.

Quengueza was greatly delighted, and exclaimed, "What kind of *ntangani* (white man) is this? He fears nothing; he cares for neither sun nor water; he loves nothing but the hunt."

The old fellow charged the people to take great care of his white man, and to defend him with their lives if need be.

We travelled all day, and about sunset came to a little river. Here we began at once to make a fire and leafy shelters for the night. Scarce was the firewood gathered, and we safely bestowed under our shelters, than a storm came up, which lasted half an hour. Then all was clear once more. We cooked plantains and smoked fish. I fried a piece of ham for myself; and, with tobacco afterwards, we were as jolly as could be. Now came stories of gorillas, to which I always listened with great interest. The natives of the whole gorilla region have like superstitions about these ferocious beasts, though each relater speaks from different authority.

"I remember," said one, "my father told me he once went out to the forest, when just in his path he met a great gorilla. My father had his spear in his hands; when the gorilla saw the spear he began to roar. Then my father was terrified and dropped his spear. When the gorilla saw that my father dropped the spear he was pleased. He looked at him, then left him and went into the thick forest. Then my father was glad, and went on his way."

Here all shouted together, "Yes! so we must do when we meet the gorilla. Drop the spear. That appeases him."

Next Gambo spoke: "Several dry seasons ago a man suddenly disappeared from my village after an angry quarrel. Some time after an Ashira of that village was out in the forest. He met a very large gorilla. That gorilla was the man who had disappeared. He had turned into a gorilla. He jumped on the poor Ashira, and bit a piece out of his arm. Then he let him go. Then the man came back, with his bleeding arm. He told me this. I hope we shall meet no such man-gorillas. They are very wicked. We would have terrible times."

Chorus: "No, we shall not meet such wicked gorillas."

Then one of the men spoke up: "If we kill a gorilla to-morrow, I should like to have a piece of the brain for my fetich. Nothing makes a man so brave as to have a fetich of gorilla's brain. This gives a man a strong heart."

Chorus (of those who remained awake): "Yes! this gives a man a strong heart."

Thus we gradually dropped off asleep.

Next morning we cleaned and reloaded our guns, and started off to the hunting ground. We had gone on about an hour when we heard the cry of a young gorilla after its mother. Etia heard it first, and at once pointed out the direction in which it was.

At once we began to walk with greater caution than before, and presently Etia and Gambo crept ahead, as they were expert with the net, and also the best woodsmen. I unwillingly remained behind, but dared not go with them lest my clumsier movements should betray our presence.

In about half an hour we heard two guns fired. Running up we found the mother-gorilla shot, but her little one had escaped. They had not been able to catch it.

The poor mother lay there in her gore, but the little fellow was off in the woods; so we concealed ourselves hard by to wait for its return. Presently it came up, jumped on its mother, began sucking at her breasts and fondling her. Then Etia, Gambo, and I rushed upon it. Though evidently less than two years old, it proved very strong, and escaped from us. But we gave chase, and in a few minutes had it fast; not, however, before one of the men had his arm severely bitten by the wicked little wretch.

It proved to be a young female. We carried it back to the mother, first securing it with some stout cords and sticks. It ran to its dead mother, and in a touching way buried its head in her bosom, and seemed really to feel grief.

We determined to go back to the camp for the day. The mother was at once skinned, and I took skin and skeleton, while the men divided the meat among them. The little one was then carried along, but proved very troublesome, making savage attempts to bite all who came near her.

The mother-gorilla was 4 feet 4 inches in height; the little one was 2 feet 1 inch high.

The little one, unhappily, lived but ten days after capture. She persistently refused to eat any cooked food, and anything, in fact, but the nuts and berries which they eat in the forest, and which my men were obliged to gather daily for her use. She was not so ferocious as the male I had before, but quite as treacherous and quite as untamable. She permitted no one to approach her without making offensive demonstrations. Her eyes seemed somewhat milder, but had the same gloomy and treacherous look, and she had the same way as my other intractable captive of looking you straight in the eyes when she was meditating an attack. I remarked also the same manœuvre practised by the other when she wished to seize something—say my leg, which, by reason of her chain, she could not reach with her arm; she looked me straight in the face, then quick as a flash threw her body on one leg and arm, and reached out with the other leg. Several times I had narrow escapes of a grip from her strong great-toe. I thought I saw sometimes that when she looked at me it was as though she were cross-eyed, but of this I could not make certain. All her motions were remarkably quick, and her strength, though so small and young, was extraordinary.

While she was alive no woman who was *enceinte*, nor the husband of such woman, dared approach her cage. They believe firmly that should the husband of a woman with child, or the woman herself, see a gorilla, even a dead one, she would give birth to a gorilla, and not to a human child. This superstition I have noticed among other tribes too, and only in the case of the gorilla.

When we returned to town I found the king making a tremendous row about the misconduct of a piece of property he had inherited from his deceased brother.

Now the piece of property which had caused Quengueza's ire was the favourite wife of the deceased king. The mourning-time was nearly over, and Quengueza had announced that the royal widows should be divided among his male relatives—cousins—he reserving to himself only one or two of the best-looking. Now the royal fancy had been set particularly upon this one in question, and she, with feminine perverseness, had been caught in an intrigue with a common—but very good-looking—fellow of the town. Quengueza was highly enraged. He swore he would not take a single one of his brother's widows. He swore revenge on the fellow who had so displaced him. The people were very much distressed. They came in a body and begged him to take at least two of his brother's wives. The town was agitated the whole day upon the important question; and I was pleased to hear at sunset that Quengueza had at last thought it best to accede to the wishes of his people. So that fuss was over.

On the 18th of March I asked Quengueza to help me forward to the interior. The Bakalai and Ashira chiefs had both asked me to come to their country, assuring me good hunts and kind treatment.

On the 22nd, we got off for up the river. Quengueza and I with my baggage were in a large canoe, which had twenty-two paddlers. The Ashira and Bakalai chiefs followed in other canoes, and after them followed several Goumbi canoes. It was intensely hot. Even the negroes suffered; and, though I had a thick umbrella over my head, and sat quite still, I had frequently to bathe my head, for I feared a sunstroke.

The river is narrow but quite deep above Goumbi, and the current is much stronger than below. It is, in fact, now a real and live river, flowing in a deep channel between high lands and hills.

The first town we stopped at was Akaka, the first of the Bakalai towns, about fifteen miles from Goumbi. From here I could see the high mountains of the far interior. They rose blue against the sky to the E.N.E.

A little before we got to Akaka we came to a holy place on the river called *Evendja-Quengouai*. Here all hands got out of the canoes to dance. It is the rule that all who have not passed up the river before shall sing a song of praise to the god of the place, and pluck a branch from a tree which must be set in the mud near the shore. This is for luck. Poor Makondai was hurried off to take his share in the devotions before I knew what was going to be done.

In the afternoon we lay by at a plantation, while a terrible rainstorm burst over the country, cooling the air deliciously. These storms, which come up at this season nearly every day, help one to bear the dreadful heat which, without this relief, would be, I believe, insupportable. To-day at noon my thermometer stood at 119° Fahrenheit in the shade of my umbrella.

When we stopped for breakfast next day, I noticed a little way from us an extraordinary tree, quite the largest in height and circumference I ever saw in Africa. It was a real monarch of even this great forest. It rose in one straight and majestic trunk entirely branchless, till the top reached far above all the surrounding trees. There at the top the branches were spread out somewhat like an umbrella, but could not give much shade, being so high. I found that this tree was highly venerated by the people, who call it the *oloumi*. Its kind are not common even here, where its home is said to be. Its bark is said to have certain healing properties, and is also in request from a belief that if a man going off on a trading expedition washes himself first all over in a decoction of its juices in water, he will be lucky and shrewd in making bargains. For this reason great strips were torn off this tree to the height of at least twenty feet.

Bakalai villages became more frequent; and I see that these people are more energetic and provident than the sea-shore tribes. At Mpopo I saw thousands of plantain trees surrounding the village. Finally we arrived at the village of Obindji, a chief who is a great friend of Quengueza's.

We came up firing guns and singing songs. When we approached the shore Obindji came down in great state, dressed in his silk hat (the crown), a coat and shirt, and a nice cloth. He was ringing his kendo, a bell, which is the insignia of kingship here and among some other tribes of Central Africa—something like a royal sceptre.

I said, "Why do you ring your kendo?" *

---

* The kendo is a rude bell of iron, fashioned with a long handle, also of iron and of the same piece, as shown in the engraving. The sound which with us announces the vicinity of a herd of cows or sheep, in Africa precedes the advent of the sovereign, who uses the kendo only when on visits of state or on business of importance. The skin represented on the cut in the opposite page, is stuffed into the bell to prevent the possibility of its sounding when not required.

He replied, "Obindji's heart is glad, and he thanks his Mboundji (fetich) that he has to-day come up higher than he ever stood before. A Mbuiri (spirit) has come to see Obindji."

When we were landed, and the two kings and I were seated in chairs, the grand reception began. Quengueza gave an account of his entire intercourse with me from the time he came down to see me to the present hour. All was said in short sentences; and the people who listened gave frequent approval. Then Obindji replied, giving, in like manner, a statement of his feelings when he heard that Quengueza was about to bring a white man to see him, etc.

The town of Obindji is about 140 miles from the mouth of the river. The clan is very powerful; but when their chief wished to remove to the river from his inland settlement, most of his people refused.

They have a few guns among them; but a man who owns a gun and some powder is rich. They were much astonished at my percussion-locks, and yet more at my revolver, which was a constant marvel to them. Revolvers of simple construction would bring almost any price among these people if they could be made with flint-locks.

KENDO.

The town, and another which lay just above, separated from Obindji's by a narrow creek, were surrounded with extensive manioc plantations. Here I notice again that the Bakalai raise better crops than the lower tribes.

One very old chief came down from his town, over a hundred miles farther up the river. When he came ashore Quengueza and I went to see him in his house, waiving ceremony on account of his age. When he saw me he started back, and was much moved. He exclaimed, "You are not a man. You are a mbuiri" (spirit). He had come the long journey, he said, to see the man who made guns and powder.

I had a laugh at Quengueza, who endeavours to teach all his neighbours the ideas he gets from me. In common with many of his subjects, the old fellow was much troubled with fleas, and when, as he stood talking with me, a flea became too troublesome, he used to adroitly catch him, and gravely *crack* him on his thumbnail. This disgusted me so that I remonstrated, and at last succeeded in reforming this one of his abuses. But no sooner had he given up the disgusting practice himself, than he at once forbade it to all his own subjects, and became a most zealous advocate of decency among our Bakalai friends.

"Why do you crack your fleas before my white man, eh? Dirty fellow! Go away! You make my white man sick!" he used to cry out. And to-day, when we had our interview with the up-river chief, Quengueza was equally zealous— though more polite—with him. But the old man replied, "Thus have I done all my life—it is now too late;" and gravely continued his massacre.

Obindji's chair is a remarkable specimen of furniture, the only question arising in my mind is to know how my friend Obindji finds comfort in such a position. It is really amusing to me to look at him while he is seated on a little stool, his back resting on the main part of the arm-chair, while his arms are supported by two of the roots. In this attitude he seems to enjoy his pipe most wonderfully, and presents a perfect type of African laziness. The easy-chair is made out of a single root of a tree.

As Obindji's village is to be our headquarters, we are having houses built. The men have gone out into the forest to collect bark, and leaves, and posts. Meantime Sunday came, and I requested Quengueza to make the men rest on this day, explaining to him the nature of our Sabbath.

The old man was puzzled for a moment, then said:—

"We are much hurried now. Suppose you put off the Sunday for three or four weeks; then we can have as many Sundays as you want."

I had a slight attack of fever, caused doubtless by the great heat we suffered from on the river. Some of the men had fever, too, and also Quengueza's brother. I gave them quinine, which cured them and relieved me too.

Up-river chiefs continue to come in with their wives, slaves, and people—all anxious to see the man who makes guns, beads, iron and brass kettles, etc.; and all rapt in astonishment at my strange appearance. Many of the chiefs are

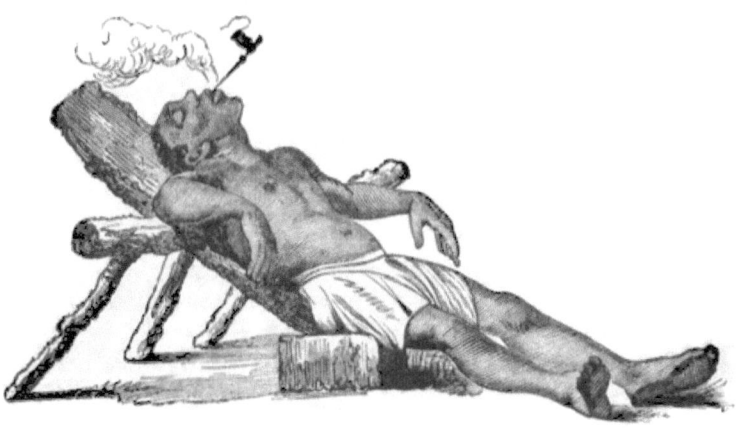

OBINDJI IN HIS EASY-CHAIR.

fine-looking fellows, well armed with spears and bows. They seem brave and warlike.

On the 30th my house was done. I had with me an American clock; and this excited the constant wonder and awe of the people, who could not be persuaded but it was a spirit, and a very powerful spirit, keeping watch over me. A Bakalai chief who is to hunt with me brought me in a female gorilla which he had killed in the woods. This female was not quite full-grown. It measured three feet eleven inches. Its canine teeth had not attained their full size. The face was intensely black, as were also the hands and feet. The hair on the crown was reddish, but not so deep a colour as in some older females I have seen. On the body the hair was a blackish-red, and no longer on the arms than on the rest of the body. The breast was covered only with very light down.

On the 2nd of April I saw another trial by ordeal performed. A little boy, son to Aquailai, the doctor who had driven the witch from the main street of Goumbi, reported that one of Quengueza's men had damaged a Bakalai canoe. The owner required to be paid for the injury. The Goumbi man denied the act, and asked for trial. An Ashira doctor was called in, who said that the only way to make the truth appear was by the trial of the ring boiled in oil. Hereupon the Bakalai and the Goumbi men gathered together, and the trial was at once made.

The Ashira doctor set three little billets of bar-wood in the ground with their ends together, then piled some smaller pieces between, till all were laid as high as the three pieces. A native pot half-full of palm-oil was set upon the wood, and the oil was set on fire. When it burned up brightly a brass ring from the doctor's hand was cast into the pot; the doctor stood by with a little va-e full of grass soaked in water, of which he threw in now and then some bits. This made the oil blaze up afresh. At last all was burned out, and now came the trial. The accuser, the little boy, was required to take the ring out of the pot. He hesitated, but was pushed on by his father. The people cried out, "Let us see if he lied or told truth."

Finally he put his hand in, seized the red-hot ring, but quickly dropped it, having severely burnt his fingers. At this there was a shout, "He lied! he lied!" and the Goumbi man was declared innocent.

I ventured to suggest that he also would burn his fingers if he touched the ring; but nobody seemed to consider this view. I judge that where an accuser has to substantiate a charge in this way information is not easily to be got.

CHAPTER XVIII.

I discover a new ape—The kooloo-kamba—Gouamba, or craving for meat—Troublesome flies—Malaouen—Numerous traces of gorilla—Killing a large male gorilla—Start for the ebony country—The ebony tree—Severe attack of fever—Take 150 grains of quinine in three days—Kindness of women during my illness—Death of a young wizard—Killing a nshiego-mbouvé—Capture of a young nshiego-mbouvé—His face is white—His mother is black—The young nshiego-mbouvé becomes tame—He turns darker as he grows older—Privileges of women—The idol said to have walked and talked.

On the 6th we set off for a two or three days' hunt. We went up-river for about ten miles, and then struck inland to a deserted Bakalai village, where we made our camp. When that was arranged we went out to look for gorilla-tracks. It was too late to hunt; but Querlaouen, my chief hunter, wanted to be ready for the morrow. I saw nothing; but Malaouen, another hunter, came in after dark, and said he had heard the cry of the kooloo, and knew where to find it in the morning. I myself on returning to the camp had heard this cry, but did not know what animal had uttered it.

Of course I asked what this kooloo was, and received for answer a circumstantial description of the animal, which threw me into the greatest excitement; for I saw that this was most certainly a new species of ape, of which I had not even heard as yet. It was called *kooloo-kamba,* by the Goumbi people, from its noise or call, " kooloo," and the Commi word *kamba,* which means " speak." The Bakalai call it simply " koola."

The kooloo was said to be very rare here, and there was a chance only that we should find that one whose call had been heard.

At the earliest streak of dawn I had my men up. We had fixed our guns the night before. All was ready, and we set out in two parties. My party had been walking through the forest about an hour, when suddenly I stepped into a file of bashikouay ants, whose fierce bites nearly made me scream.

We had hardly got clear of the bashikouays when my ears

were saluted by the singular cry of the ape I was after. "Koola-kooloo, koola-kooloo," it said several times. Gambo and Malaouen alone were with me. Gambo and I raised our eyes, and saw, high up in a tree-branch, a large ape. We both fired at once, and the next moment the poor beast fell with a heavy crash to the ground. I rushed up, anxious to see if, indeed, I had a new animal. I saw in a moment that it was neither a nshiego-mbouvé, nor a chimpanzee, nor a gorilla. Again I had a happy day—marked for ever with red ink in my calendar.

We at once disembowelled the animal, which was a male. I found in its intestines only vegetable matter and remains. The skin and skeleton were taken into camp, where I cured the former with arsenic sufficiently to take it into Obindji.

The animal was a full-grown male, four feet three inches high. It was less powerfully built than the male gorilla, but as powerful as either the chimpanzee or nshiego-mbouvé. When it was brought into Obindji, all the people and even Quengueza, at once exclaimed, "That is a kooloo-kamba."

The kooloo-kamba has for distinctive marks a very round head; whiskers running quite round the face and below the chin; the face is round; the cheek-bones prominent; the cheeks sunken; the jaws not very prominent—less so than in any of the apes. The hair is black; long on the arm, which was, however, partly bare.

Of its habits these people could tell me nothing, except that farther interior it was found more frequently, and that it was, like the gorilla, very shy and hard of approach.

Meat was now becoming scarce. Half a boar given me by Querlaouen was welcome to me, as indeed it was to Quengueza, whom we found almost crying with an affection which is common in Africa, and is called *gouamba*—but for which we, happily, have no name. *Gouamba* is the inordinate longing and craving of exhausted nature for meat. The vegetable diet here is not of a satisfying nature at best. Just now all provisions were scarce in Obindji, and even Quengueza had not tasted meat for four days. He was exhausted, nervous, and, though a stout old fellow, really whimpering. This

THE KOOLOO-KAMBA.

was *gouamba*, of which I have suffered often enough in these wilds to vouch that it is a real and frightful torture.

I came into the village just when the ceremonial dance was about to be performed which precedes the division of elephant meat. This is a thankoffering to two spirits, *Mondo* and *Olombo*, who seem to have an influence on the hunt. An Ashira doctor was leading in the ceremonies. I find here, as I have heard it said also in more civilized countries, that the prophet gains in repute the farther he travels from home. In Goumbi a Bakalai doctor was held in high esteem. In Biagano a Goumbi doctor was chief of all the prophets. Here, among the Bakalai, only an Ashira doctor was thought worthy. So it goes.

They had three pieces, cut from the hind-quarters of the elephants, boiling in large pots. Around these they danced, while the Ashira doctor chanted praises and petitions to the spirits. A piece was cut off and sent into the woods to appease the hunger of these deities (or more likely of their representatives, the leopards), and then the rest was eaten. Next came the division of the great heaps of uncooked meat. The town, the town's friends, the hunters, the hunter's friends, and *their* friends, all came and got shares. I received about fifty pounds for myself; I was glad to have it; for meat was scarce, and I had the appetite of a hunter.

The killing of an elephant is an event among the Bakalai here, not only for the meat, but because the ivory is sent down to the coast, and procures for them the cloth, powder, guns, trinkets, etc.

Hunting in the rear of the village, on the 15th, I shot a curious bird, the *Alethe castanea*—a new species. It is said by the natives to have a devil in it—for what reason I could not discover; probably for none. But its habit makes it singular. They fly in a small flock, and follow industriously the bashikouay ants in their marches about the country. The bird is insectivorous; and when the bashikouay army routs before it the frightened grasshoppers and beetles, the bird, like a regular camp-follower, pounces on the prey and carries it off. I think it does not eat the bashikouay.

Snakes are quite abundant in these woods. As we push

through the bush we often see some great anaconda hanging from a projecting bough, waiting its prey. The other day I shot a little bird which, in its fall, lodged among some vines. I was anxious to get it, and began to climb up after it. Just as I was reaching out for my bird, a snake, belonging to one of the most venomous kinds found in this part of Africa, stuck out his head at me from the thick vine foliage. I was very much startled, and dropped down to the ground without loss of time.

Fortunately I had only to drop a few feet. It was one of the narrowest escapes I had in Africa—for there is no cure for this serpent's bite, and I could literally feel its breath against my face before I saw it.

Singularly few accidents happen from snake-bites among the natives. They wander everywhere barefooted, and seem to have no dread till they see a snake, when they scamper off fast enough if it is very venomous. The python they kill because they like its meat, which, they say, makes a delicious soup.

When, as here, I am hunting regularly, I get up at five in the morning. Monguilomba then makes me a strong cup of coffee, which is served by Makondai. This drunk, daylight shows itself; I start for the bush and hunt until ten, which is my breakfast-hour. After breakfast I stuff the birds shot in the morning, and rest till three. Then out again into the bush till six, which is sunset and dark here, when I get back and find my dinner ready, with Makondai to wait on me. After dinner bird-stuffing goes on again, till all the prizes of the day are secure. That done, I go among the people and hear them talk until it is time to go to sleep.

This is the average day. Of course, when we go out on great hunts, all orderly arrangements are broken up; and I have often to sit up half or all the night to prepare my prizes, which will not keep till next day in this hot climate.

On Tuesday, the 20th of April, we set out for one of our great hunts, going up the river a short distance and then striking into the forests. We found many open spots in these woods, where the soil was sandy, and the grass was not very luxuriant, growing not more than two feet high. The sun is very oppressive in these clear spots.

We were troubled, too, on the prairie by two very savage flies, called by the negroes the *boco* and the *nchouna*. These insects attacked us with a terrible persistency which left us no peace. They were very quiet bloodsuckers, and I never knew of their attacks till I felt the itch which follows the bite when the fly has left it. This is again followed by a little painful swelling.

The next day we were out after gorillas, which we knew were to be found hereabouts by the presence of a pulpy pear-shaped fruit growing close to the ground, the *tondo*, of which this animal is very fond. I also am very fond of the subdued and grateful acid of this fruit, which the negroes eat as well as the gorilla. It is curious that that which grows in the sandy soil of the prairie is not fit to eat.

We found everywhere gorilla-marks, and so recent that we began to think the animals must be avoiding us. This was the case, I think, though I am not sure. At any rate we beat the bush for two hours before, at last, we found the game. Suddenly an immense gorilla advanced out of the wood straight towards us, and gave vent as he came up to a terrible howl of rage—as much as to say, "I am tired of being pursued, and will face you."

It was a lone male—the kind who are always most ferocious; and this fellow made the woods ring with his roar.

He was about twenty yards off when we first saw him. We at once gathered together, and I was about to take aim and bring him down where he stood, when Malaouen stopped me, saying, in a whisper, "Not time yet."

We stood therefore in silence, guns in hand. The gorilla looked at us for a minute or so out of his evil gray eyes, then beat his breast with his gigantic arms, gave another howl of defiance, and advanced upon us.

Again he stopped, now not more than fifteen yards away. Still Malaouen said, "Not yet."

Then again an advance upon us. Now he was not twelve yards off. I could see plainly the ferocious face of the monstrous ape. It was working with rage; his huge teeth were

ground against each other so that we could hear the sound; the skin of the forehead was moved rapidly backwards and forwards, and gave a truly devilish expression to the hideous face; once more he gave out a roar which seemed to shake the woods like thunder, and, looking us in the eyes and beating his breast, advanced again. This time he came within eight yards of us before he stopped. My breath was coming short with excitement as I watched the huge beast. Malaouen said only "Steady!" as he came up.

When he stopped, Malaouen said, "Now." And before he could utter the roar for which he was opening his mouth, three musket-balls were in his body. He fell dead almost without a struggle.

"Don't fire too soon. If you do not kill him he will kill you," said Malaouen to me—a piece of advice which I found afterwards was too literally true.

It was a huge old beast indeed. Its height was five feet six inches. Its arms had a spread of seven feet two inches. Its huge brawny chest measured fifty inches round. The big toe or thumb of its foot measured $5\frac{3}{4}$ inches in circumference. Its arm seemed only immense bunches of muscle, and its legs and claw-like feet were so well fitted for *grabbing* and holding, that I could see how easy it was for the negroes to believe that this animal conceals itself in trees, and pulls up with its foot any living thing—leopard, ox, or man—that passes beneath. There is no doubt the gorilla *could* do this, but that he *does* it I do not believe. They are ferocious, mischievous, but not carnivorous.

The face of this gorilla was intensely black. The vast chest, which proved his great power, was bare, and covered with a parchment-like skin. The body was covered with gray hair. Though there are sufficient points of diversity between this animal and man, I never kill one without having a sickening realization of the horrid human likeness of the beast. This was particularly the case to-day, when the animal approached us in its fierce way, walking on its hind legs, and facing us as few animals dare face man.

On the 27th of April Quengueza and I, with about twenty

slaves and some hunters, started up river for the ebony country, where the king wished to cut wood, while I hunted. All the forests up here are full of precious woods. Ebony is found in greatest plenty at the top of the hills which line, at some distance, the river-course. Bar-wood is found everywhere, and in great abundance. The natives have not yet cut much of it. The india-rubber vine is found on all hands. There are also many other varieties of hard woods, some pink, some chestnut, some yellow in colour, and all susceptible of a high polish.

The ebony-tree is not found on low ground, or near the river. It is met with all along the ridges and hills which run here north and south. It is one of the finest and most graceful trees of the African forest. Its leaves are long, sharp-pointed, dark green, and hang in clusters, producing a grateful shade. Its bark is smooth, and of a dark-green. The trunk rises straight and clean to a considerable height—often fifty or sixty feet; then large heavy branches are sent out. I have seen one of these trees which had a diameter of five feet at the base. The mature ebony-tree is always found hollow, and even its branches are hollow. Next the bark is a white "sap-wood," which is not valuable. This, in an average tree, is three or four inches thick, and next to this lies the ebony of commerce. The young trees are white or sappy to the centre; and even when they attain a diameter of nearly two feet the black part is streaked with white. Trees less than three feet in diameter are not cut down.

The ebony-tree is found intermixed with others in the forest. Generally three or four trees stand together, and none others within a little distance. Thus the cutters move through the woods constantly seeking trees.

As we were to stay a month, the king took some of his wives with him. We pulled up the river against the strong current as before.

We were bound to the town of a chief named Anguilai, whom I had met at Obindji's village. The place was called N'calai-Boumba, and was a considerable town, though very lately built. We were nearly all day on our journey. On the way we passed several villages. The river-banks all the way up are densely wooded. We saw but one monkey and a few birds the whole day.

Anguilai's town is the hottest place I had thus far been in in Africa. Most of the negroes have wit enough to build on the top of some hill, where they get a breeze. But this town was set in a hollow, and the houses were so small and close as to be quite unendurable to me. All these Rembo Bakalai are but lately come from the interior. They have been induced to move to the river by Quengueza, who makes them useful to him, and they are not yet at home there. N'calai Boumba was not yet a year old. The people were still awkward canoe-men.

On the 29th I went down to a little village called Npopo, and found the people all gone into the bush. Everything was open and exposed to thieves; chickens and goats were straying about, and I wondered to see such carelessness in the village. But in the centre, looking down on everything, stood the *mbuiti*, or idol of Npopo, a copper-eyed divinity, who, I was informed, safely guarded everything. It seemed absurd; but I was assured that no one dared steal, and no one did steal, with the eyes of this mbuiti upon him.

This uncommonly useful divinity was a rudely-shaped piece of ebony about two feet high, with a man's face, the nose and eyes of copper, and the body covered with grass.

On the last day of April I was confined to my bed with fever. In three days I took 150 grains of quinine and two heavy doses of calomel. This was the severest attack I had yet had in Africa. I suffered very much from the heat in the little houses, and was glad when Quengueza had his *shades* built on the ebony-ground and we moved thither.

While I lay sick the people came and entreated me not to hunt so much and so constantly. They said, "Look at us; we hunt one day and rest two. When we hunt three days we rest a week after it. But you go out every day!" I think they are right, and shall follow their rule.

I shall never forget the kindness of the women to me while I was sick. Poor souls! they are sadly abused by their task-masters; are the merest slaves, have to do all the drudgery, and take blows and ill-usage besides; and yet at the sight of suffering their hearts soften just as in our own more civilized lands; and here, as there, no sooner did sickness come than these kind people came to nurse and take care of me. They tried to cook nice food for me; they sat by me to fan me; they brought more mats for my bed; brought me water; got me refreshing fruits from the woods; and at night, when I waked up from a feverish dream, I used to hear their voices as they sat around in the darkness, and pitied me and devised ways for my cure. They thought some *aniemba* (devil) had entered my body, and could not be persuaded that I was not bewitched.

Poor Anguilai was sadly alarmed at my illness. He accused his people of wickedly bewitching me; and one still night walked up and down the village, threatening, in a loud voice, to kill the sorcerers if he could only find them.

On the 5th of May I was able to walk again a little, and on the 6th one of those barbarous scenes occurred in the village which show how even these kind-hearted negroes are incited to horrid cruelties by their devilish superstitions. A little boy of ten years had been accused of sorcery. On being examined, he confessed that he had "made a witch." Hereupon the whole town seemed to be seized of the devil. They took spears and knives, and actually cut the poor little fellow to pieces. I had been walking out, and returned just as the dreadful scene was over. I doubt if I could have saved his life had I been on the spot. As it was, I could not even make the wretched men feel shame at their bloody act. They were still frantic with rage, and were not quiet for some hours after.

The next day I witnessed another curious scene of superstition. One of the king's wives stood up in the open street and had herself cut on the back of her hands with knives. She bled very freely, and seemed to be very glad in her heart at the pain inflicted on her. I asked what was the reason for such conduct; and she explained, with a smiling face, that she was weakly and barren, and that now she would be strong and have children. It seems to be their method of letting blood.

On the 8th we started for the ebony-woods. Our new

location was about nine miles from the river, on the side of a long hill, and close by where a cool sparkling rivulet leaped from rock to rock down into the plain, making most pleasant music for me as I lay, weak and sick, in camp. Five huge ebony-trees lifted their crowned heads together in a little knot just above us. All around were pleasant and shady woods. It was a very pleasant camp, but proved to have one drawback: we nearly starved to death. On the 11th we began to suffer from gouamba, and got no meat. So I went out myself and shot several birds.

At last I could stand the *gouamba*, or craving for animal food, no longer, and determined to make up a regular hunting-party, and stay out till we got something to eat. Malaouen told me that if we went off about twenty miles we should come to a better game country; and so we started in the direction he pointed out, where, he thought, we should also find the gorilla, or perhaps the nshiego-mbouvé.

The men were covered with greegrees and fetiches, and had cut their hands for luck. Anguilai told me that his *ogana* (idol) had told him that to-morrow the heart of *otanga* (the white man) would be glad, for we should kill game.

For some hours after we started we saw nothing but old tracks of different wild beasts, and I began to think that Anguilai's *ogana* had been too sanguine. Finally, towards twelve o'clock, when we were crossing a kind of high table-land, we heard the cry of a young animal, which we all recognised to be a nshiego-mbouvé. Then all my troubles at once went away out of my mind, and I no longer felt either sick or hungry.

We crawled through the bush as silently as possible, still hearing the baby-like cry. At last, coming out into a little cleared space, we saw something running along the ground towards the spot where we stood concealed. When it came nearer we saw it was a female nshiego-mbouvé, running on all-fours, with a young one clinging to her breasts. She was eagerly eating some berries, and with one arm supported her little one.

Querlaouen, who had the fairest chance, fired, and brought her down. She dropped without a struggle. The poor little one cried "Hew! hew! hew!" and clung to the dead body, sucking the breasts, burying its head there in its alarm at the report of the gun.

We hurried up in great glee to secure our capture. I cannot tell my surprise when I saw that the nshiego baby's face was pure white—*very* white indeed—pallid, but as white as a white child's.

I looked at the mother, but found her black as soot in the face. The little one was about a foot in height. One of the men threw a cloth over its head and secured it till we could make it fast with a rope; for, though it was quite young, it could walk. The old one was of the bald-headed kind, of which I had secured the first known specimen some months before.

I immediately ordered a return to the camp, which we reached towards evening. The little nshiego had been all this time separated from its dead mother, and now, when it was put near her body, a most touching scene ensued. The little fellow ran instantly to her, but, touching her on the face and breast, saw evidently that some great change had happened. For a few minutes he caressed her, as though trying to coax her back to life. Then he seemed to lose all hope. His little eyes became very sad, and he broke out in a long plaintive wail, "Ooee! ooee! ooee!" which made my heart ache for him. He looked quite forlorn, and as though he really felt his forsaken lot. The whole camp was touched at his sorrows, and the women were especially moved.

All this time I stood wonderingly staring at the white face of the creature. It was really marvellous and quite incomprehensible; and a more strange and weird-looking animal I never saw.

While I stood there, up came two of my hunters and began to laugh at me. "Look, Chelly!" said they, calling me by the name I was known by among them, "look at your friend. Every time we kill gorilla, you tell us, 'Look at your black friend!' Now, you see, look at your white friend!" Then came a roar at what they thought a tremendously good joke.

"Look! he has got straight hair, just as you have. See white face of your cousin from the bush? He is nearer to you than gorilla is to us."

And another roar.

"Gorilla has not got woolly hair like we have. This one has straight hair, like you."

"Yes," said I; "but when he gets old his face is black; and do not you see his nose how flat it is, like yours?"

Whereat there was a louder laugh than before. For, so long as he can laugh, the negro cares little against whom the joke goes.

I may as well add here some particulars of the little fellow who excited all this surprise and merriment. He lived five months, and became as tame and docile as a cat. I called him Tommy, to which name he soon began to answer.

In three days after his capture he was quite tame. He then ate biscuits out of my hand; ate boiled rice and roasted plantain; and drank the milk of a goat. Two weeks after his capture he was perfectly tamed, and no longer required to be tied up. He ran about the camp, and when we went back to Obindji's village, found his way about everywhere and into the huts just as though he had been raised there.

He had a great affection for me, and used constantly to follow me about. When I sat down, he was not content till he had climbed upon me and hid his head in my breast. He was extremely fond of being petted and fondled, and would sit by the hour while anyone stroked his head or back.

He soon began to be a very great thief. When the people left their huts he would steal in and make off with their plantains or fish. He watched very carefully till all had left a house, and it was difficult to catch him in the act. I flogged him several times, and, indeed, brought him to the conviction that it was *wrong* to steal; but he could never resist the temptation.

From me he stole constantly. He soon found out that my hut was better furnished with ripe bananas and other fruit than any others; and also he discovered that the best time to steal from me was when I was asleep in the morning. At that time he used to crawl in on his tiptoes, move slyly towards my bed, look at my closed eyes, and, if he saw no movement, with an air of great relief go up and pluck several plantains. If I stirred in the least he was off like a flash, and would presently re-enter for another inspection. If my eyes were open when he came in on such a predatory trip, he at once came up to me with an honest face, and climbed up and caressed me. But I could easily detect an occasional wistful glance towards the bunch of plantains.

My hut had no door, but was closed with a mat, and it was very funny to see Tommy gently raising one corner of this mat to see if I was asleep. Sometimes I counterfeited sleep, and then stirred just as he was in the act of taking off his prize. Then he would drop everything, and make off in the utmost consternation.

He knew the hours of our meals, and was present at as many of them as possible; that is, he would go from my breakfast to half-a-dozen others, and beg something at each. But he never missed my breakfast and dinner, knowing by experience that he fared best there. I had a kind of rude table made, on which my meals were served in the open part of my house. This was too high for Tommy to see the dishes; so he used to come in before I sat down, when all was ready, and climb up on the pole which supported the roof. From this perch he attentively surveyed every dish on the table, and, having determined what to have, he would descend and sit down at my side.

If I did not immediately pay attention to him he began to howl, "Hew! hew! hew!" louder and louder, till for peace sake his wants were satisfied. Of course I could not tell what he had chosen for dinner of my different dishes, and would offer him first one, and then another, till the right one came. If he received what he did not want, he threw it down on the ground with a little shriek of anger and a stamp of his foot; and this was repeated till he was served to his liking. In short, he behaved very much like a badly-spoiled child.

If I pleased him quickly, he thanked me by a kind of gentle murmur, like "Hoohoo!" and would hold out his hand to shake mine. He was very fond of boiled meat—particularly boiled fish, and was constantly picking bones he collected about the town. He wanted always to taste of my coffee, and when Makondai brought it, would beg of me, in the most serious manner, for some, and if given without sugar he would not drink it.

I made him a little pillow to sleep on, and this he was very fond of. When he was once accustomed to it he never parted from it more, but dragged it after him wherever he went. If by any chance it was lost, the whole camp knew it by his howls; and sometimes I had to send people to look for it when he had mislaid it on some forest excursion, so that he might stop his noise. He slept on it always, coiled up into a little heap, and only relinquished it when I gave him permission to accompany me into the woods.

As he became more and more used to our ways, he grew more impatient of contradiction, and more fond of being caressed; and whenever he was thwarted he howled in his disagreeable way. As the dry season came on it became colder, and Tommy began to wish for company when he slept, to keep him warm. The negroes would not have him for a companion, for he was for them too much like one of themselves. I would not give him room near me. So poor Tommy was reduced to misery, as he seemed to think. But soon I found that he waited till everybody was fast asleep at night, and then crawled in softly next some of his black friends, and slept there till earliest dawn. Then he would up and away undiscovered. Several times he was caught and beaten, but he always tried it again.

He showed an extraordinary fondness for strong drink. Whenever a negro had palm-wine Tommy was sure to know it. He had a decided taste for Scotch ale, of which I had a few bottles, and even begged for brandy. Indeed, his last exploit was with a brandy-bottle, which, on going out, I had carelessly left on my chest. The little rascal stole in, and seeing it, and being unable to get out the cork, in some way broke it. When I returned, after some hours' absence, I found my precious bottle—it was the last, and to the traveller in this part of Africa, brandy is as indispensable as quinine

—broken in pieces, and Master Tommy coiled up on the floor by the side of the fragments in a state of maudlin drunkenness. When he saw me, he got up and tried to stagger up to me, but his legs tottered, and he fell down several times. His eyes had a glare of human drunkenness; his arms were extended in vain attempts to reach me; his voice came thick; in fact, he looked disgustingly and yet comically human. It was the maudlin and sentimental stage of human drunkenness very well represented. I gave him a severe thrashing, which served to sober the little toper somewhat; but nothing could cure him of his love for liquor.

He had a great deal of intelligence; and if I had had leisure I think I might have trained him to some kind of good behaviour, though I despaired of his thieving disposition. He lived so long, and was growing so accustomed to civilized life, that I began to have great hopes of being able to carry him alive to America. He delighted to eat with the negroes; while they were seated round the dish he used to dip his hands into it at the same time they did. As the dry season advanced, and the nights grew cooler, he became exceedingly fond of sitting near the fire with the men in the evening; and Master Tommy seemed then to enjoy himself wonderfully, and quite as much as any human being. From time to time he looked up into the faces of those round him, as if to say, " Do not drive me away ! " and the very white colour of his face contrasted singularly with the black heads around him. His eye was intelligent, and when left to himself his whole countenance had a look of sadness, sometimes painful to behold. Many times I tried to penetrate and read the inward thoughts of this wonderful little creature, which not only excited my wonder, but that of the natives. Tommy had a reputation quite as great as mine throughout the country. But alas! poor Tommy. One morning he refused his food, seemed downcast, and was very anxious to be petted and held in the arms. I got all kinds of forest-berries for him, but he refused all. He did not seem to suffer, but ate nothing; and next day, without a struggle, died. Poor fellow! I was very sorry, for he had grown to be quite a pet companion for me; and even the negroes, though he had given them great trouble, were sorry at his death.

The mother of Thomas was an adult female, aged, to judge by her teeth, which were much worn; but quite black in the face and hands. Eyebrows thin, and from half to three-quarters of an inch long. Eyelids thin and short. Upper and lower lips and chin sparsely covered with short gray hairs. Neck hairy. Thin hair on the cheeks, beginning at the temples parallel with the upper part of the ear. Ears large. The head entirely bald down to a line drawn from the middle part of the ears behind; this bald skin was quite black. On the back fine black hair. Rump partly bare, and where bare the skin was quite *white*. Hair on the chest grayish-black and thin, growing thicker on the abdomen, and grayer on the legs. Height 3 feet 9 inches. This female differed very decidedly from the female of the gorilla or chimpanzee.

Tommy turned darker as he grew older, and at his death was yellow rather than white.

My men were now getting short of every kind of provisions, and I was obliged to purchase for them from the villages. The chief articles brought were some loaves of *ndica*, a kind of bread made of the seeds of the wild mango-tree pounded and dried. It does not taste unpleasantly, but I could not live on it. There was also a clear yellow oil, which, when cool, had the colour and consistency of scorched lard, and was called *agali njavi* (njavi oil). It is made with infinite labour, from the seeds of a certain tree which is abundant here, and is one of the finest ornaments of these forests. They boil the seed, then mash it on a hollowed-out board, and then squeeze out the not very abundant oil with their hands. It makes a nice-looking oil, which is used to cook meat in; and thus prepared, meat does not taste badly.

They also mix the oil with a kind of odoriferous powder called *yombo*, and this mixture is then applied in great quantities upon their wool. They think it gives out a pleasant fragrance, but in reality it makes an abominable stench.

But another use of the oil is really sensible. When the men have been for some time out in inclement weather, or are dusty or parched with working in the sun, their skin becomes dried up, cracked, and reddish in colour. Then they come home, wash themselves clean, and smear themselves all over with this soft oil. The dried-up skin becomes in a little time smooth, and of a shiny, healthy black again. Palm-oil is used elsewhere for this purpose; but the palm-oil tree is very scarce here, and the little of the oil they have is brought from the Ashira country to the east, which is now my Promised Land, towards which I daily lift longing eyes.

On the 18th, as we were hunting, I heard in the far distance what I at first took to be muttering thunder, but presently perceived the noise to be caused by a male gorilla which was roaring to its female; who, after a while, could be heard answering with a weaker roar. The forest resounded with the tremendous voice of this animal. The echoes swelled and died away from hill to hill, until the whole forest was full of the din.

Unluckily I had gone out with my smallest gun loaded with shot to shoot birds. I put in a ball instead of the shot, and determined to follow up the animals. By-and-by I could hear the deep drum-like sound which the male gorilla causes by beating his breast with his huge fists. The jungle was quite thick, and our advance slow. Poor Makondai was in a great fright as we heard the animal, which kept up its terrible roaring, waiting at short intervals to hear the replies of its female.

Presently I heard trees cracking, and saw through the woods how every few minutes a sapling was swung about and then broken off. While I was watching these actions I suppose the animal became aware of the presence of danger, for presently a dead silence followed on the loud roars; and when, gun in hand, I broke through the wood, my gorilla was gone.

I am sure that I must have heard this gorilla's roar three miles off, and the noise of beating his breast at least a mile. No words can describe the thunderous noise which it produces.

In examining the wood where these gorillas were moving and feeding, I learned, for the first time, the cause of the great wear there is of the canine teeth of this animal, and especially of the male, which I could not before account for, and also saw some surprising evidences of their strength. Several trees, each of which was from four to six inches in diameter, had been broken down by these animals; and I found that they had bitten into the heart of these trees and eaten out the pith. Now the wood is hard, and by the peculiar form of the gnawing I saw at once that it was by this work that the very singular abrasion of the canines is caused.

The Rembo is still deep and rapid as far as we ascended, and the land becomes more mountainous, the hills approaching nearer and nearer to the banks of the river. When we returned, the town was filled with joy at our success on the hunt. Quengueza made himself sick carousing on four hams which I gave him from my share of some wild pigs we had shot. The old fellow has brought all the ebony down—a heavy job, as the pieces weighed from twenty to sixty pounds, and had to be carried on men's shoulders over a very rough and woody country.

On the 30th we started with one hundred men up the Ofoubou, the river which joins the Rembo, just above Obindji, for a Bakalai town called Njali-Coudié, the chief of which was a friend of Quengueza's, who had sent to promise me some gorilla-hunts if I would come to see him.

Obindji's town was nearly at starvation-point. The poor fellows had been very generous to us while they had food to give; but now was the time of general scarcity, when the last crop was eaten up, and the coming crop was not yet ready. They were actually living on the poor roots they could gather in the woods. In Mbango's town they were a little better off; but, even here, our advent soon created a famine. The staples of this country are plantains and manioc. New plantains, even if plucked green, will soon ripen and rot. They do not know how to dry and preserve them. Manioc may be dried, and thus made to last two months at farthest; but long before that it is poor eating. Of course, there are periods every year when these perishable provisions are eaten up.

Mbango had been informed of our approach, and had built

for me a very neat, commodious bark house, with a clay floor pounded hard, and all very clean and comfortable. The village itself is one of the neatest I have seen among the Bakalai. When I had eaten my dinner, the people came in crowds to see me. My hair was, as usual, the most singular part of my person to them. A considerable number of female strangers were in the town to celebrate the feast of *Njambai*, one of their spirits; and these could not look at me or wonder at my appearance enough.

There was such a crowd, indeed, that next day food began to grow scarce, and I had to send Makondai over, with thirty men and some articles of barter to buy some plantains. In buying food, beads are the b st currency. The women cultivate the ground and sell the surplus products, and they prefer beads above everything else. The women in all this country seem to have a good deal of privilege in this way. They are expected to feed their husbands; and Quengueza frequently tells his wives to feed him well and take good care of him, because he treats them well. But what is left or not needed of the fruits thus raised the men have no right to. The women sell and keep for themselves the articles received. Makondai returned next day with forty-five bunches of plantains and two fowls—a very good supply for the time.

Meantime the feast went on, and gave me a sleepless night, as no African feast or ceremony is complete without shouting, singing, drumming, and dancing, and playing on such a harp as is shown in the picture on p. 297. Mbango, it appears, is the head or chief of his clan or family, which includes half-a-dozen towns within thirty miles around. As chief, Mbango keeps the idol of the clan, and all come hither at regular periods to sing songs of invocation to it. It is a female figure, of wood, nearly life-size, and with cloven feet like those of a deer. Her eyes were of copper; one cheek was painted red, and the other yellow. About her neck hung a necklace of tigers' teeth. She is said to have great power, and the people believe that on certain occasions she nods her head. She is said to talk frequently—as might, indeed, be expected. She is very highly venerated by the people.

On the 30th and 31st, however, there was a dead silence

and a great darkness. No light was allowed but my own. The mbuiti (idol) was set out in the middle of the street, and the people stood all around her. She is said to have bowed, walked about, and spoken to some one, expressing her pleasure at two gazelles which had been offered her the night before. She ate some of the meat—so I was assured—and left the rest for the people.

CHAPTER XIX.

Njambai—Worship of Njambai by women only—I get a peep inside the house of Njambai—Great wrath of the women—I am in a perilous position—Mbango and Quengueza take my part—Paying a fine—Gorilla hunting—Man killed by a gorilla—His gun bent—Gambo—The ibolai and igoogouai flies—The iboco and nchouna flies—Great number of parrots—The cloway wasp—Superstition in regard to different animals as food.

On the 2nd (June) the women began their peculiar worship of Njambai, which, it seems, is their good spirit; and it is remarkable that all the Bakalai clans, and all the females of tribes I have met during my journeys, worship or venerate a spirit with this same name.

This worship of the women is a kind of mystery—no men being admitted to the ceremonies, which are carried on in a house very carefully closed. This house was covered with dry palm and banana leaves, and had not even a door open to the street. To make all close it was set against two other houses, and the entrance was through one of these. Quengueza and Mbango warned me not to go near this place, as not even they were permitted so much as to take a look. All the women of the village painted their faces and bodies, beat drums, marched about the town, and from time to time entered the idol-house, where they danced all one night, and made a more outrageous noise than even the men had made before. They also presented several antelopes to the goddess, and, on the 4th, all but a few went off into the woods to sing to Njambai.

I noticed that half-a-dozen remained, and in the course of

the morning entered the Njambai-house, where they stayed in great silence. Now my curiosity, which had been greatly excited to know what took place in this secret worship, finally overcame me. I determined to see. Walking several times up and down the street past the house to allay suspicion, I at last suddenly pushed aside some of the leaves, and stuck my head through the wall. For a moment I could distinguish nothing in the darkness. Then I beheld three perfectly naked old hags sitting on the clay floor, with an immense bundle of greegrees before them, which they seemed to be silently adoring.

When they saw me they at once set up a hideous howl of rage, and rushed out to call their companions from the bush. In a few minutes these came running in, crying and lamenting; rushing towards me with gestures of anger, and threatening me for my offence. I quickly reached my house, and, seizing my gun in one hand and a revolver in the other, told them I would shoot the first one that came inside my door. The house was surrounded by about three hundred infuriated women, every one shouting out curses at me; but the sight of my revolver kept them back. They adjourned presently for the Njambai-house, and from there sent a deputation to the men, who were to inform me that I must pay for the "palaver" I had made.

This I peremptorily refused to do; telling Quengueza and Mbango that I was their stranger, and must be allowed to do as I pleased, as their rules were nothing to me, who was a white man and did not believe in their idols. In truth, if I had once paid for such a transgression as this, there would have been an end of all travelling for me, as I often broke through their absurd rules without knowing it, and my only course was to declare myself irresponsible.

However, the women would not give up, but threatened vengeance not only on me, but on all the men of the town; and as I as positively refused to pay anything, it was at last, to my great surprise, determined by Mbango and his male subjects that *they* would make up from their own possessions such a sacrifice as the women demanded of me. Accordingly Mbango contributed ten fathoms of native cloth, and the men came one by one and put their offerings on the ground — some plates, some knives, some mugs, some beads, some mats, and various other articles. Mbango came again, and asked if I, too, would not contribute something; but I refused. In fact, I dared not set such a precedent. So when all had given what they could, the whole amount was taken to the ireful women, to whom Mbango said that I was his and his men's guest, and that they could not ask me to pay in such a matter, therefore they paid the demand themselves. With this the women were satisfied, and there the quarrel ended. Of course I could not make any further investigations into their mysteries. The Njambai feast lasts about two weeks. I could learn very little about the spirit which they call by this name. Their own ideas are quite vague. They know only that it protects the women against their male enemies, avenges their wrongs, and serves them in various ways if they please it.

On the 7th we went on a gorilla hunt. I gave powder to the whole party. Six were to go off in one direction for gazelles and whatever luck might send them; and six others, of whom I was one, were to hunt for gorillas. We set off towards a dark valley, where Gambo, Igoumba's son, said we should find our prey. The gorilla chooses the darkest, gloomiest forests for its home, and is found on the edges of the clearings only when in search of plantains, or sugar-cane, or pine-apple. Often they choose for their peculiar haunt a wood so dark that, even at midday, one can scarce see ten yards. This makes it the more necessary to wait till the monstrous beast approaches near before shooting, in order that the first shot may be fatal. It does not often let the hunter reload.

Our little party separated, as is the custom, to stalk the wood in various directions. Gambo and I kept together. One brave fellow went off alone in a direction where he thought he could find a gorilla. The other three took another course. We had been about an hour separated when Gambo and I heard a gun fired but a little way from us, and presently another. We were already on our way to the spot where we hoped to see a gorilla slain, when the forest began to resound

HUNTER KILLED BY A GORILLA.

with the most terrific roars. Gambo seized my arms in great agitation, and we hurried on, both filled with a dreadful and sickening alarm. We had not gone far when our worst fears were realised. The poor brave fellow who had gone off alone was lying on the ground in a pool of his own blood, and I thought, at first, quite dead. His bowels were protruding through the lacerated abdomen. Beside him lay his gun. The stock was broken, and the barrel was bent and flattened. It bore plainly the marks of the gorilla's teeth.

We picked him up, and I dressed his wounds as well as I could with rags torn from my clothes. When I had given him a little brandy to drink he came to himself, and was able, but with great difficulty, to speak. He said that he had met the gorilla suddenly and face to face, and that it had not attempted to escape. It was, he said, a huge male, and seemed very savage. It was in a very gloomy part of the wood, and the darkness, I suppose, made him miss. He said he took good aim, and fired when the beast was only about eight yards off. The ball merely wounded it in the side. It at once began beating its breasts, and with the greatest rage advanced upon him.

To run away was impossible. He would have been caught in the jungle before he had gone a dozen steps.

He stood his ground, and as quickly as he could reloaded his gun. Just as he raised it to fire the gorilla dashed it out of his hands, the gun going off in the fall; and then in an instant, and with a terrible roar, the animal gave him a tremendous blow with its immense open paw, frightfully lacerating the abdomen, and with this single blow laying bare part of the intestines. As he sank, bleeding, to the ground, the monster seized the gun, and the poor hunter thought he would have his brains dashed out with it. But the gorilla seemed to have looked upon this also as an enemy, and in his rage almost flattened the barrel between his strong jaws.

When we came upon the ground the gorilla was gone. This is their mode when attacked—to strike one or two blows, and then leave the victims of their rage on the ground and go off into the woods.

We hunted up our companions and carried our poor fellow

to the camp, where all was instantly excitement and sorrow. They entreated me to give him medicine, but I had nothing to suit his case. I saw that his days were numbered; and all I could do was to make him easy by giving him a little brandy or wine at intervals. He had to tell the whole story over again; and the people declared at once that this was no true gorilla that had attacked him, but a man—a wicked man turned into a gorilla. Such a being no man could escape, they said; and it could not be killed, even by the bravest hunters. This principle of fatalism and of transmigration of souls is brought in by them in all such cases, I think, chiefly to keep up the courage of their hunters, on whom such a mischance exercises a very depressing influence. The hunters are the most valued men in these negro villages. A brave and fortunate one is admired by all the women; loved—almost worshipped—by his wives; and enjoys many privileges among his fellow-villagers. But his proudest time is when he has killed an elephant or a gorilla and filled the village with meat. Then he may do almost what he pleases. The next day we shot a monster gorilla, which I suppose is the same one that killed my poor hunter, for male gorillas are not very plentiful.

The poor fellow who was hurt by the gorilla died on the 9th.

Gambo and I have been hunting for a week after another gorilla. The natives said that a monstrous animal had been several times seen in the forest some ten miles to the east. We had been on the hunt for several hours, when we came upon tolerably fresh tracks of an animal which I saw must be a very large one. These tracks we followed cautiously, and at last, in a densely wooded and quite dark ravine we came suddenly upon the beast. There were two gorillas, a male and female. Owing to the dense jungle, in a nook of which they were concealed, they saw us first. The female uttered a cry of alarm, and ran off before we could get a shot at her, being lost to sight in a moment in the bush. The male, however, whom I particularly wanted, had no idea of running off. He rose slowly from his haunches and at once faced us, uttering a roar of rage at our evidently untimely intrusion. Gambo and I were accompanied only by a single hunter and an Ashira boy, who bore an extra gun. The boy fell back, and we stood side by side and awaited the advance of the hideous monster. In the dim half-light of the ravine, his features working with rage, his gloomy, treacherous, mischievous gray eyes, his rapidly-agitated, and frightful, satyr-like features had a horrid look, enough to make one fancy him really a spirit of the damned.

He advanced upon us by starts, as is their fashion, pausing to beat his fists upon his vast breast.

We stood at our posts for at least three long minutes, guns in hand, before the great beast was near enough for a safe shot. In this time I could not help thinking of the misfortune of my poor hunter but a few days ago; and, as I looked at the gorilla before us, I could fancy the horror of the situation when, with empty gun, the poor fellow stood before his remorseless enemy, who came upon him, not with a sudden spring like the leopard, but with a slow, vindictive certainty which is like fate.

At last he stood before us at a distance of six yards. Once more he paused, and, raising his head, began to roar and beat his breast. Just as he took another step towards us we fired, and down he tumbled, almost at our feet, upon his face, dead.

Parrots, of varied colours and size, are now screaming and chattering all day in the open woods. One in particular, the gray parrot, flies in flocks of hundreds together, and makes the whole forest alive with its screams. These birds build their nests in hollow trees, and are very sociable in their nature.

In spite of all my endeavours during my former and this last journey, I have been unable to kill the guanonien, a most formidable eagle; but several times I have been startled in the forest by the sudden cry of anguish of a monkey who had been seized by this "leopard of the air," as the natives often call it, and then saw the bird with its prey disappear out of sight.

One day, hunting through the thick jungle, I came to a spot covered with more than one hundred skulls of monkeys of different sizes. Some of these skulls must have been those of formidable animals, and these now and then succeeded, it appears, in giving such bites to this eagle that they disabled him. For a while I thought myself in the Valley of Golgotha. Then I saw at the top of a gigantic tree, at the foot of which were the skulls, the nest of the bird, but the young had flown away. I was told by the natives that the guanonien comes and lays in the same nest year after year. When an adult specimen will be procured, it may be found to rival in size the condor of America.

This upper country has few mosquitoes, but, in their stead, several varieties of flies, which are exceedingly troublesome. The *igoogouai* is a small, almost imperceptible gnat, which appears in great numbers in the morning, until ten o'clock, from which time it is seen no more till four, when its operations are recommenced, and last till sunset. These little flies are most determined bloodsuckers, very sly in their approaches, but leaving behind them a bite which itches terribly and for a considerable time. Small as they are, even the thick hides of the negroes are punctured by them. In hunting they are very troublesome, and often made my men so nervous that they could hit nothing.

Another is the *ibolai*, an insect twice as large as our common house-fly. It approaches you with a sharp whistle, and its sting is long and strong enough to pierce the thickest clothes one can wear in the heat of an African summer. The sting is so sharp that I have often jumped up with the sudden pain, which was as if a pin had been stuck savagely into my person. But the bite of this insect, if painful, does not last, like that of another of the same size, which is called the *nchouna*. This fly makes no noise to warn you of its approach, and inserts its bill so gently that often it gets its fill of blood before you know you are bitten. Presently, however, the itching begins, and lasts for several hours, varied, at intervals, by sudden sharp stabs of pain, as though a scorpion had bitten you. Often this lasts the whole day. These last-named animals are found mostly on the rivers.

The *iboco*, another fly, is the size of a hornet, and very quick in its motions. Its bite is the most severe of all, and clothing is no protection from them. Often the blood has run down my face or arm from one of their savage attacks, and even the well-tanned skin of the negroes is punctured till it bleeds, so that one would think a leech had been at work on them.

But most dreaded of all is the *eloway*, a nest-building wasp which frequents the water-side, where its clay hives are hung to the pendent branches of trees. This fly is really a monster of ferocity, and the natives run from it as they do from no other animal or insect of these woods. The eloway is a little fly, shaped much like a bee, but not quite so big. The body is longer in proportion than that of a bee. Their hives are made of clay, and evidently have separate apartments, as the whole pendent bottle-shaped mass is filled with holes, each of which has a little roof over it. They generally choose a branch which is full of leaves for their *nago* or nest, and thus are hidden from view. The clay of the nest is so hard that even a bullet fired from a reasonable distance made no impression upon it, as I found by several trials. The hives seem to be very full; when disturbed I have seen them issuing in large swarms, and several from each hole.

When troubled they are very savage, and attack with a kind of blind rage. Sometimes when paddling down the Rembo a canoe accidentally strikes against a tree containing an eloway *nago*. Instantly they fall ferociously upon the men. The natives always dive into the water and swim under water for a little distance; but I noticed that if one of these venomous little insects had settled on a man, he clung to him even in the water, and had literally to be picked off. In such cases I always covered myself up with matting and lay still till they retired. Happily, they do not pursue far; and when the enemy is out of their sight they return quietly to their nests.

Their bite is exceedingly painful, and they leave in the wound an acid poison, which pains for two or three days. At intervals of an hour the poison seems to gather fresh force, the wound begins to throb, and for a little while is excessively painful. The natives fear these eloways very much, and retreat with all expedition when they have accidentally disturbed a nest. When they see a nest, also, they always paddle to the opposite side of the stream. Going nearly naked, they are very much exposed to its attacks; and its motions are so very quick that even a speedy tumble overboard does not generally save them from one or two bites.

Of snakes all this back country has a great abundance. A few are harmless; some of the large species attack the larger beasts and crush them in their folds; or, if smaller, they have poison-fangs. It is curious that the negroes have no vegetable or other remedy for a snake bite; but they are not often bitten. The snakes are easily alarmed, and the noise of an approaching hunter scares them out of his path. Sometimes they hang from the limbs of trees, waiting, probably, for prey to pass beneath, and several times such a pendent animal has given me a fright by falling down beside me as I stood under a tree. But they never attack man, so far as I have seen. I saw and killed on several occasions pythons measuring from twenty to twenty-five feet; but the largest I ever saw had been killed by a party of natives, and was just skinned as I came up. This was on the Rembo. The skin measured a little over thirty-three feet in length.

The smaller snakes feed on birds, and squirrels, and rats, which I am convinced, from frequent observation, they are able to charm with their look. This power of charming I had always doubted, but I was convinced by one day watching a venomous black snake, over four feet long, subduing and catching a squirrel which sat on the lower branch of a tree. It was in the rear of Obindji's village. I had gone out to shoot birds, and my attention was attracted by the very peculiar and continued chattering of a squirrel. When I saw it I did not know what to make of its movements. It seemed as though tied to its branch and very anxious to get away. Its head was thrust forward, its eyes fixed and glaring; but its body trembled, and was jerked about from side to side. All the time it was screaming and chattering in a really pitiable manner. Following the direction of its glance I saw the cause of its alarm. The black snake was slowly creeping out on the limb, and as steadily kept his eyes on his victim. The whole curious process went on under my inspection for at least ten or twelve minutes, during all which time the snake seemed to fix the gaze of the squirrel upon itself. The squirrel came nearer and nearer, until it reached the mouth of the snake, which made a spring, grasped its prey in its mouth, and quickly coiled its folds about it.

I have seen many such cases of charming, both of birds and squirrels; and sometimes firing my gun dissolved the charm, by diverting momentarily the gaze of the snake.

The country about here is probably one of the richest fields for an enterprising naturalist now remaining in the world. Equatorial Africa seems to have a fauna of its own. The lion, common both to North and South Africa, is not found here at all. Neither are the zebra, gnu, giraffe, rhinoceros, or ostrich, and the great number of antelopes so common in other parts of the continent, known here. There are no tame cattle, no horses, no donkeys; in fact, the only domesticated animals are goats and fowls, and a species of sheep. Several kinds of gazelles offer sport to the hunter-naturalist; and I saw several specimens of a very beautiful antelope (the Bongo), which may be considered one of the handsomest antelopes yet discovered in Africa. Swift of foot, as are all its kind, and exceedingly graceful in its motions, though more heavily built than most antelopes. Among the carnivora, the leopard takes the first rank. It is a very large and majestic animal here. There is also a hyena, whose raids among the goats are often troublesome; and several varieties of tiger-cats.

Among the most peculiar of the monkeys is the little oshingui, one of the smallest of the whole monkey tribe. It is a frolicsome and innocent little animal, and remarkable for its fondness for the water; so that where you meet one of them hopping about the branches overhead, you may be sure water is not far off. They always sleep on some tree the branches of which overhang a water-course. This little monkey is also a great favourite with the monkey-birds (*Buceros albo-crystatus*), which I often saw playing with it.

Not only was I now sick, but also poor and ragged. My clothes were torn and patched, and I looked, in reality, very little better or more civilized than my negro friends. Food was scarce; and though my friends and hunters, Querlaouen, Obindji, and others, gave me what they had, it was robbing them. So I told Quengueza we must go.

A CURIOUS SUPERSTITION.

Before leaving I had a glimpse at another curious superstition of these people. One of the hunters had shot a wild bull, and when the carcass was brought in the good fellow

THE BONGO ANTELOPE.
(*Trogelaphus albo-virgatus.*)

General colour, bright orange, with a chestnut patch between the horns and eyes, below which is a white crescent, having in the middle a dark brown stripe; but the chief features of the animal are the stripes on each side.

sent me an abundant supply of the best portions. The meat is tough, but was most welcome for a change. I had a great piece boiled for dinner, and expected Quengueza to eat as much as would make several hungry white men sick. Judge of my surprise, when, coming to the table and seeing only the meat, he refused to touch it.

I asked, why?

"It is roondah for me," he replied. And then, in answer to my question, explained that the meat of the Bos brachicheros was forbidden to his family, and was an abomination to them, for the reason that many generations ago one of their women gave birth to a calf instead of a child.

I laughed; but the king replied very soberly that he could show me a woman of another family whose grandmother had given birth to a crocodile—for which reason the crocodile was roondah to that family.

Quengueza would never touch my salt-beef, nor even the pork, fearing lest it had been in contact with the beef. Indeed they are all religiously scrupulous in this matter; and I found, on inquiry afterwards, that scarce a man can be found to whom some article of food is not "roondah." Some dare not taste crocodile, some hippopotamus, some monkey, some boa, some wild pig, and all from this same belief. They will literally suffer the pangs of starvation rather than break through this prejudice; and they very firmly believe that if one of a family should eat of such forbidden food, the women of the same family would surely miscarry and give birth to monstrosities in the shape of the animal which is roondah, or else die of an awful disease.

Sometimes I find that the fetich-man forbids an individual to touch certain kinds of food for some reason, or no reason rather. In this case the prohibition extends only to the man, and not to his family.

It is astonishing how strictly such gluttons as they are adhere to their scruples. It shows the power a superstitious faith has even over a lawless people as these are. I am certain nothing in the world would have induced the old king to eat the flesh of the wild bull, or even to eat out of a dish in which that had been cooked or otherwise contained.

CHAPTER XX.

Ants—The bashikouay ant—Its ferocity—Great moving armies of bashikouays—How they spread—Their mode of attack—They travel night and day—Every animal and insect flies before them—The white ants—Their buildings—Their habits—How they repair their houses—Their appearance—The ipi or scaly ant-eater.

In the forests of this part of Africa are found vast numbers of ants, some of whose tribes are so terrible to man, and even to the beasts of the wood, from their harsh bites, their fierce temper and voracity, that their path is freely abandoned to them, and they may well be called lords of the forest

I know of ten different species of ants found in these regions, all differing widely in their choice of food, the quality of their venom, the manner of their attack, or the

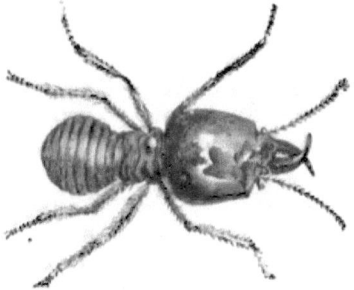

THE BASHIKOUAY ANT, MAGNIFIED TO TWICE ITS NATURAL SIZE.

time of their operation. The most remarkable and most dreaded of all is the *bashikouay*, of which I have spoken before.

They carry nothing away, but eat all their prey on the spot. It is their habit to march through the forests in a long regular line—a line about two inches broad and often several miles in length. All along this line are larger ants, who act as officers, stand outside the ranks, and keep this singular army in order. If they come to a place where there are no trees to shelter them from the sun, whose heat they cannot bear, they immediately construct underground tunnels, through which the whole army passes in columns to the forest beyond. These tunnels are four or five feet underground, and are used only in the heat of the day or during a storm.

When they grow hungry the long file spreads itself through the forest in a front line, and attacks and devours all it overtakes with a fury which is quite irresistible. The elephant and gorilla fly before this attack. The black men run for their lives. Every animal that lives in their line of march is chased. They seem to understand and act upon the tactics of Napoleon, and concentrate, with great speed, their heaviest forces upon the point of attack. In an incredibly short space of time the mouse, or dog, or leopard, or deer is overwhelmed, killed, eaten, and the bare skeleton only remains.

They seem to travel night and day. Many a time have I been awakened out of a sleep, and obliged to rush from the hut and into the water to save my life, and after all suffered intolerable agony from the bites of the advance-guard, who had got into my clothes. When they enter a house they clear it of all living things. Cockroaches are devoured in an instant. Rats and mice spring round the room in vain. An overwhelming force of ants kills a strong rat in less than a minute, in spite of the most frantic struggles, and in less than another minute its bones are stripped. Every living thing in the house is devoured. They will not touch vegetable matter. Thus they are in reality very useful (as well as dangerous) to the negroes, who have their huts cleared of all the abounding vermin, such as immense cockroaches and centipedes, at least several times a year.

When on their march the insect-world flies before them, and I have often had the approach of a bashikouay army heralded to me by this means. Wherever they go they make a clean sweep, even ascending to the tops of the highest trees in pursuit of their prey. Their manner of attack is an impetuous *leap*. Instantly the strong pincers are fastened, and they only let go when the piece gives way. At such times this little animal seems animated by a kind of fury which causes it entirely to disregard its own safety, and to seek only the conquest of its prey. The bite is very painful.

The negroes relate that criminals were in former times exposed in the path of the bashikouay ants, as the most cruel manner of putting them to death.

When on their line of march they require to cross a narrow stream, they throw themselves across and form a tunnel—a living tunnel—connecting two trees or high bushes on opposite sides of the little stream, whenever they can find such to facilitate the operation. This is done with great speed, and is effected by a great number of ants, each of which clings with its fore claws to its next neighbour's body or hind claws. Thus they form a high, safe tubular bridge, *through* which the whole vast regiment marches in regular order. If disturbed, or if the arch is broken by the violence of some animal, they instantly attack the offender with the greatest animosity.

There is another species of bashikouay which is found in the mountains to the south of the equator. It is of great size. The body is grayish-white in colour; the head of a reddish-black. Its fangs are very powerful, and it is able to make a clean bite out of a piece of flesh. It is thus a very formidable insect; but fortunately its motions are not so quick as those of its fierce brother; it does not march in such vast armies, nor does it precipitate itself upon its prey with such irresistible fury. In its motions it is almost sluggish. They do not invade villages, nor climb trees in pursuit of prey; and I do not think them nearly so voracious as their fellows before mentioned. If they were, they could doubtless clear the country of every living thing, for they are much more powerful. They are, in fact, to ants what whales are to fishes.

There are many different species of white ants (Termites), the nests of which are very conspicuous objects in the prairies.

The Mushroom-hived Termes.—They build a singular edifice, or hive, shaped like gigantic mushrooms, which are scattered by tens of thousands over the Otando prairie. The top is from twelve to eighteen inches in diameter, and the column about five inches; the total height is from ten inches to fifteen inches. After the grass has been burnt they present a most extraordinary appearance; near Máyolo they are met with almost at every step. They are not all uniformly built, as they appear at a distance, but differ in the roundness or sharpness of their summits. I opened a great number of these, and followed up my researches day after day into

NESTS OF MUSHROOM ANTS AND TREE ANTS.

the habits of their inhabitants. These and all similar edifices are built to protect the white ants against the inclemencies of the weather, and against their enemies, which are very numerous, and include many predaceous kinds of fellow ants.

The mushroom-shaped hive is not so firmly built in the ground but that it can be knocked down by a well-planted kick. It is built of a kind of mortar after being digested in the stomachs of the ants. When felled, the base of the pillar is found to have rested on the ground, leaving a circular hollow, in the middle of which is a ball of earth full of cells, which enters the centre of the base of the pillar, and the cells are eagerly defended by a multitude of the soldier class of the ants, which I took to be males, all striving to bite the intruder with their pincer-like jaws. On breaking open the ball—which, when handled, divided itself into three parts—I always found it full of young white ants in different stages of growth, and also of eggs. The young were of a milky-white colour, while the adults were yellowish, with a tinge of grey when the abdomen is full of earth. Besides these young ants, there were a great many full-grown individuals, whom I took to be females, and who appeared to be the workers or labourers. These have not elongated nippers like the soldiers, but have very bulky abdomens, and they are inoffensive. Besides these soldiers and workers, I always saw, whenever I broke a hive, a very much larger specimen than the other two, which came in from the inner galleries, looked round, and went away again. These large ants were very few in number. There were, therefore, three distinct sets of individuals. To these large ones I shall give the name of head-men or chiefs.

In order to examine the rest of the structure I often took an axe and broke the nest into several pieces; but the material was so hard that it required several blows before I succeeded. I tried then to make out the structure of the chambers and galleries of which the interior was composed. But before I could do this, I was somewhat perplexed at discovering that there was another distinct species of white ant mixed up with the proper architects of the edifice. The soldiers of this other species were much smaller and more slender, and, as I broke the pieces, these two kinds fell to fighting one another. On close inspection I found that these slender fellows came out of cells composed of a yellow earth, whilst the others inhabited cells of black earth. The yellow colour was due to a coating of some foreign substance on the walls of the cells. The chambers inhabited by the slender species did not communicate with those peopled by the lords of the manor; they seemed rather to be inserted into the vacant spaces or partition walls between the other cells. No doubt they had intruded themselves, after the building had been finished, from under the ground.

In the fight the larger kind showed no mercy to the smaller. It was quite marvellous to witness the fury with which the soldiers of the one kind seized the bodies of the

NESTS OF FOREST ANTS.

others with their powerful pincer-jaws, and carried them away into their own chambers. The soldiers of the slender kind also possessed long pincer-like jaws, and I noticed in one instance, when a worker of the larger kind had seized a small worker, who was in her last struggle for life, that one of these slender soldiers flew to the rescue, and snapping into the soft abdomen of the assailant, twice its size, let out its contents; the slender one then fell from the pincers that had gripped her, but life was extinct. The rescuer came. examined the body, and seeing that she was dead, went away and disappeared; if she had been only wounded she would probably have been carried away, as they do the young. I may here remark that, with the exception of the head, the body of the termites is exceedingly soft. On examining the structure of the soldiers, it is evident that their powerful pincer-jaws are made for wounding and piercing, while the structure of the workers shows that their pincers are made for the purposes of labour. Nothing astonished me more than this impetuous attack; my attention was intense on this deadly combat; the weaker species knew the vulnerable point of his formidable enemy, who was too busy to protect himself. A further examination showed me that the mushroom-like cap of the whole edifice was composed of both black and yellow cells. This curious mixture of two species, each building its own cells and yet contributing to form an entire and symmetrical edifice, filled me with astonishment. The wonder did not cease here, for in some of the mushroom-like heads there was still a third kind quite distinct from the other two.

The mushroom nests are built very rapidly, but when finished they last, in all probability, many years. The ants work at them only at night, and shut out all the apertures from the external air when daylight comes, for the white ant abhors daylight; and when they migrate from an old building to commence the erection of a new one, they come from under the ground. Sometimes they add to their structures by building one mushroom-head above another; I have seen as many as four, one on the top of the other. The new structures are built when the colony increases; new cells must be found for the new comers. The shelter is quite rain-proof.

I passed hours in watching the tiny builders at their daily labours in the cells, which I was enabled to do by laying open some of their cells, and then observing what went on after all was quiet. So soon as the cells are broken, a few head-men or chiefs are seen; each one moves his head all round the aperture, and then disappears into the dark galleries, apparently without leaving anything. Then the soldiers come; these do no work, but there must be some intention in these movements; they no doubt were on guard to protect the workers. I was never able, even with my magnifying glass, to see them do anything. The workers then come forward, and each of them turns round and ejects from behind a quantity of liquid mud into the aperture, and finally walls it up. They come one after the other, and all of them leave their contributions; this is done first in a row from one end of the aperture to another, then each ejection is put on the top of the other with a precision that would do honour to a bricklayer or stonemason. The question to me was to know if the same ants went away to eat more earth and came again. How much would I have given to be able to see into the dark recesses of the chambers! The apertures of the cells were only closed during the day, and during the following night the part of the structure which I had demolished was rebuilt to its original shape. Some of them brought very small grains of sand or minute pebbles, and deposited them in the mud; when demolishing their shelter, I saw several cells filled with these little pebbles, which I had also collected and preserved. Soon after others came and closed up the cell. The earth which they eat can be seen shining through the thin skins of their bodies, but I was unable to see where it was stored in the interior of the edifice. The mud is mixed with gluey matter, through the digestion, when it is ejected, and with this material the little creatures are enabled to build up the thin tough walls which form their cells, and, in course of time, the firm and solid structure of the entire nest. Sun and rain are equally fatal to the white ants; thus it is necessary that they should build a hive impervious to light, heat, and rain. I have put white ants in the sun, and they were shortly afterwards killed by its heat. I thought each cell was, perhaps, inhabited only by one ant, but the great number I saw in each mushroom-like edifice made it quite improbable that it should be so.

One may retire to bed in fancied security, with no sign of white ants about, and in the morning wake to find little covered ways overspreading the floor and chests of clothing and stores, and the contents of the chest entirely destroyed, with thousands of the busy ants engaged in cutting the things with their sharp jaw-blades. Everything made of wool or silk is, however, invariably spared. At Máyolo this kind of ant was very abundant, and was a cause of much anxiety to me.

The pangolin genus (*Manis* of zoologists) to which the Ipi

IPI, OR SCALY ANT-EATER.
(*Pholidotus Africanus.*)

belongs is a very singular group of animals. They are ant-eaters, like the *Myrmecophaga* of South America, being like them quite destitute of teeth, and having a long extensile tongue, the extremity of which is covered with a glutinous secretion, by means of which they catch their prey. But, whilst the South American ant-eaters are clothed with hair, like ordinary mammalian animals, the pangolins have an armour of large scales, implanted in the skin of the upper surface of the body from the head to the tip of the tail, and imbricated or overlapping, like the slates on the roof of a house. The animals look, at first sight, like curious heavy-bodied lizards, but they have warm blood, and nourish their young like the rest of the mammalia.

The ipi lives in burrows in the earth, or sometimes in the large hollows of colossal trunks of trees which have fallen to the ground. The burrows that I saw were in light soil on the slope of a hill. There are two holes to each gallery, one for entrance and the other for exit. This is necessary, on account of the animal being quite incapable of curving its body sideways, so that it cannot turn itself in its burrow. The bodies of pangolins are very flexible *vertically*, that is, they can roll themselves up into a ball, and coil and uncoil themselves very readily, but they cannot turn round within the confined limits of their burrows. In hunting them we had first to ascertain, by the footmark, or more readily by the marks left by the trail of the tail, which was the entrance and which the exit of the burrow, and then, making a trap at the one end, drive them out by the smoke of a fire at the other; afterwards securing them with ropes. The freshness of the tracks told us that the animal had entered its burrow the previous evening; for I must add that the ipi is nocturnal in its habits, sleeping in its burrow throughout the day. When it wanders at night the natives say that they can hear the rattling of its large scales.

I was rewarded by finding two specimens, an adult female and a young one; the skins and skeletons of both I preserved and afterwards sent to the British Museum. The adult measured about four feet and a half from the head to the tip of the tail. The flesh of the ipi is good eating. I found, on dissection, nothing but the remains of ants in their stomachs. The tail is very thick, and makes a large track on the ground in walking.

CHAPTER XXI.

Subdivision of tribes—Tribes divided into clans—Chieftainship—The elders—Two kinds of slaves—Polygamy—Religious notions of the negroes—Idols—Fetiches and charms—Rabolo's fetich—The curse of witchcraft—The doctor—Power of the doctor.

AMONG the tribes which I visited in my explorations I found but one form of government, which may be called the patriarchal. There is not sufficient national unity in any of the tribes to give occasion for such a despotism as prevails in Dahomey and in other of the African nationalities. I found the tribes of Equatorial Africa greatly dispersed, and, in general, no bond of union between parts of the same tribe. A tribe is divided into numerous *clans*, and these again into numberless little villages, each of which possesses an independent chief. The villages are scattered, are often moved on account of death or witchcraft, as I have already explained in the narrative, and not unfrequently are engaged in war with each other.

The chieftainship is, to a certain extent, hereditary, the right of succession vesting in the brother of the reigning chief or king. The people, however, and particularly the elders of the village, have a veto power, and can, for sufficient cause, deprive the lineal heir of his succession, and put in over him some one thought of more worth. In such cases the question is put to the vote of the village; and where parties are equally divided as to strength, there ensue sometimes long and serious palavers before all can unite in a choice. The chief is mostly a man of great influence prior to his accession, and generally an old man when he gains power.

His authority, though greater than one would think, judging from the little personal deference paid to him, is final only in matters of every-day use. In cases of urgency, such as war or any important removal, the elders of the village meet together and deliberate in the presence of the whole population, who finally decide the question.

The elders, who possess other authority and are always in

the counsels of the chiefs, are the oldest members of important families in the village. Respect is paid to them on account of their years, but more from a certain regard for "family," which the African has very strongly wherever I have known him.

There are two kinds of slaves in all the tribes I met. One class are domestic servants, who are not sold out of the tribe, and who, while suffering some disabilities as slaves, have yet a large portion of liberty, and a certain voice and influence in the village where they are owned. They are protected by their master; have often property of their own; and their chief duty is to provide him with food, either by hunting or by assisting in the tillage of the ground, which is the labour of free *women* and the female slaves.

Masters are seldom very severe with their slaves, because they fear that the slave will in revenge bewitch them. The slave is held to be in a very inferior position to a free man; and the master may kill his slave if he will, no one having the right of interfering between them. The laws or customs of the country protect him in this privilege, which I have myself known to be exercised. Many slaves enjoy the confidence of their masters to that degree that they are sent on long trading journeys with much valuable property. They are generally faithful to such trusts.

Polygamy exists everywhere. A man's great ambition is to have a great many wives. These cultivate the ground for him, and it is, in fact, their duty to feed him. He does not interfere with their labours on the soil. They are responsible for his daily food. The man buys his wife of her father for a sum agreed on, often when she is but a child. She becomes his wife sometimes at the age of five, and sometimes still younger. Often the young child is placed under care of the future husband's chief wife. A man's claims on his father-in-law for help in trade, or in a palaver, are rigidly respected, and this gives additional value to a great number of wives. I have found that the wives rarely disagree among themselves.

Men marry at every opportunity, and at all ages up to seventy or eighty. Obedience is the wife's first duty, and it is enforced without mercy. Such a whip as is figured below is an important instrument found in every house. It is made of the hide of the hippopotamus or manatee, and is a barbarous *weapon*, as hard and heavy as iron. This is laid on with no light hand, the worthy husband crying out, "Rascal, do you think I paid my slaves for you for nothing?" A stroke of the whip often leaves a life-long mark; and I saw very few women in all my travels who had not some such marks on their persons.

Their religious notions are of the loosest and vaguest kind, and no two persons are found to agree in any particulars about which the traveller seeks information. Superstition seems in these countries to have run wild, and every man believes what his fancy, by some accident, most forcibly presents to him as hurtful or beneficial.

They fear the spirits of the *recently*-departed; and besides placing furniture, dress, and food at their graves, return from time to time with other supplies of food. When men and women are slain over a grave, they even believe that their spirits join that of him in whose honour they have been killed. During the season appointed for mourning, the deceased is remembered and *feared;* but when once his memory grows dim, the negro ceases to believe in the prolonged existence of the departed spirit.

Ask a negro where the spirit of his grandfather or great-grandfather, whom he did not know, is, and he will reply confidently that it is "done," "gone out," no more, or that he does not know where it has gone.

I have frequently held such conversation as this—
"Do you believe there is a God?"
"Yes."
"Do you think you will see this God when you die?"
"No."
"After death all is done," is a proverb always in their

mouths. The fear of spirits of the departed seems an instinctive feeling for which they do not attempt to account to themselves, and about which they have formed no theory. They believe the spirit is near and about them; that it requires food and property; that it can and sometimes does harm them. They think of it as a vindictive thing, to be feared and to be conciliated.

I found in all the tribes I visited a faith in the existence and power of the two great spirits, one called Abambou or Ocoucou, and the other Mbuirri. They have other names in various tribes, but wherever I journeyed I found this belief. Some tribes believe them to be married to two female spirits. They are said sometimes to walk into the village by night and to let their voices be heard. These two spirits are the potent ones; they seem to be more powerful than all the others. In sickness and on other grave occasions they are always invoked.

The name *Aniambié* stands, I think, for *God*. But yet they have no idea of a Supreme and Almighty Spirit, Creator and Preserver. The word *aniemba*, which sounds much like the previously-named, and is probably derived from the same root, signifies " possessed by a witch."

The large idol of a clan is kept in a house made for the purpose, and hither come its worshippers when they are about to proceed on a hunting or other important expedition. They present food, and then invoke its protection by dancing and singing before it. Such idols are handed down from generation to generation, and are much feared. There are also *private* idols, possessed and worshipped by individuals; but these have less general authority.

Their idols, which are always repulsive figures, are believed to speak, to walk about, to eat and drink.

After the idols come the charms or greegrees, called by them *mondah*. Greegree, like fetich, is a term of European origin. In these mondahs they have implicit faith. No negro in all this region but has about his person one or more of these articles. The preparation gives a considerable revenue and much honour to the doctors, who have, however, themselves the greatest confidence in these things. The mondahs are generally worn about the neck or waist; are made of the skins of rare animals, of the claws of birds, of the teeth of crocodiles or leopards, of the dried flesh and brains of animals, of the feathers of rare birds, of the ashes of certain kinds of wood, of the skin and bones of serpents, etc. Every greegree has a special power. One protects from sickness; another makes the heart of the hunter or warrior brave; another gives success to the lover; another protects against sorcery; some cure sterility, and others make the mother's breast abound in milk for her babe. The charmed leopard-skin worn about the warrior's middle is supposed to render that worthy spear-proof; and when he has an iron chain about his neck no bullet can hit him. If the charm fails, his faith is none the less firm, for then it is considered that some potent and wicked sorcerer has worked a too powerful counter-spell, and to this he has fallen a victim.

I will here give a curious instance of their superstitious regard for fetichism. The building of a new house, which I had chosen for my residence, and which I had bought of Rabolo, a petty chief, approached completion. Nothing remained to be put up except the verandah; but an obstacle existed to its completion which my men dared not remove. This was a formidable *mondah* or fetich, which my friend Rabolo had made in his village before I purchased it, and which I now found was close to the site of my house, at what was formerly the entrance to the single street of the village. Almost all the villages in this country have something of this kind at their entrance, constructed to prevent the entry of witchcraft and death, or to bring good luck to the inhabitants. Rabolo's talisman was considered to be a very effective one, for since the village was established, twelve dry seasons ago, no one had died there. This was no great wonder, since there were only fifteen inhabitants in the place.

My builders came to me to say they dared not remove Rabolo's fetich, and prayed me not to touch it until Rabolo came, otherwise there would be a big palaver. It seemed likely I should have some difficulty, for Rabolo had already spent the purchase-money of his village, distributing the goods amongst his wives and numerous fathers-in-law. However, I was firm, and when Rabolo came I was peremptory in demanding that the rubbish should be cleared away. He submitted at last, and commenced to cut down the bushes which covered the talisman, and dig up the mysterious relics. The first thing that I saw turned up was the skull of a chimpanzee buried in the sand; then came the skull of a man, probably an ancestor of Rabolo, and a mass of broken plates, glasses, and crockery of all sorts, which had been placed there to keep company with the *mondah*. He then removed the two upright poles with cross-bar and talismanic creeper growing at their foot, which constituted the protecting portal of the village, the negroes all the while standing around with looks of blank amazement. It is the belief of the negroes that, as long as the creeping-plant keeps alive, so long will the fetich retain its efficacy. A similar plant covered both the heaps of skulls and rubbish. At the foot of this portal and underneath the creeper were more chimpanzee skulls and fragments of pottery. In the ground near the two poles were also two wooden idols. We removed the whole, and I need not tell my readers that no evil consequences ensued. As to Rabolo and his subjects, they flattered themselves that it was this powerful fetich which brought me to settle on this spot. They have, in common with all the negroes of this part of Africa, a notion that there is some mysterious connection or affinity between the chimpanzee and the white man. It is owing, I believe, to the pale face of the chimpanzee, which has suggested the notion that we are descended from it, as the negro has descended from the black-faced gorilla. I heard of other head men of villages making *mondahs* with skulls of chimpanzees associated with skulls of their ancestors, believing that these would draw my heart to them and induce me to give them presents.

The greatest curse of the whole country is the belief in *aniemba*—sorcery or witchcraft. The African firmly believes death to be always a *violence*. He cannot imagine that a man who was well two weeks ago should now be lying at death's door with disease, unless some potent wizard had interfered, and by witchcraft broken the thread of life and inflicted sickness. They have the most terrible and debasing fear of death.

"Are you ready for death?" I sometimes asked.

"No!" would be the hasty reply. "Never speak of that; ah!" with a shudder of horror.

And then a dark cloud settled on the poor fellow's face; in his sleep that night he had horrid dreams, and for a few days he was suspicious of all about him, fearing for his poor life, lest it should be attacked by a wizard.

If the African is once possessed with the belief that he is bewitched, his whole nature seems to change. He becomes suspicious of his dearest friends. The father dreads his children—the son his father and mother, the man his wife, and the wives their husband. He fancies himself sick, and really often becomes sick through his fears. By night he thinks himself surrounded with evil spirits. He covers himself with fetiches and charms, makes presents to the idol and to Abambou and Mbuirri; and is full of wonderful and frightful dreams, which all point to the fact that the village is full of wicked sorcerers. Gradually the village itself becomes infected by his fears. The people grow suspicious. Chance turns their suspicions to some unlucky individual, who is supposed to have a reason for a grudge. Finally, the excitement becomes too high to be restrained; and often they do not even wait for a death, but begin at once the work of butchering those on whom public suspicion is fastened. On the death of a *free* man, at least one or two persons are killed, but this is not generally the case when women, children, or slaves die. The law of witchcraft makes no distinction, as regards its victims, between prince, slave, or free man, male or female.

In such cases the influence of the ouganga, or doctor, is always potent for evil. He gains in power by every such scene; and it is his interest, therefore, to foster rather than to restrain the excitement. His incantations are waited upon with breathless interest, and woe to the luckless man or woman who has offended him, for now he has his revenge. His decisions follow often the prejudices of the multitude, who have suspected beforehand those that are thought to be possessed of the *aniemba*. From the doctor's decision there is no appeal but that of drinking the mboundou.

I have often endeavoured to get at the secret thoughts of the doctors or wonder-workers among these people. They lead the popular superstition in such manner that it is almost impossible to suppose they are themselves deceived, and yet it is certain that most of them have a kind of faith in it. Nevertheless, it is not likely that they are imposed upon to the same extent as the common people, and this because they are most barefaced impostors themselves. They go about covered with charms to which they themselves give importance. They relate most wonderful dreams and visions, and when they fasten a charge of sorcery on any person, it is scarce possible to conceive that in such a case they are the victims of delusions which they themselves create. Indeed, I must say, that generally for months before popular feeling points to those who are believed to be wizards. I have never found them very friendly to myself, and never disposed to assert or deny anything. One thing only I *can* assert about them: they can drink great quantities of mboundou without taking harm from it. And this is one great source of their power over the people.

The ouganga, or doctor, is a personage whose chief powers are the ability (which is real) to drink great quantities of the mboundou poison, and the power (which is imaginary) to discover sorcerers, and to confer powers on greegrees and charms, which, without his manipulations, are worthless. This personage enjoys, therefore, great consequence in his tribe or village. His word is potent for life or death. At his command—or rather at his suggestion—the village is removed: men, women, and children are slain or enslaved; wars are begun and ended.

On the eve of all the more important undertakings of the village or tribe a doctor is consulted, who pretends to be able, by certain ceremonies of divination, to foretell the issue, and by this they shape their conduct. It sometimes happens, too, that a negro, not a doctor, is seized with the belief that Obambou (a devil) is in his body. The bowels are the seat of this possession; and the possessed goes about in a wild way—sees visions, dreams, and pretends to foresee future events, gaining sometimes considerable temporary prestige.

CHAPTER XXII.

The gorilla—Habitation of the gorilla—Habits of the gorilla—His food—Shyness of the female gorilla—Fierceness of the male—His enormous strength—Height of the gorilla—His appearance—Hands and feet of the gorilla—Hanno and Pliny on the gorilla—The chimpanzee—Difference between the chimpanzee and the gorilla—Habits of young chimpanzee—The nshiego-mbouvé, or bald-headed chimpanzee—The nkengo nshiego—The kooloo-kamba.

It is my good fortune to be the only white man who can speak of the gorilla from personal knowledge; and while my experience and observation prove that many of the actions reported of it are false and vain imaginings of ignorant negroes and credulous travellers, I can also vouch that no description can exceed the horror of its appearance, the ferocity of the attack of the male, or the impish malignity of its nature.

I am sorry to be the dispeller of such agreeable delusions; but the gorilla does not lurk in trees by the roadside, and drag up unsuspicious passers-by in its claws, and choke them to death in its vice-like paws; it does not attack the elephant, and beat him to death with sticks; it does not carry off women from the native villages; it does not even build itself a house of leaves and twigs in the forest-trees and sit on the roof, as has been confidently reported of it, and the numerous stories of its attacking in great numbers have not a grain of truth in them.

It lives in the loneliest and darkest portions of the dense African jungles, preferring deep wooded valleys and also rugged heights. The high plains also, whose surface is strewn with immense boulders, seem to be favourite haunts. Water occurs everywhere in this part of Africa, but I have noticed that the gorilla is always found very near to a plentiful supply.

It is a restless and nomadic beast, wandering from place to place, and scarce ever found for two days together in the same neighbourhood. In part this restlessness is caused by the struggle it has to find its favourite food. The gorilla, though it has such immense canines, and though its vast strength doubtless fits it to capture and kill almost every animal which frequents the forests, is a strict vegetarian. I examined the stomachs of all which I was lucky enough to kill, and never found traces there of aught but berries, pine-apple leaves, and other vegetable matter. It is a huge feeder, and no doubt soon eats up the scant supply of its natural food which is found in any limited space, and is then forced to wander on in constant battle with famine. Its vast paunch, which protrudes before it when it stands upright, proves it to be a great feeder; and, indeed, its great frame and enormous muscular development could not be supported on little food.

It is not true that it lives much or at all on trees. I found them almost always on the ground, although they often climb the trees to pick berries or nuts, but after eating they return to the ground. By the examination of the stomach of many specimens, I was able to ascertain with tolerable certainty the nature of its food, and I discovered that, for all I found, it had no need to ascend trees. It is fond of the wild sugar-cane; especially fond of the white ribs of the pine-apple leaf; and also eats the pith of some trees, and a kind of nut with a very hard shell. This shell is so hard that it requires a strong blow with a heavy hammer to break it; and here is probably one purpose of that enormous strength of jaw which long seemed to me thrown away on a non-carnivorous animal, and which is sufficiently evidenced by the manner in which the barrel of the musket of one of my unfortunate hunters was flattened by an enraged male gorilla.

Only the young gorillas sleep on trees, for protection from wild beasts. I have myself come upon fresh traces of a gorilla's bed on several occasions, and could see that the male had seated himself with his back against a tree-trunk. In fact, on the back of the male gorilla there is generally a patch on which the hair is worn thin from this position, while the nest-building *Troglodytes-calvus*, or bald-headed *nshiego*, which constantly sleeps under its leafy shelter on a tree-branch, has this bare place at its side, and in quite a different way. I believe, however, that while the male always sleeps at the foot of a tree, or elsewhere on the ground, the female and the young may sometimes ascend to the tree-top, as I have seen marks of such ascension.

Of adults, I found almost always one male with one female, though sometimes the old male wanders companionless. In such cases, as with the "rogue" elephant, he is particularly morose and malignant, and dangerous to approach. Young gorillas I found sometimes in companies of five; sometimes less, but never more. The young always run off, on all-fours, shrieking with fear. They are difficult to approach, as their hearing is acute, and they lose no time in making their escape, while the nature of the ground makes it hard for the hunter to follow after. The adult animal is also shy, and I have hunted all day at times without coming upon my quarry, when I felt sure that they were carefully avoiding me. When, however, at last fortune favours the hunter, and he comes accidentally or by good management upon his prey, he need not fear its running away. In all my hunts and encounters with this animal, I never knew a grown male to run off. When I surprised a pair of gorillas, the male was generally sitting down on a rock or against a tree, in the darkest corner of the jungle, where the brightest sun left its traces only in a dim and gloomy twilight. The female was generally feeding close by; and it is singular that she almost always gave the alarm by running off with loud and sudden cries.

The common walk of the gorilla is not on his hind legs, but on all-fours. In this posture, the arms are so long that the head and breast are raised considerably, and, as it runs, the hind legs are brought far beneath the body. The leg and arm on the same side move together, which gives the beast a curious waddle. It can run at great speed. The young, parties of which I have often pursued, never took to trees, but ran along the ground; and at a distance, with their bodies half-erect, looked not unlike negroes making off from pursuit: the hind-legs moved between the arms, and those were somewhat bowed outward. I have never found the female to attack, though I have been told by the negroes that a mother with a young one in charge will sometimes make fight. It is a pretty thing to see such a mother with the baby gorilla sporting about her. I have watched them in the woods, till, eager as I was to obtain specimens, I had not the heart to shoot. But in such cases my negro hunters exhibited no tender-heartedness, but killed their quarry without loss of time.

When the mother runs off from the hunter, the young one grasps her about the neck, and hangs beneath her breast with its little legs about her body.

The strength of the gorilla is evidently enormous. That with its jaws it can dent a musket barrel, and with its arms break trees from four to six inches in diameter, sufficiently proves that its vast bony frame has corresponding muscle. The negroes never attack them with other weapons than guns; and in those parts of the far interior where no European guns had yet reached, as among the Apingi, this great beast roamed unmolested, the monarch of the forest. To kill a gorilla gives a hunter a life-long reputation for courage and enterprise even among the bravest of the negro tribes, who are generally, it may be said, not lacking in this quality of courage.

The gorilla has no cries or utterances that I have heard except those already described—the short, sharp bark, and the roar of the attacking male, and the scream of the female and young when alarmed; except, indeed, a low kind of cluck, with which the watchful mother seems to call her child to her. The young ones have a cry when in distress; but their voice is harsh, and it is more a moan of pain than a child's cry.

It uses no artificial weapon of offence, but attacks always with its arms, though in a struggle no doubt the powerful teeth would play a part. I have several times noticed skulls in which the huge canines were broken off, not *worn* down, as they are in almost all the adult gorillas by gnawing at trees which they wished to break, and which, without being gnawed into, are too strong even for them. The negroes informed me that such teeth were broken in combats between the males for the possession of a female, and I think this quite probable. Such a combat must form a magnificent and awful spectacle. A struggle between two well-matched gorillas would exceed, in that kind of excitement which the Romans took such delight in, anything in that line which they were ever gratified with.

In height adult gorillas vary as much as men. The adult males in my collection range from five feet two inches to five feet eight.

The colour of the skin in the gorilla, young as well as adult, is intense black. This colour does not appear, however, except in the face, on the breast, and in the palms of the hands. The hair of a grown, but not aged specimen, is in colour iron-gray. The individual hairs are ringed with alternate stripes of black and gray, which produces the iron-gray colour. On the arms the hair is darker and also much longer, being sometimes over two inches long. It grows upwards on the fore-arm and downwards on the main-arm. Aged gorillas, the negroes told me, turn quite gray all over; and I have one huge male in my collection whose worn-out tusks show great age, and whose colour is, in fact, a dirty gray, with the exception of the long black shaggy hair on the arm. The head is covered with reddish-brown hair, short, and extending almost to the neck, or where the neck should be.

In the adult male the chest is bare. In the young males which I had in captivity it was thinly covered with hair. In the female the mammæ have but a slight development, and the breast is bare. The colour of the hair in the female is black, with a decided tinge of red, and not ringed as in the male. The hair on the arms is but little longer than that on the body, and is of a like colour. The reddish crown which covers the scalp of the male is not apparent in the female till she is almost grown up.

The eyes of the gorilla are deeply sunken, the immense overhanging bony frontal ridge giving to the face the expression of a constant savage scowl. The mouth is wide, and the lips are sharply cut, exhibiting no red on the edges, as in the human face. The jaws are of tremendous weight and power. The huge canines of the male, which are fully exhibited when, in his rage, he draws back his lips and shows the red colour of the inside of his mouth, lend additional ferocity to his aspect. In the female these canines are smaller.

The almost total absence of neck, which gives the head the appearance of being set into the shoulders, is due to the backward position of the occipital condyles, by means of which the skull is set upon the trunk. The brain-case is low and compressed, and the lofty ridge of the skull causes the cranial

GORILLA'S HEAD.

profile * to describe an almost straight line from the occiput to the supraorbital ridge. The immense development of the temporal muscles which arise from this ridge, and the corresponding size of the jaw, are evidences of the great strength of the animal. Young gorillas have twenty milk teeth, then twenty-eight, subsequently increased to thirty-two.

The eyebrows are thin, but not well defined, and are almost

* The maximum brain of the male gorilla, as recorded up to the present time, is 34·05 cubic inches; the average of ten males, 29·70; the maximum of three females, 29·6; average of three females, 26. Maximum of three chimpanzees, which has a much smaller bony head, 26 in.; minimum, 22; nshiego-mbouvé, 22; kooloo-kamba, 25. The young nshiego-mbouvé, 21 and 18, showing the slow growth of brain (*P. B. Du C.*, 1890).

lost in the hair of the scalp. The eyelashes are thin also. The eyes are wide apart; the ears are smaller than those of man, and in form closely resemble the human ear. They are almost on the same parallel with the eyes. In a front view of the face the nose is flat, but somewhat prominent—more so than in any other ape; this is on account of a slightly projecting nose-bone. The gorilla is the only ape which shows such a projection, and in this respect it comes nearer to man than any other of the man-like apes.

The profile of the trunk shows a slight convexity. The

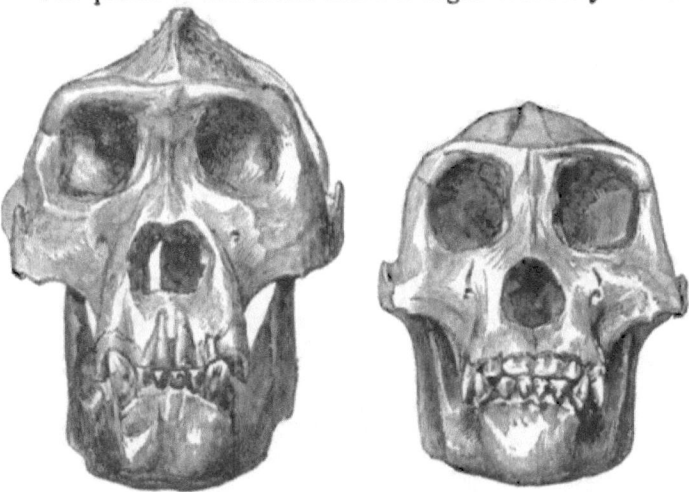

GORILLA, MALE.　　　　　　GORILLA, FEMALE.

chest is of great capacity; the shoulders exceedingly broad; the pectoral regions show slightly projecting a pair of nipples, as in the other apes and in the human species. The abdomen is of immense size, very prominent, and rounding at the sides. The arms have prodigious muscular development, and are very long, extending as low as the knees. The fore-arm is nearly of uniform size from the wrist to the elbow. The great length of the arms and the shortness of the legs form one of the chief deviations from man. The arms are not so long when compared with the trunk, but they are so in comparison with the legs. These are short, and decrease in size

278   *EQUATORIAL AFRICA.*   Chap. XXII.

from below the knee to the ankle, having no calf. The superior length of the arm (humerus) in proportion to the

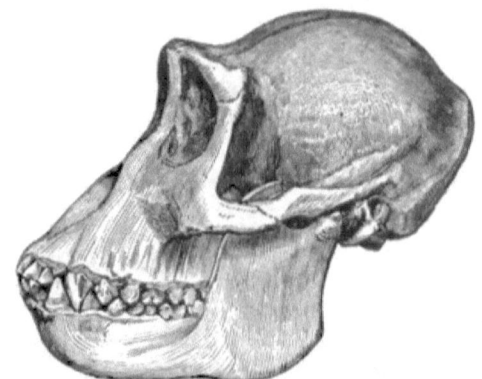

GORILLA, FEMALE (facial angle, 51).

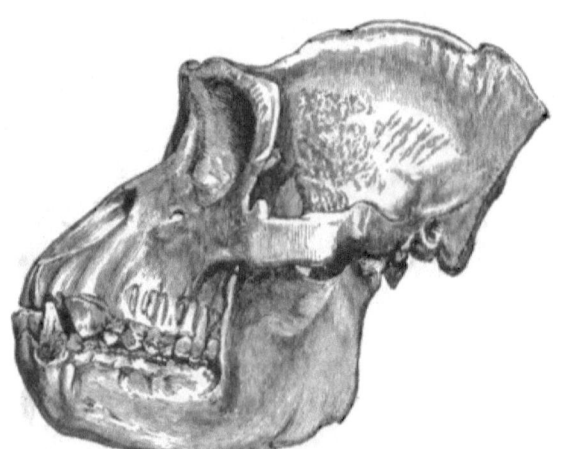

GORILLA, MALE (facial angle, 49).

fore-arm, brings the gorilla, in that respect, in closer anthropoid affinities with man than any of the other apes.

The hands of the animal, especially in the male, are of immense size, strong, short, and thick. The fingers are short and of great size, the circumference of the middle finger at the first joint being in some gorillas over six inches. The skin on the back of the fingers, near the middle phalanx, is callous and very thick, which shows that the most usual mode of progression of the animal is on all-fours, and resting on the knuckles. The thumb is shorter than in man, and not half so thick as the forefinger. The hand is hairy as far as the division of the fingers, those, as in man, being covered with short thin hairs. The palm of the hand is naked, callous, and intensely black. The nails are black, and shaped like those of man, but smaller in proportion, and projecting very slightly beyond the ends of the fingers. They are thick and strong, and always seem much worn. The hand of the gorilla is almost as wide as it is long, and in this it approaches nearer to those of man than any of the other apes.

The foot is proportionally wider than in man. The sole is callous and intensely black, and looks somewhat like a giant hand of immense power and grasp. The transverse wrinkles show the frequency and freedom of movement of the two joints of the great toe, proving that they have a power of grasp. The middle toe, or third, is longer than the second and fourth, the fifth proportionally shorter, as in man.

The toes are divided into three groups, so to speak. Inside the great toe, outside the little toe, and the three others partly united by a web. The two joints of the great toe measured, in one specimen, six and a half inches in circumference. As a whole, the foot of the gorilla presents a great likeness to the foot of man, and by far more so than in any other ape. In no other animal is the foot so well adapted for the maintenance of the erect position. Also, the gorilla is much less of a tree-climber than any other ape. The foot in the gorilla is longer than the hand, as in man, while in the other apes the foot is somewhat shorter than the hand. The hair on the foot comes to the division of the toes. With the exception of the big toe, the others present a great likeness to those of man, being free only above the second phalanx; they are slightly covered with thin hair and free.

The passage in the *Periplus*, or voyage of Hanno, in which it is supposed he alludes to the animal now known as the gorilla, reads as follows:—" On the third day, having sailed from thence, passing the streams of fire, we came to a bay called the Horn of the South. In the recess was an island like the first, having a lake, and in this there was another island full of wild men. But much the greater part of them were women with hairy bodies, whom the interpreters called gorillas. . . . . But pursuing them, we were not able to take the men; they all escaped from us by their great agility, being *cremnobates* (that is to say, climbing precipitous rocks and trees), and defending themselves by throwing stones at us. We took three women, who bit and tore those who caught them, and were unwilling to follow. We were obliged, therefore, to kill them, and took their skins off,

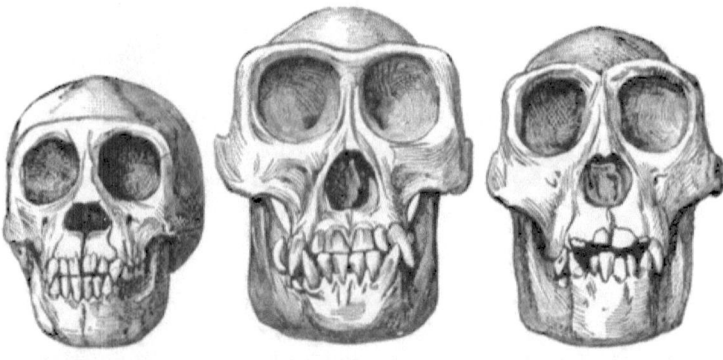

GORILLA, YOUNG (facial angle 62).   GORILLA, RED RUMP (facial angle, 51).   GORILLA, SHEDDING TEETH (facial angle, 52).

which skins were brought to Carthage, for we did not navigate farther, provisions becoming scarce."

According to Pliny, the skins were hung in the temple of Juno, and the name *gorillas* was changed to *gorgones*. Two of these skins were yet in the temple at the time when Carthage was taken. "Penetravit in eas (Gorgades Insulas) Hanno Pœnorum imperator, prodiditque hirta feminarum corpora, viros pernicitate evassisse, duarumque gorgonum cutes argumenti et miraculi gratia in Junonis templo posuit, spectatas usque ad Carthaginem captam."

Of the chimpanzee (*Troglodytes niger*), an animal long though not very thoroughly known to naturalists, I regret that I have nothing new to state. Though found in almost all the regions which I visited, it is everywhere very rare, except near the Danger, Gaboon, and Cape Lopez countries. I killed one and saw another in my Cape Lopez expedition; and I for a short time owned two young living specimens. Both of these died, however, before I was able to make any observations upon their peculiarities.

Those apes which live much in trees, as the chimpanzee, have fingers on both their fore and hind feet much longer than the gorilla's, which, indeed, approximate much nearer to the construction of the human hand and foot, and are, by reason of this different construction, less fitted for tree-climbing. Here I may state that, though young chimpanzees are often captured by the negroes of the Muni, Moonda, and Gaboon rivers, which shows that they are somewhat abundant in those regions, I never met with a single shelter there, and consequently have come to the conclusion that they make none.

The chimpanzee differs from the gorilla in these chief particulars:—It is a great tree-climber, passing much of its time among the branches of the great trees of tropical Africa. It is, though untameable when grown, still not fierce and malign like the gorilla. It has never been known to attack man, and its young are tractable and easily tamed. While the gorilla resists man, the chimpanzee flies to the densest woods: it is therefore hunted with even greater difficulty than the gorilla.

The young consort in small companies, but the adults go in pairs or singly. The young have a yellow face, which changes to an intense black as they grow older. They are difficult to keep in a state of captivity, dying almost invariably of consumption or dysentery.

I may observe that, though the negroes are very ingenious in their contrivance of traps for nearly all the greater beasts of the forest, catching by various devices not only the elephant, hippopotamus, antelope, and monkeys, but even the leopard, I know of no case in which an ape of any kind was caught in this way.

The chimpanzee is remarkable for its unusually wide geographical range. It is found from the Gambia in almost every degree of latitude down to the parallel of St. Philipe Benguela.

Its food consists of berries, leaves, and nuts. So far as I have been able to ascertain, it builds no shelter like the nshiego-mbouvé. In the Cape Lopez country I examined and inquired diligently, but could find no trace of any such habit, although the negroes are familiar with the animal. In the Gaboon country the chimpanzee is called nshiego; in the interior it is known as the nchèko, a name which very much resembles that of the leopard—n'gègo.

A negro from a neighbouring village brought me a young

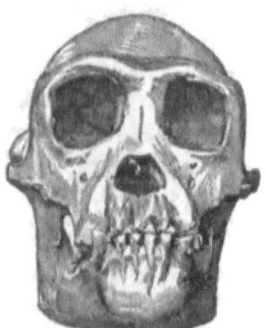
CHIMPANZEE.

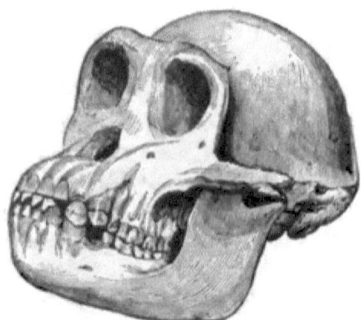
CHIMPANZEE (facial angle, 54).

male chimpanzee about three years old, which had been caught in the woods on the banks of the Npoulounay about three months previously. Thomas, for so I christened my little *protégé*, was a tricky little rascal, and afforded me no end of amusement; he was, however, very tame, like all young chimpanzees. Unfortunately, Thomas was lame in one hand, several of the fingers having been broken and healed up in a distorted position. This was caused by his having been maltreated by the village dogs, who were sent in chase of him one day when he escaped from his captors and ran into the neighbouring woods. I had Tom tied by a cord to a pole in the verandah of my hut, and fed him with cooked plantains and other food from my own table. He soon got to prefer cooked to raw food, and rejected raw plantains

NSHIEGO-MBOUVÉ AND YOUNG.
(*Troglodytes-calvus.*)

whenever they were offered to him. The difference in tamability between the young chimpanzee and the young gorilla is a fact which I have confirmed by numerous observations, and I must repeat it here, as it was one of those points which were disputed in my former work. A young chimpanzee becomes tame and apparently reconciled to captivity in two or three days after he is brought from the woods. The young gorilla I have never yet seen tame in confinement, although I have had four of them in custody, while still of very early age.

One day I witnessed an act of Master Thomas which seemed to me to illustrate the habits of his species in the wild state. A few days after he came into my possession I bought a domestic cat for my house; as soon as the young chimpanzee saw it he flew in alarm to his pole and clambered up it, the hair of his body becoming erect and his eyes bright with excitement. In a moment recovering himself he came down, and rushing on the cat, with one of his feet seized the nape of the animal, and with the other pressed on its back, as if trying to break its neck. Not wishing to lose my cat, I interfered and saved its life. The negroes say that the chimpanzee attacks the leopard in this way.

The nshiego-mbouvé (*Troglodytes-calvus*) has a much narrower range than the chimpanzee, and even than the gorilla. I found it only in the table-lands of the interior and in the densest forests. I have reason to believe that it is found indifferently in the haunts of the gorilla in the farther interior, and do not know that the two species quarrel. It differs from the gorilla in being smaller, milder, far more docile, less strong, and in the singular habit of building for itself a nest or shelter of leaves amid the higher branches of trees. I have watched, at different times, this ape retiring to its rest at night, and have seen it climb up to its house and seat itself comfortably on the projecting branch, with its head in the dome of the roof, and its arm about the tree.

The distinctive marks of the *T. calvus*, those which prove it to be a separate variety of the chimpanzee, may be stated as follows: its head is bald, and shining black; its temper is not fierce like the gorilla's; its young is *white*; while the young gorilla is black, and the young chimpanzee yellow.

Its head is nearly round, and bullet-formed; the nose is very flat; the ears larger than in the gorilla, but smaller than in the kooloo-kamba and chimpanzee; the eyes sunken; the teeth and canines small when compared with the gorilla's. The arms reach a little below the knee. The hands are long and slender; the foot shorter than the hand. The toes are *free*.

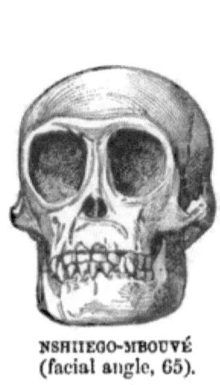
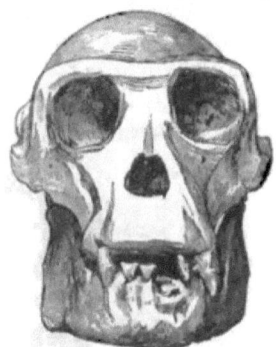

NSHIEGO-MBOUVÉ (facial angle, 65).

NSHIEGO-MBOUVÉ (facial angle, 55).

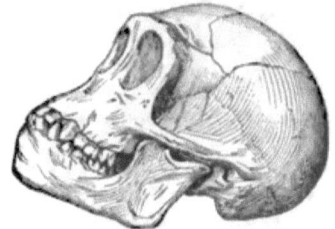

NSHIEGO-MBOUVÉ (young).

The callosities on the back of the fingers show that this animal goes commonly on all-fours, and rests its weight on the doubled-up hands. The hair is of one uniform rusty-black colour. The male is larger than the female. I have killed an old male whose skeleton seems more powerful than that of any female gorilla I have seen, but I suspect it to have been an uncommonly large specimen, it being much larger than the other adult specimen I had.

Opposite Aniambe, on the right bank of the Fernand-Vaz, I found a third species of chimpanzee of a variety new to me, and called by the natives nkengo nschiego. It is distinguished from the common form of the chimpanzee by its face being yellow. All the specimens of the old bald-headed chimpanzee that I have found had black faces, except when quite young, when the face is white and not yellow, and the common chimpanzee, although yellow-faced when young, becomes gradually black as it grows old. There are, therefore, three varieties of the chimpanzee distinguished by the negroes of Equatorial Africa. I do not here include the kooloo-kamba, which appears to be very rare.

Lastly, we come to the kooloo-kamba. This ape, whose

HEAD OF KOOLOO-KAMBA.

singular cry distinguishes it at once from all its congeners in these wilds, is remarkable, as bearing a closer general resemblance to man than any other ape yet known. It is very rare, and I was able to obtain but one specimen of it. This is smaller than the adult male gorilla, and stouter than the female gorilla. The head is its most remarkable point. This struck me at once as having an expression curiously like to an Esquimaux or Chinaman. The face is bare and black. The forehead is higher than in *any* other ape, and the cranial capacity greater by measurement proportionally to size. The eyes are wider apart than in any other ape. The nose is flat. The cheek-bones are high and prominent, and the cheeks sunken and "lank." The ridge over the eyes is well marked. The muzzle is less prominent and broader than in the other apes. The sides of the face are covered with a growth of straight hair, which, meeting under the chin like the human whiskers, gives the face a remarkably human look. The

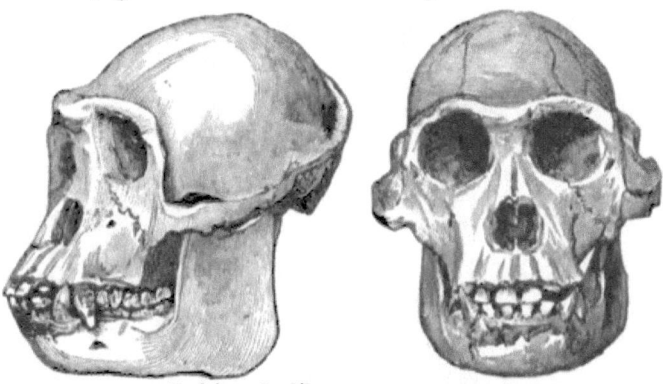

KOOLOO-KAMBA (facial angle, 57).   KOOLOO-KAMBA.

arms reach below the knee. The hair on the arms meets at the elbow, growing upwards on the fore-arm and downwards on the arm. The body is hairy. The shoulders are broad; the hands long and narrow, showing it to be a tree-climber. The arms and hands are very muscular. The abdomen is very prominent, as it is in the gorilla. The ears are very large, and are more nearly like the human ear than those of

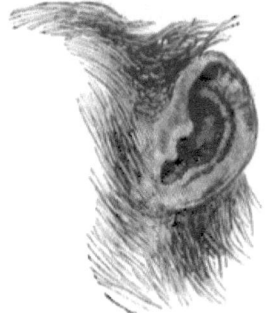

EAR OF KOOLOO-KAMBA.

any other ape. The subjoined cut is from a drawing made with great care from my specimen, and shows this singular ear very correctly.

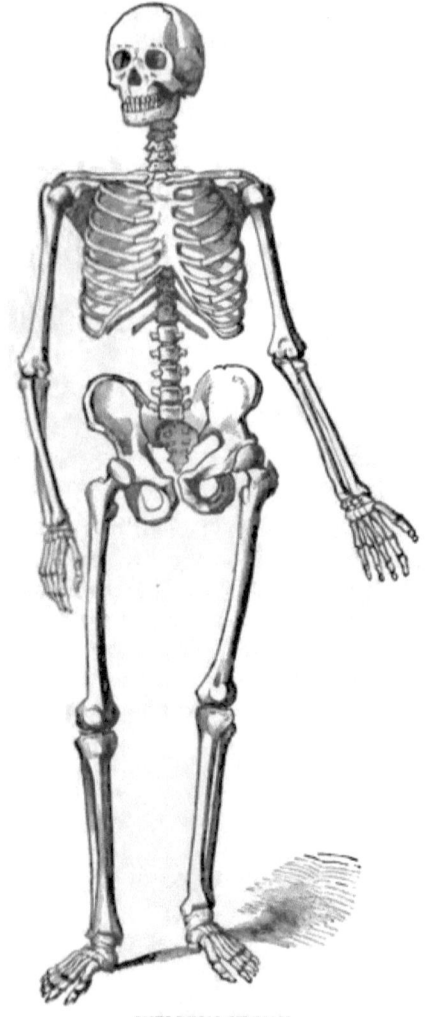

SKELETON OF MAN.

Man has

12 (and sometimes 13) pairs of ribs. 5 lumbar (sometimes 4) vertebræ.
7 cervical vertebræ.   5 sacral   do.
12 dorsal (and sometimes 13) verte- 8 carpal (wrist) bones.
 bræ.

SKELETON OF GORILLA.

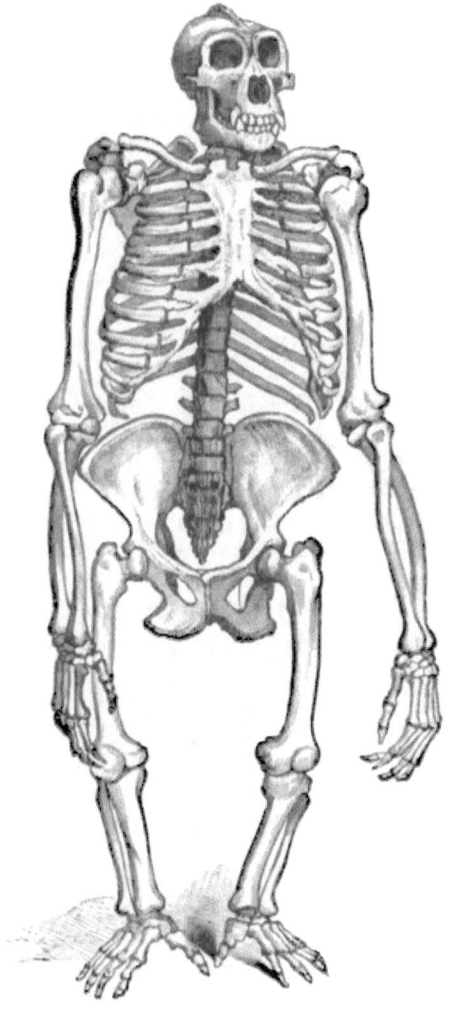

SKELETON OF GORILLA.

The Gorilla has

13 pairs of ribs.
7 cervical vertebræ.
13 dorsal do.
3 lumbar vertebræ.
6 sacral do.
8 carpal (wrist) bones.

CHAPTER XXIII.

The Bakalai people—Tribes widely intermixed—Roving tendency of the Bakalai—Instability of their villages—Their quarrelsome habits—Their war customs — Marriage customs — Negroes' knowledge of human nature—Musical instruments.

BEFORE resuming the narrative, I think it well to give the reader some account of the *Bakalai*.

The Bakalai are one of the most numerous, widely extended, and important tribes I met with in Equatorial Africa. Their settlements are widely scattered, and they are often found living in independent towns in regions chiefly occupied by other tribes. How far they reach inland I cannot tell. To the Ashira they were known as neighbours, and even the Apingi pointed eastward towards the unknown centre of the continent when I inquired for Bakalai.

These Bakalai are reputed to be very warlike, and various circumstances show that they are so. They are much dreaded by other tribes; and I find that these others have left all the right side of the river to their fighting neighbours. Those who live on the river-bank, however, are in some sort bound to keep the peace; for they have no right near the water but with the leave of Quengueza, and this they get only on promise of peaceable behaviour.

Their houses also show their prominent trait. They are not built of split bamboos, like those farther down the river, but of bark, which is peeled off large trees in slips four to five feet long and a foot wide, and securely lashed on the sides. This makes them tight. The walls always have open strips, through which an enemy can see to shoot those inside. From this danger the bark walls protect them. The houses here are small, however, not more than twelve feet long by eight wide. They are generally two rooms deep, and in the back room the family sleep, while in front their goods are kept. In war-time they change their sleeping-places in the house every night, so that the enemy may be at a loss where to fire when attacking from the outside.

The tribes of Western Africa are curiously intermixed, as

the reader will have seen ere this from the accounts of my wanderings among them. This happens because the most enterprising are always striving to get possession of the rivers, which are the only highways of the country. From these they drive away the weaker tribes, or rather portions of tribes.

One of the peculiar traits of the Bakalai is their roving character. They never stay long in one place. A Bakalai village is scarce built—often the plantations have not borne fruit the first time—when they feel impelled to move. Then everything is abandoned; they gather up what few stores of provisions they may have, and start off, often for great distances, to make with infinite pains a new settlement, which will be abandoned in turn, sometimes after a few months, though occasionally they remain a year or two, and even more, in the same place.

Many things contribute to this roving tendency, but first of all is their great fear of death. They dread to see a dead person. Their sick, unless they have good and near friends, are often driven out of the village to die in loneliness in the forest. I have twice seen old men thus driven out, nor could I persuade anyone to give shelter or comfort to these friendless wretches. Once an old man, poor and naked, lean as Death himself, and barely able to walk, hobbled into a Bakalai village where I was staying. Seeing me, the poor old fellow came to beg some tobacco—their most cherished solace. I asked him where he was going.

"I don't know."

"Where are you from?"

He mentioned a village a few miles off.

"Have you no friends there?"

"None."

"No son, no daughter, no brother, no sister?"

"None."

"You are sick?"

"They drove me away for that."

"What will you do?"

"Die."

A few women came up to him and gave him water and a

little food. But the men saw death in his eyes. They drove him away. He went sadly, as though knowing and submitting to his fate. A few days after his poor lean body was found in the wood. His troubles were ended.

When a man dies in a Bakalai village the stability of that settlement has received a violent shock. If a second dies, then the people at once move away. They think the place bewitched; they fancy death, dreaded death, stalking in their midst. A doctor is called, who goes through his incantations, and some poor wretch is condemned to drink the mboundou. Often several friendless creatures are accused and condemned in a breath, and murdered in cold blood. Then the village is broken up; the people set out again upon their wanderings, and fix upon some lonely spot for new plantations and a new home.

It is as though they were all their lives vainly fleeing from the dread face of death. This, indeed, is the refrain of all their sad songs, the burden of every fear. Having little else to lose, they seem to dread, more than any other people I ever knew, the loss of life. And no wonder; for after death is to them nothing.

"Death is the end." "Now we live; by-and-by we shall die; then we shall be no more." "He is gone; we shall never see him more; we shall never shake his hand again; we shall never hear him laugh again." This is the dolorous burden of their evening and morning songs.

And still, by a strange contradiction, they are extravagantly superstitious. Believing that there is no life beyond this, they yet fancy a ghost or spirit in every moving tree or bush after night, and in the twilight hour are sometimes overpowered with an undefinable dread, which makes them fear to come even outside their huts.

Another cause of fear is their treacherous and quarrelsome disposition. They are constantly quarrelling with their neighbours. I have already explained the singular ideas they have of retaliation. Once I was in a village, when, on a sudden, I heard great wailing among the women. I found that two women had been killed by some persons unseen, while they were standing in the neighbouring creek, washing.

The murderers were not known for some days. All was consternation in the village.

Then it somehow reached their ears that these women had been killed by men who had come from a village fifty miles off. This village had a palaver or quarrel with one nearer. They came down and killed two women of a village which they had no quarrel with, and this made the villagers, whose relatives they had thus murdered, their allies. This singular doctrine of alliance seems to be accepted by most of the tribes.

When war has really broken out in the country once, there is no rest nor safety. No man or woman in any village can take a step in any direction, day or night, without fear of death. They lay ambuscades to surprise each other's villages. They shoot through the tree-bark of which their houses are made, and kill sleeping persons. They use every unfair means of warfare; and the meaner the attack and the greater the treachery, the more glory they have won. In such times of war fires are put out after dark, because they give light to the enemy; the people keep a dead silence, lest their voices should betray their whereabouts; the hunters fear to hunt, the women and slaves to plant, and, in consequence, everybody is in a condition of semi-starvation. This lasts sometimes for months. At last whole districts are depopulated; those who are not killed desert their villages, and all, perhaps, because a man in one village stole from one in another and refused satisfaction.

While I was in Obindji's village, the Bakalai chiefs and people, to the number of several hundreds, met together to ask justice on the head of Pendé, Obindji's brother, who was charged with having stolen the bones of a dead person to make a fetich, which fetich would keep trade away from a particular town. This palaver was very violent; and I think, if Quengueza had not been on the spot, would have ended in bloodshed. Pendé denied having done what he was charged with, and I do not believe that anybody thought him guilty towards the end of the fuss. Nevertheless, to obtain quiet, the poor fellow had to give three slaves to the three chiefs who were the principal accusers.

GROUP OF BAKALAI.

The Bakalai are of the ordinary size. The men are generally well made; some are of small stature; and I have seen among them some splendid specimens of manhood. They are not very black, but have full negro features. They are not very strong, chiefly, I suppose, because they live poorly; but they have great powers of endurance, and on this account make admirable hunters.

They generally prefer to marry very young girls; and often young children are regularly bargained away. In this case they remain with their parents till the age of puberty.

When a man has chosen a girl, he calls on her parents and explains his wishes. They put a price upon her, which he pays, and then the poor girl is turned over to him. The more children she has, the more her husband loves her, and the greater is her importance in the town. The population being small in nearly all the villages, every birth is hailed with joy; and as girls have a money value, they are as highly thought of as boys, who make hunters and warriors. Few Bakalai women have many children. Those who do have their own way in many things, and are able to tyrannize over their own household and rival wives.

It is a curious fact, that, though they will take their brother's or father's wives in marriage, they will not marry a woman of the same *family* or clan with themselves. This is the case, also, among other tribes.

Those who live on the river have great fishing excursions, which furnish them with a portion of their sustenance. When the rivers recede at the approach of the dry season, the waters remain behind on the plains in pools. To one of these pools a village of Bakalai will come—men, women, and children—and, with earthenware pots and bowls, empty out the water. The poor fish, for whom no way of escape is open, struggle vainly against their enemy, who finally, having thrown out nearly all the water, rush in pell-mell and take out the fish. These are killed, and what are not eaten on the spot are smoked for future use, and thus a considerable store is often laid by for a needy time.

For hunting, almost all, even of those who live far beyond

the region where white men penetrate, make use of guns and powder. These are the chief articles of trade, and are most sought for by the natives everywhere. For the women beads are the most valued; and even the men do not despise ornaments.

The negroes, as a rule, are the shrewdest judges of human nature that ever I met. Lying is thought an enviable accomplishment among all the tribes, and a more thorough and unhesitating liar than one of these negroes is not to be found anywhere. A man does not, therefore, believe what another *says*, but watches his countenance, and forms his opinions from the other's *looks*. Now in this species of almost intuitive judgment the Bakalai excels all his brethren of the other tribes. Sometimes men came to Obindji and told him long stories on some subject of importance. The old chief would listen gravely and say nothing to the speaker, but presently would come to me and say—

"The man lies."

"But how do you know?" I would ask, knowing that the man's story was perfectly straightforward and not at all improbable.

"I watched his face," was the reply. "We Bakalai watch the face. The words are nothing; but the face tells us."

All the negroes are fond of music of certain kinds. The tam-tam is the noisiest instrument, and is used for all dances and ceremonials. But they have also a guitar, and a harp of eight strings—an ingenious instrument, on which some of the men play with a good deal of skill; and some of their airs were really pretty, though sad and monotonous. The *ombi*, as this is called, is a source of great delight to them. Often and often I have heard it played all night, while the crowd of listeners sat in silence around the fire. While the tam-tam rouses their feelings, and really throws them into a frenzy, the ombi has a soothing and softening effect upon them.

Both instruments are called *ombi*. One, which is shaped like a banjo or guitar, has but four strings. The other, with eight, is a harp. Both are made of thin pieces of a resonant wood, sometimes covered with snake, gazelle, or goat skin.

The strings are the long, fine, fibrous roots of a tree, and answer their purpose very well. The sound of the ombi with eight strings is soft and somewhat musical, and is used to accompany the voice; in such cases the airs are generally plaintive.

IBEKA: MUSICAL INSTRUMENT OF THE BAKALAI.

HARP OF BAKALAI. THE STRINGS ARE MADE OUT OF THE DRIED ROOT OF A SPECIES OF TREE.

CHAPTER XXIV.

Another journey for the interior—Meeting of the people of Biagano—
Good-bye to Biagano—Arrival at Goumbi—Death of Mpomo—
Witchcraft ceremony—Drinking of the mboundou—Execution for
witchcraft—Ilogo, a spirit living in the moon—Invocation of Ilogo—
A species of manatee.

HAVING returned from Obindji to the sea coast in order to deposit my collections in safety, I was, on the 10th of October, 1858, ready to leave Biagano, Ranpano's village, for another expedition; my health restored, my spirits in some measure recovered, and eager for the new region.

Quengueza was still too weak to travel, so I determined to start without him.

Ranpano and his people had been urging me for some time not to go; and now, when I was all ready, the old king called a grand palaver, which I attended, and of which the chief purpose was to persuade me not to venture into the interior.

My good old friend Ranpano was really solicitous about me. He made me an address, in which he informed me that he had heard the interior people wanted to get me into their power. They wanted to kill me, in order to make a fetich of my hair. They had very many fetiches already, and were very anxious to make their collection complete—so it appeared.

I replied that I had no fear of them; that, so far, I had been brought back safely to them.

Then he said, "We love you. You are our white man (ntangani). What you tell us we do. When you say it is wrong, we do not do it. We take care of your house, your goats, your fowls, your parrots, your monkeys. You are the first man that settled among us, and we love you."

To which all the people answered, "Yes, we love him! He is our white man, and we have no other white man."

Then the king said, "We know that writing talks. Write us, therefore, a letter to prove to your friends, if you do not come back, that it was not we who hurt you."

To this followed various objections to my going, to all of which I was obliged to make grave answers.

Finally, when they gave me up, all exclaimed in accents of wonder, "Ottangani angani (man of the white men)! what is the matter with you that you have no fear? God gave you the heart of a leopard! You were born without fear!"

More than a year ago the Commi gave me the title of "*makaga*," an honourable name, which only one man, and he the bravest and best hunter in the tribe, may bear. The office of the makaga is to lead in all desperate affairs. For instance, if any one has murdered one of his fellow-villagers, and the murderer's town refuses to give him up (which is almost always the case, they thinking it a shame to surrender anyone who has taken refuge with them), then it is the business of the makaga to take the best men of the villages, lead them to the assault of that which protects the murderer, and destroy that, with its inhabitants. It is remarkable that, in all the Commi country, the murder of a free man is punished with the death of the murderer. My title was rather an honorary one, as I was never called on to execute justice among them.

At last Ranpano gave me sixteen men to take me to Goumbi, from where Quengueza's people were to help me forward.

Quengueza sent orders to his brother, who acted as his vice-regent at Goumbi, to give me as many people as I wanted, and to afford me protection as far as I needed it; and especially named Adouma to be the chief of the party who were to accompany me to the Ashira country.

When all this was done, there was, according to African custom, a formal leave-taking. Quengueza's men, Ranpano's, and mine gathered before the old king, who solemnly bade us God-speed, taking my two hands in his and blowing upon them, as their custom is; saying, "Go thou safely, and return safely," and so I bid good-bye to Biagano.

We arrived at Goumbi on the 13th October, after meeting with two very heavy storms of wind and rain on the way. The people asked after their king, who had gone away well, and whom, they thought, I ought to have brought back in the same condition.

I was asked to go and see an old friend of mine, Mpomo, who was now sick. They had spent the night before drumming about his bedside to drive out the devil. But I soon saw that neither drumming nor medicine would help the poor fellow. The film of death was already in his eyes, and I knew he could scarce live through the approaching night. He held out his hand to me in welcome, and feebly said, "Chally, save me, for I am dying."

He was then surrounded by hundreds of people, most of them moved to tears at their friend's pitiable condition.

I explained to him that I had no power to save him. But he and those all around had the conviction that, if only I wished, I could cure him. They followed me to my house, asking for medicine; and at last, not to seem heartless, I sent him a restorative—something, at least, to make his remaining moments easy. At the same time I warned them that he would die, and they must not blame me for his death. This was necessary, for their ignorance makes them very suspicious.

When I awoke next morning I heard the mournful wail which proclaimed that poor Mpomo was gone to his long rest. This cry of the African mourners is the saddest I ever heard.

In the last moments of a Commi man who lies at the point of death, his head-wife comes and throws herself by him on his bed. Then, encircling his form with her arms, she sings to him songs of love, and pours out a torrent of endearing phrases, all the village standing by uttering wailings and shedding tears. Such a scene was always very touching to me.

When I went to Mpomo's house I saw his poor wives sitting in tears upon the ground, throwing moistened ashes and dust over their bodies, shaving their heads, and rending their clothes.

In the afternoon I heard talk of witchcraft.

The mourning lasted for two days. On the 17th the body, already in a state of decomposition, was put in a canoe and taken to the cemetery of the Goumbi people down the river some fifty miles. It was pitiable to see the grief of his poor wives. They seemed to have really loved him, and sorrowed for him now that he was dead, as they had carefully and lovingly attended upon him till he died. I saw them, on the night of his death, weeping over him, one after the other taking him in her arms. It was a strange sight. In these sorrowful moments there was no sign of jealousy between the poor women, that I could see. All were united by their love for the same object.

Those who have studied the African character, and know how much they are given to dissimulation, cannot be certain whether the display of love comes from real sorrow or not. Of course, every wife ought to appear much distressed, for, should they not show a profound sorrow they would certainly be accused of bewitching their husbands. I have even known cases where the mother was killed as the cause of the death of her own child.

On the day Mpomo was buried proceedings were begun to discover the persons who had bewitched the poor fellow. They could not be persuaded that a young man, hale and hearty but a few weeks ago, could die by natural causes. A great doctor was brought from up the river, and for two nights and days the rude scenes which I have already once given an account of were repeated.

At last, on the third morning, when the excitement of the people was at its height—when old and young, male and female, were frantic with the desire for revenge on the sorcerers—the doctor assembled them about him in the centre of the town, and began his final incantation, which should disclose the names of the murderous sorcerers.

Every man and boy was armed, some with spears, some with swords, some with guns and axes, and on every face was shown a determination to wreak bloody vengeance on those who should be pointed out as the criminals. The whole town was wrapt in an indescribable fury and horrid thirst for human blood. For the first time I found my voice without authority in Goumbi. I did not even get a hearing. What I said was passed by as though no one had spoken. As a last threat, when I saw proceedings begun, I said I would make Quengueza punish them for the murders done in his absence. But alas! here they had outwitted me. On the day of Mpomo's death they had sent secretly to Quengueza, who was on the sea-coast, to ask if they could kill the witches. He, poor man! sick himself, and always afraid of the power of sorcerers, and without me to advise him, at once sent back word to kill them all without mercy. So they almost laughed in my face.

Finding all my endeavours vain, and that the work of bloodshed was to be carried through to its dreadful end, I determined, at least, to see how all was conducted.

At a motion from the doctor, the people became at once quite still. This sudden silence lasted about a minute, when the loud, harsh voice of the doctor was heard—

"There is a very black woman, who lives in a house" —describing it fully, with its location—"she bewitched Mpomo."

Scarce had he ended when the crowd, roaring and screaming like so many hideous beasts, rushed frantically for the place indicated. They seized upon a poor girl named Okandaga, the sister of my good friend and guide Adouma. Waving their weapons over her head, they tore her away towards the waterside. Here she was quickly bound with cords, and then all rushed away to the doctor again.

As poor Okandaga passed into the hands of her murderers, she saw me, though I thought I had concealed myself from view. I turned my head away, and prayed she might not see me. I could not help her. But presently I heard her cry out, "Chally, Chally, do not let me die!"

It was a moment of terrible agony to me. For a minute I was minded to rush into the crowd and attempt the rescue of the poor victim. But it would have been of not the slightest use. The people were too frantic and crazed to even notice my presence. I should only have sacrificed my own life without helping her. So I turned away into a corner behind a tree, and—I may confess, I trust—shed bitter tears at my utter powerlessness.

Presently silence again fell upon the crowd. Then the

harsh voice of the devilish doctor again rang over the town. It seemed to me like the hoarse croak of some death-foretelling raven—

"There is an old woman in a house"—describing it—"she also bewitched Mpomo."

Again the crowd rushed off. This time they seized a niece of King Quengueza, a noble-hearted and rather majestic old woman. As they crowded about her with flaming eyes and threats of death, she rose proudly from the ground, looked them in the face unflinchingly, and, motioning them to keep their hands off, said, "I will drink the mboundou; but woe to my accusers if I do not die!"

Then she, too, was escorted to the river, but without being bound. She submitted to all without a tear or a murmur for mercy.

Again, a third time the dreadful silence fell upon the town, and the doctor's voice was heard—

"There is a woman with six children. She lives on a plantation towards the rising sun. She, too, bewitched Mpomo."

Again there was a furious shout, and in a few minutes they brought to the river one of Quengueza's slave-women, a good and much-respected woman, whom also I knew.

The doctor now approached with the crowd. In a loud voice he recited the crime of which these women were accused. The first taken, Okandaga, had—so he said—some weeks before asked Mpomo for some salt, he being her relative. Salt was scarce, and he had refused her. She had said unpleasant words to him then, and had by sorcery taken his life.

Then Quengueza's niece was accused. She was barren, and Mpomo had children. She envied him. Therefore she had bewitched him.

Quengueza's slave had asked Mpomo for a looking-glass. He had refused her. Therefore she had killed him with sorcery.

As each accusation was recited the people broke out into curses. Even the relatives of the poor victims were obliged to join in this. Every one rivalled his neighbour in cursing,

DECAPITATION SCENE AT GOUMBI

each fearful lest lukewarmness in the ceremony should expose him to a like fate.

Next the victims were put into a large canoe with the executioners, the doctor, and a number of other people, all armed.

Then the tam-tams were beaten, and the proper persons prepared the mboundou. Quabi, Mpomo's eldest brother, held the poisoned cup. At sight of it poor Okandaga began again to cry, and even Quengueza's niece turned pale in the face—for even the negro face has at such times a pallor which is quite perceptible. Three other canoes now surrounded that in which the victims were. All were crowded with armed men.

Then the mug of mboundou was handed to the old slave-woman, next to the royal niece, and last to Okandaga. As they drank, the multitude shouted, "If they are witches, let the mboundou kill them; if they are innocent, let the mboundou go out."

It was the most exciting scene of my life. Though horror almost froze my blood, my eyes were riveted upon the spectacle. A dead silence now occurred. Suddenly the slave fell down. She had not touched the boat's bottom ere her head was hacked off by a dozen rude swords.

Next came Quengueza's niece. In an instant her head was off, and the blood was dyeing the waters of the river.

Meantime poor Okandaga staggered, and struggled, and cried, vainly resisting the working of the poison in her system. Last of all she fell too, and in an instant her head was hewed off.

Then all became confused. An almost random hacking ensued, and in an incredibly short space of time the bodies were cut in small pieces, which were cast into the river.

When this was done the crowd dispersed to their houses, and for the rest of the day the town was very silent. Some of these rude people felt that their number, in their already almost extinguished tribe, was becoming less, and the dread of death filled their hearts. In the evening poor Adouma came secretly to my house to unburden his sorrowing heart to me. He, too, had been compelled to take part in the dreadful scene. He dared not even refrain from joining in the curses heaped upon his poor sister. He dared not mourn publicly for her who was considered so great a criminal.

Before leaving Goumbi, a grand effort was made by the people to ascertain the cause of their king's sufferings. Quengueza had sent word by my men to his people to consult *Ilogo*, a spirit said to live in the moon. The rites were very curious. To consult Ilogo, the time must be near full moon. Early in the evening the women of the town assembled in front of Quengueza's house, and sang songs to and in praise of Ilogo, the spirit of Ogouayli (the moon), the latter name being often repeated. Meantime a woman was seated in the centre of the circle of singers, who sang with them, and looked constantly towards the moon. She was to be inspired by the spirit, and to utter prophecies.

Two women made trial of this post without success. At last came a third, a little woman, wiry and nervous. When she seated herself the singing was redoubled in fury; the excitement of the people had had time to become intense; the drums beat; the outsiders shouted madly. Presently the woman, who, singing violently, had looked constantly towards the moon, began to tremble. Her nerves twitched; her face was contorted; her muscles swelled; and at last her limbs straightened out, and she lay extended on the ground, insensible.

The excitement was now intense and the noise horrible. The songs to Ilogo were not for a moment discontinued. The words were little varied, and were to this purport:—

> "Ilogo, we ask thee!
> Tell who has bewitched the king!
>
> "Ilogo, we ask thee,
> What shall we do to cure the king?
>
> "The forests are thine, Ilogo!
> The rivers are thine, Ilogo!
> The moon is thine!
> O moon! O moon! O moon!
> Thou art the house of Ilogo!
> Shall the king die? O Ilogo!
> O Ilogo! O moon! O moon!"

These words were repeated again and again, with little variation. The woman, who lay for some time insensible, was then supposed to be able to see things in the world of Ilogo, and was expected to bring back a report thereof. When she at last came to her senses, after half an hour's insensibility, she looked very much prostrated. She averred that she had seen Ilogo; that he had told her Quengueza was not bewitched; that a remedy prepared from a certain plant would cure him; and so on. I am convinced the woman believed what she said, as did all the people. It was a very curious instance of the force of imagination and extreme excitement combined.

Abuse is the negro's *forte* and his delight.

"Your chief has the leg of an elephant!" sings one; and another—

"Ho! his eldest brother has the neck of a wild ox!"

"Your women are dirty and ugly!"

"You have no food in your village, poor fellows. Ho! ho!"

And so they go on pouring out ridicule upon the discomfited foe. Nothing touches a negro so quickly as ridicule.

The morning after our arrival at Acaca we set off in small, very flat canoes, made for hunting the *Manga*. A manga doctor accompanied us. We went into the Niembai, on whose grassy bottom the manga, or manatee, dwells, and here stationed the boat among the high reeds which lined the shore. The doctor spread a powder he had in a pouch thickly on the water, and returned then towards the reeds. Presently, while we kept silence, a great beast came to the surface, and began greedily sucking in the powder. Immediately they stole upon it with the canoe, and, when they got near enough, fastened a harpoon to it. To this was attached a long strip of native rope. The animal immediately made for the bottom, but in a few minutes came to the top, and presently, after some struggles, died.

Before it was cut up the manga doctor went through some ceremonies which I did not see, and nobody was permitted to see the animal while he was cutting it up.

This manga is a new species of manatee. Its body is of a dark lead colour; the skin is smooth, very thick, and covered in all parts with single bristly hairs from half an inch to an inch in length. The eyes are very small; the paddles are without nails. The specimen we killed was ten feet long. Its circumference was very considerable, but I could not get at it to measure it. This animal feeds on the leaves and grass growing on the river-banks.

The people were greatly rejoiced. The beast weighed about 1500 pounds, as I calculate from its requiring eighteen men to drag it, and the meat is delicious—something like pork, but finer grained and of a sweeter flavour. To-night, all hands were smoking it. The doctor was greatly rejoiced at his success, and praised himself to me at a great rate. But I could not discover the composition of his powder, which was certainly quite efficacious.

CHAPTER XXV.

Arrival at Mpopo—Death of Querlaouen—Obindji enjoins Okendjo to take care of me—A cheery evening—Our entry into Ashira Land—Arrival at Akoonga—King Olenda sends men to fetch me—Extraordinary appearance of King Olenda—He receives me with great honour—The Ashira plain—Numerous villages—Appearance of the Ashira people—Dress—Mode of dressing the hair—Women's toilette—Pernicious effect of smoking wild hemp—Story of a leopard attacking a gorilla—Shelter of the nshiego-mbouvé—Starvation—Scramble for my cut hair.

On the 24th of October, 1859, we started for the interior. When we got to Mpopo I found my men would not be able to carry all my luggage. I had to hire more. The chief asked his wives to furnish some slaves for me, but they asked such a price for their services that I would not give it. It is curious how seldom a husband in this country interferes with that property which he has given to his wives. The women jealously guard their rights in this respect, and so long as they feed their husbands and make them comfortable, they are not, in many things, subject to male rule at all.

As we approached Obindji's village, we came to the plantation of my old friend Querlaouen. I got out of the canoe, and went ashore to greet the good old African and his wife and children, for whom I had brought presents such as they wished. But alas! I found no house or plantation. The place was deserted; the jungle was thickest where his little clearing had been, and I walked back with disappointed and foreboding heart. On the river-bank I met a Bakalai, who told me poor Querlaouen's story. Some months before the old hunter had gone out after an elephant. His slave who was with him heard the report of the gun, and, finding that his master did not return, set out to seek him. He found him in the forest, dead, and trampled into a shapeless mass by the beast, which he had wounded mortally, but which had strength enough left to rush at and kill its enemy. The poor body was brought in and buried. But now came in the devilish superstitions of the Africans. This family really loved each other. They lived together in peace and unity. But the people declared that Querlaouen's brother had bewitched him and caused his death. The brother was killed by the mboundou ordeal, and the women and children had gone to live with those to whom they belonged by the laws of inheritance, and were thus scattered in several villages.

On the 26th we got to Obindji's village. The old fellow was rejoiced to see me, and here I got several Ashira men and two Bakalai, which makes my troupe up to thirty-two men all told, and sets me on my way rejoicing.

One of the Ashira fellows was here last spring when I was here. He had brought a slave to Obindji to sell for him, and he had been waiting for the proceeds ever since. He might have waited a year or two longer if I had not come, and he would have done so quite willingly. The creditor in such case lives with the debtor. Okendjo was fed by Obindji's wives; and to comfort and cheer him while he was waiting, Obindji gave him one of his own wives—a hospitable custom in this part of Africa, which a man is always expected to observe towards his visitors. Whenever I entered a strange village, the chief always made haste to place apart, and often his whole harem at my service. Time was literally of no account to Okendjo. Obindji's village was as jolly a place as any village of his own country. And perhaps in a few months his goods would come. So the days went on pleasantly with him.

When he heard my destination mentioned, he at once conceived the brilliant idea of having the honour of guiding the first white man to his king, and thus gaining imperishable renown to himself. I was very glad to have him, as he was a very intelligent negro.

Early on the 27th we were awakened by the voice of Obindji, who was recommending Okendjo to take great care of " his white man," and see that nothing hurt him. We were soon under weigh. Our road led up the Ofoubou for some three miles and a half. Then we struck off due east, and after half an hour's arduous travel we got through the marshy bottom land which bounds the river, and stood at the foot of a mountain ridge, along which lay the route to Ashira-land. Here we gave three cheers, and with great hopes I led the way into a new terra incognita.

By five that night, when we encamped, we had advanced in a straight line about twenty miles from the Ofoubou. The country was mountainous, very rugged, and very thickly wooded with great trees. The ground was in many places thickly strewn with the immense boulders which I had noticed in my journey to the Fans, only here quartz rock was more abundant. Numerous streams of the purest and most crystalline water rolled in every direction, tumbling over the rocks in foaming cascades, or purling along in a bed of white pebbles.

Our camp was full of life this evening. The men were rejoicing in anticipation of great trade in slaves and ivory, and gave their imagination full swing. When trade was exhausted, they rejoiced over the wives they would get among the Ashira, where they expect, as strangers from a far land, to be sumptuously entertained. And at last Okendjo capped their pleasure by promising them great feasts of goats and plantains, the Goumbi and Bakalai regarding Ashira-land as the country of goats and plantains.

We were kept awake between one and three o'clock by the roarings of a leopard, which, however, could not face the fire, which we had kept bright, so he could not make his breakfast upon one of us as he desired. But neither did I think it quite safe to venture into the gloom after him.

This day the country was much as yesterday. Ebony grows in great abundance. The poorer the soil, the taller the trees, and the more numerous do these trees become. In many places the rains had washed away the soil from the immense and wide-spreading roots which ran along the ground looking like huge serpents. To-day we saw for the first time a tree new to me, and which my men called the *indoonoo*. It has an immense girth, and is a much taller and better shaped tree than the baobab, which is not found in this part of Africa. I measured one, of only moderate size, which had fallen down, and found it, at some feet from the base, eight feet in diameter.

The blocks of quartz grow larger and larger as we proceed. To-day there were some which were really stupendous masses, and it was a most curious sight to see our caravan filing between two such ponderous blocks, looking like pigmies alongside of these huge boulders.

Towards evening, at last, we began to see signs of a change in the face of the country. Plantations could be seen from time to time; the soil became more clayey; and at last we emerged from the immense forest. I saw spread out before me the great Ashira prairie-land, dotted plentifully with villages, which looked in the distance like ant-heaps. I stood for a long time on the edge of a bluff, taking in this, one of the finest landscapes I ever saw in my life. Far as the eye could reach was a high rolling prairie. As I afterwards discovered, the plain is about fifty-five miles long by ten wide. All over this vast plain were scattered collections of little Ashira huts. The hills and valleys were streaked with ribbon-like paths, and here and there the eye caught the silver sheen of a brook winding along through the undulating land. In the far distance loomed up mountains higher than any I had yet seen, and whose peaks were lost in the clouds. It was a grand sight.

To make our entry into Ashira-land properly, Okendjo sent two men ahead to announce that "the spirit" was coming to see them, and that he (Okendjo) had been selected as his guide. Soon, in the nearest village, we began to see people moving about hurriedly, and in half an hour the whole plain knew something had occurred. Meantime those nearest us came out to meet us, and we moved forward to them. When they saw me, all stopped, and the majority turned back with awe and alarm depicted on their faces. We continued to advance slowly. It was nearly dusk when we entered the nearest village. But very few of the people dared to approach me; and even those took to flight if I fixed my eye upon them, evidently fearing I would do them a mischief.

Okendjo walked ahead of me, proclaiming, in a most magniloquent manner, the many virtues of the great white man or spirit whom he had brought to see his countrymen. And the crowd answered to his words in shouts, "Then tangani has come! The spirit has come to see our land—our land, which he never saw before!"

It happened luckily that the chief of the first village we came to was a brother of Okendjo. Akoonga met us at the entrance of his place, and said, "Is it true, Okendjo, what I hear, that you bring to us this man? Is it not an hallucination of my mind, occasioned by too much palm-wine? Is he the spirit who makes the guns, the cloth, the beads, the brass rods, and the copper rings?"

Okendjo replied, "He is the man. This is he of whom you have heard so much. He comes from a far country to see us."

Then the people shouted. A house was given me, and when I had taken possession the chief came, followed by ten of his wives, each bearing two bunches of plantains, which, with fear and trembling, they deposited at my feet. Next were brought four goats, twenty fowls, several baskets of ground-nuts, and many bunches of sugar-cane.

When these were delivered, Akoonga said to Okendjo, "Tell the spirit that I thank him that he stays in my village a night. Tell him he is welcome, and all those who follow him. He is the master while he is here. This food is for him. As for his people, my women will cook for them."

I thanked him.

Then, showing me the house, he said, "It is your house; my wives are yours; my slaves are yours; my people are yours."

After supper, being tired, I lay down, but was not yet asleep when I heard the chief say to his people, "Be silent; do not trouble the spirit; do not speak lest you awake him. Neither our forefathers nor ourselves ever saw such a wonder as this."

The consequence of this kind and very unusual forethought was that I enjoyed a very good night's rest.

By my reckoning, the village of Akoonga is two hundred and forty miles east from Cape Lopez.

Early next morning the rush of people began. They were less afraid than on the evening before, and crowded around me in such masses that I was nearly stifled. As usual, my hair was the great object of wonder to them. I stood it as long as I could, but at last had to ask the chief to send them away. Not to disappoint their curiosity too much, I consented to walk through the streets at intervals of an hour or two, and thus give all an opportunity to look at me.

In the morning, Olenda, the king or head chief of the Ashiras, sent two messengers with presents of goats and plantains, and a desire that I should come to his town. I sent back word that I would the day after to-morrow; to-day my feet were too sore.

The king sent word that I should be carried if I would come.

I replied that I would come on the day I had appointed. That I never broke my word nor ever changed my mind.

Accordingly, on November 2nd, early in the morning, I was aroused by King Olenda's people, who had come to escort me with singing and dancing. I took leave of Akoonga, giving him a present of one hundred yards of cloth, and some beads, and an old shirt, whereat he was vastly delighted.

My men had now easy times. My baggage was carried altogether by the Ashira, who marched ahead singing wild songs celebrating my arrival among them. After a journey of ten miles over the grassy prairie we came to Olenda's village, which may be called the capital of the tribe. I was conducted to the best house in the place; and, after waiting half-an-hour, the ringing of the *kendo* announced the approach of the king.

At last King Olenda stood before me—a most surprising object indeed. He was an old, old man, with wool as white as snow, face a mass of wrinkles, and body thin, lean, and bent almost double with age. He had painted his haggard old face red on one side, and white on the other, in streaks, and, as he stood before me, I wondered as much at his appearance as did he at mine.

When we had looked at each other for some five minutes he made me a formal address in Ashira, which was translated for me by Okendjo. He said, "I have no bowels. I am like the Ovenga River; I cannot be cut in two. But also I am like the Niembai and Ovenga rivers, which unite together. Thus my body is united, and nothing can divide it."

This gibberish, which may possibly have had some mystic significance, I afterwards discovered was the regular and invariable salutation of the Ashira kings, Olenda's predecessors, time out of mind. Each chief and important person has such a salutation, which they call *kombo*.

Then he continued: "You, the spirit, have come to see Olenda. You, the spirit, have put your feet where none like you have ever been. You are welcome."

Here the old king's son, also a very old negro, with snow-white wool, handed over to the king two slaves, which the king formally presented to me, together with three goats, twenty bunches of plantains, twenty fowls, five baskets of ground-nuts, and several bunches of sugar-cane.

"This," said he, "is to salute you. Whatever else you want, tell me. I am the king of this country. Whatever else you wish, let it be known to me."

I replied that slaves I did not want.

Then more of the old man's children came; all old, and wrinkled, and white-headed men. They stood before me, regarding me with wonder and awe; while the people, of whom thousands were gathered from all the villages of the prairie, looked on in silence, and expressed their surprise in whispers.

At last the old king turned to his people and said, "I have seen many things in my life, and many wonderful things, and now I am ready to die, for I have seen the spirit from whom we receive all things. It will always be said in our nation by those coming after us, that in the time of Olenda the spirit first appeared and dwelt among us. You are welcome" (turning to me). "Keep this spirit well" (to his people); "he will do us good."

Nov. 9th.—The last week has been devoted to seeing and being seen. From all the one hundred and fifty villages of the plain the people have streamed to Olenda's town to see "the spirit." They come in the night, sleep on the ground outside the town, and in the morning crowd about me, following me with curious gaze, wondering at my hair, and trying, unobserved, to get a glance at my eyes. The moment I look at them they run off, especially the women and children. The African has a great dread of the steady look of a white man's eye. They believe it has an evil-working influence, and it is certainly a potent weapon to reduce a refractory or turbulent crowd. Even the bravest warrior will quail beneath the steady glance of a white man.

My clock is an object of constant wonder to them. They think it watches over me. Its constant ticking day and night is noticed, and this, to them, denotes the watchfulness of my familiar. Nothing could persuade them that a musical-box, which I sometimes wound up and caused to play for them, was not a very powerful devil in my employ. And, though they have a few guns and knew their use, my revolver excited not only their admiration, but a superstitious kind of reverence. They could not comprehend a machine which could fire time after time right ahead without stopping.

The Ashira plain, which I have in this week to some extent explored, is the finest and most delightful country I had seen in Africa. The soil is light, but tolerably good. The undulations of the prairie, which is, in fact, a table-land surrounded on all sides by higher mountains, give the landscape a charming variety. The surrounding mountains, the splendid peak of the Nkoomoo-nabouali on the north, the Andele and Ofoubou to the south, the peaks of Ococoo to the east, are all covered with dense masses of forest, and lend a solemn majesty to the scene, from whatever point it is viewed. They thoroughly disclose the great prairie, their forests reaching to the very feet of the hills.

I learned from the natives that beyond the Nkoomoo-nabouali range a superb cataract was known. A stream called the Rembo Ngouyai runs through a high defile, and finally falls into the plain down an abrupt precipice, resuming its course around the very base of the mountain. Its roar fills the whole surrounding country, and its vapour rises along the sides of the mountain into a magnificent rainbowed column visible at a great distance. This great fall is called the Samba Nagoshi.

The villages were so scattered at random that I could not

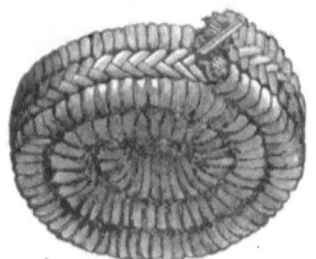

A ROLL OF ASHIRA TOBACCO.

make an accurate count of them, but there are between 150 and 200. They are the neatest I have seen in Africa. The houses are small, but cleanly, and built of tree-bark. The village is generally composed of one long street, with houses on each side. The streets are kept very clean; and this is the only tribe where the ground at the back of the houses is also cleared off. The villages are surrounded by thousands of plantain trees, and regular paths connect them with each other. I learned that villages are removed, as among other tribes, for death or witchcraft, but not beyond the plains.

Behind every village, in particular near the boundary of the forest, are great plantations, carried on with much industry, and where tobacco, peanuts, plantains, yams, and sugar-cane are grown in quantities which make this a land of plenty, where no man starves. Bushes of wild cotton were seen now and then, but not in great plenty. As I stood on one of the highest hills which diversify the plain, and cast my eyes over the scene, the yellow waving grass and cane fields contrasting with the dark green of the forest, reminded me strongly of the harvest fields of my home, and gave the landscape a charm of homely rural beauty which is lacking elsewhere in this part of Africa, where all is wild and grand, but where the traveller's heart often aches for something which shall remind him of home.

The people are among the finest I had seen in Africa. They are evidently a distinct people, for the Bakalai and other tribes who surround them are much lighter coloured. The Ashira are invariably coal-black. The women, in particular, have fine forms, and, though they have full negro features, many of the young women have a grace of carriage

ASHIRA THREAD AND NEEDLE.

and a sprightliness of manner which is something quite un-African.

The dress of the men and married women consists of a flowing garment called a ndengui, which is made of a kind of cloth woven by them, and which I found, in many cases, of very fine and tolerably even texture. The thread which is used is obtained from a species of palm. They take the leaf, which is from two to three feet long, and strip off from it the thin cuticle, which is then dried, and becomes a tolerably firm yarn. They told me that this tree is very short-lived, dying after having borne fruit once. The loom is a complicated structure, which is suspended between two trees, or poles, at the front of the house. It is worked on the same principle on which seamen make their mats on board ship, having two sets of "dividers," to separate the web and admit the shuttle with the warp.

22

They sew very neatly with a wooden needle and thread, a skein of which is here represented.

By a singular fashion, which I never saw elsewhere, girls and young women, till they are married, are not allowed to wear any clothing except the narrow grass-cloth girdle about the middle. They wander about as freely as a total absence of the sentiment of modesty can let them. Their scant toilet was simply a fashion of such long standing that it was taken as a matter of course.

The men, who are not nearly so finely-built as the women, though they too are superior to the men of the surrounding tribes, wear on their heads caps of grass-thread knit in a most

ASHIRA IRON WEAPONS.

beautiful manner, something in the style of the crochet-work which is the amusement of our ladies. The cap is called *ashita*. From their shoulders hangs a bag, not unlike the fashion of our game-bags, with a mass of pendent strings surrounding the bag. It is a very pretty thing, and is used to carry whatever they may have, which we would put in our pockets.

Both men and women are very fond of copper ornaments, such as bracelets and anklets, which they manufacture from the copper brought hither by the Bakalai from the sea-shore.

Some of their grass-cloth retains its natural colour, which is a dark buff. Other articles are dyed black in a very

CHAP. XXV. DYEING NATIVE CLOTH. 319

ingenious manner. A beautiful bush, which grows in abundance here, bears a profusion of small berries in which the dye is secreted. To obtain it, however, it is necessary first to rub the cloth thoroughly with clay until it is quite covered, and then put it to soak for a day in running water. After soaking twenty-four hours it is put in a kettle with

ASHIRA BELLES.

water and the berries and bark, and some leaves of the same tree. The whole is boiled for three or four hours. When the cloth is taken out it is of a light black or brown colour. It does not turn of the peculiar deep shining black till it is once more rubbed in clay and soaked in running water.

The Ashira women dress their hair in a very curious way,

and quite differently from any negroes I have seen. The pictures here given make an explanation unnecessary, except to say that the protuberance on the top of the head and the projecting horns are their own wool, made stiff by being strung over such substances as plantain-leaves or sticks. The toilet of an Ashira lady's head is rather a complicated affair; but then a head "lasts" a good while. The hair is covered with palm-oil.

The women paint their bodies red with the dye obtained from the barwood-tree. They are particularly fond of wearing copper rods about their necks, which makes them look as though ready collared for the slave-market. Both men and women file their teeth slightly in the middle, and it does not produce an unpleasant effect on the stranger. Occasionally I saw an old man with teeth filed to a point, as is the savage custom in many of the African tribes. It gives the countenance a peculiar look of ferocity which is not soon forgotten.

Seeing no slaves, although I had been some days at Olenda's town, I began to think they had none. But I soon discovered that the poor slaves, on hearing of my arrival, had been panic-struck. They thought, poor fellows! that I had come to carry them off to the sea-shore to be fattened, and then carried off to the white man's country to be eaten, and that I myself intended to eat a few, which is the use they fancy we make of slaves. Accordingly they retreated to the plantations, where they hid themselves, and resolutely refused to make their appearance; nor would any assurances or entreaties of mine induce them to come forth. Their masters only laughed.

The women are very industrious, and seemed to me milder mannered, as they certainly were healthier, than elsewhere in Africa. They do not become wives till they have arrived fully at the age of puberty, which is one sufficient reason for the greater beauty of the little nation, and for its intellectual superiority, as denoted by the cloth manufactures, and the settled and provident mode of life. Polygamy, of course, prevails; and parents sometimes sell their children, which is not thought a crime.

This whole country is well watered. Along every distant mountain-side rivulets are dancing downward, and are lost in the plain, or eventually fall into the Ovenga or Ovigui, which flow past, the last emptying into the Rembo Apingi.

While I was resting in one of the villages, a poor crazy fellow came capering and singing along the street. I was so much amused at his antics, and at the forbearance of the people with him, that I gave him an old torn coat I had with me. At this he was vastly delighted, and redoubled his jumps and songs, while the villagers were also much pleased. The poor fellow followed me for several days, and tried to show his gratitude by dancing and singing for my diversion. In this part of Africa idiots—those who are dull, stupid, senseless, and gloomy—are much disliked and soon got rid of. Generally they are sold to another tribe as slaves. But such poor light fellows as this was are kindly treated, and I think regarded with a certain superstitious reverence. I have seen but three such in all my journeys, but have seen many brutish idiots. I may as well add here that cases of deafness are very rare. I do not remember to have met any, except very aged people. Among the Bakalai I found one mute, and I have seen in another tribe two humpbacks—both, by the way, remarkably cunning fellows. I do not remember a single case of blindness in all my journeys, not even among the very aged.

I found in these hill villages a plant they call the *liamba*, and which the men cultivate with great care. The leaf is used to smoke in their clay pipes, and has powerful exhilarant and narcotic effects. From some leaves which I brought home I have discovered that this liamba is nothing else than the well-known *Cannabis Indica*, or Indian hemp, from which the far-famed Eastern drug *hasheesh* is made.

One day I found a village in great excitement. One of the men had been smoking liamba leaves, and had run out to the forest in an insane state, and it was feared he would be eaten by wild beasts. Such cases are not uncommon in the Ashira country. Under my own observation afterwards, one liamba-smoker became furiously and permanently insane, and I saw many who were miserably debilitated by the habit.

There are among the Ashira many confirmed liamba-smokers, and the habit seems very quickly to fix itself with a fatal tenacity. Beginners I have seen fall down in convulsions from the first few puffs. Practised smokers are seen laughing, talking, quarrelling, and acting in all respects like drunken persons. Insanity is often its ultimate result on those who persist in its use. I have several times seen men run into the forest under the influence of a few whiffs of liamba, perfectly unconscious and raving.

LIAMBA LEAF, OR WILD HEMP.

The negroes acknowledge its pernicious effects, but yet its votaries increase; and though the plant is yet unknown to the sea-shore tribes, they will soon fall under its subjugation, for it is making gradual but sure advances. I never saw the leaf on the sea-shore, but once saw a few of the seeds in the possession of a slave in a slave-factory. He was carefully preserving them, intending to plant them in the country to which he should be sold.

The negroes choose for the liamba a soil humid, rich, and

near the summit of a hill, in a sunny exposure, where it may secure the greatest amount of heat.

Hasheesh and the *Cannabis Indica* are so well known that it is not necessary to say anything about them here. The plant is a native of Abyssinia, Persia, and Hindostan, and is not, in my opinion, indigenous to this part of Africa. This I think, because I nowhere heard of its growing wild, and because the Ashira and Apingi, the only people I met with who use it, cultivate it with considerable care. How it came thither, or how they first came by a knowledge of its qualities, I could not learn.

On the 12th I took with me to hunt a number of Ashira, who covered themselves with fetiches, as usual, and gashed their hands for good luck. They were in high spirits because a fetich had given indications that we should get much game. When we had camped that evening, and after a rain-tornado had passed and left us in quiet in our leafy shelters, the men began to tell stories of the gorilla. Some of these were such as the reader has already met with in this volume; but two were told of quite a different kind. One of these related how a gorilla was walking in the forest, when suddenly he met a *ngègo* or leopard. The gorilla stopped, and so did the leopard. The latter, being hungry, crouched for a spring at his foe, whereat the gorilla set up a hideous roar. Undismayed by this, the leopard made his leap, but was caught in mid-air by the gorilla, who seized his foe by the tail, and whirled him round his head till the tail broke off, and the animal escaped, leaving his brush in the hands of the gorilla!

The leopard ran away to his companions, who, when they saw him, asked, "What is the matter?" whereupon the unfortunate beast recounted his defeat. At this the chief ngègo howled and howled till all the leopards of the forest came, who, when they saw their brother's injury, vowed vengeance, and set out to find the gorilla.

They had not long to hunt. When the gorilla saw them coming he broke down a tree, of which he made a club, which he swung round and round his head, and kept the troop of leopards at bay. At last, however, he grew tired, and then the leopards rushed on him with one accord and soon killed him.

Next came a story of a gorilla and an elephant, told with a good deal of dramatic force. As the gorilla was walking in the forest with his wife and baby, they came suddenly upon a huge elephant, who said, " Let me pass, gorilla, for these woods belong to me."

"Oh, oh!" said the gorilla. " How do the woods belong to thee? Am I not master here? Am I not the man of the woods? Do I not roam where I please?"

And, ordering his wife and baby to go aside, he broke down a large tree, and brandishing it like a club, made at the elephant, whom he soon killed. The body of the elephant was found by a man a few days afterwards, with the club of the gorilla lying by its side.

This story, the narrator assured me, was a fact; and I think he firmly believed it.

The next morning I succeeded in bagging several wild boar. These animals are not only very savage, but singularly active. When I brought down the boar, three others which were with him were much startled, and, in their fright, made a leap which must have measured over ten yards. I have seen them repeatedly leaping across the Ovenga, where, by my own measurement, it was more than eight yards across. Once I saw one miss the opposite bank, and I shot it in the water.

This wild boar is peculiar to this part of Africa, and is a new species. I have called it *Potamochœrus albifrons*. The animal looks somewhat like the *Potamochœrus penicillatus*. It is a very remarkable-looking animal, attaining a great size, and conspicuous for a curious white face, adorned with several large warty protuberances on each side, half-way between the nose and eyes. These, and the singular long bristles which surround the eyes and the long ears, ending in a tuft of coarse hair, give the animal a very remarkable expression. The colour of the body is red.

We got no gorillas on this hunt, but I killed a very remarkable animal, the *Cynogale velox*, resembling a small otter, and the only animal of this genus known, as yet, I believe, in Africa. I have called it *velox* because of the extreme rapidity with which it darts through the water after its prey.

At sunset of the third day we heard the call of a nshiego-mbouvé (*Troglodytes calvus*). I immediately caused my men to lie down, and was just getting into a hiding-place myself, when I saw, in the branches of a tree at a little distance, the curious nest or bower of this ape; hard by, on another tree, was another shelter. We crept up within shot of this nest, and then waited, for I was determined to see once more the precise manner in which this animal goes to rest. We lay flat on the ground, and covered ourselves with leaves and brush, scarce daring to breathe, lest the approaching animal should hear us.

CYNOGALE VELOX.

From time to time I heard the calls. There were evidently two, probably a male and female. Just as the sun was setting I saw an animal approach the tree. It ascended by a hand-over-hand movement, and with great rapidity; crept carefully under the shelter, seated itself in the crotch made by a projecting bough, its feet and haunches resting on this bough; then put one arm about the trunk of the tree for security. Thus, I suppose, they rest all night; and this posture accounts for some singular abrasions of hair on the side of the nshiego-mbouvé. At a little distance off I saw another shelter made for the mate.

No sooner was it seated than it began again to utter its call. It was answered, and I began to have the hope that I should shoot both animals, when an unlucky motion of one of my men roused the suspicions of the ape in the tree. It began to prepare for descent, and unwilling to risk the loss of this one, I fired. It fell to the ground dead. It proved to be a male, with the face and hands entirely black.

As we were not in haste, I made my men cut down the trees which contained the nests of these apes. These are made by the animal to protect it from the nightly rains. When the leaves begin to dry to that degree that the structure no longer sheds water, the owner builds a new shelter, and this happens generally once in ten or fifteen days. At this rate the nshiego-mbouvé is an animal of no little industry.

On the 18th I told Olanda that I wished for men to help me ascend the high peak of Nkoomoonabouali, which was about forty miles off. He laughed, and said I could not do it; I should starve, in the attempt; besides, there was a mighty spirit living there which would prevent us from passing. However, I had set my heart on ascending this peak; and though it proved impossible to draw the slaves from their concealment, I managed to bribe a sufficient number of freemen to be my guides through the impenetrable forest which lay between the prairie and the mountain-top, and to help me in the ascent. The negroes are excellent woodmen, and are very rarely lost, even in a forest where they are strangers.

On the night of the 22nd a tremendous rain-storm put out our fires and left us most uncomfortable. Next morning we heard the roar of a gorilla, and killed it.

By the evening of the 24th we had ascended I could not tell how far up the mountain-side. The woods were still dense; every step was attended with difficulties. The negroes were suffering from hunger, and we had but one day's provisions left. My poor rags could no longer be kept together, and at every advance my bleeding body bore witness to the difficulties of a farther ascent; so I determined not to risk certain death by starvation, but rather to return.

So, on the 25th, we set out on our way back, praying only

NSHIEGO-MBOUVÉ IN HIS SHELTER.

that we might not starve by the way. Fortunately, one of the men discovered a bees' nest in a tree, and we ate up their wormy store of honey; and in the afternoon we shot a leopard, which lay in a tree just ahead of us as we were passing along, and I dare say hoped to make his dinner off one of our party. It was a splendid beast, and very large. We lost no time in cutting it to pieces, and had a satisfactory supper from leopard-steak.

But there was only a bite a-piece for the party, and we were half-famished. The next morning we rose weak and depressed. I could scarce stand. We picked a few berries for breakfast, and again made for the plain. I took a last mouthful of brandy, and, to encourage the men, walked in advance, and assumed a degree of high spirits which I did not in reality possess.

27th.—This morning I could only with great difficulty rise from my poor bed of leaves. We set forward without breakfast. I dared not send the men into the forest for berries, for every hour was precious, and they might not find any after all. So we walked on with empty stomachs, praying for a sight of the plain.

On, and on, and on, through the gloomy jungle, no man saying a word to the other, and every one looking anxiously for the first sign of the prairie-land, which now seemed a very fairy-land to me.

At last, in the afternoon, about three o'clock, a sudden lighting up of the forest's gloom gave us hope, and after another hour's anxious marching the wide plain lay before us. With a simultaneous renewal of strength and hope, we set off on a run, nor stopped till we had reached a village at the very bounds of the bush. Here the people were at first very much alarmed at our appearance and our frantic actions. "Food, food, food!" was all that any of us could cry out. When they discovered that we did not mean mischief, they approached, and, learning our necessities, made haste to supply us with all manner of food in their possession. One came with yams, another with plantains, others with little baskets of cassava; and all expressed sorrow that they had nothing better to offer. The chief killed a goat for me, which we ate up as fast as it could be cooked. I feared I should be sick from putting too large a share on my so long empty stomach; but, happily, the goat did not disagree with any of us. Probably there was not enough of it.

The weather has been very hot lately; and, as my hair was too long for comfort, I told Makondai one day to cut it for me, giving him a pair of scissors I had in my kit. He

OGANA: AN ASHIRA HOUSEKEEPER.

did not do it very artistically, but in the interior of Africa one comes to care little for looks or fashions. When he had done he gathered up the cut hair and threw it out into the street. I was not attending to what was going on, and was surprised presently at a noise of scuffling and fighting in front of my house.

I looked out and beheld a most laughable scene. The men

were busily picking up the scattered hairs, and those who could not get at them were disputing possession with their luckier neighbours. Even the old king, Olenda, was in the midst, eager for a share. As each got what he could, he would tie them up carefully in the corner of his ndengui, and walk off very contentedly.

I called Olenda and asked what was the use of this hair. He replied, "Oh, spirit! these hairs are very precious; we shall make mondas (fetiches) of them, and they will bring other white men to us, and bring us great good luck and riches. Since you have come to us, oh spirit! we have wished to have some of your hair, but did not dare to ask for it, not knowing that it could be cut." I was happy that it had not occurred to them to appropriate violently my whole head, hair and all, and was glad enough to let the old king walk off with his precious lock of a white man's hair.

CHAPTER XXVI.

Preparations to go to the Apingi country—The Ovigui river—A dangerous bridge—The primeval forest—Beautiful brooks and rills—Travellers' shelters—Leopard attacking a buffalo—Remaudji, king of the Apingi—A big river—Crossing the Rembo Apingi—Offer of a negro for supper—Stories about a cloven-footed race—I am made king—Am invested with the kendo—The kendo, the emblem of royalty—Tattooing—Supposed to be married to an Apingi woman—Industrious habits of the Apingi—Ownership in trees—Their knowledge of weaving—Powerful fetich to kill leopard.

My determination to go farther into the interior has aroused the jealousy of the Ashiras. All the chiefs came in to Olenda and expressed their disapproval of my project. They do not wish their trade interfered with, and are fearful, if a white man once reaches the far East beyond them, those people will not be content to trade with the Ashira longer. I stated my objects, and that I did not go as trader, but as traveller, and to collect new animals. At last Olenda said, "This white man must go where he wishes. He has been sent to me by my friend Quengueza. He must do what he pleases."

CHAP XXVI.   I TAKE LEAVE OF OLENDA.

Then the wily chiefs asked me what I would give them as presents if I was permitted to go. To this I put on a show of anger, and asked if I was not their guest, their stranger, and why they were so mean as to beg me for my goods? They seemed much ashamed. Of course I gave them some trifles afterwards for good will.

It is curious to see how greatly slaves are trusted in this country. The owners of these fellows had no security for their return, nor for the goods they intrusted to them; for I, of course, would not become responsible for them. But they were sure to return. They, who were originally themselves from an interior tribe, have come to feel greatly attached to Goumbi, and look down with contempt on the Ashira, whom they call "men of the woods."

Dec. 4th.—Food has been collected and cooked for my trip. I am to give the Ashira men six fathoms of cloth each to go with me to the Apingi country and wait for me there. Olenda gave me a numerous band, including three of his sons to accompany me, Minsho, Iguy, and Aiaguy, the latter a very common name here.

It rains nearly every day, and every few days we have tremendous storms of wind and rain. All the rivers are swollen, and the prairie looks very green and beautiful.

We set out on Dec. 6th. Early in the morning Olenda called us around him, and after telling his sons to take good care of me, the venerable old man proceeded formally to bless us, wishing us good success. It was a touching scene. At the close he took a sugar-cane, bit a piece of the pith, and spat a little of the juice in the hand of each one of the party, at the same time blowing on the hand. Then he said solemnly, "Let all have good speed with you, and let it be as smooth (pleasant) as the breath I blow on your hand." Then Minsho received the cane, which he is to bring back.

I found that the prairie was much more swampy to the eastward, towards the foot of the hills, than I had supposed. We had to walk through much mud, and often to wade through considerable pools and swamps of standing water, produced by the constant heavy rains. In one of these swamps we had to wade up to our middles in muddy water, and some of the party slipped down on the roots with which the bottom is covered.

The forest beyond the line of the prairie is also inhabited. We passed over a dozen villages, the people of which flocked out to see the "white spirit." They were all Ashira.

Towards noon we approached the Ovigui River, a mountain-torrent, which was to be crossed by a rude and very dangerous bridge. This bridge I had dreaded all day, and when at last I saw it I was by no means reassured. The stream was about thirty yards wide, and rushed through the forest, overflowing its banks. The waters were very swift, and I saw that even a good swimmer would be helpless here, and would soon be dashed to pieces against the fallen trees which jutted out in every direction. Now I swim but very little.

The bridge was a complicated, shaky structure, of which the engraving will give the reader some idea.

It appears that the Ovigui had its bed, till some years ago, not here, but some hundreds of yards on the other side. This is a trick that some of the mountain-streams of Africa have. Now in the new bed stood certain trees which native ingenuity saw could be used as the piers for a bridge. In this place two trees, standing each about seven or eight yards from one side, were chosen. Other trees opposite on the banks were so cut as to fall into these. Thus were formed two portions of the bridge, and these, though sufficiently rude, were not seriously bad for a traveller. It now remained to unite the still open space in the centre, between the two "piers," and here came the tug. Unable to transport heavy pieces of timber, they had thrown across this chasm a long, slender, bending limb, which sagged down in the middle until, when it bore a man's weight, its centre was three feet below the surface of the rushing tide. Of course no one could walk on this without assistance, so a couple of strong vines had been strung across for balustrades; but as these vines were of necessity so slack as to be parallel with the bamboo, they were of the very slightest assistance.

My heart failed me as I stood looking at this rickety concern. To add to the pleasurable excitement of the scene,

Minsho told me that this was a much better crossing than some others they had lower down, but admitted that even here some half-dozen of their people had been drowned within a year.

RUDE BRIDGE OVER THE OVIGUI.

I watched the party crossing with great interest. One man slipped when midway, but luckily recovered himself. He dropped only a box of mine containing two pairs of shoes. Another, who was carrying a gun, so narrowly escaped falling as to drop that, which was also swept off and lost. Meantime I wondered if I should follow in the wake of my shoes and gun.

At last all were across but Minsho. I had stripped to my shirt and trousers, and set out on my trial, followed by Minsho, who had a vague idea that if I slipped he *might* catch me. It was an unpleasant suspense in every way; and as I crossed the centre part, and felt the current beating against my legs and almost seeming to have a hold on me, with purpose to drag me away, I vowed I would never try such an enterprise again. However, I managed to hold on to the vine and drag myself up, very weak and pale with excitement, but outwardly necessarily calm, as it would not do to let these natives see me make a difficulty of anything they could do.

Again we plunged into the primeval forests of ebony, barwood, india-rubber vines, and other strange trees and shrubs. After about two miles of travel we came to a curious little *strip* of prairie, which was five or six miles long, but only a few hundred yards wide. This they called *Odjiolo*. It was not inhabited.

A few miles farther on the path led over a curious steep mount called Mount Ocoucou. We had to climb the almost perpendicular sides, and I had to grasp branches or vines as I ascended the face of this high hill. Having surmounted that and three others, with intervening plains and valleys, all covered with dense forests, we at last found ourselves on the banks of another little purling mountain-brook which skirted the base of our last hill, the Aloumy. Here we lit fires, built shelters, and camped for the night. This day we made but twenty miles, fifteen of which were due east.

Dec. 7th.—As we advance the country becomes more rugged and mountainous. On every side brooks and rills and small streams are wending their way down to the Ovigui, or towards the Apingi river, and very frequently we have to march along the bed of a purling brook, the only way which the broken and rocky country affords us. This day was exceedingly trying for our feet. We picked our way through a dense and gloomy forest, every step obstructed by rocks and broken ground. This is evidently the favourite haunt of gorilla. Several times during the day we heard his roar in the distance. We heard also the cry of a nshiego-mbouvé.

As we advanced, the scenery became even more grand and picturesque. We were already on a high plain or table-land, but our route led us continually to higher levels by regular gradations of ascent. Some of the hills we had to surmount were from two to three thousand feet high. The higher we got, the vaster became the piles and boulders of quartz and granite, which seem to have been scattered over the face of all this country by some vast convulsion of nature ages ago.

This country is very abundantly watered, and we passed some considerable streams. One of these we traced upwards for several miles, as it ran along the foot of some huge hills which we had to ascend one after another. The highest peaks of this range were called the Kayambi and the Boundou, and another called the Okoukouè. We crossed the Louvendji, which is one hundred and twenty feet wide.

Passing this, we came at sunset to a *bando*—a travellers' house—a rude shelter left by former caravans at the foot of a high hill called Konngon.

The bando was occupied by a party of Apingi, who, when they saw me, instantly ran off, very much scared. It was only after many persuasions that they could be brought back. Presently a tremendous tornado came up, followed by rain, which made us glad we had reached shelter. Such storms frequently do great damage to the woods, and are very dangerous to travellers, as trees are uprooted, and branches fall on every side.

The bando here was roofed with peculiar and very large leaves from two trees, which are called here the *shayshayray* and the *quaygayray*.

To-day we travelled about twenty-five miles in a general direction of east.

Dec. 8th.—This day the country was less wild, and the hills very few. We saw in the distance about mid-day some Bakalai villages, situated on a little prairie, but my people were afraid to approach them. No persuasions of mine would induce them to go near. They were afraid, Minsho said, of trouble with the Bakalai.

THE LEOPARD AND HIS PREY.

Dec. 9th.—Last night, fortunately for me, it was clear and bright starlight. About midnight our camp was awakened by a tremendous roaring, and, jumping up, I saw in the plain before me a grand and exciting scene. A wild buffalo had been wandering in the woods, and a leopard had leaped upon him. The poor animal rushed, with roar after roar of agony and fright, into and across the plain, vainly plunging and striving to loose the claws of his enemy, who sat upon his hump, and was, as we could see, sucking the blood from his neck. The poor beast doubtless fell a victim to the leopard, whose attack is generally fatal. It was a splendid sight, though it lasted but for a few minutes.

This day, and also the next (10th), we journeyed along to the eastward, hurried onward by a lack of food. As usual in Africa, all the provisions we could carry could not be made to last above three days.

On the afternoon of the 10th, as we were passing through a dense wood, we heard people talking not far from us, and presently we stood before Remandji, a king of the Apingi tribe. He was a fine-looking old negro. At sight of me he and his company stood silent and amazed for a few minutes, looking at us. Then the king began on a sudden to dance about in a most unroyal and crazy manner, shouting again and again, "The spirit has come to see me! the spirit has come to see my country!"

When he was a little pacified he told us he came to fish, and must now go for his wives, whom he had sent on before, and who had food. We were directed to go on to a bando not far off, whither he would return for the night, as his town was too distant.

We went on, hoping that the women would have food for us. Meantime night came on; it grew darker and darker; and as we did not reach our rendezvous, and I was half-famished, I pushed ahead, to try if I could not kill a stray gazelle for supper.

Presently I thought I perceived an animal a little off the path, and, stepping towards it, suddenly pitched head foremost into an elephant-trap, a hole about eight feet long by six feet wide and ten deep; a wretched place, where I lay helpless, momentarily expecting to see some huge serpent fall on the top of me. I cried out lustily, and fortunately was heard by my people and dragged out with a creeper, which they cut and let down to me.

In these holes the Apingi catch their elephants. I saw many of them afterwards. They are ingeniously covered with brush and leaves, but are evident enough to a man who has once seen or fallen into one.

Finally we reached the camp, and when Remandji came he had but a few fish to eat, therefore we poor half-famished fellows had to go to sleep supperless. All night we endured torments indescribable from mosquitoes, which must be of a new kind, for their sting was like that of a bee. In the morning our bodies were swollen as though we had been beaten all over. Smoke and fire seemed to have no effect upon them. I never suffered such torture in my life.

The next morning we started off again, and, after a three hours' march, came at last, by a sudden opening of the forest, upon a magnificent stream, the Rembo Apingi. It was much larger than I had been led to expect—about three hundred and fifty yards wide, as far as I could guess, and evidently a considerable body of water. As I stood in delight, looking down upon the beautiful river, whose waters were gliding down towards the great sea, a tremendous cheer from a crowd which had quickly collected about me announced to the people on the other side, where the villages were, that "the white man" had come. The cheer was responded to by gathering crowds on the opposite bank, and presently some exceedingly frail, narrow canoes and several rafts were pushed across to ferry us over. The Apingi have villages only on the farther bank of the river.

I got into a canoe, which was managed by the Apingi boatmen with much skill. The Ashira know nothing of boating. The rafts were composed of several logs tied together. Their motion was very slow.

The shouting continued until I was safely housed in the largest house in Remandji's village. This was a little hut, with, fortunately, a piazza in front; for, when I had secured my goods inside, there was scarce room for me to turn.

Presently Remandji came to me, followed by all the old men of his village and the chiefs from neighbouring villages. He brought me two dozen fowls, and some bunches of plantains, and baskets of cassava, which being laid at my feet, he addressed me, saying, "I have beheld what our forefathers never saw, what I never saw before. I bid welcome to thee, oh white man! oh spirit! I thank your father," turning to Minsho, "for sending this spirit to me, for nothing greater could happen to us."

Then he said, "Be glad, oh spirit! and eat of the things we give thee."

Whereupon, to my astonishment, a slave was handed over to me bound, and Remandji said, "Kill him for your evening meal; he is tender and fat, and you must be hungry." It took me a moment to recover from my astonishment. Then I shook my head, spat violently on the ground, and made Minsho tell them that I abhorred the people who ate human flesh, and that I and my people never did so.

To which Remandji replied, "We always heard that you white men eat men. Why do you buy our people? Why do you come from nobody knows where, and carry off our men, and women, and children? Do you not fatten them in your far country and eat them? Therefore I gave you this slave, that you might kill him, and make glad your heart."

It was a difficult matter to explain to the king that he was much mistaken, and that we do not eat our slaves.

When at last my meal was cooked and served for me, Remandji came in to taste of what was provided, and to drink of the water that was set for me. This is a custom observed in every tribe I have visited, and is to show the guest that he runs no risk of being poisoned. Even the wives taste of the food they set before their husbands, they not being permitted to eat with the men.

I may add here that the negroes have no prejudices on the subject of meat which has died a natural death. Even if it is very high they relish it, and if the beast has died of disease, that makes no odds to their tolerant stomachs.

As usual, the people are full of wonder at my appearance. They avoid my glance, they admire my wonderful straight hair, my white skin (which is pretty black by this time), and my clothing; and at last several urgently requested me to take off my "foot coverings," that they might see if I had toes like them.

I asked with surprise why they had a doubt upon the subject, and was then informed that they had thought perhaps I was like a people far away in the interior, whom they call the *Sapadi*, and who have cloven feet, like antelopes.

Now, wherever I have been in Africa, I have heard this legend; and the nation called *Sapadi* are always situated in much the same place—in Central Equatorial Africa. At Cape Lopez slaves from the interior had told me of such a people; among the Commi the curious legend is devoutly believed; Quengueza's people mentioned them; and now these Apingi proved believers.

Remandji immediately called one of his slaves and a man of the Shimba tribe, both of whom declared positively, and with a look of great truthfulness, that they had *seen* the *Sapadi*; that they were people, black, and in all things like themselves, only they had feet split like an antelope.

I asked why they did not capture these people and send them to the coast as slaves; to which was answered that they were so far off that they did not reach them.

That there was a nation cloven-footed they were firmly persuaded, and no reasoning could shake their belief. Indeed, I suppose my white skin and straight hair were quite as wonderful to them as a Sapadi's cloven foot.

It is curious that wherever I have heard of this people they have had the same name, *Sapadi*. But the negro has so vivid an imagination that all conjectures as to the origin of the superstition are vain. Some fellow may have dreamed it, and afterwards infected the country with his dream. Among the Commi many people believe that the whites who make the cloth which traders bring them are not like us, but a race with but one eye, and that in the middle of the forehead.

Dec. 16*th.*—Yesterday I wound my musical-box and set it on an Apingi stool in the street, in the midst of a great crowd who had come in to see "the spirit." They were infinitely surprised and afraid at the sweet sounds, and particularly when I went away from it and left it to play alone. They looked from me to the box, and back, and finally exclaimed, "Lo! the devil speaks to him!" My clock is kept on the piazza, and its constant *tic-tac*, particularly in the still night, when it can be heard over the village, seems to strike them with awe. They say the spirit watches over me, especially when I sleep, and would kill any one who should try to injure me or my property.

When they saw me write they at once exclaimed that I was about to make cloth, and this was the pattern. Whereupon ensued a council of about thirty Apingi chiefs, who, after due deliberation, came, Remandji at their head, and addressed me, saying, "Spirit, you are our king. You have come to our country to do us good. You can do everything." And then requested that I would now proceed to make for them a pile of beads as high as the highest tree in the village (pointing to it), that they and their women and children might go and take as much as they wished. Also cloth, and brass kettles, and copper rods, and guns, and powder. And all the people, who had gathered around, to the number of several thousands, to listen, answered "Yo! yo!" as a sign of approval.

They believed fully that I made by night all the articles which I gave them day after day in return for fruits and food, and that I hid them in the forest during the day, to be produced as occasion required. Nor could I convince them that I had not the power to make these articles by a simple operation of the will. It was a severe disappointment to all who had gathered from many miles around to witness the expected miracle. Most of the Apingi chiefs had come hither bringing whole villages of people with them, who encamped in the forest in such numbers that starvation soon began to appear in the camp. Even an Ashango chief had come from a hundred miles eastward, so quickly does great news travel, bringing some of his people to carry away a share of the goods which I was to create so miraculously. As they approached, the faces of the great crowd were beaming with satisfaction, and they had so little doubt, that if, indeed, I had done the wonder they asked, these poor heathen would scarce have been surprised. It was a most strange and curious

APINGI MAN AND WOMAN WITH NDENGUI OR GREEN CLOTH.

scene to me. They went away grieved, because, as they thought, I refused to do them a kindness.

As the people from all the neighbouring villages came to look at me, I got a good idea of them without going about myself. The women seem to be very fruitful, more so than with any tribe I have before seen in Africa. Almost every woman I see has three or four children. But they are hideously ugly, rather small, compared with the men, and tattooed all over in a manner which they think beautiful, but which is to me hideous. Both men and women file their front teeth to a sharp point, which gives their faces a frightfully savage appearance.

In colour they are rather a yellowish black. Indeed, I have remarked that, in all parts of the continent, from the bounds of the Sahara to the Apingi, the natives of the mountainous regions of the interior are much lighter than the people of the seaboard and the plains or desert.

On the 17th we went into the forest to construct a trap for leopards, two goats having disappeared the night before from a flock belonging to Remandji. The trap was a very singular and most ingenious structure. They cut a great many sticks, which were firmly put into the ground close together, and in two lines or rows, about two feet apart. To make them more firm, they were tied together with grape-vines, and then more sticks were laid across the top, and also strongly lashed down. One end of the row was left open; the other was closed, a live goat having first been fastened there. This, by its bleating, was to lure the leopard, who, crawling into this *cul de sac*, had not sense enough to get out again, the space being purposely made too narrow to admit of his turning round. This kind of trap is also used to catch the small gazelle (ncheri), and other small animals of the woods; and I afterwards saw such traps for the smaller beasts, quite a mile long, with various openings, all turning inward, and admitting, but not emitting the bewildered prey.

On the 18th I was formally invested with the kendo, which is here, also, the insignia of the head-man or chief ruler. Remandji put the kendo over my shoulder, which gave me like power with himself. It was done in the presence of an immense crowd, who shouted out their approval, and promised to obey me. Remandji said, "You are the spirit, whom we have never seen before. We are but poor people when we see you. You are of those whom we have often heard of, who come from nobody knows where, and whom we never hoped to see. You are our king and ruler; stay with us always. We love you, and will do what you wish." Whereupon ensued shouts and rejoicings; palm-wine was introduced, and a general jollification took place, in the orthodox fashion at coronations. From this day, therefore, I may call myself Du Chaillu the First, King of the Apingi. Few sovereigns have assumed rule with so general approval of their subjects, I imagine. Of course, I would not submit to the ill-usage which the king elect has to undergo here, as among the Gaboon or other tribes, before his investiture; therefore it was omitted in my case.

The kendo used here is made by the Shimba, a tribe still farther east, who are reputed the greatest workers in iron in all this region. From them all these interior tribes obtain the few iron articles they possess.

This country is full of palm-trees, of the kind the fruit of which yields oil. I had never seen such vast quantities of palms, all hanging full of ripe nuts. Much oil might easily be made here, and transported on rafts by water to the seaboard, if only the trade could once be opened. The Apingi eat the nuts, and seem to thrive upon them. They make but little oil, and use that chiefly to rub on their heads and bodies. The Ashira are their only customers, and that to the extent of only a few calabashes of oil annually, for which they pay such a trifle that it is not worth their while to make it.

They are fond of the palm-wine, and go out regularly into the forest to obtain it. In my wanderings and hunts, I often saw the calabash hung to a tube inserted in the tree; the owner comes for it early in the morning, and generally drinks it in the forest alone, lest, if he took it into the village, some thirsty friend might beg a drop. They do not kill the tree to get the juice, as do many other tribes. The men love to get drunk. I have seen half the men in a town drunk at the same time. But it must be said for the women that they are much more temperate, though sometimes they also get drunk.

The women have a particular form of tattooed lines which

is thought most beautiful. A broad stripe is drawn from the back of the neck along the shoulders, across the breasts, meeting in an acute angle in the hollow of the chest. Other stripes are drawn in curves along the back, and from the breast down over the abdomen. The more of these marks, the greater is the beauty. They are permitted to wear only two of the little squares in which the Apingi grass cloth is made, and consequently go nearly naked, while their husbands are often fully covered. I cannot divine the origin of this custom; but it has robbed the women of any remnant of modesty which exists naturally in other tribes. Remandji's head-wife or queen, a rather pretty young woman, after the Apingi custom, came with her husband one day to see me. I gave her a piece of bright cotton cloth, which delighted her so much that she immediately began, to my great dismay, to disrobe herself, in order to put on my present. But when she had reduced herself to a state of nature, something else of my goods attracted her attention, and she began to talk and look around her with the most complete unconcern for some time, before she bethought her of the neglected cloth, with which she endued herself very leisurely.

I had a little adventure with another of the women. The king, on my arrival, signified to me, with the usual liberality of African kings, that any of his wives, or any of anybody else's wives that pleased my eyes, I was requested to consider my own. I, of course, replied that in our country we did not marry in this off-hand way; which he could not at all understand. As, however, the women are the housekeepers, when I was settled a little I chose one of the oldest and ugliest that I saw, and installed her as my housekeeper, cook, and maid-of-all-work. For two or three days all went well. But one morning I was waited upon by a deputation of men and women, who hailed me with much joy as their relative; thanked me for the honour I had done them in taking their relative to wife; and gravely asked me for presents to make their hearts glad on such a joyful occasion.

I confess that for once I lost my temper. I took a stick and drove my new relatives out of the village, packed off my slandering housekeeper after them, and heaped all the abuse upon them I was master of in Apingi. They fled with the utmost consternation.

When I told Remandji of the affair, he laughed and said, "You see—why don't you take my advice?"

The Apingi are, for Africans, a very industrious people. The men do some *work* here, and this is an extraordinary sight in this part of Africa. They make fine grass-cloth, for which they are noted among all the tribes. It is called mbongo when in squares, and, by the tedious course of trade from tribe to tribe, comes even to the sea-shore. The other tribes farther eastward also make this cloth.

The men are the weavers among the Apingi. The loom is a complicated instrument, much resembling that used by the Ashira. The loom is stretched under the verandah of the house, and it is a very pretty and cheering sight, as one walks along the street, to see a number of busy weavers weaving this fine and very useful cloth.

The Apingi have the reputation of making the softest grass-cloth in all this region. Some of their coloured patterns are very pretty. The pieces, owing to the short staple of the fibre used, and their inability to give it a longer twist, are never more than three feet long by about two wide. To work in colours, they first dye the threads, and very ingeniously work them in the weaving. It is a day's work to make one plain square or mbongo; and to make a coloured one takes two, and sometimes three days. The square is about two feet long and eighteen inches in width. When sent off to be sold they are tied up in packages of twenty or thirty. In this shape they find their way even down to the coast, and are everywhere used for garments, and also for mosquito-bars. My bars were always of this stuff. The natives prefer it to our common trade-cottons; and here, in Apingi-land, the people did not care to exchange their cloth for mine, for which I did not blame them.

To make a ndengui several of the mbongo pieces are sewed together with thread and a wooden needle, and the sewing is done quite as neatly as ours. The men are the tailors. From six to nine cloths go to a ndengui. The dandies among the Apingi wear sometimes a cloth thrown over the shoulder, more for ornament than use. The women are strictly restricted to the very moderate costume I have already described.

The holding of property in trees of any kind is something new to me in Africa, and shows that the Apingi have made a very important step in advance of the Bakalai and Shekiani, and all the other tribes I have met. Moreover, an Apingi village stands and remains in the same place, at least for a long time. They are a settled people, and need only flocks and cattle to make them a very prospering nation. Among the other tribes described in this book, a town is only a temporary resting-place, abandoned at the first death; land and trees, of whatever kind, are free to any one; and even with the Mpongwe of the Gaboon, who have long been under trading influence, though they cannot afford to remove a whole town, the house in which a man has died is destroyed, never to be raised again on the same spot. The reader will appreciate the delight with which I hailed a people who live on the same spot for several generations; who cultivate and acknowledge private property in trees; and who make cloth.

18*th*.—Yesterday I told Remandji I wanted to go on a leopard-hunt. He immediately brought me a man who had a fetich which enabled him to kill leopards *ad libitum*, and without personal danger. I laughed. The man said, " Laugh, oh white man! but you will see."

He went through a mass of ceremonies, then told me I must not accompany him, but the next day I should see a leopard. His big mondah would help him.

This morning he started, and, to my surprise, came in the afternoon with a handsome leopard. He asked so much for the skin, which they value for ornaments, that I would not buy it. I suppose they must be plentiful in the forest, and shall go out and kill some for myself.

The strip of skin cut from the head along the spine to the tail is used here as a war-belt, after being charmed by the fetich-man or ouganga. This makes the weaver invulnerable, they say. No spear, or arrow, or bullet can hit a man who has such a belt on. Of course, as only one belt can be made from each skin, and nothing but a leopard's skin will answer, these bear a high price, every warrior placing a great account upon his personal safety.

CHAPTER XXVII.

The ceremony of bongo—Ascending the Rembo Apingi—Apingi canoes—Apingi villages and houses—Great reputation of the Apingi fetiches—Quaint customs in regard to getting a wife—Spiders—Upsetting of a canoe—Apingi woman in the water—Customs regarding the dead—The Samba Nagoshi Falls—Grand and beautiful sight—Legend regarding the falls—The Rembo Okonda and the Rembo Ngouyai—Different tribes—Eastward from the Apingi country—No more shoes—Bleeding feet—Starvation—Farewell to the Apingi country.

ON the 20th, as I was speaking with Remandji, a man came and laid his hands on the chief's head. He said, "Father, I want to serve you. I choose you for my master, and will never return to my old master."

This ceremony is called *bongo*, and is a curious phase of African slavery. It obtains more or less in all the tribes. When a slave gets hard treatment from his master, and has reason to be dissatisfied, he slips off to another village and chooses for himself a new master. This man is obliged to accept and protect him. He cannot refuse. Nor is any "palaver" made on this account. No one, for instance, could hold Remandji responsible for this act. He may even visit immediately the village from which the slave has run away; only the slave himself must not go back thither, else he exposes himself to be reclaimed. The bongo is given always to a person of another village, and always to one of another family or clan in the same tribe. The technical term is to "beat bongo," in allusion to the laying on of hands. This singular custom has a marked influence on the condition of the slaves, who have always open to them this legitimate and tolerably easy avenue of escape from tyranny. It prevents families being separated, in particular, for nothing will make a slave leave his master so quickly as having his wife sold away from him. Even solitary freemen avail themselves of this custom to secure protection.

To-day canoes were being procured for an ascent of the river. They got quite a little fleet together for me; but all are small, and so easily capsized, that navigation is by no means comfortable to me, who can scarce swim a stroke. However, there was no help for it, so I prepared for accidents by tying my compass to a cord fastened about my neck, then tied my gun fast by a long rope to the canoe, which would float in any case, and took, besides this, only a little box containing a change of clothes and two pairs of shoes (the most necessary article hereabouts to the traveller). Then Remandji, myself, and a paddler, got in and started, followed by the fleet.

The canoes are quite flat in the bottom, float almost entirely above water, and are very well designed to stem the swift current of this river, which runs, at this time of the year, at the rate of four or five miles per hour.

Before we started necessity compelled me to spend a morning at the river-side washing my clothes. The negroes have so little idea of even the commonest cleanliness, that they never wash their scanty garments.

We ascended the river at a very slow rate, passing the shores at the rate of about two or three miles the hour. The people sang as they paddled. I sat very still and very uncomfortably in the bottom of the boat.

We passed several villages in about three hours after starting. These Apingi villages are not as pretty to look upon as those of the Ashira. In the latter I find always a verandah next the house, where the cooking is done; while in the Apingi house the same room has to serve as store-room, bedroom, and kitchen. They are built of bark, as those of the Ashira and many other tribes, and are covered with a matting made of palm leaves. There is generally one larger house in the village, which belongs to the chief. The villages have no high fence or pickets, which is an evidence that the people are not warlike.

We landed at the village of Agobi, a chief I had seen before. He gave me some fowls, but complained that the

leopards had eaten up all his goats. I saw here the largest *ashangou*-tree I ever saw. It was hung full of the olive-shaped fruit. This is larger than our olives, quite fleshy, and, when ripe, of a dark red colour. This tree, and a number of others, Agobi told me had been planted by his grandfather, which shows that property has been respected among these people for at least two or three generations. Most of these villages are surrounded by groves of these trees. The fruit is boiled, and has then an agreeable acidity both pleasant and wholesome in this climate.

I find that the superstitions of this people are as great as those of the tribes nearer the sea. They hold that death is caused by witchcraft; but yet they do not remove after every death as do the Commi, Shekiani, Bakalai, and the other tribes. Among the sea-shore tribes the Apingi have great repute as wizards, and Apingi-land is the land of *aniemba*, where any one may learn to become a powerful sorcerer. Consequently, the Apingi fetiches are very highly valued by the coast tribes, especially those professing to remove barrenness. I had special instructions from a number of childless fathers in my town on the sea-shore to bring them some Apingi mondahs.

In the evening we had a dance, and Agobi, bent on the utmost civility, sent some women to dance for my especial delectation. I quickly sent them back, preferring to take my amusements with the mass. The African dances are much alike everywhere, and had long ceased to amuse me.

To-day I inquired of a young man, who had for wife the prettiest woman in the Apingi country, why he was so ragged; his ndengui being all torn and worn out. He calmly answered, "This woman has entirely ruined me." I asked how it happened, and he replied that in order to get possession of her from her husband, he had been obliged to give all he possessed in the world. From this conversation I learned that it was customary in the Apingi country, that when a man fell in love with his neighbour's wife, and she in her turn loved him, the lover might secure her for himself by giving the same amount in goods or slaves to the husband as he had given to obtain her in the first instance. Under such circumstances he cannot refuse, and the woman becomes the wife of another.

As I was walking through the forest on a hunt the next day, I was bitten by one of the immense yellow-spotted spiders which are so numerous in all the African woods and openings, and in the huts of the natives as well. Some of the spiders of this country grow to an immense size. I have frequently seen them with a body as large as a sparrow's egg. The house-spider, which lives chiefly on flies and cockroaches, is mostly of a dull grey, which conceals its approach in the gloom of the hut. One species of house-spider does not make a web for its prey, so far as I have been able to discover. It conceals itself during the day in the crevices of the hut, and preys only by night. At the approach of evening, the cockroaches, which swarm in every African hut, come forth to act their part of scavengers. Then, by the dim light of a torch, and half-smothered with the heat, I have, for hours at a time, watched the motions of this spider. It comes out very carefully from its lair, and, having got a good station, remains perfectly rigid and motionless often for half-an-hour, waiting for some unlucky cockroach to pass by. At last the cockroach rushes past. In an instant the spider has pounced upon him. Now ensues a tug and battle which is of the greatest interest, and which is often prolonged for half-an-hour. The great African cockroach grows to the size of an almost full-grown mouse, and is a strong and somewhat formidable animal to the spider. The latter fastens on its back, and, to prevent being borne off, clings with two of his hairy legs to the floor or sides. All the cockroach's endeavours are to escape. He tugs and jerks, and often succeeds in dragging his enemy off for some distance. Then the spider manages to catch hold with his feet again, and once more the struggle is renewed. All this time, however, the spider is sucking away at the juices of the cockroach, and so presently the struggles grow weaker and weaker, and the poor cockroach succumbs: whereupon his enemy drags off the body to some corner, where it can be finished at leisure.

Another very large house-spider spins a web, and catches its prey of flies and cockroaches as ours do.

But the largest and most numerous species are found in the forest. The large black and yellow spotted one by which I was bitten spins its web in every wood. The web is a bright yellow, like the same colour in the spider's body. It is generally placed in an open space between two shrubs, and is often three feet in diameter. The thread is very coarse, and so strong, that when walking rapidly, I have inadvertently run against such a web, I have felt a very perceptible resistance to my progress. The bite of this insect is very painful, but not poisonous. The pain, which is like running a red-hot needle into the flesh, is soon over, and the wound heals up immediately. I have been several times bitten by this spider.

One or two species have very short legs, and flat, oval bodies, surrounded by pointed spurs, looking, when taken from their webs, more like bugs than veritable spiders. All the wood-spiders use webs to entangle their prey. They are of many colours; but none are poisonous to man, so far as I have been able to discover, by the personal trial of being bitten, or by the report of the natives.

Also, during my stay at Agobi's village, I shot two remarkable little animals. One, called by the Apingi the *kendo*, is a squirrel, and the smallest, by far, yet known. I have called this new species, *Sciurus minutus*.

When my guide saw my shot, and the poor little thing tumbling to the ground, he was greatly amazed at such skill; and when we got back to the village, the negroes told me, with astonishment, that this was the first time they had ever known a kendo killed. They concluded that I had a very powerful *mondah*, by whose aid alone I could accomplish such wonders. Many have begged me to make them *mondahs* to give them skill in the hunt.

On the 20th we made about thirty miles up stream. No rapids impeded our progress, and, though the current was strong, the water was everywhere of good depth, averaging from three to four fathoms. This is the rainy season. The songs of numerous birds resounded gaily over the waters, and the busy hum of insect life came with a gentle buzz to us as we voyaged along. Everything was clad in brightest green. The river-bank, down to the very water's edge, was a mass of verdure.

In the afternoon, near sunset, the accident which I had provided against happened. A canoe, attempting to cross the rapid river, was borne down by the current, and, before

THE KENDO SQUIRREL (*Sciurus minutus*)—*natural size*.

we could get out of the way, swept down upon us. In a moment both frail boats were capsized, and the men were swimming for the shore. As for poor me, I dared not trust my unskilful self to the stream. I clung to the canoe. Happily, we were not far from shore, and Remandji and my paddler soon dragged the boat to where I could get a footing and wade out. I could not help laughing at the old woman whose canoe had caused the accident. She swam off down stream like a buoy, shouting continually, "Where is my bunch of plantains? Give me my plantains!" Climbing out at a bend of the river, she waited for her capsized canoe to float along, secured that, and then got in again and paddled off, full of complaints at losing her plantains. All these Apingi swim like so many fishes, and, I suppose, have occasion enough for the accomplishment, with their little cockle-shell boats.

Wet as I was, and with my little box of clothes and rifle soaking, we marched off to a village near which we were capsized. As we entered, my nostrils were assailed by a most horrible and loathsome smell. On inquiry, I learned that it proceeded from the putrid corpse of a man who had died seven days ago. It is their custom to keep the body just as long as it will hold together. It lies in the house in which it died, and the only wonder is that the stench does not breed a disease.

I at once told Remandji that I could not stay there unless they buried the corpse immediately. I was accordingly conducted to the windward end of the village, where the air was but little tainted. Judge of my astonishment when, presently, a man appeared, bearing upon his shoulders the nearly naked and festering body. They had determined that it was well to humour my prejudice, and this was the funeral *cortège*. They make no coffin, but always bear the corpse out on the shoulders of the nearest male relative. No man follows the deceased to his last resting-place. There is no cemetery, and they leave the body at but little distance from the village. No grave is dug, but it is laid in a clear space, and near it are placed some tusks of ivory, or some of the bracelets or other ornaments of deceased.

While I was in this village a woman gave birth to twins, and one of the children was immediately killed, the negroes of this and most of the other tribes holding that if both are permitted to live the mother will die. In Obindji's town I once saw two boys, seven years old, who had both escaped, and their mother too; but all the people looked upon her as a remarkable woman.

Salt is very scarce here, and bears a high value. It is all brought from the sea-shore, the Cape Lopez people making considerable quantities yearly, which is then scattered over the interior. Here, among the Apingi, it is so scarce that ten pounds of poor salt will buy a boy slave. It is a great luxury; I have little doubt that they suffer for the lack of it. I think the frequency of skin-diseases and ulcers here is caused, partly, by lack of salt.

On the 24th, having procured the largest, stoutest canoe I could find, I set off down the river to try to get a glimpse of the great wonder of this region, the great fall of *Samba Nagoshi*, of which I had already heard so much. I was accompanied by a dozen canoes full of negroes. The stream is very rapid. This was the rainy season, and the banks were filled, the water turbid and yellow, and the current swift, running at the rate of about five miles an hour. We swept rapidly down stream past the villages of the Kamba, Aviia, Osounga, and Njavi tribes.

The scenery grew grander and bolder as we advanced. The mountains neared; the banks became high and precipitous; the force of the current increased; and every mile of downward progress seemed to bring us to a more magnificent country. At last we could hear the dull boom of the fall in the distance. The negroes told me it was still a long distance off—as near as I could tell, at least five or six miles; but even here the river began to break up into rapids, and navigation in the small Apingi canoes became too dangerous to risk it farther. So I pulled the canoe to shore, and called a halt. By this time it was nearly dark. We had come down from Remandji's about sixty miles. We made our camp by the side of the stream, and in hearing of the fall, which I determined to see the next day by an overland journey.

We took, for some distance, a path which followed the course of the river, and then descended a steep bank to the margin of the river itself. Here we beheld the first rapids. The bed of the stream was encumbered with boulders of rock of various sizes, through which rushed the water with great force. We followed the river margin for about two hours, scrambling over rocks.

At length we emerged on the brink of the stream, and saw before us a broad seething torrent, madly rushing down between steep and rocky banks with deafening roar. It was not a cataract, but a torrent of fearful velocity and grand proportions, leaping in huge billows, as though the whole of the water of the river dropped into a chasm and bounded out again, over ridges of rock; the scene was rendered more magnificent by the luxuriant tropical foliage of the banks, and the steep hills rising on each side, and clothed to their summits with glorious forest. The width of the stream was not so great as at Luba, and the torrent roared along one mass of foam as far as the eye could reach.

The stream here was about 150 yards in width, but a rocky island in the middle, covered with trees, breaks the fall of water into two unequal parts, only one of which could be seen from either side. The right-hand Fall was about seventy yards wide, the water rushing in immense volume down a steep incline. Besides the island several detached islets and masses of rock divided this body of water, so that the cataract did not present one imposing sheet of water, as I had expected, and the total fall was only about fifteen feet. The rocks were of red granite, both in the middle of the Falls and on the mainland.

The sight was wild, grand, and beautiful; but it did not quite impress me with the awe that the rapids below inspired. We see here the River Ngouyai, after flowing through the Apingi valley in the interior, and receiving the waters of the Ovigui and many other streams, bursting through the barrier of the hilly range which separates the interior of Africa from the coast-land. The high ridges which have been broken through by the river rise on each side, covered with varied forest, and the shattered fragments encumber the bed of the stream for miles. The falls and rapids must vary greatly according to the season and the amount of water in the river. At the foot of Fougamou my aneroids gave an altitude of 347 feet above the sea-level.

Like all other remarkable natural objects, the Falls of the Ngouyai have given rise, in the fertile imaginations of the negroes, to mythological stories. The legend runs that the main Falls are the work of the spirit Fougamou, who resides there, and was in old times a mighty forger of iron; but the rapids above are presided over by Nagoshi, the wife of Samba, who has spoiled this part of the river in order to prevent people from ascending and descending. The Falls to which the name Samba is given lie a good day's journey below the Fougamou, but, from the description of the natives, I concluded they were only rapids, like Nagoshi above. The Fougamou is the only great fall of water. It takes its name from the spirit (mbuiri) who is said to have made it, and who watches it constantly, wandering night and day round the Falls. Nagoshi, the rapid above, takes its name from a spirit said to be the wife of Samba, as I have already stated.

A legend on this subject was related to us by our Aviia guide, to the following effect: In former times people used to go to the Falls, deposit iron and charcoal on the riverside, and say, "Oh, mighty Fougamou, I want this iron to be worked into a knife or hatchet" (or whatever implement it might be), and in the morning when they went to the place they found the weapon finished. One day, however, a man and his son went with their iron and charcoal, and had the impertinent curiosity to wait and see how it was done. They hid themselves, the father in the hollow of a tree, and the son amongst the boughs of another tree. Fougamou came, with his son and began to work, when suddenly the son said, "Father, I smell the smell of people!" The father replied, "Of course you smell people; for does not the iron and charcoal come from the hands of people?" So they worked on. But the son again interrupted his father, repeating the same words, and then Fougamou looked round and saw the two men. He roared with rage, and to punish the father and his son, he turned the tree in which the father was hidden into an ant-hill, and the hiding-place of the son into a nest of black ants. Since then, Fougamou has not worked iron for the people any more.

My men told me that before the moving hither of the savage and treacherous Bakalai, the Apingi used to penetrate down river as far as the Anenga tribe, who command the junction of the Rembo Ngouyai and the Rembo Okanda. The tribes on this bank of the river are named, commencing above, the Njavi, Evili, Ngaloi, and Anenga.

I was assured that the Rembo Okanda was much larger than the Rembo Ngouyai, and I know that its shores must be populous, for from there are brought a great many of the slaves which supply the Cape Lopez market. Remandji, who had been over the ground, informed me that the Rembo Okanda was five or six days' journey off, to the north or north-west, and that the intervening country was very mountainous. He named the following tribes as inhabiting this fine river: the Meouandji, the Mosheho, the Madouma, the Njavi, the Npovi, and the Moshobo.

Beyond these lie the Njavi, and in their country a great fall or rapid obstructs the river, which is even there a very large stream. Beyond the Njavi is an unknown land even to the Apingi, who had never been as far as there, but from which they hear through their slaves.

On the 28th I set out on an exploration of the mountain-range, which extends almost due east so far as I can see from the highest point near Remandji's village.

On the first day we made twenty-five miles due east. We stopped for the night in an Apingi village where we were received with shouts of welcome. Most of the people had already seen me on my first arrival in Remandji's village. The next morning we set out again, and, travelling eastward about twenty miles, reached at nightfall an Isogo village, the chief of which was one of Remandji's numerous fathers-in-law.

The men armed and stood on the defensive, and the women screamed and ran away when they saw me coming. If Remandji had not been with me, I suspect I should have had difficulty in explaining my wishes.

The air is tolerably pure and cool on these high mountains; my spirits were high; I was now going straight east, and, though I had not goods enough with me to pass me very far, yet my depôt at Remandji's village was sufficiently supplied to pay all I might owe. My hopes were bright that I might now penetrate at least 400 miles direct east, and settle the questioned extension of this hitherto unknown mountain-range so far across the continent.

We started on the 29th. The way was somewhat rocky, and the forest dense. Roads there were not, and my companions did not even know the country. We travelled by compass, avoiding the eminences, and keeping, the greatest part of the time, the rocky rivulets for our paths. Of course such paths were terrible for my shoes. The first day I wore out a pair of shoes, the heels giving way. Fortunately, I had provided a spare pair, and I was able to go on the next day. On the first night, as we slept around our fire, we were awakened by the scream of a leopard, which did not, however, come within shot, nor did we venture after it, as man has no fair chance with this animal by night. When the leopard ceased his cries, a terrible tornado came up, which broke down trees and branches all around us, and this was followed by a heavy rain-storm, with strong lightning, which lasted till five o'clock A.M.

The next morning, donning my fresh pair of shoes and making a frugal breakfast of plantains, we set out again. The majestic forest through which we travelled seemed to be quite devoid of life, except indeed insect life.

As we were travelling through the forest I suddenly started a flock of monkeys. One of my young men, Ishoungi by name, was with me. Ishoungi, who was as black as a crow, had, in *less than a minute*, become covered all over with blotches, which gave him a ghastly spotted appearance, frightful and sickening to the view. It was a complete and most singular metamorphosis. The swellings extended under my own observation, and in less than five minutes scarce a spot on his whole body was left in its pure black state. Even his face was covered. His lips were disfigured, his nose put out of shape, his eyes closed.

This singular disease is known to the Ashira by the name of *etita*. The swellings are large, but of different sizes and shapes, and look much as though the subject had been badly scalded. The skin is raised, and a thin matter collects beneath it. An intolerable itching pain follows, which makes the poor sufferer scream with agony. I dropped my monkey and led poor Ishoungi to a little brook not far off, where I sprinkled him with water, which seemed somewhat to ease his pain. Presently one of the Ashira men came along, and, seeing his condition, took out some yellow bark of a tree, unknown to me, from a pouch he carried. This he made fine, then chewed it with water in his mouth. When he had chewed it a little he spat the juice on the other's body, and Ishoungi rubbed and spread it gently. Wherever it touched, the swelling went down. In little more than twenty minutes —certainly less than half an hour—the swellings were gone, leaving scarce any mark upon his body.

The gloom of the woods was something quite appalling to the spirits. It seemed a fit place for the haunt of some sylvan monster, delighting in silence and the shades of night. I was on the look-out for gorillas; but the natives did not seem to expect to find even many of them here, though they knew the animal.

These lifeless forests, so different from the teeming brush

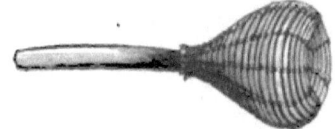

WICKER-WORK RATTLE TO DRIVE THE DEVIL OUT.

of Southern Africa, fill the traveller with awe. Dependent in a great degree upon his rifle for his living, the miserable explorer finds himself here in momentary danger of starvation. For of the cumbrous provision of the negroes it is quite impossible to carry an adequate supply. With starvation staring us in the face, we pushed on energetically, and by the evening of the second day had made, by my reckoning, about sixty-five miles from the last Isogo village, in a crooked direction, or a little more than a hundred from Remandji's town.

The ground had been getting rougher all the day before; our paths were the course of streams; and now, about two in the afternoon, occurred what I had been dreading. My last pair of shoes gave out completely. They were torn, both upper and sole, and at every step my bleeding feet were more and more torn, till at last the agony grew too great, and I could not set a step forward without almost an accompanying scream.

The pain obliged me to lie down near a brook where I had stopped to bathe my wounded feet. We built a fire, and, keeping my gun in readiness for any passing game, I sent my men ahead to see if they could spy out a village. Evidently the vague report of a three days' journey was a delusion and a snare.

The good fellows were gone two hours. They came back with a small monkey and a serpent nearly twelve feet long, of the boa species. The monkey they gave me. The snake made them a meal, and something over.

Then, finding it impossible to advance farther, I sent two men to climb the highest tree in sight, and fasten the American flag at its top. When it floated out on the breeze, I made my men give three cheers for the star-spangled banner.

Of the journey back I have but a dim and feverish recollection. I remember that my feet got worse instead of better; that when the wretched shoes were beyond even tying together with vines, I cast them away, and bandaged the feet with what remained of my shirt. That on the second and third day we had not even a little bird to eat, but plunged forward in a stupid apathy of hunger and pain. That on the fourth morning one of the men espied a gorilla, who came roaring towards us, beating his vast chest, and waddling up to the attack with fierce utterances and soul-freezing aspect, eyes glaring, and the monstrous face distorted with rage. I remember that when my gun-carrier shot the huge beast, the men rushed upon it, and tore rather than cut it up, to stifle with its flesh the hunger which was gnawing at their vitals.

Then we went on, relieved for a time from starvation, I dragging my bleeding, bare, and swollen feet over the rough and thorny ground, till at last, at noon of the fifth day, we came to the Ishogo towns.

Here I lay but half-conscious for three days. The people

brought me food; the kind women bathed and oiled my feet.

When I could walk once more, though not without pain, I returned to Remandji's, packed up my few goods and journals, and set out on the way back. For the first time in my life I was home-sick—really and thoroughly home-sick.

When I told Remandji that I must return, he called Minsho and said, " The spirit must go back. We are sorry; but as it is his will, we must submit. Wait, however, that we may get him food, that he may not be hungry on the way." Thereupon the people brought me fowls, plantains,

APINGI TOOLS.—1. AXE; 2. MPAŠO.

and manioc. The kendo I was requested to keep, "that when you come back you may be our master."

Remandji also gave me two beautiful grass caps done in fine crochet-work, and which have excited the admiration of many ladies in this country for the neatness of their work.

I gave the old chief my knife and fork, and afterwards, at his own special request, covered the walls of his hut inside with some New York papers which I had received on my way to the Ashira, and whose columns had helped to while away my inactive days here in the far interior. He was very proud of this, and promised to preserve them till the next white spirit came to see him, to whom it will doubtless be a curious spectacle. He said, " When, in after years, I tell the people from far away that a white spirit came to see me and was my friend, they will say, ' You lie.' Then I will show them these things which you have left me. Then they will believe."

I was presented with a large anvil of iron, used by the Apingi in their blacksmithing operations; but it was too heavy to carry off, and moreover, as iron is the gold of these people, it would have been cruel to rob them. They work iron very neatly, but not to so great an extent as the Fan, who are the best blacksmiths I saw in Africa.

CHAPTER XXVIII.

A long absence—Wrecked in the breakers—Once again with my faithful Commi—Sangala, Makombé, Binkimongani dead—Ranpano and his superstitions—I receive fresh supplies—Departure for the interior—Arrival at Goumbi—Quengueza invokes the spirits of his ancestors—Departure from Obindji—Advice of Quengueza to my men—Once more in Ashira-land—A whole group of gorillas—Quarrels between my men and the Ashira—The small-pox—A terrible plague—Departure of Quengueza—Fearful effects of the plague—Death of King Olenda—A valley of the dead.

AFTER a long absence I found myself on the Guinea coast in the beginning of the year 1863 prepared to make further explorations. I was once more among my faithful Commi on the banks of the Fernand Vaz river, but at a standstill; for I had had the misfortune before landing to be upset in the terrific breakers which line the coast here, and had lost many useful and valuable objects, among them my scientific instruments. I had only been saved from a watery grave through the superhuman efforts of my canoe-men, who were splendid swimmers.

Death had been busy during my absence. Old Sangala, the chief of Elindé, at the mouth of the river, was dead, and his widows had all married again; but they gave me a warm welcome, especially the old kondé (head wife), who cooked my food for me whilst I stayed, and became eloquent in recalling the events of the good old times when Sangala was alive. Her husband showed no jealousy at this discourse, for here widows are allowed freely to praise their former husbands.

At the village of Makombé I found that the chief was dead, and that Ilougou, his heir, who had helped me to build my former settlement of Washington, had been accused of having caused his death by witchcraft, and forced to drink the mboundou ordeal, which ended in his own life being sacrificed. It is dangerous in this unhappy country to be the heir of any man who sickens and dies.

Rinkimongani was also dead. I felt the loss of the honest old fellow, who, the natives told me, was continually talking of me during my absence, counting the seasons as they rolled past, and carefully guarding the house and gardens, in the firm hope that I should soon return. It was universally believed, of course, that he had been bewitched through jealousy of my friendship for him.

I went to the burial-ground to see his grave. The road to it from my hut led across the prairie and through a few groves of trees to the margins of one of those pretty islands of wood which diversify the sandy grass-land of the Fernand Vaz. The cemetery was recognisable from a distance by the numerous poles fixed in the ground. Rinkimongani's body had been placed in a box or coffin; it is only, however, the head men who are laid in boxes, and they are not interred in the earth, but laid, according to the old native habit, on the surface, or inserted a small depth into the ground. The wood of my old friend's coffin was decayed, and I could see his mouldering bones inside, together with the remains of his valuables that were buried with him, consisting of jugs and pots, a quantity of brass buttons, the remains of a coat, and an old umbrella-stick, which was all that was left of this article, a present from me, and which he always carried about with him.

Old Ranpano had some strange notions about witchcraft,

spirits good and bad, which I think were peculiar to him. One day he took into his head that he should die if he entered my hut, for he had been told that some one having an aniemba (a witch) had made a *mondah*, and had put it under the threshold of my door, so that, should he enter my hut, the witch would go into him and he would die.

No persuasion of mine could induce the old chief to come into my hut, and after a time I got angry with him, and told him that he ought not to refuse to come and see me. The good old chief immediately sent for some doctors, who, of course, at once declared that it was true that some one wanted to bewitch him, and had put a mondah at my·door to kill him. But they said it could be removed now that the people knew that there was one.

Immediately the ceremonies for banishing the witch began. For three consecutive days they danced almost incessantly, and invoked the good spirits; and one fine morning, whilst I was occupied in writing inside the hut, unaware that any one was approaching, Ranpano came to my door, fired a gun, and entered the hut in a great hurry, muttering invocations and curses; he then became easier in his manners, having, as he thought, thus cleared the moral atmosphere:

One day a schooner appeared in the offing, and soon afterwards the news came that the little vessel was for me. My friends, Messrs. Thomas Baring, Joshua Bates, and Russell Sturgis, of the firm Baring Brothers, had at my request despatched this small craft loaded with all the necessaries for my expedition without knowing even if I should ever be able to repay them; but soon afterwards the vessel sailed back to them loaded with a cargo of ebony which Quengueza and Obindji had cut in the meanwhile while I was waiting, and also a young live gorilla was consigned to them, which unfortunately died on the voyage.

At last I was enabled to start for Goumbi. Quengueza was to accompany me as far as the Ashira-land.

The day before my departure, on the 28th October, I was awakened by the beating of the kendo, the voice of the old chief invoking, in loud tones, the spirits of his ancestors to protect us on our journey.

Quengueza appeared with his body, face, forehead, and arms marked with patches of different colours from the ochre cakes of his alumbi house. These cakes had, according to custom, been saturated, some of them generations before, by the decaying heads of his ancestors.

The roll of his ancestors was a formidable one—Igoumbai, Wombi, Rebouka, Ngouva, Ricati, Olenga Yombi, and many others.

From Goumbi we proceeded to Obindji, where, on the eve of our departure into new countries, old Quengueza made a speech to my men. "You are going into the great forest," said he; "you will find there no one of your tribe; look up to Chaillie as your chief, and obey him. Now, listen to what I say. You will visit many strange tribes. If you see on the road, or in the street of a village, a fine bunch of plantains with ground-nuts lying by its side, do not touch them, leave the village at once; this is a tricky village, for the people are on the watch to see what you do with them. If the people of any village tell you to go and catch fowls or goats, or cut plantains for yourselves. say to them, 'Strangers do not help themselves; it is the duty of a host to catch the goat or fowl, and cut the plantains, and bring the present to the house which has been given to the guest.' When a house is given to you in any village, keep to that house, and go into no other; and, if you see a seat, do not sit upon it, for there are seats which none but the owners may sit upon. But, above all, beware of the women! I tell you these things that you may journey in safety." The speech of the old sage was listened to with great attention. Like most other good advice, it was not followed; if it had been, many of my subsequent troubles would have been avoided.

I chose for my body-guard ten faithful negroes. It was on these men that my own safety, among the savage and unfriendly tribes we might expect to meet within the far interior, depended. I knew I could thoroughly rely upon them, and that, come what might, they would never hurt a hair of my head. It would have been better if I could have obtained twenty-five Commi men, but this was not possible. Many were willing to go, but their parents objected.

The best of them were Macondai, now grown a stalwart

OPAITAI, OR PORTER'S BASKET.

young man and completely devoted to me, and my hunter Igala, a good and faithful friend. Igala I considered my right-hand man. He was a negro of tall figure and noble bearing, cool and clear-headed in an emergency, brave as a lion, but with me docile and submissive. In our most troublesome marches he used to lead the van, whilst I brought up the rear to see that the porters did not run away with their loads. I could always rely upon him; and, with twenty such as he, there would be little difficulty in crossing Africa. He was also my taxidermist, for I had taught him to skin and preserve animals. His reputation was great amongst the Commi as a hunter, and he used to make quite a trade by selling fetiches to the credulous people who wished to possess his skill and good luck in this respect. Igala, however, had a weakness; he was too amorous, and his intrigues with the wives of chiefs gave me no end of trouble. Another good man was Rebouka, a big strapping negro, whose chief faults were bragging and a voracious appetite. Then there were Igalo, next to Macondai the youngest of the party, a light-coloured negro, excitable and tender-hearted; and Mouitchi, Retonda, Rogueri, Igala (the second), Rapelina and Ngoma —six slaves which belonged to the interior given to me by the various chiefs whose friendship I had acquired on the banks of the Fernand Vaz. I dressed my men all alike in thick canvas trowsers, blue woollen shirts and worsted caps. Shirts being the more important article of dress, they had three each. Trousers I had found it quite necessary for negroes to wear on a march, as they protected the legs from the stings of insects, from thorns, and many other injuries to which they are liable. Moreover each man had a blanket to keep him warm at night. All the six slaves had volunteered to accompany me; they were not forced to go, against their will, at the command of their masters. Most of these men now handled fire-arms for the first time, and the possession of a gun to the six men who had been slaves all their lives was one of the inducements which made them willing to accompany me.

Quengueza never travelled without his fetich, which was an ugly little pot-bellied image of wood, with a row of four cowries embedded in its abdomen. As he generally wore an old coat when he travelled with me, he used to keep this dirty little thing in one of the pockets. Waking or sleeping the fetich was never suffered to be away from him. Whenever he ate or drank he used to take the image and gravely pass its belly with the row of projecting cowries over his lips, and when I gave him anything to drink he would always take it out and pour a libation over its feet before drinking himself. It used to puzzle me where the four sacred cowries came from; I believe they came across the continent from Eastern Africa.

Next morning we marched over a wild, hilly, and wooded country until eleven o'clock, when we emerged on the pleasant undulating grass-land of Ashira. An extensive prospect here lay before us; to the south extended the Igoumbi Andele and Ofoubou Orere ranges of hills, and to the north the lofty ridges of the Nkoumou Nabouali, near which lie the Falls of Samba Nagoshi. At two p.m. we entered, in the midst of the firing of guns and great hubbub, the village of Olenda, where we were received with great demonstrations of joy.

An assembly of the head-men of Ashira-land, presided over by King Olenda, was held to discuss the important subject of my journey towards the east.

I learnt, in the course of the palaver, the cause of Olenda's opposition. It appeared that after I had left the Apingi, the people could not comprehend what had become of me, and Remandji their chief had much trouble with them. They declared he had hid me in the forest, with the intention of keeping me for himself. So they came in a body to ask him what had become of me. They also demanded that he should give them some of the presents I had given him. A few days afterwards Remandji died, and his son shortly followed him. The cry of witchcraft of course was raised, one party saying that some of the neighbouring people had killed their chief, through envy of his possession of the ntangani, whilst others (and these prevailed) said that I had killed him, wishing, on account of the friendship I had for him, to carry him with me to my own country. The present chief, I afterwards learnt, had secretly sent messengers to Olenda to warn him against forwarding me through his country. He said that he did not want to follow the "spirit," as Remandji and his son had done, but would prefer to stop at home and eat plantains. The present world was good enough for him.

After a long discussion it was decided that I should go through the Otando country, and that Olenda should send forthwith a messenger to the chief, apprising him of the intended visit, and requesting him to send a party of men to help in carrying my baggage. This is the best, and, indeed, the only plan of getting from place to place in this part of Africa.

One of my excursions in the neighbourhood of Olenda was to the village of my former friend the chief Angouka.

The most remarkable feature about his place was the great extent of his plantain-groves. It was the largest plantation of this tree I had ever seen in Africa; there being, according to my calculation, about 30,000 trees, most of them planted about five feet apart. Each tree would bear, on an average, half a dozen shoots, which would in time grow to trees, but the natives generally cut all these away except two or three. The bunches of plantain produced by each tree weighed from 20 to 40 lbs., but I found many weighed as much as from 80 to 120 lbs. No cereal could give in the same space of ground so large a supply of food. There were many varieties; some bear about six months after the sprouts are planted, others eight or ten months, and others again not before eighteen months; these last generally bear the largest-sized bunches. The sight of this great plantation, with the magnificent foliage covering the gentle hollows and slopes, was most pleasing.

While in the Ashira prairie I made different explorations of the forest. In one of the excursions my men were tired with the exertions of the day before, for we had been wet all day, so, to keep them up to the speed, I led the column myself. We were soon buried again in the shades of the forest. It was a wild, desolate district, and I marched along in anything but a cheerful mood. I was a little ahead of my party, when my reverie was suddenly disturbed by a loud crashing and rustling in the trees just before me. Thinking it might be a flock of monkeys feeding on some wild fruit-tree, I looked up, peered through the thick foliage, and was thoroughly roused by seeing on a large tree a whole group of gorillas. I had nothing but a walking-stick in my hand, but was so struck at the sight that I was riveted to the spot. Meantime the animals had seen me, and began to hurry down the tree, making the thinner boughs bend with their weight. An old male, apparently the guardian of the flock, alone made a bold stand, and stared at me through an opening in the foliage. I could see his hideous black face, ferocious eyes, and projecting eyebrows, as he glared defiance at me. In my unarmed condition I began to think of retracing my steps, but the rest of my party coming up at the moment, with clatter of voices, altered the state of things. The shaggy monster raised a cry of alarm, scrambled to the ground through the entangled lianas that were around the tree-trunk, and soon disappeared into the jungle in the same direction as his mates.

The first days of the New Year were spent by me in much anxiety of mind. There were, in the first place, many unpleasant disputes with the Ashira people, on account of the intrigues of my Commi men with the native women, and these led to a quarrel between me and Mpoto, Olenda's nephew, who was very violent. Mpoto was a hot-headed negro, never well disposed towards strangers. He came, with the intention of making a disturbance, one morning from his village, which was within a short distance from Olenda, and singling out my head-man, Igala, pointed a loaded gun at his head. I was obliged to interfere, otherwise blood would have been shed, and only prevented him from firing by levelling a revolver at him. All my men had seized their arms, and a general *mêlée* was imminent. Igala behaved like a brave fellow as he was, facing the enraged Mpoto when the muzzle of the gun was within a few feet of his head, and you could not see a muscle move in his fearless countenance. Olenda interposed afterwards as peace-maker, and Mpoto was so terrified at the old man's threatening to curse him, that he bent down, and, taking hold of the patriarch's feet, implored his forgiveness. I threatened and chastised my men, but all my endeavours to put a lasting end to the evil were fruitless.

GORILLAS SURPRISED IN THE FOREST.

Whilst we were engaged in collecting a sufficient number of Ashira porters to aid in transporting my baggage, a most serious cause of anxiety arose.

Elanga, one of Olenda's nephews, was taken ill with a disease which the natives had never before seen. It was described to me, and I thought I recognised in the description the symptoms of small-pox. The next day the news came from a neighbouring village that Elanga had died. There was a great deal of mourning and wailing among the people; and all the inhabitants of Olenda, with the exception of the old king, went to join in the wild manifestations of grief. Now, Elanga was one of the Ashira men who had been to Obindji to fetch my baggage, and a suspicion of foul play or witchcraft, as usual, arose in the minds of the Ashira people, which, in addition to the other causes of unfriendliness, threatened to embarrass my movements. After the lapse of a few days, two other cases of the disease occurred, also in men who had carried my goods from the Bakalai country. I began to be alarmed, for I knew what havoc such a pestilence would cause amongst these people if it gained head. But I had no fear for myself, for I had been, fortunately, re-vaccinated in London a fortnight before I left England, little thinking what I should have afterwards to pass through.

The first step I took was to keep my Commi men away from the places where the disease had shown itself. This was remarked by the people, and their suspicions were strengthened. They began boldly to accuse me of having introduced the *evira* (thing that spreads, *i.e.*, the plague), or, as they sometimes called it, the *opunga* (a bad wind), amongst them; they declared that I had brought death with me instead of bringing good to the people; that I was an evil spirit; that I had killed Remandji, king of the Apingi, and so forth.

At length the calamity which I had so much dreaded came upon us; the plague broke out with great violence in Olenda village, causing obstacles to the progress of my expedition which had well-nigh proved fatal to it. The first victim was the head wife of Olenda himself. The awful scourge spread with a rapidity that frightened me. Several of the mourners who had been to Elanga's funeral had fallen ill of the disease. This was not to be wondered at, considering their style of mourning, the relatives and neighbours all surrounding the corpse, touching and even embracing it, whilst crying out, "Do speak to us—do not leave us! Oh, why do you die?" I had urged Olenda not to allow these mourning ceremonies to take place, telling him of the results that would follow. None of the people of the surrounding villages would come near us. In a few days more than half the people of Olenda caught the infection. I became alarmed for the safety of the noble old Quengueza and his men; and my first desire was to see him free from the danger, and returning to his own country. But he refused to leave me. "Chaillie," said he, "I cannot go back. I came here to see you through this country, and I should feel shame to leave you in your troubles."

It was in vain, however, that I tried to get Quengueza to send away his little boy. When I went to see him, I found, to my horror, that he had got the boy in his hut, laid on a mat near his own, and was nursing him with the tenderest care. If the noble old fellow had caught the disease himself, it would have completely put an end to my expedition; besides, many of his own people were going in and out of the hut, and all my quarantine regulations were totally upset. To my expostulations the old man only replied, "If I get the plague, it will be God's (Aniembié's) palaver."

Three times I had mustered porters for my onward journey, and had each time been disappointed through the poor fellows falling ill of the epidemic before even the packing of the loads was completed. I had now given away a large quantity of my goods, and had much reduced my baggage; but still it would require more men to carry it than were now in a condition to work in Olenda's village. Thirty men were all that could be mustered at the command of Olenda, and they are so proud that they would not go to another clan to get porters from among their friends. The bargaining for pay was the most difficult I had ever experienced. The rascals knew the difficulty I was in, and increased their demands accordingly. When settling the price of their services, all the older men took my part in the haggling match, beating down the demands of the younger ones; of course looking forward to the natural reward of their partisanship in higher pay for themselves.

My plan now was to get all my own men away from the small-pox by sending them on first with part of the goods to the Otando country, under the guidance of Arangui, myself intending to follow with the rest of the baggage on Arangui's return. To this arrangement my faithful lads would not agree at all. They conferred together, and then told me they would not leave me here alone. "Who," said they, "in the midst of this fearful sickness, is to cook for you and wash your clothes? These Ashira may poison you, by putting the gall of a leopard into your food. Some of us must remain with you, come what may!" I was obliged to accede to their wishes, and chose five of them to remain with me, Macondai, Ngoma, Igala (Quengueza's slave), Igalo, and Rétonda. The rest, Igala, Rebouka, Monitchi, Rapelina, Rogueri, together with the porters, who comprised all the disposable men of Olenda's clan, departed on the following morning. This division of my party was a great mistake on my part; it tempted the Ashira people to form a plot to plunder me.

Quengueza now left me to return to Goumbi. He believed I was now well on my way to the white man's country, and told me not to forget to bring him back a big bell, a silver sword, a brass chest, and plenty of fine things. On parting he took my two hands in his own, blew on them, and invoked the spirits of his ancestors to take care of me.

After Quengueza's departure the small-pox increased its ravages. Not a day passed without its victims, each fresh death being announced by the firing of guns, a sound which each time pierced through me with a pang of sorrow. From morning to night, in my solitude, I could hear the cries of wailing, and the mournful songs which were raised by the relatives round the corpses of the dead. The curses of the natives fell thick on me as the author of their misfortunes. To these miseries another one was soon added in the shape of famine. There was no one left to gather food; and my men in searching for it in the neighbouring villages were driven back and threatened with death by the terror-stricken inhabitants, who believed that we were the carriers of the plague and of the famine.

All Olenda's wives were down with the disease; but, happily, the king himself remained my friend, and as long as he had food he shared it with us. But sorer trials than famine were in store for us. One wretched night a sudden wailing burst forth, and soon became general throughout the village. It was the announcement of the death of Mpoto, the favourite nephew and heir-apparent of Olenda. The tremulous and feeble voice of poor old Olenda was heard in the early morning singing the plaintive songs of grief. The death of Mpoto was imputed by the people to me, on account of the quarrel I had had with him; and a general complaint was made that, whilst all the Ashira were falling ill, the white man's people were untouched. We were in great danger of being attacked by the enraged people of Mpoto, and had to keep watch for some time with loaded revolvers ready at hand. He was the last of his clan to be struck down with the disease, if, indeed, it was the small-pox of which he died. In fact, he, Macondai, and I, were the only people remaining well at that time, for my three other faithful lads had, to my infinite grief, fallen ill with the worst type of the infection; Ngoma, especially, was a great sufferer, for the skin sloughed off his body in large patches; his face was swollen up, and the putrid smell that came from his body was dreadful. He lay beside my bed; for there was no hut but my own in which I could put him. Igala, Quengueza's slave, was in almost as bad a state.

Soon after this came the final blow—Olenda himself sickened and died! No one can imagine the anxiety I felt when, one morning, he complained to me of burning heat and thirst. The fever increased in the course of the next two days, and with it weakness and drowsiness, but without any external appearance of small-pox. When I sat by his bedside, the old man, seeing my sorrowful countenance, would say, "Do not grieve, Chaillie; it is not your fault; you have not caused my illness, I know it." On the third night a sudden cry of anguish from house to house in the village, the meaning of which I knew too well, told me that my only remaining friend was no more.

Happily, matters took a better turn than I expected. His relatives consoled me, saying that although Olenda was dead, his clan had not died with him; he had left people behind him, and they would carry out his wishes, and see that I had porters to take my baggage to Otando. This day Macondai fell ill. A high fever, the precursor of the small-pox, seized him, and for a week I knew not whether I should lose my beloved boy. And now I was indeed alone, with no one to help me. I had to fetch water, to search for firewood, and to cook for myself, as well as for all my poor stricken followers.

The villagers exerted themselves to procure food for me. Those who were now well enough crept towards the plantation to get plantains for me; and even the invalids, men and women, sent me offerings of food, saying, "We do not want our stranger to be hungry."

Poor Olenda was buried in the cemetery of the chiefs of the Ademba clan, the clan of Ashira over which he had been the head. The cemetery was in a little grove of trees just outside the village. I gave the people powder to fire a salute at the funeral, and they came and begged from me an umbrella to bury with him, this being an article which it was thought very necessary and desirable to bury with their chief. There was great grief on the burial day; the women shaved their heads, dressed themselves in rags, and besmeared their bodies with ashes; and as the body was carried out of the village, cries of anguish and lamentation were heard; all the people shouting out, "He will not take care of us any more—he will not speak to us any more. Oh, Olenda, why have you left us! Oh, Olenda, why have you left us!" The corpse of the old chief was placed on the ground, in a sitting posture, enveloped in a large European coat which I had given him, and by his side was the umbrella; the head looked already like a skull, covered with dry, wrinkled, parchment-like skin. By his side lay a chest containing the various presents

I had given him, and also plates, jugs, cooking utensils, his favourite pipe, and some tobacco, and a fire was burning, which the people keep alight day and night by the corpse of a chief, sometimes for many weeks. There was also a plate of victuals, brought, according to the custom of these people, for the corpse to eat, and renewed daily for some time. All around lay the bones of the ancestors of the Ademba chief. For several mornings after his burial the people came to me and declared that they had seen Olenda the previous evening, walking in the village, and that he had told them that he had not left them entirely, but would come from time to time to see how they were going on.

The once cheerful prairie of Ashira had now become a gloomy valley of the dead; each village was a charnel-house. Wherever I walked, the most heartrending sights met my view. The poor victims of the loathsome disease in all its worst stages lay about in sheds and huts; there were hideous sores filled with maggots, and swarms of carrion flies buzzed about the living but putrid carcases. The stench in the neighbourhood of the huts was insupportable. Some of the sick were raving, and others emaciated, with sunken eyes, victims of hunger as well as of disease. Many wretched creatures from other villages were abandoned to die in the bush. How I bewailed my hard fate, and wished myself back, even though it were only as a street-sweeper, in one of the cities of Europe!

The small-pox gradually diminished from sheer lack of victims for further ravages; but the Ashira people had grown more distrustful, and something was evidently going wrong. At length three of my men suddenly made their appearance from Máyolo. They had left all well, but, to my surprise, told me that Arangui had left two days after their arrival in Máyolo, and must therefore have long ago arrived in Ashira. Some underhand movement was evidently going on, probably with a view to plunder me, and I suspected Ondonga to be at the bottom of it, as it was he who had repeatedly told me that Arangui still remained in Otando. I soon learnt, on further inquiry, that several of the loads had never reached Máyolo at all, that the porters had gone back to their plantations with them, no doubt by order of Arangui, who would have a large share of the spoil afterwards; the porters had scattered themselves along the forest road, some sleeping in one place and some in another, and almost every load had been rifled of part of its contents. My followers had been tired of waiting for me, and they told me that the Otando messengers, who had returned in such hot haste, were driven from Ashiraland by the threats of Arangui, who had seized one of them, and made him prisoner; and thinking that something was wrong, my men had resolved to despatch three of their number, well armed, to know the cause of my detention.

CHAPTER XXIX.

Departure from the Ashira country—Crossing the Ovigui again—A village of slaves and their plantations—I am plundered—Illness of Macondai —He is left behind—A beautiful forest tract—Robbed again by my porters—The Koola nut—Hunger—The Mpegni nut.

AT length, after several months of weary delay, the hour arrived for our departure from the Ashira settlement. I had suffered in this unfortunate place more than words can describe; racked with anxiety on account of the fearful epidemic which had dogged my footsteps. My party of ten men had become reduced to seven. Retonda was dead; Igala (Quengueza's slave) was left behind, although much better; and Rogueri, the slave given to me by Makaga Nchango, had run away. But as he was an inveterate thief, I did not regret his loss. Yet I should have been happy, if I could have felt that the dreaded plague was left behind us, for we were now again *en route* towards countries never before visited by a European.

About a mile or so east of Olenda commences the great forest which bounds the eastern side of the Ashira prairie; and just within its borders flows the impetuous Ovigui. I crossed by a bridge—a slippery log lying across the torrent, with a rope of lianas stretched from tree to tree to hold on by. There had been a very heavy rain the previous night, and the Ovigui had overflowed its banks, forming three channels separated by islands.

A march of about a mile beyond the river brought us to a large plantation, the chief slave settlement of the late King Olenda. The plantation extended over a picturesque and undulating tract of ground, with brooks of crystal water in the hollows. In places where these cool streams flowed under the shade of trees, their banks were most delightful, being overgrown with rich vegetation, and the trunks and branches of the trees overhead covered with vines and parasitic plants. The great quantity of plantain-trees in the open ground, with their gigantic, glossy leaves, the patches of ground-nuts, and the light green blades of the sugar-cane, gave a pleasant aspect to the place, and hid the charred trunks and stumps of trees which are otherwise so unsightly in these clearings.

The slave village had its chief, himself a slave, and all called themselves the children of Olenda. He was an Ashango man, a chief in his own country, and probably sold into slavery on account of witchcraft. He was a savage of noble bearing, and apparently of good disposition. He had several wives and a large family of children. The other slaves called him father, and he exercised quite a patriarchal authority over them.

We spent the night here, and early the next morning Ondonga arrived with the porters. The first disagreeable news I heard was that several of them had run away before starting, taking, of course, their pay with them. I next discovered that three of my boxes were missing. Notwithstanding the protestations of Ondonga, I was convinced that he was at the bottom of another plot to rob me in the midst of my troubles. He appeared, however, rather alarmed at what had been done, and in the course of the day the boxes were brought in, but they had been opened and rifled of half their contents. At this, Ondonga pretended to be in a violent rage with the unknown thieves, and declared in a loud voice that there should be war against those who had dared to rob his white man. For a moment I thought he was sincere, and that, being young, his authority as successor to Olenda was not sufficiently established over his unruly clan to prevent me from being robbed by his subjects. The old slave-chief joined in the well-acted cry of indignation, and actually put spears into the hands of his sons, and bid them go forth with the rest to demand the restitution of my property. They then all hurried out of the place, shouting, cursing, and vowing death to the thieves.

A greater calamity to me than the loss of my property, and the desertion of several frightened porters which followed, was the illness of Macondai, who had been at last struck down with the small-pox. We could not delay our journey, and I was very reluctant to leave him behind, on many accounts. When we resumed our march he tried to walk with us, but he became so ill that we were forced to come to a stand. I held, as was my custom in cases of difficulty concerning the safety of our party, a palaver with my faithful body-guard, but to my proposition that I should remain behind and take care of Macondai they opposed a decided negative. The poor lad himself prayed us to leave him. "All your porters will desert you," said he, "if you do not go on, and you will never reach Máyolo." We finally decided to leave Igala with him at a plantation in the neighbourhood, and Ondonga promised, with every appearance of good-will, to send people to take care of him.

We now continued our march. The country became more and more picturesque at every step. We were seven days on the road between the slave village and Máyolo; but this included considerable stoppages, for the road is a narrow path through a most varied and picturesque but dense forest, clothing the hills and valleys of the mountain range, which extends in a north and south direction, between the Ashira and the Otando territories; a continuous ridge, broken up into a great number of hills, of greater or less elevation, with steep slopes and narrow valleys; the highest elevation at which I crossed the range was about 1,200 feet. The hills are of primitive rock; and numerous blocks of quartz lay strewed along the path nearly all the way. Quartz crystals also covered the beds of the sparkling brooks that flowed at the bottom of every valley, all running in a northerly direction. It was impossible to see far on either side of the path; in many places there was a dense growth of underwood, including a dwarf species of palm-tree, and the ground was strewn all over with wrecks of the forest in the shape of broken and rotting branches, upturned trees, and masses of decaying leaves.

It was most toilsome marching up the steep hills, encumbered with the weight of our loads. A few miles southeast of the plantation, we came unexpectedly upon a most enchanting sight. One of the numerous tributaries of the Ovigui here descends from the upper valleys, down the broken hill-side, in a most lovely cascade, filling the neighbouring forest with spray and favouring the growth of countless ferns and glossy-leaved plants. There was, however, throughout the whole march a great scarcity of animal life.

But guides and porters alike were bent on plundering me. I found it impossible to keep them all together. All sorts of excuses were invented for lagging behind, and I soon made the discovery that they were hiding their provisions in the bush—a sign that they intended to rob me and run away by the same road.

On the first and second nights I ordered all the loads to be piled up near to the shed under which I slept, but on the third night, when we were assembled together to sleep, Mintcho and several of the porters were not forthcoming. They had stayed behind and did not overtake us till the next morning. On their arrival, Mintcho took the bull by the horns and told me to look into some of my boxes, for he thought they had been opened and plundered. He accused others of being the thieves, and mutual recriminations ensued, which ended in several of the porters laying down their loads and running away, and the rest (including some of the thieves) declared that it was of no use going any further, as the white man had been robbed and would not give them their pay. On opening some of the boxes I found a great number of valuable articles had been stolen. I was imprudent enough, at first, to accuse Mintcho of knowledge of the thefts, a step which nearly led to my being left alone in the wilderness. I was obliged to retract, and allay his fears by saying that I did not hold him responsible. Towards the evening of the fourth day we came to a standstill; so many porters had run away, that there were no longer men enough to carry our goods.

The weather was stormy, and it was almost impossible to shelter ourselves from the rains which fell every night. We could find no large leaves to make a good thatch for our sheds. As time went on, hunger came to add to our miseries. We were now reduced to very slender rations indeed.

I gathered our party together, and consulted with them as to what was best to be done. To my suggestion that some of the Ashira men should go forward to Máyolo and ask for porters, Mintcho and his friends opposed a decided negative. Neither would they allow two of their men and two of my Commi boys to go to Máyolo. I finally resolved to send Mouitchi, with the Otando man who had been Arangui's prisoner. He departed with the promise of returning in two days with men to carry our goods, and a supply of food.

I was now left with the Ashira rascals, eight in number, and with only two of my faithful Commi men to aid me in keeping watch over them. We were encamped in a small open space in the loneliest and gloomiest part of the forest, on the top of a long sloping path which led into a deep valley on the Otando side. We were absolutely without food, myself and my two men Rebouka and Ngoma having agreed to watch in our turns the Ashira, who pretended to be asleep on the opposite side of the road. My baggage, alas! still too large and the cause of all my troubles, lay piled up beside our camp fire in front of us.

We whiled away the early hours of night in talking of Quengueza and the country by the sea-shore, or in relating and listening to legends and fables.

The following legend, connected probably with some natural phenomenon in one of the neighbouring rivers, is a sample of these African stories:—

Atungulu Shimba was a king who attained the chief authority in his village by right of succession, and built eight new houses. But Atungulu had sworn that whosoever should quarrel with him he would eat him. And so it really happened until, finally, after eating his enemies one after the other, he was left alone in his dominions, and he then married the beautiful Arondo-ienu, daughter of a neighbouring king.

It was Atungulu's habit, after his marriage, to go daily into the forest to trap wild animals, with the Ashinga net, leaving his wife alone in the village. One day Njali, the eldest brother of Arondo-ienu—for Coniambié (King of the Air), their father, had three sons—came to take back his sister out of the clutches of Atungulu Shimba; but the king arrived unexpectedly and ate him up. Next came the second brother, and he was also eaten. At last came Reninga, the third brother, and there was a great fight between him and Atungulu, which lasted from sunrise to midday, when Reninga was overpowered and eaten like his two brothers before him.

Reninga, however, had a powerful fetich on him, and came out of Atungulu alive. The king, on seeing him, exclaimed, "How have you contrived this, to come back?" He then smeared him and Arondo-ienu with *alumbi* chalk, and putting his hands together, blew a loud whistle, saying afterwards, "Reninga, take back your sister." He then went and threw himself into the water, to drown himself, through grief for the loss of his wife.

Before dying, Atungulu Shimba declared that if Arondo-ienu ever married again she would die; and the prophecy came true, for she married another man and died soon after. Her brother Reninga, thereupon, through sorrow for the loss of his sister, threw himself into the water in the place where Atungulu died, and was drowned.

At the spot where Atungulu Shimba died a stranger sees, when he looks into the deep water, the bodies of the king and Arondo-ienu side by side, and the nails of his beautiful wife all glittering like looking-glasses. From that time, water had obtained the property of reflecting objects, and has ever since been called by the name of Arondo-ienu, and people have been able to see their own images reflected on its surface, on account of the transparency given to it by the bright nails of Arondo-ienu.*

Hunger came, but there was no food to be had. There was no help for it, but to divide our party and go in search of something to eat in the forest; some, therefore, went to look for *Koola* nuts, and others took their guns and wandered in search of monkeys, or any other game they might find. The whole day passed, however, without anything being found, and we again went supperless to bed.

It was unfortunate for us that Koola nut-trees were so scarce in the part of the forest where we now lay, for this valuable nut is generally an unfailing resource at this season of the year. The natives never think of taking with them much food on a journey in the season when Koola nuts are ripe, but trust in finding their daily bread, as it were, under the trees. The tree is one of the tallest and finest in these forests. It grows singly, or in small groups, and yields so abundantly that, when the nut is ripe, the whole crown appears one mass of fruit. The nut is quite round, and has a very hard shell, so hard that it has to be broken with a stone. The kernel is about as large as a cherry, and is almost as compact in substance as the almond. It is very nourishing and wholesome; about thirty nuts are enough for a single meal. The wild boar feeds on them in the nut season, and becomes extremely fat with the nutritious diet.

The next day I went also myself into the bush, accompanied by an Ashira boy, and leaving Rebouka armed to the teeth to watch my baggage. I was so much weakened by hunger and anxiety that I could scarcely walk. For a long time I could find no traces of game of any kind.

I returned weary and hungry to the camp, and tried to sleep under my shed. But I could not sleep, and, in my prostrate condition, visions passed through my mind of the many good dinners I had eaten at the hospitable boards of my friends. Dinners which I had entirely forgotten now recurred to my memory with an almost morbid vividness. I could tell every dish, and recalled the pleasant savour of many good things.

* Ienu means "looking-glass" in the languages of tribes near the sea.

But things began to mend. The Ashira returned from their chase successful, having killed two monkeys. These men who had so remorselessly plundered me, and with whom my relations had been for a long time none of the pleasantest, came forward with great disinterestedness and gave the whole of the meat up to me. I refused however to take it, and told them that they were to divide it among themselves. They insisted, however, upon giving me the lion's share, which I did not a second time refuse, and a most hearty and refreshing meal we made off our monkey.

On the following day, hour after hour passed and no arrival from Otando. The Ashira men began to feel uneasy. They thought something was in preparation against them; that Máyolo was mustering a force to come and punish them for their treachery to the white man, and for their imprisonment of an Otando subject. I had great difficulty, as the day wore on, to prevent them from leaving me.

At length voices were heard in the valley on the Otando side, then the report of a gun, and up bounded the long line of Otando men, headed by Rapelina, to the rescue, laden with provisions, and merry as crickets. Máyolo had sent for my own use a stock of *Mpegui* nuts, two fowls, and plenty of plantains. The arrival was most welcome, for we were again helpless with hunger. We had been again without food all day, and it was now evening.

Mpegui nuts are the product of a large tree which grows abundantly in some parts of the forest, but is nowhere planted by the natives. The nut is quite different in form from the Koola nut already described. It is round, but the kernel is three-lobed and full of oil. The oily nature of the nuts enables the natives to manufacture them into excellent cakes, by pounding them in a wooden mortar, and enclosing the pulp in folded leaves, and then subjecting it to the action of smoke on a stage over a wood-fire. They eat it generally with meat as we do bread, but when animal food is scarce it forms a good reserve, and is very palatable, seasoned with a little salt and pepper.

CHAPTER XXX.

Arrival in the Otando prairie—Máyolo—Present of food—Máyolo makes a speech—Illness of Máyolo—Arrival of Macondai—Surgical practice of the Otandos—A female doctor—The legend of Akenda Mbani—Protecting the village against witchcraft—My speech to Máyolo—Speech of Igala—Máyolo gets tipsy—Monkeys as food—I send men to Apono-land—Their reception—The people wonder at my powerful magnet—The Otando people—Native dogs.

ON the evening of the 24th March we emerged from the gloom of the forest into an open tract of grass-land, the Otando prairie. A wide stretch of undulating country lay open before us; the foreground of which was formed by prairie, the rest appearing as a continuous expanse of forest with long wooded ridges in the distance, one behind the other, the last and highest fading into blue mist in the far distance. As we approached the village of Máyolo, we fired off the customary signal-shots, and these brought a response of the same kind. The chief of the village possessed only one old Tower-marked musket, *minus* the stock, which had long been worn out; it was still, however, a good gun. Powder was a scarce article in this inland country, and nothing but the hope of getting more from me could have induced Máyolo to waste his small stock.

A number of men soon made their appearance, and led us, with loud cheers, to the palaver-house of the village. The beating of the kendo was then heard, and Máyolo himself was seen in the street advancing towards us; his body streaked with alumbi chalk, and muttering mysterious words as he slowly marched along. On being seated, and after stopping the beating of the kendo, he looked towards my Ashira guides, and exclaimed, "So here he is at last, the great spirit with his untold wealth!" Then, turning to me, he told me of the great trouble he had had with the Otando people, who had tried all they could to dissuade him from receiving me, saying that I brought the plague and death wherever I came.

Máyolo was the principal chief of the Otando country. He was a man of striking appearance; tall, broad-shouldered, and very light-coloured for a negro. His eyes were small and piercing, and there was in them far more intelligence than is usually seen in negroes. His right hand had lost several of its fingers through the bursting of a gun, for he had been, in his younger days, a great elephant-hunter, and his bravery was well known all over the neighbouring country. He had a pleasant expression of features, notwithstanding that his face was daubed with ochre-coloured chalk of various shades; one cheek being red and the other nearly white, including the circuit of the eyes. His people seemed to regard him with great reverence.

After Máyolo retired, a present of a large goat and two enormous bunches of plantains was brought in. We had a great feast that evening. It was astonishing to see the quantity my Commi men could consume. Negroes can stand hunger well for a few days, but they make amends for it when food is put before them in abundance.

At a gathering of the head men of the neighbouring villages, belonging to Máyolo's clan, there was much speechifying and excitement. Máyolo swelled with pride on introducing the white man to them, and as I spread out the goods I intended for each of them as payment for the men they had sent to my assistance, he exclaimed, pointing at the goods: "Look! this is the sort of plague the white man brings among us. Would you ever have had any of these fine things if I had not invited him to come?" The appeal was not to be resisted. They all went away at the end of the palaver in good humour, and the next morning brought into the village presents of fowls, goats, ground-nuts, and plantains. After this there were more speeches, and then the important ceremony, for me, of making return presents to all the donors. I had previously shown Máyolo what I intended to give, and he had remonstrated with me for giving them too much, saying they did not know the value of the things. I adhered, however, to my purpose, and was rather astounded to hear Máyolo, on coming out of the hut, tell the chiefs that he had been persuading me to give each of them a good present! On their side they tried to look dissatisfied, and demanded more. This I resisted, and made a show of taking back the whole. They all laughed and said, "No, we were only trying it on;" and looking at one another, they added, "He *is* a man!" which means he is not to be humbugged, and is a high compliment.

We had been only four days in Otando-land, when, to my great sorrow and vexation, Máyolo fell seriously ill. Thus it was my fate to see another chief cast down after my arrival in his country. Should Máyolo die, I felt that my expedition must come to an end, for it would be impossible to drive the idea out of the heads of the superstitious negroes that my presence was the cause of the death of their chiefs. The heat in the shade was about 92° Fahr., and in the sun it reached 130° or 135° Fahr. I took, at night, several lunar observations, ascertaining the distances between the moon and Venus and between the moon and Spica, and obtained also several meridian altitudes of stars. It was fortunate that the scoundrels had not robbed me of all my stock of quinine and calomel.

The great heat of the weather culminated on the evening of the 5th of April, and we then had a most terrific storm, with claps of thunder exploding over our heads that made the whole place shake with the concussion. Deluges of rain accompanied the electric explosion, and the weather became much cooler.

April 8th. To-day one source of anxiety was taken off my mind in the arrival of Igalo with my poor boy Macondai. The state of Macondai was, however, a great drawback to my rejoicing. I was horrified on beholding him. His head was swollen and covered with pustules, the nose seemed literally eaten up, and his body was in the same state. But the worst sight was one of his legs; it was so swollen that it looked more like the foot of an elephant than that of a human being.

On the 22nd of April I saw a curious example of the surgical practice of the Otando people. In the stillness of the afternoon, when the heat of the vertical sun compels every one to repose, I was startled by loud screams, as though some unfortunate being was being led to death for witchcraft. On going to the place, I found a helpless woman, who was afflicted with leprosy, and suffering besides under an attack of lumbago, undergoing an operation for the latter disease at the hands of the Otando doctor and his assistants. They had made a number of small incisions in the back of the poor creature with a sharp-pointed knife of the country, and were rubbing into the gashes a great quantity of lime-juice mixed with pounded cayenne-pepper. The doctor was rubbing the irritating mixture into the wounds with all his might, so that it was no wonder that the poor creature was screaming with pain, and rolling herself on the ground. It is wonderful to observe the faith all these negroes have in lime-juice mixed with cayenne-pepper. They use it not only as an embrocation, but also internally for dysentery, and I have often seen them drink as much as half a tumblerful of it in such cases. The pepper itself I believe to be a very useful medicine in this climate, for I have often found benefit from it when unwell and feverish, by taking an unusual quantity in my food.

I must relate what I saw afterwards in the course of Máyolo's illness. I knew the old chief had been regularly attended by a female doctor, and often wondered what she did to him. At length one morning I happened to go into his house when she was administering her cures, and remained, an interested spectator, to watch her operations. Máyolo was seated on a mat, submitting to all that was done with the utmost gravity and patience. Before him was extended the skin of a wild animal. The woman was engaged in rubbing his body all over with her hands, muttering all the while, in a low voice, words which I could not understand. Having continued this wholesome friction for some time, she took a piece of alumbi chalk and made with it a broad stripe along the middle of his chest and down each arm. This done, she chewed a quantity of some kind of roots and seeds, and, having well charged her mouth with saliva, spat upon him in different places, but aiming her heaviest shots at the parts most affected. Finally, she took a bunch of a particular kind of grass, which had been gathered when in bloom and was now dry, and, lighting it, touched with the flame the body of her patient in various places, beginning at the foot and gradually ascending to the head. Máyolo smarted with the pain of the burns, when the torch remained too long. When the flame was extinguished the woman applied the burnt end of the torch to her patient's body, and so the operations ended.

I was much amused one evening, whilst my men and a number of villagers were lying about the fires near our encampment, by a story or parable related by a very talkative old fellow who seemed to be the wag of the village. It was as follows :—

AKENDA MBANI.

Redjioua had a daughter called Arondo, and she was very beautiful. Redjioua said, "A man may give me slaves, goods, or ivory to marry my daughter, but he will not get her; I want only a man that will agree that when Arondo falls ill, he will fall ill also, and that when Arondo dies, he will die also." Time went on; and, as people knew this, no one came to ask Arondo in marriage; but, one day, a man called Akenda Mbani ("never goes twice to the same place") came, and he said to Redjioua, "I come to marry Arondo, your daughter; I come, because I will agree that when Arondo dies, I will die also." So Akenda Mbani married Arondo. Akenda Mbani was a great hunter, and, after he had married Arondo, he went hunting, and killed two wild boars. On his return, he said, "I have killed two boars, and bring you one." Radjioua said, "Go and fetch the other." Akenda Mbani said, "My father gave me a *nconi* (a law) that I must never go twice to the same place." Another day he went hunting again, and killed two antelopes; on his return, he said to Redjioua, "Father, I have killed two kambi (antelopes), I bring you one." The king answered, "Please, my son-in-law, go and fetch the other." He answered, "You know I cannot go twice to the same place."

Another time he went hunting again, and killed two bongos (a kind of antelope). Then Redjioua, who saw that all the other animals were being lost, said, "Please, my son-in-law, show the people the place where the other bongo is." Akenda Mbani replied, "If I do so I am afraid I shall die."

In the evening of the same day a canoe from the Orounou

country came with goods, and remained on the river side. Akenda Mbani said to his wife Arondo, "Let us go and meet the Oroungous." They saw them, and then took a box full of goods and then went back to their own house. The people of the village traded with the Oroungous; and, when the Oroungous wanted to go back, they came to Akenda Mbani, and he trusted them ten slaves, and gave them a present of two goats, and many bunches of plantains, mats, and fowls; then the Oroungous left. Months went on; but, one day, Arondo said to her husband, "We have never opened the box that came with the Oroungous. Let us see what there is in it." They opened it, and saw cloth; then Arondo said, "Husband, cut me two fathoms of it, for I like it." Then they left the room; then Arondo seated herself on the bed, and Akenda Mbani on a stool, when suddenly Arondo said, "Husband, I begin to have a headache." Akenda Mbani said, "Ah, ah, Arondo, do you want me to die?" and he looked Arondo steadily in the face. He tied a bandage round her head, and did the same to his own. Arondo began to cry as her headache became worse; and, when the people of the village heard her cry, they came all round her. Redjioua came, and said, "Do not cry, my daughter; you will not die." Then Arondo said, "Father, why do you say I shall not die? for, if you fear death, you may be sure it will come."* She had hardly said these words than she expired. Then all the people mourned, and Redjioua said, "Now my daughter is dead, Akenda Mbani must die also."

The place where people are buried is called Djimai; the villagers went there and dug a place for the two corpses, which were buried together. Redjioua had a slave buried with Arondo, besides a tusk of an elephant, rings, mats, plates, and the bed on which Akenda Mbani and Arondo slept; the cutlass, the hunting bag, and the spear of Akenda Mbani were also buried. The people then said, "Let us cover the things with sand, and make a little mound." When Agambouai (the mouth-piece—the speaker of the village) heard of this, he said to Redjioua, "There are

* When an African is ill, his friends consider it will cause his death to say he will die.

leopards here." Then Redjioua said, "Do not have a mound over my child's burial-place, for fear that the leopards might come and scratch the ground and eat the corpse of my child." Then the people said, "Let us then dig a deeper hole," and they took away Arondo and Akenda Mbani, and placed both on stools, and then dug and dug, and put back the things that were to be buried with Arondo, and then laid her in her place. Then they came to Akenda Mbani, who then awoke and said, "I never go twice to the same place; you put me in the tomb and you took me away from it, though all of you knew that I never go to the same place again." When Redjioua heard of this he became very angry, and said, "You knew that Akenda Mbani never goes twice to the same place; why did you remove him?" Then he ordered the people to catch Agambouai, and cut his head off.

MORAL.

Formerly it was the custom with married people that when the woman died the man should die also, and *vice versâ*. But since the time of Akenda Mbani the custom is altered, and the husband or the wife no longer die with their partners.

To protect the village from the wizards who might enter it from the neighbouring villages, and who had been accused as the cause of Máyolo's troubles, the doctor, accompanied by the whole of the people, went to the paths leading to Máyolo from other villages, and planted sticks at intervals across them, connecting the sticks by strong woody creepers, and hanging on the ropes leaves from the core of the crowns of palm-trees. It is a recognised law among these people that no stranger can come within these lines. When I asked Máyolo what he would do if any one was to force the lines, he said there would then be a grand palaver, but that there was no fear of such an event, for it never happened.

I learnt to-day that the Otando man, who had accompanied me from Olenda, had since died of the plague, and the people of other villages had naturally come to the conclusion that his being in contact with me was the cause. He was one of Máyolo's fathers-in-law.

I now called my people, and Máyolo and his people, together, and made a formal and resolute demand to be furnished with guides and porters to the Apono country. The speech which I made on this occasion was in the following words:—

"Máyolo, I have called you and your people together, in order that you may hear my mouth. When one of your people goes to the Ashira country to make trade, his heart is not glad until his friends there have given him trade, although he may have been well treated in the meantime, had plenty given him to eat, and a fine woman lent him as a wife. When you go to the Apono country in order to get a slave on trust from your friend the chief, or some large tusk of ivory from an elephant he has killed, you are not satisfied until he has sent you back to your village with the slave or the ivory; and your friend never fails to send you back with your desire granted. It is the same if you go to a man whose daughter you are very fond of, and who has promised to give her to you as a wife. For if, when you go to his house to get his daughter, instead of her he gives you plenty of food, your heart is not glad, though you have plenty to eat. The food will taste bitter, for it is not what you came for!

"So it is with me: I am not happy. I have not come to you, Máyolo, to make trade, to get slaves and ivory, or to marry your daughters. If I had come for these things, I am sure they would have been given to me long ago. (The assembly here all shouted 'Yes! they would have been given to you long ago!')

"But you all know that I have not come for these things. I told you when I came, and you knew it before, that I wanted to go further away. I love you and your people. (Interruptions of 'We know you love us.') You have been kind to me and to my men. Though some of them have slept with your women, you have done nothing to them. You have given us plenty to eat; you have stolen nothing from my men or from me; I have been here as if in my own village. (Here they cried out, 'It is your own village; you are our king,' Máyolo leading the chorus.) If I wanted to get angry with you, I could not find a single cause for it. (At this Máyolo stiffened himself up and looked around, quite proud.) A few days after my arrival you, Máyolo, fell ill. You have a good head; you know that I did not make you ill. I was very sorry to see you ill, for I have a heart like yourself. How could I like to see Máyolo, my only friend, ill? (Here Máyolo smiled, and looked prouder than ever.) I love you, and I love your people for your sake. (Shouts of 'We are all your friends.') I am not an evil spirit; I do not delight in making people ill; I do not bring the plague, for it was in your country before I came. (Loud shouts of 'Rovano!'—it is so.) My own people have also been ill; how could I make them ill? If you wanted to go amongst other tribes, would you spread illness before you? So it is with me; to go into the interior I must make friends. The plague goes where it likes and asks nobody. The people are afraid of me; they do not see that I bring them fine things: beads, looking-glasses, cloth, and red caps for their heads. These are things that I wish to leave with the people wherever I go.

"Now, Máyolo, you are getting better. You have a saying among yourselves that a man does not stand alone in the world; he has friends, and there are no people who are without friends. You Otando have friends among the Apono and Ishogo people, where I want to go. If you ask trade of these friends, they give it to you. I come to you to ask you the road. Come and show me the road through the Apono country; it is the one I like the best, for it is the shortest. I will make your heart glad, if you make my heart glad. I have things to give you all, and I want the news to spread that Máyolo and I are two great friends, so that after I am gone people may say, ' Máyolo was the friend of the Oguizi.'"

The last part of the speech was received with tremendous shouts of applause, and cries of "Rovano! Rovano!" Máyolo joining in with the rest.

Máyolo deferred his answer to the next day. The men were seated round in a semi-circle, the women forming a cluster by themselves, and in front was stationed a boy holding a goat, by the side of which were two bunches of plantains; my own people were also present. Máyolo began his speech, and, as is customary, addressed a third person, Igala, saying:—

"When a hunter goes into the forest in search of game, he is not glad until he returns home with meat. So Chaillie's heart will not be glad, until he finishes what he wishes to do. I have heard what Chaillie has told me. I am *a man*. Chaillie, the Oguizi (spirit) has come to Máyolo; I am Máyolo; there is no other Máyolo but me. I am ashamed at this long delay; I have a heart, and Chaillie shall go on. The people are afraid of Chaillie; we all know that he is a spirit; from the time of our fathers were born, his like has never been seen. I am Máyolo, and Chaillie shall go on his way, and then his heart will be glad."

Then turning to me, he said: "During the days you have to wait, take this goat and these two bunches of plantains, and eat them. We shall soon be on the *long road*, but I must feel the way first; we must do things little by little. You cannot catch a monkey, unless you are very careful in going to it."

I answered one of their sayings. "If you had said 'Wait, wait,' and I saw that you were not telling me the truth, the goat you have just given me could not be good, and I would have returned it to you, for it would taste bitter; but I believe you."

Thus I had to content myself whilst Máyolo was exerting himself to open the way for me into Apono-land. In the afternoon I made Igala cut, with a lancet, into the abscess on Máyolo's shoulder, which gave him great relief after the discharge of the matter. The good fellow thanked me very much, and we became better friends than ever. Next day he was so much elated with the improvement in his health, that he got tipsy on a fermented beverage made with ripe plantain. All the people of the village had a jollification in the evening to celebrate the recovery of their chief; Máyolo being the most uproarious of all, dancing, slapping his chest, and shouting "Here I am alive; they said I should die because the spirit had come, but here I am."

He had several of the jars of the country full of the

fermented beverage. Fortunately, he was very inoffensive when under the influence of drink. Scarcely able to stand steady, he came up to me, crying out, "Here I am, Chaillie, well at last. I tell you I am well, Oguizi!" and, in order to prove it to me, he began to leap about and to strike the ground with his feet, saying, "Don't you see that I am well? The Otando people said, the Apono said—as soon as they heard that you had arrived in my village—'Máyolo is a dead man!' As soon as I fell ill, they said, 'Máyolo will never get up again!'"

Throughout the month of April I frequently regaled myself with what I used to consider a very good dinner: that is, a haunch of monkey cooked on the grill. Formerly I had always had a great aversion to eating monkeys (not, however, from any ideas about their relationship to man), but hunger and the scarcity of other animal food had compelled me lately to make many a meal on these animals. This is the height of the monkey season in Otando-land, the season lasting through March, April, and May, during which months they are so fat that their flesh is really exquisite eating. I know of no game better or more relishing; the joints must be either roasted or grilled, to bring out the flavour of the meat to perfection. At all other times of the year except these three months monkeys are lean, tough, and tasteless. Many wild fruit trees are now in full bearing and the monkeys have splendid feed. I finished my dinner with pine-apple as dessert.

The whole country is very rich in spiders; they are of wonderful diversity of form. Some of them are so large, and their webs so strong, that birds are said to be caught in them. There are house-spiders, tree-spiders, ground-spiders. These spiders are exceedingly useful, and rid the country of many unpleasant flies. How many times I have seen them overpower prey which seemed much stronger than themselves! The web-spiders seemed to have but a few enemies, but the house and wall-spiders, which make no web, have most inveterate enemies in the shape of two or three kinds of wasps. During the day I have seen these wasps travelling along the walls with a rapidity that astonished me, and, finally, when coming to a spider, immediately pounce upon the unfortunate insect and overpower it by the quickness of the movements of their legs, and succeed in cutting one after the other the legs of the spider close to the body, and then suck it, or fly away with it to devour it somewhere else.

Oshoumouna and the men sent by Máyolo to open the way for me into Apono-land, returned, frightened away by the reception they had met with from the people of the Apono village to which they had gone, and which is situated on the right bank of the Rembo Ngouyai. As soon as they said who they were, and that they had beads with which to buy some salt—for the Apono trade a good deal in salt, paying for it in slaves—the villagers shouted out, "Go away! go away! We don't want to have anything to do with the Oguizi, or with the people who have come in contact with him! We do not want your beads! We want nothing that came with the Oguizi!"

Many people of Máyolo's clan came to see, before I left the country, the many wonderful things I had brought with me. I got out a galvanic battery, and experimented on such of them as I could persuade to touch the handles. When they felt the shock they cried out "Eninda!" this being the name of a species of electric fish found in the neighbouring streams. They all cried, "Why did you not show us these things before?" I exhibited my large magnet, which I knew would astonish them. I asked one man to come near with his Apono sword, and staggered him by taking it out of his hand with the magnet. I asked for other swords and knives. All were handed to me at arm's length, for they were afraid of approaching the magical instrument, to which the red paint gave additional terrors. When they saw their knives and swords sticking to the magnet without dropping, sometimes by the edges and sometimes sideways, they all shouted out: "He is surely an Oguizi (spirit) to do these things." I invited them to take the instrument in their hands, but they dared not; Máyolo's curiosity eventually overcame his fears, and he handled the magnet with the air of a man who is doing something very courageous.

As the time approached for our departure, a marked increase of attention and kindness was noticeable on his part. Every day a present of eatables came to my hut cooked by his head wife—one day a plateful of yams, another day a dish of cassava, and so forth. But I suspected a trick was being played upon me, having recently become acquainted with an African custom, of which I had not previously heard, and which consisted in serving, in dishes given to a guest, powder from the skull of a deceased ancestor, with a view to soften his heart in the matter of parting presents. This custom is called the *alumbi*.

I had long known of the practice of preserving in a separate hut the skulls of ancestors, but did not know of this particular use of the relics. In fact, a person might travel in Africa for years without becoming aware of this singular custom, as no negro will divulge to you the whole details of such a matter, even should he be one of your best friends.

The Otando people are not very dark-skinned. They had various fashions as regards their teeth. Many file the two upper incisors in the shape of a sharp cone, and the four lower ones are also filed to a sharp point. Others file the four upper incisors to a point. A few among them have the two upper incisors pulled out. They tattoo themselves on the chest and stomach, but keep the face smooth. Among the young people very few have their teeth filed; the custom is dying out.

The native dogs are trained to be useful for hunting. One day, in my rambles near Máyolo, two of them had a severe fight with a very large white-nosed monkey (*cercopithecus*), and came back to me in a dreadful state, especially my dog Andeko, who, being always the first in a fray, generally came off worse than his comrade. In this encounter with the white-nosed monkey, he had the flesh of his fore-leg bitten through to the bone, and his upper lip was cut in two by a terrible gash. Andeko was famous for his courage. He had at different times taken alive young gorillas, young chimpanzees, and young boars.

These native dogs are keen, active animals; they are seen in the interior of purer blood than in the Commi country, where they have become much changed by crossing with

European dogs of various breeds, brought by trading vessels. The pure-bred native dog is small, has long straight ears, long muzzle, and long curly tail—very curly when the breed is pure. The hair is short and the colour yellowish, the pure breed being known by the clearness of this colour. They are always lean, and are kept very short of food by their owners; in fact, they get no food except what they can steal. Although they have a quick ear, I do not think highly of their scent. They are good watch-dogs, but are often destroyed by leopards in the night. Hydrophobia is unknown in this part of the continent. I have only now to confirm that statement; it appears, therefore, conclusive that heat is not the cause of this terrible disease.

CHAPTER XXXI.

Start for Apono-land—An Apono village—Fright of the people—King Nchiengain—The village of Mouendi—The story of the sun and of the moon—Nchiengain and Máyolo drunk with palm wine—Their enthusiasm for going inland—The Aponos a merry people—They love to get tipsy—Leaving Nchiengain's village—Cross a large river—Ishogo and Apono villages—The village of Dilolo—A war cloud—A great meeting—The Apono village of Mokaba—Appearance and dress of the Aponos—The Aponos a warlike people—Iron workers—Their weapons—Aponos accompany me to the Ishogo country—Nchiengain returns to his country—Arrival among the Ishogos—The villages of Igoumbié and Yengué.

WE left Máyolo on the 30th of May, in the morning. The good chief accompanied us, and our party consisted of about thirty men, including twenty porters, all heavily laden with my baggage. My own load was, besides a double-barrelled gun and two revolvers, fifty ball-cartridges, thirty bullets, six pounds of shot, and a quantity of powder and caps: altogether about forty pounds weight.

As we left the village, they all shouted, "The Oguizi is going! the Oguizi is going! we shall never see him more!"

Marching onwards, always in an easterly direction, we

arrived, at half-past four, at the village of the Apono chief Nchiengain, which is called Mouendi. The territory of the Apono tribe lies chiefly to the south-east of this place.

We halted before entering the village, at the request of Máyolo, to arrange the order of going in, for it was necessary to avoid anything that might give alarm to the timid savages, who had never before received a similar visitor. The passage of inhabited places would henceforward be the most difficult part of our journey; as long as we had nothing but forests, rivers, and mountains to traverse, provided we could get plenty of food, all would go well; but to contend with the superstitious fears and greedy avarice of the chiefs and villagers was a serious matter. It was settled that Máyolo, who was the friend and *nkaga* (born the same day) of Nchiengain, should go first, and that the rest should follow at intervals one by one. We marched towards the entrance of the village in dead silence.

As we approached, the people who first caught sight of us began to flee. The women cried out as they ran with their babes in their arms, "The Oguizi! (spirit) the Oguizi! He has come, and we shall die!" They wept and shrieked; I heard their cries with dismay, but did not know till afterwards that the small-pox had already swept through this village.

When we reached the middle of the village, there was not a soul remaining except Nchiengain himself and two men, who stood with fear depicted in their countenances near the ouandja (a kind of house open in front) of the chief. Nchiengain, however, had given his consent to our coming, and seemed to have inwardly resolved to brave it out. He had fortified himself against evil by besmearing his body with great streaks of the alumbi chalk, and hanging all his fetiches around him.

The persuasive tongue of Máyolo soon calmed his fears. He gathered courage to look me steadily in the face. I then addressed him in the Ashira language, and recounted the treasures in beads, caps for the head, coats, and cotton prints that I had brought for him; finally he began to smile and took my proffered hand. Beads were promised to the women, and gradually the people came back to their houses. Towards evening I went round the village, looked into the huts, laughed with the people, and distributed beads. Good humour was restored, and the remark became general that the Oguizi was a good spirit after all.

Nchiengain is a tall, slender old negro, with a mild and timid expression of features. He is the leading chief of the Apono tribe in these parts; but his clan is now, I hear, almost extinguished. His village is one of the finest and cleanest I have yet seen, the houses being neat, built chiefly of bamboo, or strips of the leaf-stalks of palm-trees, and arranged in symmetrical lines. I have measured the street, and find it to be 447 yards long and 18 broad. The houses are small and quite separate from one another; the height of the roof is about seven feet; and each house has its little verandah in front, under which the inhabitants take their meals and sit to smoke and chat. I notice that many of the men have their two middle upper incisor teeth pulled out, and the two next to them filed to a point. Some of the women beautify themselves in a similar way; they also endeavour to improve their looks by tattooing themselves in long scars on their foreheads, between their eyebrows, and on their cheeks in a line with the middle of the ear.

Although the chief seems to be of a good disposition, I found him no better inclined to forward my journey than any of the others I had dealings with. Like the Olenda people, he wanted the chief who had brought me to his place to leave me in his hands; this being the first step necessary to enable the rapacious negroes to get all they could out of me at their leisure. Máyolo was firm in his demand to have me forwarded across the Rembo in two days. Our palavers lasted all this day and the next. I gave him a quantity of goods, but, as was to be expected, he expressed his dissatisfaction, with a view to get more out of me. I left Máyolo with him, and by some means or other he persuaded him to be contented. What could I do with a man who believed that I made all these things myself, by some conjuring process? for it is thus that that Nchiengain argued with Máyolo: "The cloth and beads and guns cost him no trouble to make; why does he not give me more of these things which do me so much good?" "Máyolo," he would continue in course of his many palavers with him, "you eat me with jealousy. Why do you want yourself to take the Oguizi to the Ashango country? why not go back and leave him to me? I want it to go far and wide that the Oguizi and Nchiengain are big friends."

June 1st. A number of Apingi men came up the river to-day from their villages, which are situated a few miles lower down the river banks, towards the north or north-west. They fraternised with the Apono, and we had great noise, tam-tamming, drinking, and confusion.

Sometimes I used to be amused by the ideas of the people about the heavenly bodies. Like all other remarkable natural objects, they are the subjects of whimsical myths among them. According to them, the sun and moon are of the same age, but the sun brings daylight and gladness and the moon brings darkness, witchcraft, and death—for death comes from sleep, and sleep commences in darkness. The sun and moon, they say, once got angry with each other, each one claiming to be the eldest. The moon said: "Who are you, to dare to speak to me? you are alone, you have no people; what! are you to consider yourself equal to me? Look at me," she continued, showing the stars shining around her, "these are my people; I am not alone in the world, like you." The sun answered, "O moon, you bring witchcraft, and it is you who have killed all my people, or I should have as many attendants as you." According to the negroes, people are more liable to die when the moon first makes her appearance and when she is last visible. They say that she calls the people her insects, and devours them. The moon with them is the emblem of time and of death.

Some of the inhabitants of a neighbouring Apono village, who had been most hostile to my coming to their country, having since heard that I had brought no evil or sickness with me here, now came to see me. As soon as my friend Nchiengain saw them, he went up to them in great anger, crying out, "Go away, go away! Now that you have smelt niva (my goods or present), you are no longer afraid, but want to come!" So the men went away without my speaking to them.

June 2nd. Towards evening both Nchiengain and Máyolo got drunk with palm wine, and their ardour to go forward with me was something astonishing. They say they are going with me far beyond the Ashango; they are *men;* they will even travel by night, as there will be the moon with us.

Many of the people are drunk to-night, following the example of the two chiefs. I had always heard from the slaves near the coast that the Apono were a merry race, and I now find it so with a vengeance. Since my arrival here there is nothing but dancing and singing every night.

June 3rd. We left Mouendi with a great deal of trouble this morning. Nchiengain and Máyolo wanted to renew their libations of the previous evening, and, in fact, were half-drunk soon after daylight; but I went to the hut where the symposium was going on, and, kicking over the calabashes of palm-wine, sent the chiefs and their attendants to the right-about. I could not, however, get Nchiengain away, and we started without him. I wondered afterwards at the good-nature of these people, who saw with composure a stranger knocking over so large a quantity of their cherished beverage. They did not resent my act, but only grumbled that so much good liquor was spilt instead of going down their throats.

We reached the banks of the river, distant about three miles from the village. The Ngouyai was here a fine stream, from ten to fifteen feet deep, flowing from the S.S.W.

It was now the dry season, when the water is about ten feet below the level of the rainy season. I could not but admire the magnificent trees, which towered above the masses of lower trees and bushes growing from the rich soil; some of them grew on the very brink of the stream, and their trunks were supported by erect roots, looking like maypoles, eight or ten feet high, and projecting in places over the water.

Nchiengain's flat-bottomed canoe carried my party and baggage across in seven journeys. Nchiengain arrived at the river-side, reeling drunk, just as we were shoving off with the last load, and I told the men to pretend not to hear his shouts for the return of the canoe to embark him, so he had to come over alone when we had all landed on the other side.

4*th*. We left the banks of the river at a quarter past six a.m. Shortly afterwards we passed through an Apono village, and at half-past eight a.m. came to three Ishogo villages close together. It was no new feature to find a settlement of a tribe living in the middle of a district belonging to another tribe.

The Ishogos of these villages knew that I was to pass through the places. They had heard of the untold wealth I brought with me, and were annoyed when they perceived my intention to pass on without stopping. The villages are built in an open grassy space; and as soon as the caravan came in sight the excitement was intense. Women, children, and armed men came around, shouting and entreating; some running along the line of march, with goats in tow, offering them as presents if I would stay with them, even if it was only for a night. It is the custom in all these villages to offer a present of food to a stranger if the inhabitants wish him to stay with them; and the acceptance of the present by the stranger is a token of his intention to remain in the place for a time. They offered also ivory and slaves, and the more I refused the offers, the more pertinacious they became. Their sole wish, of course, in asking me to stay, was to get as much as they could of the coveted goods I brought with me. Our Apono companions mourned over the goats that I might have had.

The direct easterly path from here led to a number of Apono villages; these we wished to avoid in order to escape a similar annoyance to that which we had undergone in the morning from the Ishogos, and so struck a little more southerly, or S.S.E. by compass. Our road lay for three hours over undulating prairie land, with occasional woods; one of the open spaces was a prairie called Matimbié irimba (the prairie of stones) stretching S.E. and N.W.

At the S.E. end of the prairie we came to a village called Dilolo. Our reception here was anything but friendly. We found the entrance to the one street of the village barricaded and guarded by all the fighting men, armed with spears, bows and arrows, and sabres. When within earshot, they vented bitter curses against Nchiengain for wanting to bring the Oguizi, who carries with him the plague into their village, and probibited us from entering if we did not want war. The war drums beat, and the men advanced and retired before us, spear in hand. We marched forward, nevertheless, and the determined fellows then set fire to the grass of the open space leading to the village barricade. Wishing to avoid an encounter, and also the fire which was spreading at a great rate over the prairie, we turned by a path leading round the village; but when we had reached the rear of the place, we found a body of the villagers moving in the same direction to stop our further progress. Most of them appeared half-intoxicated with palm wine, and I now felt that we were going to have a fight. Presently two poisoned arrows were shot at us, but they fell short. Nchiengain then came up and walked between my men and the irritated warriors, begging me not to fire unless some of us were hit. The villagers, seeing that we made no display of force, became bolder, and one of them came right up and with his bow bent threatened to shoot Rapelina. My plucky lad faced the fellow boldly, and, showing him the muzzle of his gun, told him he would be a dead man if he did not instantly put down his bow. All my Commi boys came up, and ranging themselves on the flanks of our caravan with their guns pointed at the enemy, protected the train of porters as they filed past. I was glad to see also our Apono companions taking our part; they got enraged with the villagers, and some of them laid down their loads, and rushed to the front waving their swords. I watched the scene calmly, and surveyed the field where war might at any moment break out. Behind us the country was all in a blaze, for the fire had spread with great rapidity. The Apono porters being so resolutely on our side, I had no fear as to how the conflict would end. It is a point of honour with these primitive Africans that they are bound to defend strangers whom they have undertaken to convey from one tribe to another, though they may rob him. We went on our way, Nchiengain shouting from the rear to the discomfited warriors that there would be a palaver to settle for this when he came back.

I was prouder than ever of my boys after this, and profited by the occasion to strengthen them in their determination to go forward. There was no going back after this, I told them; they all shouted, "We must go forward; we are going to the white man's country!"

We continued our march till half-past four p.m., when we encamped for the night in the middle of a wood, where there was a cool spring of water, close to a cluster of Apono villages. In the evening we heard the cries of the people, the weeping of the women, and the beating of the war drums. The burthen of their lamentations was, "O Nchiengain, why have you brought this curse upon us? We do not want the Oguizi, who brings the plague with him. The Ishogo are all dead, the Ashango have left; it is of no use your taking the white man to them; go back, go back!" We slept with our loaded guns by our side.

June 5th. At daylight this morning I got up and looked out over the broad prairie, and, to my agreeable surprise, I saw no signs of war. Shortly afterwards a deputation of three men came from the village to try to persuade Nchiengain not to pass through, on account of my bringing death wherever I went. But the trusty and sensible old chief, in a long speech, showed them that it was a foolish alarm about my bringing the *eviva*, and that the plague came quite independent of me, for it had passed through his village long before the Oguizi had come near it. The argument seemed to have a good effect; they retired, and shortly afterwards both Nchiengain and Máyolo were sent for to the village; this was followed by a messenger arriving for me.

When I came into the open space chosen for the meeting, at some distance from the village, I was not a little surprised to see about 200 of the villagers assembled, all gravely seated on the grass, in a group of a semi-circular form. As I advanced towards them, I was amused to see the front row getting uneasy and wriggling off into the rear, followed by the next row, and so on. Nchiengain addressed me, saying that he had sent for me to tell me that the villagers wished me to leave the wood in which I was encamped, and to move to the top of a grassy hill a little further off. If I did that all the people would come and see me, and bring me food, and on the following day would be willing that I should continue my journey.

Late in the afternoon, three head men of neighbouring villages came to invite us to their respective villages. One of the elders was from a large place not far distant, called Mokaba, and **Máyolo** recommended me to go to this village in preference to the others, because its representative had offered us the greatest number of goats, namely, three. Nchiengain was too far gone in intoxication, having had a drinking bout with the chiefs of the village where we now were, to accompany us. After a short march we entered the friendly town of Mokaba, amidst the shouts of the whole population.

My own men now enjoyed much better health than they did at the commencement of our expedition; for, strange to say, these negroes cannot bear as much fatigue and hardship as I do, and generally after a long march or a hunt they fell ill. But I could never make them come and tell me as soon as they felt the first symptoms of being unwell, so, at fixed periods—once a fortnight, or once a month, according to the season—they were summoned to my "dispensary" to be dosed all round. I had fixed days for the different medicines: one day was castor-oil day, another was blue-pill or calomel day, a third was the "feast of Epsom salts." They all had to come up in single file, and, one after the other, were ordered to swallow their dose. Now and then one or two of them tried to escape the medicine parade; and, when I called them up, each had some ready excuse for his non-attendance, but in vain. This was generally on castor-oil day, for they said that they did not mind the other medicines, but that this was "so bad;" and many were the wry faces that were made before the dose was swallowed by the entire company. However, I found that my plan had very good results, as my men had much better health than they had before I adopted it.

CHAPTER XXXII.

The Apono country—The village of Mokaba—Large quantity of palm trees—Palm wine a favourite drink—Many men with scars—The Ocuya performance—The Apono people—Fashion—Weapons of the Aponos—From Mokaba to Igoumbié—A large village—Singing at night.

June 6th. Mokaba and most of the other villages of the Apono tribe are situated in an open tract of undulating country, partly wooded and partly open prairie. The distance of the town from Máyolo is not more than twenty-seven miles in a direct line, and within a short distance of the Ngouyai.

I liked the Aponos, and got on very well whilst in their country. They showed themselves to be honest, and were faithful in carrying out the engagements they entered into with me, in spite of the numerous palavers we had. I lost none of my property by theft whilst I was amongst them.

The village of Mokaba is large and well arranged; it was the prettiest village I have ever seen in Africa. There are upwards of 130 houses or huts, which, as in other West-African villages, are so arranged as to form one main street. But, in Mokaba, several houses are connected so as to form a square, with a common yard or garden in the middle, in which grow magnificent palm-trees. Behind the houses, too, are very frequently groups of plantain and lime-trees. The village being thus composed of a series of small quadrangles and back-gardens containing trees with beautiful foliage, the whole effect is very charming. In the rear of the houses, amidst the plantain-groves, they keep their goats, fowls, and pigs. This was the only village where I saw tame pigs. I was struck with the regularity of the main street; but, besides this, there was another narrower street on each side of the village, lying between the backs of the houses and the plantain-groves, and kept very neat and closely-weeded. Each house has in front a verandah, or little open space without wall, occupying half the length of the house; the other half, in equal portions on each side, forms apartments in which the owners sleep and keep their little property.

MOKABA. AN APONO VILLAGE.

When a man marries, he immediately builds a house for his new wife; and, as the family increases, other houses are built; the house of each wife being kept separate. The palm-trees in the quadrangles are the property of the chief man of each group of houses; and, being valuable property, pass on his death to his heir, the next brother or the nephew, as in other tribes. Some of these palm-trees tower up to a height of fifty feet, and have a singular appearance in the palm-wine season from being hung, beneath the crown, with hollowed gourds receiving the precious liquor.

The large quantity of palm-trees in and around the village furnish the Aponos of Mokaba with a ready supply of their favourite drink, palm-wine; they are a merry people, and make a regular practice of getting drunk every day as long as the wine is obtainable. I often saw them climb the trees in early morning, and take deep draughts from the calabashes suspended there. Like most drunken people, they become quarrelsome; and being a lively and excitable race, many frays occur. Happily, the palm-wine season lasts only a few months in the year: it was the height of the drunken season when I was at Mokaba. I saw very few men who had not scars, or the marks of one or more wounds, received in their merry-making scrimmages. Their holidays are very frequent. Unlimited drinking is the chief amusement, together with dancing, tam-tamming, and wild uproar, which last all night.

They are very fond of the *ocuya* performances. The ocuya is a man supporting a large framework resembling a giant, and whimsically dressed and ornamented, who walks and dances on stilts. In Mokaba, he appears in a white mask with thick open lips, disclosing the rows of teeth *minus* the middle incisors, according to the Apono fashion. The long garment reaches to the ground, covering the stilts. It struck me as a droll coincidence that his head-dress resembled exactly a lady's bonnet; it was surmounted by feathers and made of the skin of a monkey. Behind, however, hung the monkey's tail, which I cannot say has its parallel in European fashions.

The curiosity of the Mokaba people is most troublesome.

The way they come upon me is sometimes quite startling; they sidle up behind trees, or crawl up amongst the long grass until they are near enough, and then, from behind the tree trunks, or above the herbage, a number of soot-black faces suddenly bob out, staring at me, with eyes and mouth wide open. The least thing I do elicits shouts of wonder; but if I look directly at them they take to their legs and run as if for their lives.

The Mokaba people took alarm at night in seeing me look at the stars with my instruments; and the chief, accompanied by his people, came and told me they would build a shed for me at a distance from the houses.

The Aponos are no doubt a branch of the great Ashira nation, like the Ashira Kamba, the Ashira Ngozai, and the Otando, all of whom, as well as the Aponos, speak the Ashira language. The Ashangos also speak the Ashira language, although they are divided from the Aponos by the Ishogo, who speak an entirely different language. But the Aponos are distinguished from all the other branches of the Ashira nation by their sprightliness of character; and they are clean and well-looking. Their villages are larger, better arranged, and prettier than those of the Otando and Ashira Ngozai. Each house is built separate from its neighbours, and they attend to cleanliness in their domestic arrangements. Their country is an undulating plain, varied with open grassy places covered with a pebbly soil, and rich and extensive patches of woodland well adapted for agriculture, in which they make their plantations. I cannot make an estimate of the total population of the tribe; their villages were numerous along our line of march from Mouendi.

Both men and women are distinguished by their habit of taking out the two middle upper incisors and filing the two others, as well as the four lower incisors, to a point. The women have for ornament tattooed scars on their forehead; very often these consist of nine rounded prominences similar in size to peas, and arranged in the form of a lozenge between their eyebrows, and they have similar raised marks on their cheeks and a few irregular marks on the chest and abdomen, varying in pattern in different individuals. They also rub themselves with red powder derived from the common barwood of trade. They dress their hair in many ways. They do not practise tattooing so much as the Apingi, who decorate their chests and abdomens with various kinds of raised patterns. The Apingi and the Ishogos speak the same language.

The Aponos are a warlike people, and are rather looked up to with fear by the Apingi and the Ishogos, whose villages are close to theirs. They are not such skilful workers in iron as the Fans, or as some other tribes further to the east. The iron-ore which they use is found plentifully in some parts of their prairies: it occurs in lumps of various sizes, and is dug from the soil; the deeper they dig the larger and purer are the lumps. They melt it in little thick earthenware pots, holding about a pint each, and use, of course, charcoal in tempering the metal. Their anvils are large and well made, but the construction of them is apparently beyond their ability, as all the anvils which I saw came from the Abombo and Njavi tribes, who live further towards the east. The Abombos and Njavis manufacture also a superior kind of straight sword four feet long, the handle of which is made of wood and is in the shape of a dice-box, through the middle of which the handle-end of the sword passes.

The bows of the Aponos are very different from the crossbows of the Fans, which I have described; they are not nearly so powerful, but, at the same time, not so clumsy; they are of very tough wood, and bent nearly in a semicircle, with the chord measuring about two feet, and the string of vegetable fibre. The arrow is rather heavy; the head is of tempered iron, triangular in shape, and prolonged in a tubular form for the insertion of the shaft; the shaft is not secured into the head, so that when the arrow enters into the body of a man or animal, the sharp triangular lance-head, coated with poison, remains in the wound, whilst the shaft drops out. The arrows are kept in cylindrical quivers made of the bark of a tree, and not in bags.

Their spears, also, are different from those of the Fans, and are similar to those described by Burton, Grant, Speke, and other travellers, as used by the tribes of Eastern Equatorial

Africa. They are much heavier and clumsier than the spears of the Fans, and cannot, therefore, like them, be thrown to a great distance. The head is lance-shaped, without barbs, and a foot in length. In fight they are used for thrusting, at close quarters. Sabres are the most common weapons with these people; they are curved, and have wooden handles. The metal of which the blades are made, although pretty well tempered, by means of the charcoal used, is full of flaws. Some of the people use round shields made of wicker-work. Each of my Apono porters carried a sabre, besides his bow and quiver of arrows. The possession of a sword is a mark of manhood with these people, and all the young men think it honourable to obtain a sword before they acquire a wife. In fact, the chief things coveted by the young dandies of the tribe are a sword, a grass-web cap of the country, and a handsome *dengui*, or garment of striped grass-cloth. The red worsted caps which I carried, as part of my stores, immediately drove their native caps out of fashion, and, indeed, created a perfect *furore*. It was a sure way of gaining the good will of an Apono man to present him with one of these caps.

The Aponos are industrious weavers of grass-cloth, which forms the clothing of both sexes. The cloth is woven in small pieces with a fringe, called *bongos*, and is sometimes beautifully fine; when several *bongos* are sewn together, the garment is called a *dengui*; the women wear only two pieces, or *bongos*, one on each side, secured at the top over the hips, and meeting in front at the upper edge.

It might be supposed, from the frequency with which I met with villages on the march, that the Apono country was thickly inhabited, especially as the villages were large, a few of them containing about a thousand inhabitants. But it must be recollected that the pathways, along which we were obliged to march, were the roads leading from one village to another. I travelled, therefore, through the peopled part of the country. Away from these main pathways there were vast tracts of prairie and some wooded land remaining in their original desert condition.

It is settled that nineteen Apono porters are to accompany

me to the Ishogo country with their chief Kombila.*
Nchiengain returns to his own place. Before he left me we
assembled all our new men, and he made a speech to them
whilst I distributed the pay. He told them how Olenda had
delivered me to Máyolo and Máyolo to him, and that now
they must take me safe to the Ishógo people, who would pass
me over to the Ashango, and so on. They were to see that I
had plenty of goats and plantains, and then if their task was
well done they would receive their reward as he and his
people had done.

June 10th.—We pursued a direction a little north of east.
The ground soon began to rise, and we entered on a richly-
wooded hilly country, in which were numerous plantations
and villages of slaves belonging to the head-men of Mokaba.

We continued our journey to the south-east, and at half-
past three arrived at a large Ishogo village called Igoumbié.
We did not intend to stay, and marched straight through;
the people all hiding themselves in their huts, with the exception of a few men bolder than the rest, who stood staring
at us, without uttering a word, as we marched along. When
we had passed through the village, we stopped near the road
or pathway on the other side, about fifty yards beyond.
Then Kombila and some of our Apono men went back to the
village, and spoke to the people. One of the elders of the
place was a great friend of Kombila's, and they all knew the
Mokaba people. So Boulingué, Kombila's friend, came back
with him to our encampment, and begged me to come and
stay in the village, saying that they did not wish us to pass
their place without their giving us something to eat.

I could not ascertain who was the chief of this village, if
there was any. Since I have left Mouendi I cannot find out

---

* As proper names may be of some utility in the study of the native
languages, I subjoin the names of my porters :—

Head man, Kombila.   Second in command, Mbouka.

Ipandi,	Kassa,	Boushoubou,
Foubou,	Mondjego,	Djembé,
Batali,	Mombon,	Boulingué,
Njomba,	Badinga,	Nchago,
Mozamba.	Miyendo,	Noueti,
Mousoumbi,	Mafoumbi,	Momelou.

that there are any head-men or chiefs in the villages, but there seemed to be a certain number of elders, who hold authority over their respective villages. Here three elders, beating the kendo, came and presented me, each one, with a goat and several bunches of plantains — prefacing their presents with three tremendously long speeches.

At a glance I perceived that I was among quite a different tribe from those I had hitherto met with. The mode of dressing the hair, both with men and women; the shape of their houses, each with its door; the men smeared with red powder; all these points denoted different customs.

I was very much amused with these Ishogos, especially with the women. When they thought I was not looking at them, they would partially open the door of their hut and peep out at me. As soon as I looked at them, they immediately closed the door, as if greatly alarmed. When they had to go from one house to another, and had to pass the hut in which I was located, and at the door of which I was seated, they hurriedly crossed to the other side of the street, putting their hand up to the side of their face so that they might not see me—apparently with a view to avoid or avert the "evil eye."

June 11*th*.—Igoumbié is the largest village I have met with yet, and forms one long and tolerably broad street. I counted 191 huts; each hut has a wooden door, and is divided into three compartments or chambers. The houses are generally placed close to each other, not wide apart like the houses of the Aponos. There are many of the curious alumbi houses scattered about. A large mbuiti, or idol house, stands about half way down the street, with a monstrous wooden image inside, which the villagers hold in great reverence. The village being so large, the inhabitants seem to have thought it required several palaver-houses, for I noticed four or five. The palaver-house is an open shed, which answers the purpose of a public-house, club-room, or town-hall, to these people; they meet there daily to smoke and gossip, hold public trials or palavers, and receive strangers. What was most remarkable, there was here an attempt at decorative work on the doors of many of the houses. The huts, neatly built, with walls formed of the bark of trees, had their doors painted red, white, and black, in complicated and sometimes not inelegant patterns. These doors were very ingeniously made; they turned upon pivots above and below, which worked in the frame instead of hinges. Each house is of an oblong shape, about twenty-two feet long by ten or twelve feet broad; the door being in the middle of the front, three

ISHOGO HOUSES OF IGOUMBIÉ, WITH ORNAMENTED DOORS.

and a half feet high and two and a half feet broad. The walls are four and half feet high and the highest part of the roof is about nine feet.

I could not sleep last night on account of the noise made by these Ishogos. They sang their mbuiti songs until daylight, marching from one end of the village to the other. When at a distance their singing did not sound unpleasant, but when close by it was almost deafening. During the day

I made friends with the Ishogos, and gave them sundry small presents. Many of the women came and gave me bunches of plantains, sugar-cane, and ground-nuts, and seemed much pleased when I tasted them.

June 12*th.* We took leave of Igoumbié a little before 8 A.M. The people seemed unwilling to let us go, and the elders begged us to stay another day.

Some tampering took place with my Apono porters, and I had great difficulty in preventing them from throwing down their loads and going back. It was an awkward position to be placed in; but, by dint of coaxing and promising extra pay if they would accompany Kombila to the place to which he and they had agreed to take me, they resumed their loads, and we continued our march.

We passed two Apono villages near together; and halted for breakfast by a small stream of water near the second one. We were soon surrounded by villagers bringing fowls and plantains. The noise and confusion were so great that I went away alone for a walk in the thick of the forest, leaving my men to bargain for fowls and eggs. All the villagers wanted to get some of my beads.

We resumed our march at half-past twelve. Kombila annoyed me much by slinking behind, and getting drunk with another of my men, named Mbouka, an elder of Mokaba, who at the last moment said he would accompany us for *a walk.* Under one pretext or another they had remained behind; and as they had told the villagers to follow them "with the drink," when they knew that I was far enough off, they took their libations. They both made their appearance after causing a long delay, and Mbouka had a calabash of palm wine in one of the country bags, which I detected, the bag being of a great size. I was resolved to put a stop to this, so forced the man to give up his bag, and poured the wine out on the ground, to the great dismay of Kombila, and to the extreme indignation of Mbouka, who grieved that the earth should receive the wine that would have so rejoiced his stomach. He protested that I ought to pay him back the beads he had paid for the wine. This palm-wine drinking had been a great annoyance to me. Our porters squandered their pay (which consisted chiefly of beads) in buying wine at the villages, and were thus spending all their money before we reached the journey's end.

The Apono porters threatened again to leave their loads unless I gave them an increase of pay; but I was determined to resist this imposition, and declared I would shoot down the first man that mutinied.

CHAPTER XXXIII.

From Igoumbié to Yengué—Discovery of a deserted village of the dwarfs—Curious houses of the dwarfs—Yengué—The king makes his appearance—Popularity of my red woollen caps—Presented with goats and fowls—Superstitions in regard to twins—The village of Mokenga—I am said to have moved a huge granite block—A village fetich-tree—Leopards—King Quembila—Panic among the Ishogos—Dismiss my Apono porters and guides—The Ishogo tribes—Appearance of the people—Women's head-dress—Wealth of an Ishogo man—The Ishogos are celebrated weavers.

WE were now bound for Yengué, and on our way thither, in traversing the wild forest through which runs the highway of the country, we came suddenly upon a cluster of most extraordinary diminutive huts, which I should have passed by, thinking them to be some kind of fetich-houses, if I had not been told that we might meet in this district with villages of a tribe of dwarf negroes, who are scattered about the Ishogo and Ashango countries and other parts further east.

I had heard of these people in the Apingi country, under the name of Ashoungas; they are called here, however, Obongos. From the loose and exaggerated descriptions I had heard, I had given no more credence to the report of the existence of these dwarf tribes than to that of men with tails, who had stools with a hole in them for their tails to be put through, or to the stories of the Sapadi, or cloven-footed men. The sight of these extraordinary dwellings filled me with curiosity, for it was really a village of this curious people. I rushed forward, hoping to find some at least of their tenants inside, but they had fled on our approach into the neighbouring jungle. The huts were of a low oval shape, like a gipsy tent; the highest part—that nearest the entrance—was about four feet from the ground; the greatest breadth was about four feet also. On each side were three or four sticks for the man and woman to sleep upon. The huts were made of flexible branches of trees, arched over and fixed into the ground at each end, the longest branches being in the middle, and the others successively shorter, the whole being covered with large leaves. When I entered the huts, I found in each the remains of a fire in the middle of the floor. We scoured the neighbourhood for some distance, but could find no traces of them. (A fuller account of these strange creatures will be found in a subsequent chapter.)

Finally, we came to Yengué, an Ishogo village, almost as large as Igoumbié, situated on the banks of a river called Ogoulou, one of the affluents of the Ngouyai.

Before entering the village, we stopped until all the porters were collected together. Then Kombila and I took the lead, followed by my Commi men. We marched through the street of the village—the villagers looking at us, open-mouthed—until we reached the large ouanja, which was almost at the farthest extremity of the village; Kombila all the time exclaiming to the alarmed villagers, "Do not be afraid; we have come to see you as friends!"

Kombila then went and spoke to some of the elders, who came to me, and presented fowls and plantains.

As usual, the king was not at Yengué. But one of the elders took great care of me; so after a while I called him into my house, and made Kombila tell him that I had not come to do them harm, but good. Then I put on his head a bright shining red cap, and round his neck a string of very showy beads. As he came out of my hut, the shouts of the people were deafening. I then distributed a few beads among the women. My Aponos did the same, and to-night the ice is partly broken, and the people are very friendly with me. Kombila having told the women that I was very fond of sugar-cane and ground-nuts, they brought me some, laying them at my feet. In return I gave them beads, and chatted with as many as I could get to talk to me.

June 14*th.* The man whom I suppose to be the head chief of Yengué arrived in town this afternoon. It appears that he had fled through fear at my approach, and had gained confidence only on hearing that I was not such a dreadful being as he had imagined. The news of the red cap I had given to the elder had reached his ears; for the first thing he asked me was whether I would give him one also. Last night I heard a man walking in the streets of the village and saying, in a tone of voice like that of a town crier, " We have the Oguizi amongst us. Beware ! There is no mondah to prevent us from seeing him during the day, but let no one try to see him in his house at night, for whoever does so is sure to die."

After the arrival of the chief, things looked quite promising. A formal reception palaver took place in the open street, the Apono guides seated in a row on one side, and the Ishogos on the other. Kombila stated at great length, as usual, the objects of my journey, and the king answered in a speech of greater length still. The chief gave to Kombila, as presents for me, two goats, ten fowls, nine bunches of plantains, and a native anvil. The ceremony finished in a kind of war-dance, in which the Aponos took part.

The singing and dancing during this uproarious night were partly connected with a curious ceremony of this people, namely, the celebration of the *mpaza,* or the release from the long deprivation of liberty which a woman suffers who has the misfortune to bring forth twins.

The custom altogether is a very strange one, but it is by no means peculiar to the Ishogos, although this is the first time I witnessed the doings. The negroes of this part of Africa have a strange notion or superstition that when twins (mpaza) are born, one of them must die early ; so, in order, apparently, to avoid such a calamity, the mother is confined to her hut, or rather restricted in her intercourse with her neighbours, until both the children have grown up, when the danger is supposed to have passed. She is allowed during this time to go to the forest, but is not permitted to speak to any one not belonging to her family. During the long confinement no one but the father and mother are allowed to enter the hut, and the woman must remain chaste. If a stranger goes in by any accident or mistake, he is seized and sold into slavery. The twins themselves are excluded from the society of other children, and the cooking utensils, water vessels, etc., of the family are tabooed to everybody else.

The house where the twins were born is always marked in some way to distinguish it from the others, in order to prevent mistakes. Here in Yengué it had two long poles on each side of the door, at the top of which was a piece of cloth, and at the foot of the door were a number of pegs stuck in the ground, and painted white. The twins were now six years old, and the poor woman was released from her six years' imprisonment on the day of my arrival. During the day two women were stationed at the door of the house with their faces and legs painted white—one was the doctor, the other the mother. The festivities commenced by their marching down the street, one beating a drum with a slow measured beat, and the other singing. The dancing, singing, and drinking of all the villagers then set in for the night. After the ceremony the twins were allowed to go about like other children. In consequence of all this trouble and restriction of liberty, the bringing forth of twins is considered, and no wonder, by the women as a great calamity. Nothing irritates or annoys an expectant mother in these countries so much as to point to her and tell her that she is sure to have twins.

The river Ogoulou, on the banks of which Yengué is situated, is a fine stream forty or fifty yards broad, and of great depth in the rainy season. It is now about ten feet deep, and I perceived that it was fifteen feet lower than the highest water-mark. The banks of the river show signs of a very considerable population; for about a mile on each side of the valley is full of plantations both new and old; the most extensive plantations of ground-nuts I ever saw in Africa are found here—they extend along the slopes of the banks of the river for miles.

The Yengué people were afraid I should take their canoes by force to cross the Ogoulou, and when I was about to start had hidden them in the jungle. It required a long parley to bring them to reason. At length three ferry-boats were brought, one old and rotten. The owner of this last boat was an old man, who knew how to drive a very hard bargain—he required four measures of powder for the loan of the boats, and when I had given him four asked five, when I had given him five he raised his demands to six, and so on. It finished at last in the usual way by my indignantly refusing his demands: he then came round to more moderate terms,—the more readily because he saw that the other two boat-owners were ready to take us at my price—and we embarked, all Yengué crowding down to the water-side to see us off, the chief himself leading me to the boat.

Before we had emerged from the river valley we passed through several Ishogo villages; the country then began to rise, and we marched over a hilly district, all covered, as usual, with impenetrable jungle. The forest paths were narrow, and the most varied and strange forms of vegetation rose on either side. We were delayed some time on the way. At two p.m. we reached an elevated plateau, and a little before three arrived at the Ishogo village of Mokenga, about six miles to the eastward of Yengué.

The village was surrounded by a dense grove of plantain-trees, many of which had to be supported by poles, on account of the weight of the enormous bunches of plantains they bore. Little groves of lime-trees were scattered everywhere, and the limes, like so much golden fruit, looked beautiful amidst the dark foliage that surrounded them. Tall, towering palm-trees were scattered here and there. Above and behind the village was the dark green forest. The street was the broadest I ever saw in Africa; one part of it was about 100 yards broad, and not a blade of grass could be seen in it. The *Sycobii* were building their nests everywhere, and made a deafening noise, for there were thousands and thousands of these little sociable birds.

Mokenga, being on the skirts of the interior mountain ranges, its neighbourhood is very varied and picturesque. The spring from which the villagers draw their water is situated in a most charming spot. A rill of water, clear and cold, leaps from the lower part of a precipitous hill, with a fall of about nine feet, into crystal basin, whence a rivulet brawls down towards the lower land through luxuriant woodlands.

Not far from Mokenga there was a remarkable and very large boulder of granite perched by itself at the top of a hill. It must have been transported there by some external force, but what this was I cannot undertake to say. I thought it possible that it might have been a true boulder transported by a glacier, like those so abundant in northern latitudes. Although I visited it and examined it closely, I found no traces of grooves upon it. On my way from Mokaba to Yengué, I saw no boulders of quartz or granite.

My visits to this enormous block of granite were so numerous that they attracted the notice of the natives, and I was not a little surprised, one fine morning, to find the village in a state of great excitement about the rumour that the boulder was not in the same place as it had always been, and that the Oguizi had moved it.

In almost every Ishogo and Ashango village which I visited there was a large tree standing about the middle of the main street, and near the mbuiti or idol-house of the village. The tree is a kind of Ficus, with large, thick, and glossy leaves. It is planted as a sapling when the village is first built, and is considered to bring good luck to the inhabitants as a talisman: if the sapling lives, the villagers consider the omen a good one; but if it dies they all abandon the place and found a new village elsewhere. This tree grows rapidly, and soon forms a conspicuous object, with its broad crown yielding a pleasant shade in the middle of the street. Fetiches, similar to those I have described in the account of Rabolo's village on the Fernand Vaz, are buried at the foot of the tree. The tree, of course, is held sacred. An additional charm is lent to these village trees by the great number of little social birds (*Sycobius*, three species) which resort to them to build their nests amongst the foliage. These charming little birds love the society of man as well as that of their own species. They associate in these trees sometimes in incredible quantities, and the noise they make with their chirping, chatting, and fuss in building their nests and feeding their young is often greater even than that made by the negroes of the village.

The place appeared deserted when we entered, all the doors were closed, and we took possession, undisturbed, of a large unoccupied shed. A few men soon afterwards were seen peeping at us from afar with frightened looks. Kombila shouted to them, "How is it that when strangers come to your village you do not hasten to salute them?" They recognised some of the Aponos, and shouted back, "You are right, you are right!" Then they came to us and gave us the usual salutation of the Ishogos, which is done by clapping the hands together and stretching them out, alternately, several times. We returned the compliment in the same form, and then ensued much tedious speechifying on the part of Kombila, who related all that had happened to us since we commenced our expedition.

The "M'bolo" salutation, common to the Mpongwés of the Gaboon and all the tribes of the Ogobai, is unknown in this interior country.

June 17th. Last night as some of my men were fixing their mosquito nets outside the huts, they were told by the Mokenga people that they had better sleep inside and secure well the doors, as leopards were roaming about the village, and had lately killed many of their dogs and goats. They added that in a neighbouring village a leopard had killed several people. So careful were they of my safety, that a body-guard of three of my men came to protect me whilst I was out taking meridian altitudes. One of them fell asleep before my work was half done, and made the rest of us laugh by snoring most boisterously. This sort of thing generally happened when any of the negroes pretended to keep watch whilst I was out in the night taking observations. I was once startled at midnight by hearing a formidable snore close to where I stood. Looking on the ground I saw my man Igalo fast asleep, his gun by his side. Kicking him gently, I asked him why he was not in his hut. He replied, "Do you think I could leave you here alone at night amongst people who use poisoned arrows? No; I keep watch."

June 18th. The king Quembila made his appearance to-day,

thinking that the bad wind or plague I had brought with me had now had time to blow away. He was clad in grass-cloth, and wore a covering on his head in shape somewhat resembling a turban. On his arrival a grand palaver was held; the Ishogo people ranging themselves on one side, and my Apono attendants and Commi body-guard on the other.

June 19th. A panic seized the Ishogos at night. The news somehow spread through the village (no one could tell who brought it) that in all the villages I had gone through the people were dying fast, especially those to whom I had given things. The fear was so great that many of the women took the beads I had given them and threw them away in the woods. Happily, Quembila took my part. I assembled the villagers together, and addressed him in the usual way by parable. "When you marry a woman," I said, " she loves you, she brings you plenty of food, she presents you with the fish she catches in the forest stream; are you then to flog her? (Cries of 'No, no!') But it is this which happens when I come to your village. You give me food, you give me a house to live in, your women are kind to me—how, then, can I bring evil on you?" They all shouted: "You are right. The Ishogos are jealous of us; they spread bad news to prevent us getting some of your good things." Many of the young men came forward and offered themselves as porters to take me to the Ashango country; while the chief and the elders came and presented me with a goat as a peace-offering.

It being thus agreed that the Ishogos should take me to the Ashango country, I dismissed my Apono party.

These people do not seem to sleep at night, for they sing and dance and beat their tam-tams until morning. They seem to be afraid of darkness, believing that night is the time when the spells of witchcraft are the most potent.

The Ishogos are a fine tribe of negroes; they are strongly and well built, with well-developed limbs and broad shoulders. I consider them superior to the Ashiras in physique, and I remarked that they generally had finer heads, broader in the part where phrenologists place the organs of ideality. With some of them their general appearance reminded me of the Fans. The women have good figures; they tattoo themselves in various parts of the body—on the shoulders, arms, breast, back, and abdomen—and some of them have raised pea-like marks, similar to those of the Apono women, between the eyebrows and on the cheeks. Both men and women adopt the custom of pulling out the two middle incisors of

ISHOGO FASHIONS.—OBLIQUE CHIGNON.

the upper jaw, but this mode of adding to their personal attraction is not so general as among the Aponos; many file their upper incisors and two or three of the lower ones to a point.

The men and women ornament themselves with red powder, made by rubbing two pieces of bar-wood together; but their most remarkable fashions relate to the dressing of the hair. Three different ways of hair-dressing are most prevalent among the Ishogo belles. In order to give shape to the chignon, they make a framework, generally out of old pieces of grass-cloth, and fix the hair round it.

One tower, instead of being perpendicular to the crown, is inclined obliquely from the back of the head, and the head is clean shaven almost to the middle. The neck is also shorn closely up to the ears.

The whole structure must require years of careful training before it reaches the perfection attained by the leaders of

ISHOGO FASHIONS.—HORIZONTAL CHIGNON.

Ishogo fashion. A really good chignon is not attained until the owner is about twenty or twenty-five years of age. It is the chief object of ambition with the young Ishogo women to possess a good well-trained and well-greased tower of hair of the kind described. Some women are far better dressers of hair than others, and are much sought for—the fixing and cleaning of the hair requiring a long day's work.

Once fixed, these chignons remain for a couple of months without requiring to be re-arranged, and the mass of insect life that accumulates in them during that period is truly astonishing. However, the women make use of their large iron or ivory hairpins in the place of combs. They wear no

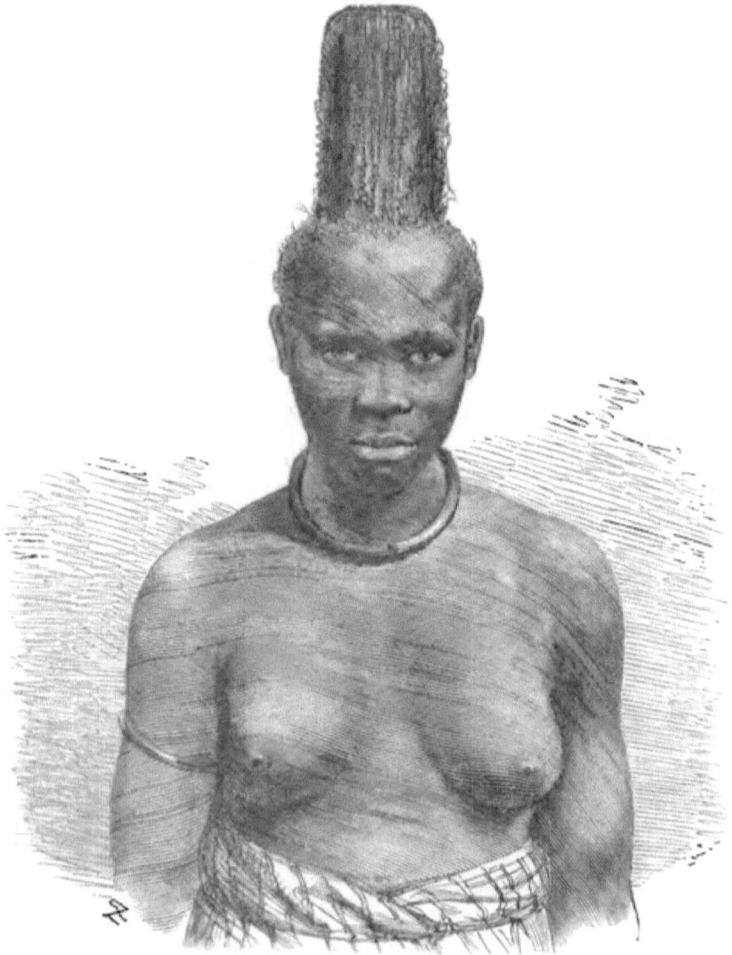

ISHOGO FASHIONS.—VERTICAL CHIGNON.

ornaments in the ears, and I saw none who had their ears pierced; they are very different from the Apingi in this respect. Like the women of other tribes, they are not allowed to wear more than two denguis, or pieces of grass-cloth. This stinted clothing has a ludicrous effect in the fat dames, as the pieces do not then meet well in the middle.

The men also have fancy ways of trimming their hair.

ISHOGO FASHIONS.—MALE HEAD-DRESS.

The most fashionable style is to shave the whole of the head except a circular patch on the crown, and to form this into three finely-plaited divisions, each terminating in a point and hanging down. At the end of each of these they fix a large bead or a piece of iron or brass wire, so that the effect is very singular. The Ishogo people shave their eyebrows and pull out their eyelashes.

The native razor, with which both men and women shave themselves, is a kind of curved and pointed knife made of iron, well worked and tempered with charcoal, the cutting edge being the convex side. It is four or five inches long and has a wooden handle. Slabs of slaty stone are used as whetstones.

The wealth of an Ishogo man, contained in his hut, consists of numerous baskets and dishes or large plates made of wicker-work, and a large stock of calabashes to contain water, palm oil, and palm wine, all which are suspended from the roof. The baskets and wicker-work plates are made either of reeds or of the rind of a kind of wild *rotang*, divided into thin strips. The calabashes are hardened by long exposure to smoke, in order to make them more durable. A highly-valued article is the cake of tobacco, carefully enveloped in leaves and suspended, like the rest of the property, from the roof. Numerous cotton-bags and cooking vessels are hung about, or stored away, and on the walls are the bundles of the cuticle of palm-leaves, of which their bongos are woven.

The Ishogos are a peaceful tribe, and more industrious than tribes who live nearer the sea-shore. Very few of them bear scars or signs of hostile encounters. Offensive weapons are not common; at least, they are not carried about on ordinary occasions. I saw very few spears and bows and arrows carried in that way, but sabres are more general, and they carry these along with them in their friendly visits from one village to another. Their villages are surrounded with palm-trees, and they are not sparing of the favourite intoxicating beverage obtained from them; it must be said to their discredit that they are far more given than the Aponos to sell their kindred into slavery. The Ishogos speak the same language as the Apingi, which, as I have already remarked, is quite distinct from the Ashira idiom.

The people are noted throughout the neighbouring tribes for the superior quality and fineness of their *bongos*. They are industrious and skilful weavers. In walking down the

ISHOGO WEAVERS.

main street of Mokenga a number of ouandjas, or houses without walls, are seen, each containing four or five looms,

ISHOGO LOOM AND SHUTTLE.

with the weavers seated before them weaving the cloth. The weavers, as you pass by, are sure to be seen smoking their pipes and chatting to one another whilst going on with their work. The weavers are all men, and it is men also who stitch the bongos together to make denguis or robes of them. The bongos are very often striped, and sometimes made even in check patterns; this is done by their dyeing some of the threads of the warp, or of both warp and woof, with various simple colours; the dyes are all made of decoctions of different kinds of wood, except for black, when a kind of iron ore is used. The bongos are employed as money in this part of Africa.

CHAPTER XXXIV.

I leave Mokenga—Engage Ishogo porters—The home of rain—The story of the rainy and dry seasons—Strike among the Ishogos for more pay—Drastic measures threatened—Among Ashango villages—Our entrance into Niembouai—Why chiefs do not show themselves at first—The Njavi, Abombo, and Ashangui tribes—Hear of a large river—A village idol—The mbuti men, or doctors.

June 21st. I engaged eighteen Ishogo porters, paying them, as customary, their wages beforehand, and promising them further pay if they performed their engagements to my satisfaction. I also gave a present to each of the elders who had given me goats, fowls, or plantains. King Quembila is too old and feeble to accompany me, so I am to have as guide one of the leading men, named Mokounga.*

Soon after leaving Mokenga the country became more and more mountainous as we travelled onward; but the path led through thick forests, and we could not obtain extensive views except in places where trees had been felled for plantations.

Our road led us over Mount Migoma, and from it I had a

* The following are the names of my Ishogo party:—
Head man, Mokounga.

Mokanbi,	Nchiengani-orere,	Maboungo,
Mokanbiyengo,	Mondjo,	Moquiá
Nchiengani,	Doutai,	Mandolo,
Maduta,	Morgangué,	Medjambi,
Makima,	Matomba,	Nchando.
Madibako,	Mandja,	

magnificent view of the country to the south and south-east. Ranges of hills, all wooded to the summit, stretched away as far as the eye could reach. By compass, I found the ranges to tend N.W. by W. and S.E. by E.

The Ashango mountains seem to be, if I may use the negro expression, the home of the rain. I doubt very much whether in any other country in the world it rains more than in the mountainous regions of the interior. On the western coast, near the equator, there are only two seasons, the rainy and the dry.

The rain begins in September and ends in May.

As I advanced into the interior the prospect became apparent of a continuous rainy season, for the books of Burton, Speke, and Grant showed me that I had probably nothing other to expect.

I was once much amused by the story one of the men related about the dry and wet seasons. The remarkable dryness of the present season had been talked over a good deal, and it was this conversation that led to the story. As usual with the African, the two seasons were personified, *Nchango* being the name of the wet, and *Enomo* that of the dry season. One day, the story went, Nchanga and Enomo had a great dispute as to which was the older, and they came at last to lay a wager on the question, which was to be decided in an assembly of the people of the air or sky. Nchango said, "When I come to a place rain comes." Enomo retorted, "When I make my appearance the rain goes." The people of the air all listened, and, when the two disputants had ceased, they exclaimed, "Verily, verily, we cannot tell which is the eldest, you must both be of the same age."

June 23rd. We forded the Odiganga—which was by no means an easy task, owing to the strength of the current—and reached the village of Magonga.

At this Ashango village my Ishogo porters found many friends and fathers-in-law; and, although we had marched only five miles to-day, they pleaded fatigue in order to have an idle day with them. Mokounga made all sorts of excuses to put a stop to the march. The villagers, to propitiate me, brought me as a present a goat and some plantains.

After much ado, we succeeded in leaving the village.

After breakfast the porters came to me in a body, and mildly asked me to give them each a few beads to enable them to purchase ground-nuts in the Ashango villages. I opened my bags and distributed a few beads amongst them; but I was not a little surprised immediately afterwards to find that a mutiny had been resolved upon. They began to complain that I had been more liberal to the Aponos than to them—that I had given them a great many things, for they saw them; and the chief spokesman, the same man who had been the chief cause of our troubles at the last village, had the impudence to say to his comrades, "If he will not give us more beads, let us leave him." The whole body then laid down their loads, and said they would return to their homes. This was a critical moment; I felt that an energetic step was necessary to put an end to such insubordination. I gave the order to my Commi men to arm, and in a few moments, the resolute fellows stepped forward and levelled their guns at the heads of the offenders. I told them to go now, and they would see how many would reach the other side of the brook alive. The movement had its due effect—they all held out their hands and begged to be forgiven. These little mutinies I found were all arranged beforehand; they are attempts at extortion, and the rascals in planning them agree not to proceed to extremities.

In the course of time we arrived at a large Ashango village, called Oyégo or Moyégo, through which we passed without stopping; the inhabitants, who seemed to be more astonished at my lace-boots than at anything else, cried out, "Look! he has feet like an elephant!"

We reached another Ashango village, of which I was unwilling to accept the hospitality owing to the noise and annoyance caused by the villagers; in fact, I felt that my head would not stand it, and so fixed my camp at a short distance from it; erecting as usual slight sheds of poles thatched with leaves.

The altitude was 1480 feet above the sea-level. The thermometer at six A.M. marked 72° Fahr., and at noon only 73°. In the early morning a thick mist lay over the magnificent woodlands, and half hid the village and surrounding palm-trees from our view.

It is very curious that one side of the street of this village is peopled by the Ashango, and the other side by the Njavi tribe. This was the only opportunity I had of seeing people of the Njavi tribe. It appeared that they had been driven westward to this place by the enmity of a powerful tribe, the Ashangui—whose country lies near theirs on the east; for the territory occupied by the Njavi lies between Ashango-land and the country of the Ashangui. These Njavi were the shyest and most timid negroes I had met with. They would never allow me to enter their houses.

The streets of all the Ashango villages I have yet seen are less broad than those of the Ishogo villages. As to the inhabitants, my first impressions were unfavourable. They brought us no food either for sale or presents. My Ishogo men began to show signs of discontent, this time not against me but against the villagers; they said, "If there is nothing to eat, let us be off. We do not stop at villages where goats are not given to the Oguizi!" I fed my porters well, for many were induced to come from hearing the stories told by the Aponos of the great number of goats they had eaten while with me. It is a great task that I have undertaken. The ordinary difficulties of the way, the toilsome marches, the night watches, the crossing of rivers, the great heat, are as nothing compared with the obstacles and annoyances which these capricious villagers throw in our way. I begin to dread the sight of an inhabited place. Either the panic-stricken people fly from me, or remain to bore me by their insatiable curiosity, fickleness, greediness, and intolerable din. Nevertheless I am obliged to do all I can think of to conciliate them, for I cannot do without them.

June 26th. At length we were again *en route.* For several miles we continued to ascend; and whenever we could obtain a view through breaks in the forest we saw higher ground towards the east and south-east. Huge rocks of ferruginous sandstone bordered the line of our route. Our entry into Niembouai was a pleasant affair compared with our reception at most of the other villages. This was chiefly owing to one of the elders of Niembouai having been at Mokenga while I was there; and who, having returned before us, had prepared the inhabitants. The best house in the village had been prepared for me. It belonged to the elder who had met us at Mokenga, and who now claimed me as his guest, and, according to the custom of the country, no one disputed his claim.

June 27th. The king of Niembouai, like most of the other monarchs of these regions, did not show himself on my arrival—he was absent until about noon to-day. I have now been told that the reason why the chiefs keep away from the villages until I have been in them some time is, that they have a notion that I bring with me a whirlwind which may do them some great harm; so they wait until it has had time to blow away from the village before they make their appearance.

Presents and food for sale came in early, and we were well supplied.

June 28th. The ground is soaked after so many hours of steady rain, and this is in the middle of the dry season on the coast. There is evidently no sharp distinction between the seasons in these high inland regions.

I was told to-day, and it was repeated to me in every place afterwards, that there is a tribe called Ashangui, very numerous, and clever workers in iron, who live a few days' march further on towards the east, on the banks of a large river. This river must either be the Congo or some unknown stream flowing towards the great river. It is remarkable that the people in most of the Ashango villages were very anxious to get gunpowder from me; the porters wanted to be paid partly in powder, and many of the villagers were provided with a little measure made of a hollowed gourd expressly for the purpose of measuring the powder that they received from me in payment of food and so forth. I wondered at first why they were so anxious to obtain gunpowder, as they had no guns. They replied that a tribe called Ashangui, living beyond the Njavi and Abombo, bought it and gave them iron for it; that all the iron they had came from there; that there was a good deal of iron "*in the land;*"

that all the anvils came from there, and that their swords, spears, and arrow-heads—in fact, all their edged implements were made of iron bought from that country.

We must conclude, from their buying the powder, that the Ashangui are in possession of guns, which they obtain from traders on the Congo. From Niembouai eastward I found beads were not uncommon, and these must have been obtained by way of the Congo and through the Ashangui; in fact, all the natives told me they came up the large river.

June 29th. The sky in this elevated region is almost constantly clouded or hazy. All day yesterday it was either clouded or overspread with a thick haze; the sun was dimly seen only for a few minutes about four o'clock, and at night the moon did not remain visible long enough to enable me to take lunar observations.

A grand palaver was held to-day. The elders of Niembouai were all mustered, seated in a half-circle on the ground, and smoking their long pipes—which are about three feet in length—with imperturbable gravity. The great number of old people seen here was quite remarkable, and the fact speaks well for the healthiness of the climate or the absence of wars and deaths on account of witchcraft. The people here, and also among the Ishogos, seemed to have more respect for old men than in other tribes. It required a long explanation by Maduta and Mokounga to convince the wise men that I had not come to their country to buy slaves and ivory, but simply to travel from one tribe to another. Maduta is related to some of the villagers by marriage, and this favoured our arrangements. He finished a long rigmarole, which took him about an hour to deliver, by saying that the Ishogos had now fulfilled their duty in bringing me safely to Ashango-land, and that the duty, or, as their language expressed it, the "shame" (or point of honour) remained with the Niembouai people to carry me on a stage further.

The Ashangos unanimously shouted "We have shame, we will pass the Oguizi on."

This evening I went to see the village idol, or mbuiti, and to witness a great ceremony in the mbuiti-house. As with the Aviia and other tribes, the idol was a monstrous and indecent representation of a female figure in wood; I had remarked that the further I travelled towards the interior, the coarser these wooden idols were, and the more roughly they were sculptured. This idol was kept at the end of a long, narrow, and low hut, forty or fifty feet long and ten feet broad, and was painted in red, white, and black colours. When I entered the hut, it was full of Ashango people, ranged in order on each side, with lighted torches stuck in the ground before them. Amongst them were conspicuous two mbuiti men, or, as they might be called, doctors, dressed in cloth or vegetable fibre, with their skins painted grotesquely in various colours, one side of the face red, the other white, and in the middle of the breast a broad yellow stripe; the circuit of the eyes was also daubed with paint; these colours are made by boiling various kinds of wood, and mixing the decoction with clay. The rest of the Ashangos were also streaked and daubed with various colours, and by the light of their torches they looked like a troop of devils assembled in the lower regions to celebrate some diabolical rite; around their legs were bound white leaves from the heart of the palm-tree; some wore feathers, others had leaves twisted in the shape of horns behind their ears, and all had a bundle of palm-leaves in their hands.

Soon after I entered, the rites began. All the men squatted down on their haunches, and set up a deafening kind of wild song. There was an orchestra of instrumental performers near the idol, consisting of three drummers with two drum-sticks each, one harper, and a performer on the sounding stick, which latter did not touch the ground, but rested on two other sticks, so that the noise was made the more resonant. The two mbuiti men, in the meantime, were dancing in a fantastical manner in the middle of the temple, putting their bodies into all sorts of strange contortions. Every time the mbuiti men opened their mouths to speak, a dead silence ensued. As the ceremony continued, the crowd rose and surrounded the dancing men, redoubling at the same time the volume of their songs, and, after this went on for some time, returning to their former positions. This was repeated several times. The mbuiti men, I ought to mention, had been sent for from a distance to officiate on the occasion. The mbuiti men, like the witchcraft doctors, are important persons among these inland tribes; some have more reputation than others, but in general those who live furthest off are most esteemed.

June 30*th*. The altitude of Niembouai I found to be 1896 ft. above the level of the sea. The village lies in 1° 58′ 54″ S. lat. and 11° 56′ 38″ E. long.

CHAPTER XXXV.

The dwarfs, or Obongos—Villages of dwarfs—Another deserted village of dwarfs—A new village—We approach with great caution—Flight of the dwarfs—Meeting some dwarfs—Their shyness—Leaving the dwarf village in despair—Return to their village—The people had fled—Cunning of the dwarfs—Laughable scene when measuring some of them—Appearance of the dwarfs—Modes of burial of the dwarfs—The dwarfs great trappers and hunters of game—Mode of life of the dwarfs—They are scattered all over the equatorial forests towards the east.

I HAD heard that there was a village of the Obongos, or dwarfed wild negroes, somewhere in the neighbourhood of Niembouai, and one of my first inquiries on arriving at the place was naturally whether there was any chance of my seeing this singular people, who, it appears, continually come into their villages, but would not do so while I was there. The Ashangos themselves made no objection, and even offered to accompany me to the Obongo village. They told me, however, that I had better take with me only a very small party, so that we might make as little noise as possible. Two guides were given me, and I took only three of my men. We reached the place after twenty minutes' walk. In a retired nook in the forest were twelve huts of this strange tribe, scattered without order, and covering altogether only a very small space of ground. The shape of the huts was the same as that I have before described in the deserted Obongo village near Yengué. When we approached them no sign of living creature was to be seen, and, in fact, we found them deserted. The huts are of such slight construction, and the Obongos so changeable, that they frequently remove from one place to another. The abodes were very filthy; and whilst my Commi men and myself were endeavouring to examine them, we were covered with swarms of fleas and obliged to beat a retreat. The village had been abandoned by its inhabitants.

Leaving the abandoned huts, we continued our way through the forest; and presently, within a distance of a quarter of a mile, we came on another village, composed, like the last, of about a dozen ill-constructed shelters, scattered about, without any regular order, in a small open space. The dwellings had been newly made, for the branches of trees of which they were formed had still their leaves on them, quite fresh. We approached with the greatest caution, in order not to alarm the wild inmates, my Ashango guides holding up a bunch of beads in a friendly way, and shouting "Do not run away; the spirit has come with us to give you beads;" but all our care was fruitless, for the men, at least, were gone when we came up. Their flight was very hurried. We hastened to the huts, and luckily found three old women and one young man, who had not had time to run away, besides several children, the latter hidden in one of the huts.

The little holes which serve as doors to the huts were closed by fresh-gathered branches of trees, with their foliage, stuck in the ground. My Ashango guides tried all they could to calm the fears of the trembling creatures; telling them that I had come to do them no harm, but had brought some beads to give them. I finally succeeded in approaching them, for fear seemed to have paralysed their powers of moving. I gave them some beads, and then made my Ashango guides tell them that we should come back the next day with more beads, to give some to all the women; so they must all be there. One of the old women, in the course of a short time, lost all her shyness and began to ridicule the

APPROACH TO THE CAMP OF THE PIGMIES

men for having run away from us. She said they were as timid as the nchende (squirrel), who cried "Qué, Qué," and in squeaking she twisted her little body into odd contortions, with such droll effect that we all laughed.

When I brought out my tape to measure her, her fears returned; thinking perhaps that it was a kind of snake that I was uncoiling out of its case, she trembled all over. I told her I was not going to kill her, but it required another present to quiet her again. I accomplished my task at last. I also measured the young man, who was adult, and probably a fair sample of the male portion of his race.

We then returned to Niembouai. I had waited an hour, in the vain hope that the men might come back to their huts. By the way, the Obongo women seem to know how to tell lies as well as their country-women of larger growth; for when I inquired where the rest of the people were, they at once replied that they were gone into the forest to fetch firewood and to trap game.

The next day (*July 1st*) I went again to their village, and saw only one woman and two children. I had not come early enough, the birds had flown. Luckily, the woman was one of those I had seen the day before. I gave her and the children a number of beads. Then suspecting that the mother of the children was in the hut close by where they stood, I went to it, took off the branch that had been put at the entrance to signify that the owner was out, and then putting half of my body into the hut, in the best way I could, I finally succeeded in seeing in the dark something which soon after I recognised as a human being. My Ashango man called to her, telling her not to be afraid. I succeeded in getting hold of one of her legs and pulled her out of her abode. She seemed terribly frightened as I looked at her, and avoided my direct glance. I was then told that she had lost her husband a few days before, when they lived in the now deserted village which I had seen on my way hither. She had over her forehead a broad stripe of yellow ochre.

I desired my Ashango guide to ask the women where they

buried their dead; but he told me I had better not ask the question, as they might get frightened, and the woman who had just lost her husband might cry.

I gave the poor widow some beads, and then left them again; my old friend Misounda (for she told me her name) inviting me to come back in the afternoon, as the men would then have returned from the woods. I accordingly returned in the course of the afternoon, but no men were to be seen.

On a subsequent visit I found the village deserted by the women as well as by the men—at least, as we approached it, the women, who had heard us, ran into their huts; among them I caught sight of my old friend Misounda running to hide herself. This was doubly disappointing, as I had flattered myself that I had quite tamed her. When we entered the village not a sound was to be heard, and the branches of the trees had been put up at the doors of all the huts, to make us believe that the people had all gone into the woods. My Ashango guide shouted aloud, "We have come to give you more beads; where are you?" Not a whisper was heard, no one answered our call; but there was no room for any mistake, as we had seen the women enter the huts. I therefore went to the hut of my old friend, Misounda, took off the branch, and called her by name, but there was no answer. It was so dark inside that I could see nothing; so I entered, and tumbled over the old woman. Finding that she was detected, she came out, and pretended that she had been fast asleep. Then she called out to the other women, saying that I was not a leopard come to eat them, and that they need not be afraid.

In the course of other visits which I made to the village during my stay at Niembouai I succeeded in measuring five other women. I could not help laughing, for all of them covered their faces with their hands; and it was only in the case of Woman No. 1 that I could get any measurements of the face. Unfortunately, I could not take the same measurements for all. I did the best I could under such circumstances. In order to allay their fears, I tried to measure one of my Ashango guides, but he refused, being as much frightened as the women. The measurements are as follows:—

		Ft.	In.
Woman No. 1, total height		4	4¼
,, between the outer angles of the eyes		0	5¼
,, No. 2, total height		4	7¼
,, No. 3, considered unusually tall		5	0¼
,, round the broadest part of the head		1	9¼
,, from the eye to the ear		0	4
,, No. 4, total height		4	8
,, round the head		1	10
,, from the eye to the ear		0	3¾
,, No. 5, total height		5	0
,, round the head		1	9
,, from the eye to the ear		0	4¾
,, No 6, total height		4	5
,, round the head		1	10⅝
,, from the eye to the ear		0	4½
Young man, total height		4	6

The colour of these people was a dirty yellow, much lighter than the Ashangos who surround them, and their eyes had an untamable wildness about them that struck me as very remarkable. In their whole appearance, physique, and colour, and in their habitations, they are totally unlike the Ashangos, amongst whom they live. The Ashangos indeed are very anxious to disown kinship with them. They do not intermarry with them; but declare that the Obongos intermarry among themselves, sisters with brothers, doing this to keep the families together as much as they can. The smallness of their communities, and the isolation in which the wretched creatures live, must necessitate close interbreeding; and I think it very possible that this circumstance may be the cause of the physical deterioration of their race. Their foreheads are exceedingly low and narrow, and they have prominent cheek bones; but I did not notice any peculiarity in their hands or feet, or in the position of the toes, or in the relative length of their arms to the rest of their bodies; but their legs appeared to be rather short in proportion to their trunks; the palms of their hands seemed quite white. The hair of their heads grows in very short curly tufts; this is the more remarkable, as the Ashangos

and neighbouring tribes have rather long bushy hair on
their heads, which enables them to dress it in various ways;
with the Obongos the dressing of the hair in masses or plaits,
as is done by the other tribes, is impossible. The young
man had an unusual quantity of hair also on his legs and
breast, growing in short curly tufts similar to the hair of the
head, and all the accounts of the Ashangos which I heard
agreed in this, that the Obongo men were thickly covered
with hair on these parts of their body; besides, I saw myself,
during the course of my stay at Niembouai on my return,
male Obongos in the village, and although they would not
allow me to approach them, I could get near enough to notice
the small tufts of hair: one of the men was black. The
only dress they wear consists of pieces of home-made cloth
which they buy of the Ashangos, or which these latter give
them out of pure kindness, for I observed that it was quite
a custom of the Ashangos to give their old worn *denguis* to
these poor Obongos.

The modes of burial of these savages, as related to me by
my Ashango companions, are curious. The most common
habit is to place the corpse in the interior of a hollow tree in
the forest, filling up the hole with branches and leaves
mixed with earth; but sometimes they make a hole in the
bed of a running stream, diverting the current for the
purpose, and then, after the grave is covered in, turning
back the rivulet to its former course. I cannot, however,
vouch for the accuracy of this story.

The Ashangos like the presence of this curious people near
their villages because the Obongo men are very expert and
nimble in trapping wild animals and fish in the streams, the
surplus of which, after supplying their own wants, they sell
to their neighbours in exchange for plantains, and also for
iron implements, cooking utensils, water-jars, and all
manufactured articles of which they stand in need. The
woods near their villages are so full of traps and pitfalls that
it is dangerous for any but trained woodsmen to wander
about in them; I always took care not to walk back from
their village to Niembouai after nightfall; for in the path
itself there were several traps for leopards, wild boars, and

antelopes. From the path, traps for monkeys could be seen everywhere: and I should not at all have relished having my legs caught in one of these traps. I was surprised at the kindness, almost the tenderness, shown by the Ashangos to their diminutive neighbours. On one of my visits to the village I saw about a dozen Niembouai women, who had come with plantains to exchange for game, which they expected to be brought in by the men. As the little hunters had not returned from the forest, they were disappointed in this errand; but seeing that the Obongo women were suffering from hunger, they left nearly all the plantains with them as a gift, or, perhaps, on trust, for outside the hut they were cooking roots of some tree, which did not seem to me very nourishing.

The Obongos never remain long in one place. They are eminently a migratory people, moving from place to place whenever game becomes scarce. But they do not wander very far; that is, the Obongos who live within the Ashango territory do not go out of that territory—they are called the Obongos of the Ashangos—those who live among the Njavi are called Obongo-Njavi—and the same with other tribes. Obongos are said to exist very far to the east, as far, in fact, as the Ashangos have any knowledge. They are distinct from the people amongst whom they live, yet living for generations within the confines of the same country. They plant nothing, and depend partly for their vegetable food on roots, berries, and nuts, which they find in the forest; indeed, the men spend most of their days and many of their nights in the woods, and it was partly on this account, and their excessive shyness, that I was unable to examine them closely. When they can no longer find wild animals in the locality where they have made their temporary settlements, they are sometimes apt to steal food from their more civilized neighbours, and then decamp. Their appetite for animal food is more like that of a carnivorous beast than that of a man. Often they satisfy their hunger with meat alone.

One day I enticed the old woman, whose heart I had gained by many presents of beads, to Niembouai simply by promising her a joint of goat-flesh. I had asked her if she was hungry

—without answering me, she drew a long breath, drawing in her stomach, to make me understand that it was very empty. When she came, I tried to put her off with a bunch of plantains, but she stuck tenaciously to my hut until I had fulfilled my promise of giving her some meat, repeating the word, *etava, etava* (goat, goat). Through her and an Ashango interpreter I took down a few words of the Obongo language; it contains words of Ashango; indeed their dialect is a mixture of what was their own original language and the languages of the various tribes among whom they have resided for many years past. I was told that now and then one of them will leave his people, and come and live among the Ashangos. My guides were kind enough to inform me that, if I wanted to buy an Obongo, they would be happy to catch one for me.

CHAPTER XXXVI.

Departure from Niembouai—Onwards towards the east—A queer ferry—Appearance of the country—The village of Niembouai Olomba—Numerous beehives—Ashangos—The Apono and Ashira languages the same—Appearance of the Ashangos—Attacked by Bashikouay ants—Leave Niembouai Olomba—The village of Mombana—Outfit of a bride—Presentation of Ntchiugo, or red powder—Three different paths to the Njavi country.

July 5th. We were delayed three more days in Niembouai through the illness of Ngoma, one of my Commi boys. I paid the Ashango porters on the 2nd, and had some difficulty in getting them away after the two days' delay without giving them more.* Besides these we had eight porters to

* The names of my Ashango porters were as follows:—

	Magonga—Head man.	
Adoombo,	Mayombon (the 2nd),	Mokela,
Mayombon,	Moushagou,	Madoungou,
Bishelo,	Ibalo,	Maniaga,
Moquangué,	Dibako,	Mamagué,
Divangui,	Dishelo,	Badinga,
Moshelekai,	Bengouin,	Mayoubon.

carry the loads of my Commi men, and a varying number followed to carry the provisions and kettles. We had also generally with us three or four old fellows who followed us from village to village, expecting to feed well on the road, and at the end of a few days to get something for speech-making; for they thought they helped me wonderfully in this way. With them departed Mokounga.

We started, led by Magonga, an influential man of Niembouai. The path gradually descended into the valley of the Ouano, a river which falls into the Odiganga. I found on reaching its banks, about three miles east of Niembouai, that we had descended more than 600 feet, the altitude being 1285 feet. The Ouano was about 30 or 40 yards wide, and too deep to be forded.

We crossed this stream by a singular kind of ferry. The boat or raft was formed of two logs of light wood, fifteen feet long, and a flooring of laths, tied by their ends to the logs, so as to form a rude vessel four or five feet broad. The boat was propelled by the ferrymen across the current, and, to prevent its being swept down stream, it was attached, by means of a stout creeper looped at the end, to a rope stretched between trees across the river. Upright sticks were fixed in the side-beams of the raft for the standing passengers to hold on by. Our party were transported across the stream by means of this contrivance in five journeys. In the rainy season, when the current is exceedingly strong, this ferry must be very useful. I had never before seen a ferry of this kind in Africa.

We ascended a high hill called Mogiama, the summit of which was 2264 feet above the sea-level. Soon after, we passed a small Ashango plantation, with a few huts on its borders and patches of the wild tobacco-plant and of the hemp. The tenants of the huts had fled at our approach, and we cooked our dinner at the forsaken fires of the settlement. My Ashango porters insisted upon killing their goat here. When I asked them why they had not killed and eaten it at Niembouai, they replied that they were afraid their own people would have asked them for some of the meat. I then asked them why they did not wait until we had reached the village to which we were going. Their reply was the same—the people there also would ask them for some of the meat. They succeeded in eating the whole of the goat at one meal; after which they came to me saying, "You see we have eaten the whole of it. Ashango people have big stomachs."

The country continued very hilly, and we made *détours* to avoid the steep ascents. At length, a little before the sun

AN AFRICAN GROUP.* DRAWN FROM LIFE BY A. H. H. M.

set, we reached the village of Mongon, 12° 3' 37" E. long., latitude 1° 56' 45" S. Many of my porters had relatives here, and we were received in a friendly manner. We passed the night in the village, and the place is 2488 feet above the sea-level.

* This goat, parrot, hen, and idol were brought over by me, and presented to the children of my publisher, under whose care the three former lived for a considerable number of years.

We left at about eight A.M. the next day, and after two hours' march arrived at a small village called Niongo, where we stopped for breakfast.

July 6th. The importunities of the villagers and their chief delayed us here nearly three hours. I was getting annoyed at these repeated delays. It was now nearly a year since I left the coast. At last, I told the chief that if he was so fond of me I would tie him with ropes and carry him with us: we were allowed, after this, to depart without further trouble. Of course I refused the proffered goat; for it is an universal rule with these tribes that, a present being received by a stranger from the villagers, he is bound to make some stay in the place. The refusal of the present of food is a token that you do not wish to remain, hence the pertinacity of these people in trying to force goats and so forth upon us, when we are passing a village. I was again brought to a standstill by the porters laying down their loads and demanding more pay. This was the Ishogo scene over again, and terminated in the same manner, by the vigorous measure of bringing my Commi men up with the muzzles of their guns levelled at the heads of the offenders, followed by their sudden repentance, and their laughing over the affair, as usual, saying, "Let us stop a while and have a smoke. Do you think we would leave you in the woods? People may be left in a village, but not in the forest."

About four P.M. we reached the village called Niembouai Olomba, or "Further Niembouai," to distinguish it from the other place of the same name which I will call Niembouai West for the sake of distinction. We had made but eight miles in a direct line in four hours' march; but the road lies over a succession of hills, everywhere thickly wooded; and travelling is most toilsome, heavily-laden as we all were.

We were received with great joy by the chief, who is the "father," head chief, or king of this clan of Ashangos. Houses were allotted to us; presents of goats and plantains were laid at my feet; and I was glad to find that the old chief had not run away. He had one of the mildest expressions of face I had seen; was tall, and about 60 years old.

The people of Niembouai Olomba were shy, but many of

them had seen me at Niembouai West. Like all the villages in these mountains, it is surrounded with groves of plantain-trees. Goats are very abundant, and the goat-houses are scattered here and there throughout the village. Swallows were flying over the streets, and numerous birds were singing, perched on the surrounding tall trees, behind the plantain-groves. In the street of the village is seen, now and then, the stump of an old tree, which time has not been able to destroy; for here, wherever the people settle or plant, the trees have to be cut down, and the stump and roots are left to perish by the action of time. Niembouai Olomba is a large village containing about 184 houses. Formerly this and Niembouai West constituted one town (*i.e.*, the population all lived in one place). Nearly all the houses have bee-hives fixed to the walls, and the honey is beautifully white and well-flavoured. Wax is very abundant in Ashangoland, and of a fine quality: the beehives were made simply of the bark of trees, rolled up so as to form a cylinder, thus imitating a hollow tree in which bees make their hives in the wild state. The ends of the cylinder are closed with pieces of bark, in which holes are made for the entrance and exit of the bees; wooden hoops are fixed at each extremity to keep the cylinder in shape.

Although the Ashangos are certainly quite a distinct tribe from the Ishogos, for they speak a different language, I did not notice any striking difference in their appearance or habits. Their language is the same as that of the Ashira. In one particular they contrast advantageously with the tribes nearer the coast, namely, in the amplitude of their clothing. All are well clothed with the beautiful native cloth of this region. I did not even see any naked children. The denguis or robes of chiefs are of unusually large size, and are worn generally very gracefully. They seem to tattoo themselves rather more than the Ishogos do; the women do not pierce their ears for ear-ornaments; their head-dress is the same as that of the Ishogo women. Although the streets of the Ishogo villages were broader, the houses of the Ashangos are larger than those of their neighbours. Both tribes adopt the custom of taking out their two middle upper incisors, and of filing the other incisors to a point; but the Ashangos do not adopt the custom of filing also the upper incisors. Some of the women have the four upper incisors taken out. They submit to this process, in order to be considered the leading belles of the village. All of them, both male and female, shave off their eyebrows and pluck out their eyelashes, and both tribes smear themselves with ntchingo, or red powder.

Beating the woman is here of very rare occurrence, I am told; and I have not, myself, seen a single case of woman-beating. In fact, the women have their own way in many things. Almost every Ashango carries a sabre made by the Shimba and Ashangui tribes. Their other weapons are spears and poisoned arrows. They do not forge any iron here, but get it from tribes further east. They have the reputation of being more quarrelsome than the Ishogos, and of being greater liars. This sin of lying is, unfortunately, thought of little matter in this part of the world.

July 8th. Last night, as I was quietly lying on my bed, I was aroused by a rustling and scratching noise in the hut and the flying of numerous cockroaches, some of them alighting on the back of my neck, which, by the way, produces one of the most unpleasant sensations I know of. I knew it must be an invasion of Bashikouay ants, and started up and called my men. The active creatures were already on my bed, and I was lucky in making my escape without being half devoured by them. They were attracted, no doubt, by a quarter of goat's meat hanging in the chamber, for, unfortunately, my sleeping room is obliged to be also my store-room. The men hastened to fetch hot ashes to spread over the floor, which was black with the shining bodies of these most destructive ants, who come to their work in dense masses. Had their progress not been checked they would have finished our goat-meat in a very short time, for they were already climbing the walls, and we had to sweep them down on the hot cinders, not daring to apply a torch to the wall of such a combustible edifice as an Ashango hut. In the afternoon I ascended one of the hills which form so grand a feature in the landscape close to Niembouai.

An almost perpetual mist shrouds the summit of this hill, which is called Birogou Bouanga. I found the altitude to be 2574 feet above the sea-level.

From the summit of Birogou Bouanga I could see the country for many miles round. The mountains appeared to be, for the most part, of nearly equal height.

July 12th. We did not leave Niembouai Olomba without trouble. First, my porters of Niembouai West wanted an increase of pay; then the people of Niembouai Olomba wanted them to leave me with them, and to go back to their own country, saying that they could take care of me. Magouga retorted that he also could take care of me. On their referring the matter to me, in order to please both parties, I said I would take half my porters from Niembouai West, and the other half from Niembouai Olomba.

When at length we started, Magouga and the chief of Niembouai Olomba were both with me, and with Rebouka we formed the rear-guard of the caravan. I kept constantly on the alert, and took care always to make one of these two leading men walk before me, for, in so wild a country, one cannot be too careful.

We were now on our march to the country of the Njavi tribe, who live to the east of Ashangoland. My Ashango porters were to convey me to the principal village of the Njavi, and I had hoped that all would go smoothly, now that we had left Niembouai and were again on the road. But further troubles were in store for me. Several of the porters went on ahead, and, concealing themselves in the forest, let us pass them, and then made off to their own village. When we halted to rest the porters, I discovered that several of them were missing. The absentees all belonged to Niembouai West. We waited for them, but in vain. Both they and their loads were gone.

Being determined to check this new evil at its commencement, I ordered a halt near Mobana, and, seizing Magouga, placed three of my Commi men as guard over him, with orders to shoot him if he attempted to escape ; and I told him that I should not release him until the lost property was restored by the Niembouai porters under his leadership. In the meantime the old chief of Niembouai Olomba, with his people, came to me, and said, "I have nothing to do with this—here are all my people, here are all their loads. Why did you not take my people only? We do not steal in my village."

Mobana is a large village situated on the top of a high hill, at a height of 2369 feet above the level of the sea. The range, at the foot of which Niembouai is situated, is the highest of the four ranges, reckoning from the coast. The houses are like those of Niembouai. Numerous beehives hang against the houses or are scattered among the plantain-trees. Goats are plentiful; some of them are of great size, and very fat. While here, I assisted at the departure of a young woman who had been given in marriage to a man of a neighbouring village. Her father was to take her there, with all the marriage outfit. It consisted of eight wooden plates; two large baskets for carrying plantains from the plantations, or calabashes full of water from the spring; a great number of calabashes; a large package of groundnuts; a package of squash seeds; two dried legs of antelope; some fine nchandas (the name given to the denguis here), and her stool. Several members of her family carried this elaborate outfit. The bride-elect was smartly dressed; her headdress had been *built up* most elaborately the day before. As she left the village, the people remarked to each other, "Her husband will see that the Mobana people do not send away their daughters with nothing!"

Her old mother accompanied her to the end of the street, and then returned to her home, looking proud and happy at having seen her daughter go with such an outfit.

After we entered Mobana, the villagers wanted my men to smear themselves with *ntchingo* or red powder, bringing for this purpose several of their wickerwork dishes, on which was placed a quantity of the pigment. This I found a general custom amongst the Ashangos when a host wishes to welcome a guest; and a visitor to a village or a house is only too happy when the elders or the owner of the house request him to make himself red, for it is a sign of their good will. As we were entering the village we met a

Niembouai man coming out quite furious about something or other, and venting threats and curses; on asking him what was the matter, he said that the Mobana people had not offered him the *ntchingo*, and he was going back to the place whence he came.

At the foot of the hill on which Mobana stands, there is a stream called Bembo, flowing in a north-easterly direction. The natives pointed towards the east when I inquired as to its further course.

I have at last succeeded in hiring porters. Rakombo and his men have sworn to carry me to the Njavi country. The good old chief of Niembouai Olomba has taken his departure to return to his old village.

The country, as far as I am able to see eastward and south-eastward, continues hilly, the hills being of moderate elevation. There are three paths from Mobana leading into the Njavi country; one towards the north-east, one nearly due east, and a third south-east. Mobana is 1° 52′ 56″ S. lat.; longitude, by my dead reckoning, I place about 12° 27′ E.

July 21*st*. We proceeded in an easterly direction, passing several villages, one of which was called Kombo; and after a march of nearly four hours we reached the village of Mouaou Kombo.

CHAPTER XXXVII.

Arrival at Mouaou Kombo—True Ashango clans—Troubles brewing—Departure of the Niembouai and Mobana people—Retire from the village—A palaver—Peace made—Return to the village—Promise to take me to the Njavi tribe—A terrible accident—A man accidentally killed—Great panic among the natives—War drums beating.

The first events on my arrival at Mouaou Kombo were not encouraging; but still the difficulties I encountered were only of the ordinary sort which every African traveller meets with, and were nearly overcome, when the event happened which brought my further progress to an end. In the first place, I found that Rakombo and his Mobana porters intended to break through their agreement to take me to the

Njavi country. The Mouaou people belonged to a different clan from the Mobanas, and there appeared not to be a cordial understanding although there had been a good many intermarriages between them. We had no sooner arrived at the village—the elders of which at first behaved well, giving me a large house to stay in—than the Mobana porters, having laid down their loads, gave us the slip; one by one, on some pretence or other, they sneaked off amongst the trees which surround the village, and we saw them no more. It was in vain that I threatened Rakombo. I could see nothing to enable me to fix the blame on him; he declared that the Mouaou people would not allow him to take me onward.

On the second day after my arrival (July 23rd), the head chief, named Kombo, made his appearance, and gave me presents of goats and plantains to indicate that I was welcome, then he called the villagers together and made them a long speech, to the effect that the Niembouai and Mobana people having left the " Spirit " in their hands, it fell to their duty to take me onward to the Njavi country; and that they were not to rob me, for, if they did, they would surely die, as had happened to the Niembouaians. It was then that I learnt that the thieves must have been tasting my arsenic, or had probably mixed it with the salt they had stolen. I soon made friends with the people, engaged porters, and paid them, and all seemed to be going on well for a fresh start.

On the day following I found no signs of readiness for departure. The chief came to me, and explained that the men were obliged to go to the forest to cut firewood to leave with their wives. It is true that this is the custom of these people; for, amongst the Ishogo and Ashango, the men on leaving their wives have to gather a sufficient quantity of firewood to last their families during their absence. Kombo, addressing himself to Igala—for, when holding a palaver, these people never address themselves directly to the person for whom the speech is intended—said, " I see by the look of the Oguizi that he thinks I am deceiving him, and that I lie: he must not judge me so harshly. A man may have a fine body, yet, if his heart is bad, he is an ugly man; therefore, if a man's heart is good, people should not look at his body. To-morrow the Oguizi will see whether I have a good heart or a bad heart: Kombo will take him to the Njavi country."

In the afternoon the village street became deserted. I walked down it, but could see no one. I called my men together; Igala shook his head, and said that they were all gone to "mogoua oroungo" (hold a secret meeting), and that it boded no good.

Such was indeed the case. When the meeting broke up all the men of the village assembled before my hut, and the chief began a long rambling speech, the purport of which was that I must give them more goods before I could leave the place. He said the Niembouai Mobana people had left me because they were unable to take me to Njavi; that he alone could help me forward, and I must therefore pay him at least as much as I had paid the people at other places. He asked particularly for the pieces of a large brass kettle which I had broken yesterday, and also for many measures of gunpowder.

The question of more pay was not, however, what had drawn the people to their secret meeting. The true cause was the arrival of a deputation, from some villages further ahead, to threaten the Mouaou people with war if they came with me through their villages. The aim of the embarrassed Kombo was to gain time, during which he might settle his outstanding palavers with the hostile villagers further on.

The next day (July 25th), on finding there was no chance of our departure, I made up my mind to retire for a time from the village, and show my displeasure in that way this being an effective mode of bringing them to reason, for I knew they would come and humbly promise everything I wanted to induce me to come back. I made all the porters return the pay in beads that I had given them, and then with my men transported my baggage to a distance in the woods, on the borders of one of those beautifully clear streams which are so frequent in this mountainous region. The amount and weight of my baggage were still very great. The path down to the place of our retreat was very steep, and, from what I could gather by a survey of our position, I found we should be on the main eastern road from Mouaou. The villagers looked on at our proceedings in mute amazement.

Before evening the whole of the baggage was removed. My men erected sheds, and collected firewood to cook our supper. The place was a very pleasant one, under the shade of magnificent trees whose closely interwoven crowns would protect us from the night mist, which dissolves in a soaking drizzle almost every night in this humid country. The path near our encampment was a broad and well-trodden one, showing that it was one of the highways of the district.

As soon as we had finished, I sent Igala and two other men, well armed, along the path to try to find the next village, and ascertain, if possible, why they did not wish us to pass through. My messengers returned in about two hours, Igala laughing whilst describing to me the ignominious way in which the warriors of the village, armed to resist our progress, ran away at the sight of him and his two companions. The villagers told him that they had no quarrel with me, but had an old feud with the Mouaou people about two slaves that were owing to them, and that they were determined not to let them pass until the debt was paid. "If that is the case," said Igala, "why don't you come and fetch our luggage and take us on yourselves?" To this they returned evasive answers; they would call a council of the people to consider the matter, and give us an answer to-morrow, &c., &c.

It was impossible to get at the truth of the case. How I wished I had an armed party, strong enough to force my way through the barriers which the caprice and trickery of these savages opposed to my progress! With twenty men like Igala and Macondai, I would have set all these vapouring fellows at defiance, and have been half-way across the continent by this time. Before we laid down to rest I had branches cut from the trees and strewed all around our encampment, to prevent, by the noise and impediments they would cause, a nocturnal surprise, which I thought very likely to happen, for parties of men from time to time sneaked through the woods, and after talking to us and taking note of our position, quietly went back again. They were armed with bearded spears similar to those carried by the Fans, and which they get from the Ashangui tribe. I did not sleep all night. My negroes kept watch, taking it in turns, three sleeping and three waking, and I made them tell stories one after the other, speaking loud, so as to show the people we were awake and watchful.

July 26th. Early in the morning, as I had expected, a deputation from Mouaou, consisting of all the elders of the village, came to me, and with sorrowful countenances asked why I had deserted them. They prayed me to come back, and repeated that it was not their fault that my journey had been delayed, but the fault of the next village ahead. They promised earnestly that if I came back they would send me forward in two days, and by another route, to the south-east, so as to avoid the hostile villages, the people of which, they said, had made up their minds now to take me, but had laid a plan to leave me in the middle of the forest and run away with the baggage.

As the promised answer did not come from the other village, and the Mouaou elders seemed to be sincere, I agreed to go back. In a few moments all my baggage was shouldered by strong men, and, with shouts of rejoicing, we marched up the hill to the village. All the population was then out to receive us. The chief came in state, with his countenance painted and his royal bell ringing, and, after repeating what the elders had said, made us presents of goats and plantains. Soon after, the *kondé*, or head wife, of the chief came to tell us that she was cooking a large pot of the koa root for me and my men, and all went pleasantly. The villagers were thoroughly sincere this time, and I felt happy, for there were not likely to be any more obstacles in my way before arriving in the Ashangui country, on the banks of the large river, which every one was now telling me of. I had heard that in one day we should get through the districts on this side of the Ashangui country; that in a few hours after leaving Mouaou Kombo we should be among the Njavi tribe; and that we could, in the same day, pass through the country of the Abombos.

But four men from the hostile village, arrayed in warrior's attire and brandishing plantain-leaves over their heads, came in. They said they had held their palaver this morning and had decided not to let the Oguizi pass; there would be war if the Mouaou people attempted to bring me.

Kombo, who was seated by my side, told me to hide myself in my hut, so as not to give the strangers the pleasure of seeing me; he then ordered my men to make a demonstration with their guns to intimidate these vapouring warriors. I laughed as I saw the men taking to their heels as soon as Igala advanced towards them, firing his gun in the air. But my men got excited, and hurrying forward into the open space to fire their guns in the air, one of the weapons loaded with ball went off before the muzzle was elevated. I did not see the act; but, immediately after the report of the guns, I was startled to see the Mouaou villagers, with affrighted looks and shouts of alarm, running in all direction. The king and his head wife, who were both near me, fled along with the rest.

"Mamo! Mamo!" (the untranslatable cry of anguish of these poor Africans) was now heard on all sides. I rushed out, and not far from my hut saw, lying on the ground, the lifeless body of a negro: his head shattered and his brains oozing from his broken skull. Igala ran to me with terrified looks, saying, "Oh, Chaillie, I could not help it; the gun went off!" The inevitable consequences of the deed flashed across my mind. The distrust of my motives amongst these people, which had only just been overcome, would now return with redoubled force. They would make common cause with the enraged warriors of the neighbouring villages; hundreds of men, armed with poisoned spears and arrows, would soon be upon us. I called to the king to come back and not be afraid; but already the war drums were beating. Kombo shouted: "You say you come here to do no harm and do not kill people; is not this the dead body of a man?" It was out of the question our trying to make our way eastward; without goods and without escort, there was no help for it but to go back to the Ishogo country as fast as we could.

I got my men together, seven in number, and gave a few hasty directions about the baggage with which our hut was filled. I did not know what to do. The thought flashed across my mind that it would be best to set fire to the hut; but I dreaded the further sacrifice of life that might be caused by the explosion of so much gunpowder. Our main purpose now was to get away on the forest path before the warriors, who would otherwise impede our advance and rouse other villages ahead. Ammunition was what was most necessary to us now; I served out a good supply of bullets and powder to each man; loaded some of them with my most valuable articles, my journals, photographs, natural history specimens, and a few of my lighter goods, and took, for my share of the burdens, five chronometers, a sextant, two revolvers, rifle, with another gun slung at my back, and a heavy load of ammunition. "Now boys," I said, "keep together, do not be afraid, and do not fire until I give the order; if it is God's will that we should die, we must die; but let us try our best, and we may reach the sea in safety!" The brave lads, although struck with terror, and fully comprehending the gravity of the situation, stood their ground.

CHAPTER XXXVIII.

A momentous pause—The head wife of a friendly chief killed—A general shout of war—The order of retreat—A deadly struggle commences—Igala and I are wounded—My men narrowly escape—Making a desperate stand—Long rifle firing—Tumultuous shouting—Devotion of my Commi men—Throwing away our heavy loads—Another stand—The enemy is cowed—Troubles threatened among the natives—Advice to my men in case I am killed or die—Passing Niembouai Olomba at night—Travelling through the forest in darkness—Arrival at a plantation—Friendly welcome—Stories of our struggles—The war-dish prepared between the people of Mobana and Mouaou-Komba—I am supposed to change my shape during the fight—Leaving Igoumbié—Farewell to the Ishogos—On our way towards the sea-shore—Meeting with Quengueza.

For a moment there seemed a chance of the affair being patched up. Igala had explained in shouting to the frightened Kombo and the elders, that it was all an accident and that I would pay the value of twenty men in goods if they would listen to me. I had hurriedly taken out a quantity of beads and cloth and spread it on the ground in the middle of the street, as the price of the life. One of the head men had even come forward, saying, "It is good, let us hold the palaver." The war drums had ceased beating. But it was but a gleam of sunshine in the midst of a storm; at that moment a woman came rushing out of a hut, wailing and tearing her hair—the head wife of a friendly head man had been also killed by the fatal bullet which, after killing the negro, had pierced the thin wall of her hut!

A general shout arose of "War!" and every man rushed for his spear or his bow. I gave the order for the retreat; for I saw at once that there was no chance of peace, but that a deadly struggle was about to commence. Away we went; Igala took the best of our remaining dogs, and led the van; I bringing up the rear. It was not an instant too soon; before we were well on the forest path leading from the village, a number of arrows were discharged at us; Igala was hit in the leg, and one of the missiles struck me on the hand, cutting through one of my fingers to the bone. Macondai and Rebouka, in leaving the village, narrowly escaped being transfixed with spears, and only succeeded in repelling their assailants by pointing their guns at them. If I had not stopped them from firing, they would have shot a number of them. Wild shouts, and the tramp of scores of infuriated savages close behind us, put us on our mettle. I shouted to my men not to fire, for we were in the wrong, and to the villagers that we would not shoot them if they did not pursue us to the forest, but that if they followed us we should certainly kill them.

Our pursuers had the disadvantage that they were obliged to stop every time they wanted to shoot, to adjust the arrow and take aim, and in the forest paths we were often out of sight round turnings in the road before they could deliver their shot. Moreover, their bravest men durst not come up to close quarters with us, although they often came near enough to make us hear their shouts of defiance; they cried out that it was of no use our attempting to escape from them, that we did not know the road through the bush, and should never get out of it alive. They seemed to be most bitter against Igala, whom they called *Malanga*. "You have tasted blood," they shouted out, "and your own blood must be shed." They dodged about, took short cuts through the jungle, and we were in constant fear lest some spear or arrow should come from behind the trees on our flanks, and finish us for good. Besides it would be impossible long to keep up the pace at which we ran. After behaving so steadily at starting, a sudden and unaccountable panic seized my men when we were some distance on the road, and for about ten minutes no shouts of mine could make them stop. To lighten themselves they threw load after load into the bush, and the toil of months was irrecoverably lost.

After we had retreated some four or five miles, finding that our enemies still pursued us, I felt that it was time to make a stand and give them a specimen of our power, for if we allowed them to go on in this way there would be danger of their rousing against us the villagers ahead. I ordered a halt. Mouitchi, one of our number, was missing, and we concluded he had fallen a victim; our pursuers, before we left the village, had shouted to us that they had killed him; poor Igala, my best and bravest man, complained sorely of the wound in his leg. He believed the lance was poisoned. There was time only for a few words of encouragement; our pursuers were in sight, and a number of men were threading the jungle apparently with a view of flanking us. I shouldered my long-range rifle, and, as the leader advanced adjusting his bow, I fired. His right arm dropped broken and powerless by his side, and the next man behind fell with a crash amongst a mass of fallen leaves and branches. Rebouka also fired at a man in the bush, who disappeared suddenly, as if shot, down a steep bank. This served as a check for the present, and we jogged on more leisurely.

We had not gone far when a tumultuous shouting was heard behind us and a large number of warriors hove in sight, more furious than ever. The path was most difficult, over one steep hill after another, and the village of Mobana, likely

RETREAT FROM ASHANGO-LAND.

to be hostile to us, was only about a mile from us. We increased our speed, but our pursuers were within range, and a paralysing thud, accompanied by a sharp pain, told me that I had been again struck. This time it was in my side! I had no time to stop to take the arrow out, and the barbed head having gone through the leather belt of my revolvers, the point was working in my flesh every step I took, causing the most acute torture. Had its force not been arrested by the resistance of the leather, it would probably have killed me. After I was struck, Igala, the unfortunate cause of all our woe, who kept close by me during our flight, turned round and by a quick and well-directed shot laid the too skilful bowman low. The unfeigned sorrow and devotion of my men at this juncture were most gratifying to me. I was getting weak from loss of blood, and a burning thirst was tormenting me. They asked what was to become of them if I should die? I told them to keep together, come what might; and, if they escaped, to deliver all my journals and papers to the white men. Wherever we stopped for a few minutes during this disastrous day, they came round me and asked me how I felt, and what they could do for me.

My strength began to fail me, and I had myself to follow the example of my men in throwing away things to lighten the load I carried. To my great sorrow I had to throw into the bush my beautiful double-barrelled breech-loading rifle, a magnificent weapon, carrying a two and a half ounce steel-pointed ball.

Another check was necessary. Igala said, "I know I am going to die, but let me kill a few of these fellows first." He concealed himself behind a tree, whilst we continued forward to draw on the men, for we had found that the tactics of our pursuers were to send to the van their most expert bowman to get as near to us as they safely could, while the rest of them remained behind, shouting loudly, to make us believe that they were all far off. The foremost was not long in coming within Igala's range, who fired, and the man fell.

At last we crossed the difficult stream near Mobana called the Bembo, and commenced the ascent of the steep hill on which the village is situated. It was a critical stage in our retreat. We thought it likely messengers might have gone by other paths to rouse the people against us, as the men who pursued us shouted out, "Men of Mobana, do not let the Oguizi's people pass! they have killed our people!" As we expected, we found the fighting men all ranged in battle array at the further end of the village. Our road, however, lay a little out of their way; we passed quickly, and were soon again immersed in the shade of the forest path.

So far from being free, we were now followed by the Mouaou and Mobana warriors united. The path led at first down the hill and we hurried along it at full speed so as not to be caught at a disadvantage. A little further on, halfway up another hill, Igala and Rapelina stayed behind and shot another man, wounding him only, and sending him howling back to his companions.

After this there was a lull for a short time. We stopped and considered what was best to be done. We were all tired with our long run over the rugged hilly forest road. I had wished to escape without causing any further sacrifice of life if possible, but it was plain that unless we killed more than we had done we should be unable to free ourselves from our enemies before nightfall, and then they might surround us and massacre us all. My men and myself agreed that we should here choose a place to make a last stand, and give them a lesson that should put a stop to them.

We had leisure to look out for a good position, for we knew the district, and remembered every hill. On the slope of one of the hills there was a place where a number of trees grew close together. We stationed ourselves each behind a broad trunk, but all within a short distance of each other, and there waited the arrival of our pursuers. As usual, the bowman came on first, but we heard the noise of a multitude not far behind them, all bellowing forth curses on our heads. As soon as a good number were visible down the broad and tolerably straight road, Igala and Rapelina both fired. One man fell, evidently dead, and another was wounded in the face, to all appearance his jaw broken. Ngoma then took his aim, but his shot fell wide. The fellows seemed to be cowed at this unexpected onslaught, and when we suddenly emerged from behind the trees and showed ourselves, they all beat a retreat. It was our last combat, and although we heard them for a long time afterwards, it was always at a great distance.

We now breathed more freely. We halted, laid down our loads and rested, keeping a sharp lookout at the same time. My clothes were quite saturated with blood; but the flow of blood appeared to have carried off the poison, for I felt no further ill effect from the wound except the pain, and it was healed three weeks afterwards.

The action of the poison used by the natives is not very rapid; it causes corruption of the flesh around the wound, discharge of matter, and eventually gangrene; when an arrow or spear penetrates into the bowels, death is, of course, certain to ensue, but if the wound is only an external one it is very seldom fatal. The arrow-head which had pierced my side was found, when wrenched from the wound, to have been poisoned; but the coating of poison had been fortunately scraped off it in passing through the leather, and my wound, though extremely painful, was not a dangerous one.

As we were again shouldering our *otaitais* (now almost empty) to resume our march, we descried a man a short distance off, walking stealthily through the bushes up the hill and occasionally hiding himself. He was coming towards us, and we were at once on our guard again. Igala volunteered to go down and watch his movements. We waited the result in dead silence. The man came nearer, and we saw that he had a gun in his hand: it was Mouitchi, whom we had given up for lost! He had escaped without a scratch, by running along by-paths in the forest within sound of the noisy crowd of our pursuers. He told us that the men we had hit in the last encounter were dead, and that our pursuers had resolved to desist from following us, saying that they should all be killed one by one if they went on.

The forest after this resumed its accustomed stillness, undisturbed by the savage war-cries and still more savage curses of the infuriated Ashangos. We had another village to pass, Niembouai Olomba, where I thought we might be attacked. Before we reached the place we met two women in the path belonging to Mobana. Igala wanted to shoot them, but I prevented him and gave him a sharp reprimand for thinking of such an act. I had given him an order at starting that if any women, old men, or children should be met with on the road he must let them pass unhurt, but that he was to shoot down armed men without mercy, this being necessary for our safety. Igala did not like this style of making war; he said this was not the white man's country, and we ought not to fight in white man's fashion.

Thus we went on till sundown. We were then near the village of Niembouai Olomba, and had travelled at least over twenty miles of ground without food since nine o'clock in the morning.

I thought it unsafe in our exhausted state to run the gauntlet of this large and possibly hostile village, through which lay the only path we knew, and my men agreed with me that our best plan would be to retire into the forest, some distance from the main road, and sleep there till midnight. We might then pass through before the fighting men were aroused and seized their weapons.

The plan was carried out. We plunged into the dense part of the forest, and then lay down on the ground to sleep, in a small open space, muzzling our dog that he should not betray our hiding-place. Darkness had closed in: silence was broken only by the mournful cry of a solitary owl. My exhausted men thought neither of leopards, nor poisonous snakes, nor hostile savages, but slept soundly; as for myself, I was too anxious to sleep, and Igala distressed me by his moaning from time to time, although he tried all he could to suppress it.

The night air was misty and cold. As I lay awake on the damp ground, I thought of kindred and friends, of the many happy hours I had spent in happy homes, amidst every luxury of civilized life; and I felt desolate.

At last I thought it must be near midnight. I looked at my watch. I was right; so I awoke my men and sent two of them into the path that leads to the village, telling them to go and see if all was quiet. They returned with a favourable report. Then calling them all close to me, I said, "My boys, I have fought for you as hard as I could, but the time may be near at hand when I shall not be able to do so any more. I may be killed to-night, or I may not be strong enough to fight much longer. Whatever happens, remain together; listen to Igala, your chief, and do not throw away my Journals.* Even if you have to throw away everything else, do not throw them away, but deliver them into the hands of the white men on the coast."

My men clung close round me as I spoke, and all, with voices full of love, said, "Chaillie, you are not to die! You are not to die! We will bring you alive to our people! You shall always be with us." I answered, in a laughing tone, in order to cheer them up: "I do not say I am to die to-night; but only that I might die. Don't you know that Chaillie knows how to fight?" They all said, "Yes, yes; and we also know how to fight—we are men!" We then shouldered our bundles and guns, and struggled through the entangled thicket, tearing ourselves with thorns, into the path, and thence to the village street. We here paused, and called each other in a low voice to make sure we were all together; for it was so intensely dark that we could not see a yard before us. It was necessary to guard against a possible ambush, for the villagers must have been aware that we were near their place, and they knew that we could not venture to travel except along the main path of the country, which passed through their village. We then stepped forward, like desperate men. We took the middle of the street, which was a very long one, treading cautiously, with our guns cocked, and ready at the slightest warning. At one house we heard people playing the native harp inside; we crossed lightly to the opposite side of the street, and passed without having alarmed the inmates. We then came near the end of the street, and were thinking that all danger was passed, when suddenly a bright fire blazed up

* One of the volumes of the journal, together with my route-maps, numerous notes, and two copies of astronomical and meteorological observations, had already been lost in the retreat.

right before us! As we stood motionless waiting for the next move, a kind voice spoke out in the darkness—"It is the Oguizi's people; go on! go on! there is no harm to you in my village; pass on! you will find the path smooth; there is no war for you!" It was the voice of the old king, who was thus, with some of his people, waiting our passage, with the good intention of speeding us on with kind words.

On we went in the darkness of the night; through swamps and water-courses, over stony hills and thorny brakes, often losing the path, and wandering about for some time before finding it again. At about three o'clock in the morning we came to a field of cassava. We halted, made a fire, gathered some of the roots, and roasted them to eat, for we had had no food since our flight began the preceding morning, and were quite worn out with fatigue and hunger. This renewed our strength, and I offered up a silent prayer to that gracious Providence who had so marvellously preserved my little band.

July 27th. A little before daylight (as soon as we could see our way through the forest), we resumed our march, Igala limping along with his lame leg, and I marching among the men encouraging them with hopeful words. After going a short distance we came to a place where two paths diverged, and a dispute arose amongst my men as to which was the right way. Rebouka, who was now leading us, fixed upon one way as the right one, and Ngoma declared the other was the proper path; he knew it, he said, by a monkey trap by the side of the road, which we had passed on coming to Niembouai Olomba. The majority declared in favour of Rebouka, and so we took his path.

We continued on this road till midday, when it was necessary to halt and make a search for something to eat, for we were all ravenous with hunger. Some of the men dispersed on foraging expeditions, and two of them soon returned successful, having found a small grove of plantains from which they gathered several bunches. We made a fire on the margin of a pretty rivulet under the shade of trees, and cooked and ate our meal. Soon after, having resumed our onward march, we arrived at a small village surrounded by plantains, which we knew at once we had not seen on our outward journey. Ngoma was now triumphant, and Rebouka and his followers discomfited. I was obliged to interfere to put an end to their dispute, and we then boldly walked into the village and spoke to the people.

The place proved to be a plantation of one of the head men of Niembouai Olomba, next in influence to the king. He was a fine old fellow, with snow-white hair, and with that genial expression of features which is often seen in negroes of a better sort. He received us with great kindness, inviting us to stay and eat something; and, on our accepting his offer, ordered his women to cook us a fowl and some plantains. The women gave my men sugar-cane and mpegui nuts, and the old man apologized for not having a goat to offer us.

The people of the village naturally asked us why we had returned so soon. My men were not behindhand in satisfying their curiosity; but they took care to conceal the fact that we were the aggressors, though through no ill-intention on our part. They said we had been attacked, and had had to fight our way back. Each of them boasted of his own feats and prowess, saying how many of the warriors of Mouaou Kombo he had beaten off.

Whilst we were thus engaged, our old guide Magouga came in. The arrival of this faithful old man was most fortunate for us. He proved himself to be a real friend in need. He had heard, when he got up in the morning at Niembouai, that we had passed in the middle of the night, and had immediately set off to overtake us. He must have walked very fast. He seemed overjoyed to see us, and said he had returned to Niembouai Olomba from Mobana, intending to remain until he had heard of our safe passage through the Njavi country; for he had anticipated that we should have great difficulties with the people of Upper Ashangoland, who were a bad set. Magouga seemed not to have heard a correct account of the Mouaou affair. All he knew was that the people had driven us away, and that we had killed many of their warriors. He told us that one of the men shot by Igala was the head warrior of Mobana, and that this was likely to be made a *casus belli* between the Mobana villagers and the people of Mouaou Kombo, who were held to be the cause of the death. The Mobanas were already cooking the " war dish " in order to march against the village of Mouaou Kombo.

The " war dish " is the pot of magic herbs and fetiches which is cooked with a great deal of mystery and ceremony on the eve of going to meet an enemy. The mess is cooked in a very large vessel, and the affair is presided over, as a matter of course, by the most renowned fetich doctor of the tribe. So soon as the cooking is completed, the warriors swallow part of the contents of the vessel, and smear their bodies over with the rest; when they have succeeded in exciting themselves to the requisite pitch, they rush forth to attack the village they intend to assault.

It was evident from the confused statements of Magouga that the country was all in a ferment behind us. He said the Mouaou people had abandoned their village and retired to the forest, fearing lest I should return and burn it. They said all the arrows they had shot at me would not pierce me, but had rebounded from my flesh; and they were filled with superstitious fears of the power of so mysterious a being I must here add that my men and myself kept the fact of my having been wounded a secret from all the negroes on our homeward march; my men knew as well as myself how important it was that I should maintain the reputation of being invulnerable; and it was universally believed that the arrows of the Ashangos glanced from my body without hurting me. Magouga said he had heard that at one time I had turned myself into a leopard, and hid myself in a tree, and had sprung upon the Mouaou people as they came to make war on my men; that at other times I turned myself into a gorilla, or into an elephant, and struck terror and death among the Mouaou and Mobana warriors. Magouga finished his story by asking me for a " war fetich," for he said I must possess the art of making fetiches, or I and my men could not have escaped so miraculously.

After a good rest and a hearty meal we left the good old chief of the plantation-village, and continued our homeward march, now under the guidance of Magouga. On parting I gave the old chief a quantity of beads out of our remaining stock, and also a red powder flask, which latter present delighted him beyond measure, and he said he would keep it in remembrance of me.

* * * * * *

August 5th. We left Igoumbié to-day, to the great sorrow of the villagers, who wished me to stay longer with them.

The Ishogòs are the kindest-hearted and the gentlest negroes I ever met with. As soon as my men had shouldered their *otataïs*, and the people saw that we were ready to start, the whole population came out. This time we had to pass through the whole length of the village. They followed behind us—the women were the most conspicuous. They all shouted out, "Go on well, go on well; nothing bad shall happen to you!" When we reached the end of the village, and just before turning into the path that would take us out of their sight, I turned round, and, taking off the remnant of what was once a good Panama hat, I waved it in the air. Immediately a dead silence succeeded to the noise, and I shouted, "Farewell, good Ishogos!" As I disappeared from their view among the trees of the forest we were entering, suddenly a wild and sorrowful shout of the multitude reached our ears. They all cried out with one voice, "We shall see the good Oguizi no more! We shall see the good Oguizi no more!" Then all became again silent, and once more we trod the path of this gigantic forest on our way to the sea-shore, traversing, but without any guide, the same countries through which we had passed on our way to the interior.

* * * * * *

On reaching Quengueza's encampment on the river Ovenga we were received with a most hearty welcome; the loyal old chief hugged me to his breast, and I am sure I reciprocated the joy he felt at our meeting. He beat his *kendo*, and, in a kind of solemn chant, thanked the spirits of his ancestors, whom he had invoked when I left Goumbi with him for the Ashira country, for my safe arrival.

* * * * * *

In September, 1866, I quitted the shores of Western Equatorial Africa for the last time with many regrets, leaving behind me many kind friends and bearing away with me many warm remembrances.

www.ingramcontent.com/pod-product-compliance
Lightning Source LLC
Chambersburg PA
CBHW021417300426
44114CB00010B/527